Get the eBooks FREE!

(PDF, ePub, Kindle, and liveBook all included)

We believe that once you buy a book from us, you should be able to read it in any format we have available. To get electronic versions of this book at no additional cost to you, purchase and then register this book at the Manning website.

Go to https://www.manning.com/freebook and follow the instructions to complete your pBook registration.

That's it!
Thanks from Manning!

grokking
Machine
Learning

Luis G. Serrano

Foreword by Sebastian Thrun

MANNING
SHELTER ISLAND

grokking

Machine
Learning

Luis G. Serrano

Foreword by Sebastian Thrun

MANNING

SHELTER ISLAND

For online information and ordering of this and other Manning books, please visit
www.manning.com. The publisher offers discounts on this book when ordered in quantity. For more
information, please contact

>Special Sales Department
>Manning Publications Co.
>20 Baldwin Road, PO Box 761
>Shelter Island, NY 11964
>Email: orders@manning.com

Manning Publications Co.   Development editor: Marina Michaels
20 Baldwin Road   Technical development editor: Kris Athi
Shelter Island, NY 11964   Review editor: Aleksander Dragosavljević
                                  Production editor: Keri Hales
                                  Copy editor: Pamela Hunt
                                  Proofreader: Jason Everett
                                  Technical proofreader: Karsten Strøbæk, Shirley Yap
                                  Typesetter: Dennis Dalinnik
                                  Cover designer: Leslie Haimes

ISBN: 9781617295911
Printed in the United States of America

contents

foreword

Did you think machine learning is complicated and hard to master? It's not! Read this book!

Luis Serrano is a wizard when it comes to explaining things in plain English. I met him first when he taught machine learning on Udacity. He made our students feel that all of machine learning is as simple as adding or subtracting numbers. And most of all, he made the material fun. The videos he produced for Udacity were incredibly engaging and remain among the most liked content offered on the platform.

This book is better! Even the most fearful will enjoy the material presented herein, as Serrano demystifies some of the best-held secrets of the machine learning society. He takes you step by step through each of the critical algorithms and techniques in the field. You can become a machine learning aficionado even if you dislike math. Serrano minimizes the mathematical *kauderwelsch* that so many of us hard-core academics have come to love, and instead relies on intuition and practical explanations.

The true goal of this book is to empower you to master these methods yourself. So the book is full of fun exercises, in which you get to try out those mystical (and now demystified) techniques yourself. Would you rather gorge on the latest Netflix TV show, or spend your time applying machine learning to problems in computer vision and natural language understanding? If the latter, this book is for you. I can't express how much fun it is to play with the latest in machine learning, and see your computer do magic under your supervision.

And since machine learning is just about the hottest technology to emerge in the past few years, you will now be able to leverage your new-found skills in your job. A few years back, the *New York Times* proclaimed that there were only 10,000 machine learning experts in the world, with millions of open positions. That is still the case today! Work through this book and become a professional machine learning engineer. You are guaranteed to possess one of the most in-demand skills in the world today.

With this book, Luis Serrano has done an admirable job explaining complex algorithms and making them accessible to almost everyone. But he doesn't compromise depth. Instead, he focuses on the empowerment of the reader through a sequence of enlightening projects and exercises. In this sense, this is not a passive read. To fully benefit from this book, you have to work. At Udacity, we have a saying: You won't lose weight by watching someone else exercise. To grok machine learning, you have to learn to apply it to real-world problems. If you are ready to do this, this is your book—whoever you are!

Sebastian Thrun, PhD
Founder, Udacity
Adjunct Professor, Stanford University

preface

The future is here, and that future has a name: machine learning. With applications in pretty much every industry, from medicine to banking, from self-driving cars to ordering our coffee, the interest in machine learning has rapidly grown day after day. But what *is* machine learning?

Most of the time, when I read a machine learning book or attend a machine learning lecture, I see either a sea of complicated formulas or a sea of lines of code. For a long time, I thought that this was machine learning, and that machine learning was reserved only for those who had a solid knowledge of both math and computer science.

However, I began to compare machine learning with other subjects, such as music. Musical theory and practice are complicated subjects. But when we think of music, we do not think of scores and scales; we think of songs and melodies. And then I wondered, is machine learning the same? Is it really just a bunch of formulas and code, or is there a melody behind it?

Figure 1 Music is not only about scales and notes. There is a melody behind all the technicalities. In the same way, machine learning is not only about formulas and code. There is also a melody, and in this book, we sing it.

With this in mind, I embarked on a journey to understand the melody of machine learning. I stared at formulas and code for months. I drew many diagrams. I scribbled drawings on napkins and showed them to my family, friends, and colleagues. I trained models on small and large datasets. I experimented. After a while, I started listening to the melody of machine learning. All of a sudden, some very pretty pictures started forming in my mind. I started writing stories that go along with all the machine learning concepts. Melodies, pictures, stories—that is how I enjoy learning any topic, and it is those melodies, those pictures, and those stories that I share with you in this book. My goal is to make machine learning fully understandable to every human, and this book is a step in that journey—a step that I'm happy you are taking with me!

acknowledgments

First and foremost, I would like to thank my editor, Marina Michaels, without whom this book wouldn't exist. Her organization, thorough editing, and valuable input helped shape *Grokking Machine Learning*. I thank Marjan Bace, Bert Bates, and the rest of the Manning team for their support, professionalism, great ideas, and patience. I thank my technical proofers, Shirley Yap and Karsten Strøbæk; my technical development editor, Kris Athi; and the reviewers for giving me great feedback and correcting many of my mistakes. I thank the production editor, Keri Hales, the copy editor, Pamela Hunt, the graphics editor, Jennifer Houle, the proofreader, Jason Everett, and the entire production team for their wonderful work in making this book a reality. I thank Laura Montoya for her help with inclusive language and AI ethics, Diego Hernandez for valuable additions to the code, and Christian Picón for his immense help with the technical aspects of the repository and the packages.

I am grateful to Sebastian Thrun for his excellent work democratizing education. Udacity was the platform that first gave me a voice to teach the world, and I would like to thank the wonderful colleagues and students I met there. Alejandro Perdomo and the Zapata Computing team deserve thanks for introducing me to the world of quantum machine learning. Thanks also to the many wonderful leaders and colleagues I met at Google and Apple who were instrumental in my career. Special thanks to Roberto Cipriani and the team at Paper Inc. for letting me be part of the family and for the wonderful job they do in the education community.

I'd like to thank my many academic mentors who have shaped my career and my way of thinking: Mary Falk de Losada and her team at the Colombian Mathematical Olympiads, where I first started loving mathematics and had the chance to meet great mentors and create friendships that have lasted a lifetime; my PhD advisor, Sergey Fomin, who was instrumental in my mathematical education and my style of teaching; my master's advisor, Ian Goulden; Nantel and François Bergeron, Bruce Sagan and Federico Ardila, and the many professors and colleagues I had the opportunity to work with, in particular those at the Universities of Waterloo, Michigan, Quebec at Montreal, and York; and finally, Richard Hoshino and the team and students at Quest University, who helped me test and improve the material in this book.

To all the reviewers: Al Pezewski, Albert Nogués Sabater, Amit Lamba, Bill Mitchell, Borko Djurkovic, Daniele Andreis, Erik Sapper, Hao Liu, Jeremy R. Loscheider, Juan Gabriel Bono, Kay Engelhardt, Krzysztof Kamyczek, Matthew Margolis, Matthias Busch, Michael Bright, Millad Dagdoni, Polina Keselman, Tony Holdroyd, and Valerie Parham-Thompson, your suggestions helped make this a better book.

I would like to thank my wife, Carolina Lasso, who supported me at every step of this process with love and kindness; my mom, Cecilia Herrera, who raised me with love and always encouraged me to follow my passions; my grandma, Maruja, for being the angel that looks at me from heaven; my best friend, Alejandro Morales, for always being there for me; and my friends who have enlightened my path and brightened my life, I thank you and love you with all my heart.

YouTube, blogs, podcasts, and social media have given me the chance to connect with thousands of brilliant souls all over the world. Curious minds with an endless passion for learning, fellow educators who generously share their knowledge and insights, form an e-tribe that inspires me every day and gives me the energy to continue teaching and learning. To anyone who shares their knowledge with the world or who strives to learn every day, I thank you.

I thank anyone out there who is striving to make this world a more fair and peaceful place. To anyone who fights for justice, for peace, for the environment, and for equal opportunities for every human on Earth regardless of their race, gender, place of birth, conditions, and choices, I thank you from the bottom of my heart.

And last, but certainly not least, this book is dedicated to you, the reader. You have chosen the path of learning, the path of improving, the path of feeling comfortable in the uncomfortable, and that is admirable. I hope this book is a positive step along your way to following your passions and creating a better world.

about this book

This book teaches you two things: machine learning models and how to use them. Machine learning models come in different types. Some of them return a deterministic answer, such as yes or no, whereas others return the answer as a probability. Some of them use equations; others use if statements. One thing they have in common is that they all return an answer, or a prediction. The branch of machine learning that comprises the models that return a prediction is aptly named *predictive machine learning*. This is the type of machine learning that we focus on in this book.

How this book is organized: A roadmap

Types of chapters

This book has two types of chapters. The majority of them (chapters 3, 5, 6, 8, 9, 10, 11, and 12) each contain one type of machine learning model. The corresponding model in each chapter is studied in detail, including examples, formulas, code, and exercises for you to solve. Other chapters (chapters 4, 7, and 13) contain useful techniques to use to train, evaluate, and improve machine learning models. In particular, chapter 13 contains an end-to-end example on a real dataset, in which you'll be able to apply all the knowledge you've obtained in the previous chapters.

Recommended learning paths

You can use this book in two ways. The one I recommend is to go through it linearly, chapter by chapter, because you'll find that the alternation between learning models and learning techniques to train them is rewarding. However, another learning path is to first learn all the models (chapters 3, 5, 6, 8, 9, 10, 11, and 12), and then learn the techniques for training them (chapters 4, 7, and 13). And of course, because we all learn in different ways, you can create your own learning path!

Appendices

This book has three appendices. Appendix A contains the solutions to each chapter's exercises. Appendix B contains some formal mathematical derivations that are useful but more technical than the rest of the book. Appendix C contains a list of references and resources that I recommend if you'd like to further your understanding.

Requirements and learning goals

This book provides you with a solid framework of predictive machine learning. To get the most out of this book, you should have a visual mind and a good understanding of elementary mathematics, such as graphs of lines, equations, and basic probability. It is helpful (although not mandatory) if you know how to code, especially in Python, because you are given the opportunity to implement and apply several models in real datasets throughout the book. After reading this book, you will be able to do the following:

- Describe the most important models in predictive machine learning and how they work, including linear and logistic regression, naive Bayes, decision trees, neural networks, support vector machines, and ensemble methods.

- Identify their strengths and weaknesses and what parameters they use.

- Identify how these models are used in the real world, and formulate potential ways to apply machine learning to any particular problem you would like to solve.

- Learn how to optimize these models, compare them, and improve them, to build the best machine learning models we can.

- Code the models, whether by hand or using an existing package, and use them to make predictions on real datasets.

If you have a particular dataset or problem in mind, I invite you to think about how to apply what you learn in this book to it, and to use it as a starting point to implement and experiment with your own models.

I am super excited to start this journey with you, and I hope you are as excited!

Other resources

This book is self-contained. This means that aside from the requirements described earlier, every concept that we need is introduced in the book. However, I include many references, which I recommend you check out if you'd like to understand the concepts at a deeper level or if you'd like to explore further topics. The references are all in appendix C and also at this link: http://serrano.academy/grokking-machine-learning.

In particular, several of my own resources accompany this book's material. In my page at http://serrano.academy, you can find a lot of materials in the form of videos, posts, and code. The videos are also in my YouTube channel www.youtube.com/c/LuisSerrano, which I recommend you check out. As a matter of fact, most of the chapters in this book have a corresponding video that I recommend you watch as you read the chapter.

We'll be writing code

In this book, we'll be writing code in Python. However, if your plan is to learn the concepts without the code, you can still follow the book while ignoring the code. Nevertheless, I recommend you at least take a look at the code, so you get familiarized with it.

This book comes with a code repository, and most chapters will give you the opportunity to code the algorithms from scratch or to use some very popular Python packages to build models that fit given datasets. The GitHub repository is www.github.com/luisguiserrano/manning, and I link the corresponding notebooks throughout the book. In the README of the repository, you will find the instructions for the packages to install to run the code successfully.

The main Python packages we use in this book are the following:

- **NumPy:** for storing arrays and performing complex mathematical calculations
- **Pandas:** for storing, manipulating, and analyzing large datasets
- **Matplotlib:** for plotting data
- **Turi Create:** for storing and manipulating data and training machine learning models
- **Scikit-Learn:** for training machine learning models
- **Keras (TensorFlow):** for training neural networks

About the code

This book contains many examples of source code in line with normal text. In both cases, source code is formatted in a `fixed-width font like this` to separate it from ordinary text. Sometimes code is also **`in bold`** to highlight code that has changed from previous steps in the chapter, such as when a new feature adds to an existing line of code.

In many cases, the original source code has been reformatted; we've added line breaks and reworked indentation to accommodate the available page space in the book. Additionally, comments in the source code have often been removed from the listings when the code is described in the text. Code annotations accompany many of the listings, highlighting important concepts.

The code for the examples in this book is available for download on the Manning website (https://www.manning.com/books/grokking-machine-learning), and from GitHub at www .github.com/luisguiserrano/manning.

liveBook discussion forum

Purchase of *Grokking Machine Learning* includes free access to a private web forum run by Manning Publications where you can make comments about the book, ask technical questions, and receive help from the author and from other users. To access the forum, go to https://livebook.manning.com/#!/book/grokking-machine-learning/discussion. You can also learn more about Manning's forums and the rules of conduct at https://livebook.manning .com/#!/discussion.

Manning's commitment to our readers is to provide a venue where a meaningful dialogue between individual readers and between readers and the author can take place. It is not a commitment to any specific amount of participation on the part of the author, whose contribution to the forum remains voluntary (and unpaid). We suggest you try asking the author some challenging questions lest his interest stray! The forum and the archives of previous discussions will be accessible from the publisher's website as long as the book is in print.

about the author

LUIS G. SERRANO is a research scientist in quantum artificial intelligence at Zapata Computing. He has worked previously as a Machine Learning Engineer at Google, as a Lead Artificial Intelligence Educator at Apple, and as the Head of Content in Artificial Intelligence and Data Science at Udacity. Luis has a PhD in mathematics from the University of Michigan, a bachelor's and master's in mathematics from the University of Waterloo, and worked as a postdoctoral researcher at the Laboratoire de Combinatoire et d'Informatique Mathématique at the University of Quebec at Montreal. Luis maintains a popular YouTube channel about machine learning with over 85,000 subscribers and over 4 million views, and is a frequent speaker at artificial intelligence and data science conferences.

In this chapter

- what is machine learning

- is machine learning hard (spoiler: no)

- what do we learn in this book

- what is artificial intelligence, and how does it differ from
  machine learning

- how do humans think, and how can we inject those ideas
  into a machine

- some basic machine learning examples in real life

1

I am super happy to join you in your learning journey!

Welcome to this book! I'm super happy to be joining you in this journey through understanding machine learning. At a high level, machine learning is a process in which the computer solves problems and makes decisions in much the same way as humans.

In this book, I want to bring one message to you: machine learning is easy! You do not need to have a heavy math and programming background to understand it. You do need some basic mathematics, but the main ingredients are common sense, a good visual intuition, and a desire to learn and apply these methods to anything that you are passionate about and where you want to make an improvement in the world. I've had an absolute blast writing this book, because I love growing my understanding of this topic, and I hope you have a blast reading it and diving deep into machine learning!

Machine learning is everywhere

Machine learning is everywhere. This statement seems to be truer every day. I have a hard time imagining a single aspect of life that cannot be improved in some way or another by machine learning. For any job that requires repetition or looking at data and gathering conclusions, machine learning can help. During the last few years, machine learning has seen tremendous growth due to the advances in computing power and the ubiquity of data collection. Just to name a few applications of machine learning: recommendation systems, image recognition, text processing, self-driving cars, spam recognition, medical diagnoses . . . the list goes on. Perhaps you have a goal or an area in which you want to make an impact (or maybe you are already making it!). Very likely, machine learning can be applied to that field—perhaps that is what brought you to this book. Let's find out together!

Do I need a heavy math and coding background to understand machine learning?

No. Machine learning requires imagination, creativity, and a visual mind. Machine learning is about picking up patterns that appear in the world and using those patterns to make predictions in the future. If you enjoy finding patterns and spotting correlations, then you can do machine learning. If I were to tell you that I stopped smoking and am eating more vegetables and exercising, what would you predict will happen to my health in one year? Perhaps that it will improve. If I were to tell you that I've switched from wearing red sweaters to green sweaters, what would you predict will happen to my health in one year? Perhaps that it won't change much (it may, but not based on the information I gave you). Spotting these correlations and patterns is what machine learning is about. The only difference is that in machine learning, we attach formulas and numbers to these patterns to get computers to spot them.

Some mathematics and coding knowledge are needed to do machine learning, but you don't need to be an expert. If you *are* an expert in either of them, or both, you will certainly find your skills will be rewarded. But if you are not, you can still learn machine learning and pick up the mathematics and coding as you go. In this book, we introduce all the mathematical concepts we need at the moment we need them. When it comes to coding, how much code you write in machine learning is up to you. Machine learning jobs range from those who code all day long, to those who don't code at all. Many packages, APIs, and tools help us do machine learning with minimal coding. Every day, machine learning is more available to everyone in the world, and I'm glad you've jumped on the bandwagon!

Formulas and code are fun when seen as a language

In most machine learning books, algorithms are explained mathematically using formulas, derivatives, and so on. Although these precise descriptions of the methods work well in practice, a formula sitting by itself can be more confusing than illustrative. However, like a musical score, a formula may hide a beautiful melody behind the confusion. For example, let's look at this formula: $\sum_{i=1}^{4} i$. It looks ugly at first glance, but it represents a very simple sum, namely, $1 + 2 + 3 + 4$. And what about $\sum_{i=1}^{n} w_i$? That is simply the sum of many (n) numbers. But when I think of a sum of many numbers, I'd rather imagine something like $3 + 2 + 4 + 27$, rather than $\sum_{i=1}^{n} w_i$. Whenever I see a formula, I immediately have to imagine a small example of it, and then the picture is clearer in my mind. When I see something like $P(A|B)$, what comes to mind? That is a conditional probability, so I think of some sentence along the lines of "The probability that an event A occurs given that another event B already occurs." For example, if A represents rain today and B represents living in the Amazon rain forest, then the formula $P(A|B) = 0.8$ simply means "The probability that <u>it rains today</u> given that <u>we live in the Amazon rain forest</u> is 80%."

If you do love formulas, don't worry—this book still has them. But they will appear right after the example that illustrates them.

The same phenomenon happens with code. If we look at code from far away, it may look complicated, and we might find it hard to imagine that someone could fit all of that in their head. However, code is simply a sequence of steps, and normally each of these steps is simple. In this book, we'll write code, but it will be broken down into simple steps, and each step will be carefully explained with examples or illustrations. During the first few chapters, we will be coding our models from scratch to understand how they work. In the later chapters, however, the models get more complicated. For these, we will use packages such as Scikit-Learn, Turi Create, or Keras, which have implemented most machine learning algorithms with great clarity and power.

OK, so what exactly is machine learning?

To define machine learning, first let's define a more general term: artificial intelligence.

What is artificial intelligence?

Artificial intelligence (AI) is a general term, which we define as follows:

> **artificial intelligence**   The set of all tasks in which a computer can make decisions

In many cases, a computer makes these decisions by mimicking the ways a human makes decisions. In other cases, they may mimic evolutionary processes, genetic processes, or physical processes. But in general, any time we see a computer solving a problem by itself, be it driving a car, finding a route between two points, diagnosing a patient, or recommending a movie, we are looking at artificial intelligence.

What is machine learning?

Machine learning is similar to artificial intelligence, and often their definitions are confused. *Machine learning* (ML) is a part of artificial intelligence, and we define it as follows:

machine learning   The set of all tasks in which a computer can make decisions *based on data*

What does this mean? Allow me to illustrate with the diagram in figure 1.1.

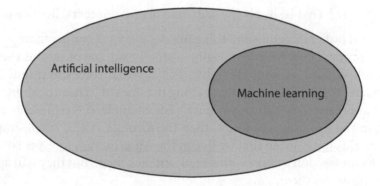

Figure 1.1   Machine learning is a part of artificial intelligence.

Let's go back to looking at how humans make decisions. In general terms, we make decisions in the following two ways:

- By using logic and reasoning
- By using our experience

For example, imagine that we are trying to decide what car to buy. We can look carefully at the features of the car, such as price, fuel consumption, and navigation, and try to figure out the best combination of them that adjusts to our budget. That is using logic and reasoning. If instead we ask all our friends what cars they own, and what they like and dislike about them, we form a list of information and use that list to decide, then we are using experience (in this case, our friends' experiences).

Machine learning represents the second method: making decisions using our experience. In computer lingo, the term for *experience* is *data*. Therefore, in machine learning, computers make decisions based on data. Thus, any time we get a computer to solve a problem or make a decision using only data, we are doing machine learning. Colloquially, we could describe machine learning in the following way:

Machine learning is common sense, except done by a computer.

Going from solving problems using any means necessary to solving problems using only data may feel like a small step for a computer, but it has been a huge step for humanity (figure 1.2). Once upon a time, if we wanted to get a computer to perform a task, we had to write a program, namely, a whole set of instructions for the computer to follow. This process is good for simple tasks, but some tasks are too complicated for this framework. For example, consider the task of identifying if an image contains an apple. If we start writing a computer program to develop this task, we quickly find out that it is hard.

Figure 1.2 Machine learning encompasses all the tasks in which computers make decisions based on data. In the same way that humans make decisions based on previous experiences, computers can make decisions based on previous data.

Let's take a step back and ask the following question. How did we, as humans, learn how an apple looks? The way we learned most words was not by someone explaining to us what they mean; we learned them by repetition. We saw many objects during our childhood, and adults would tell us what these objects were. To learn what an apple was, we saw many apples throughout the years while hearing the word *apple*, until one day it clicked, and we knew what an apple was. In machine learning, that is what we get the computer to do. We show the computer many images, and we tell it which ones contain an apple (that constitutes our data). We repeat this process until the computer catches the right patterns and attributes that constitute an apple. At the end of the process, when we feed the computer a new image, it can use these patterns to determine whether the image contains an apple. Of course, we still need to program the computer so that it catches these patterns. For that, we have several techniques, which we will learn in this book.

And now that we're at it, what is deep learning?

In the same way that machine learning is part of artificial intelligence, deep learning is a part of machine learning. In the previous section, we learned we have several techniques we use to get the computer to learn from data. One of these techniques has been performing tremendously well, so it has its own field of study called *deep learning* (DL), which we define as follows and as shown in figure 1.3:

deep learning The field of machine learning that uses certain objects called *neural networks*

What are neural networks? We'll learn about them in chapter 10. Deep learning is arguably the most used type of machine learning because it works really well. If we are looking at any of the cutting-edge applications, such as image recognition, text generation, playing Go, or self-driving cars, very likely we are looking at deep learning in some way or another.

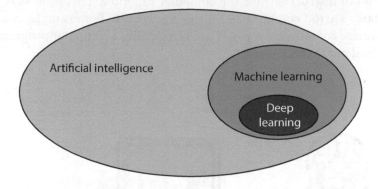

Figure 1.3   Deep learning is a part of machine learning.

In other words, deep learning is part of machine learning, which in turn is part of artificial intelligence. If this book were about transportation, then AI would be vehicles, ML would be cars, and DL would be Ferraris.

How do we get machines to make decisions with data? The remember-formulate-predict framework

In the previous section, we discussed that machine learning consists of a set of techniques that we use to get the computer to make decisions based on data. In this section, we learn what is meant by making decisions based on data and how some of these techniques work. For this, let's again analyze the process humans use to make decisions based on experience. This is what is called the *remember-formulate-predict framework*, shown in figure 1.4. The goal of machine learning is to teach computers how to think in the same way, following the same framework.

How do humans think?

When we, as humans, need to make a decision based on our experience, we normally use the following framework:

1. We **remember** past situations that were similar.

2. We **formulate** a general rule.

3. We use this rule to **predict** what may happen in the future.

For example, if the question is, "Will it rain today?," the process to make a guess is the following:

1. We **remember** that last week it rained most of the time.

2. We **formulate** that in this place, it rains most of the time.

3. We **predict** that today it will rain.

We may be right or wrong, but at least we are trying to make the most accurate prediction we can based on the information we have.

Figure 1.4 The remember-formulate-predict framework is the main framework we use in this book. It consists of three steps: (1) We remember previous data; (2) we formulate a general rule; and (3) we use that rule to make predictions about the future.

Some machine learning lingo—models and algorithms

Before we delve into more examples that illustrate the techniques used in machine learning, let's define some useful terms that we use throughout this book. We know that in machine learning, we get the computer to learn how to solve a problem using data. The way the computer solves the problem is by using the data to build a *model*. What is a model? We define a model as follows:

model A set of rules that represent our data and can be used to make predictions

We can think of a model as a representation of reality using a set of rules that mimic the existing data as closely as possible. In the rain example in the previous section, the model was our representation of reality, which is a world in which it rains most of the time. This is a simple world with one rule: it rains most of the time. This representation may or may not be accurate, but according to our data, it is the most accurate representation of reality that we can formulate. We later use this rule to make predictions on unseen data.

An *algorithm* is the process that we used to build the model. In the current example, the process is simple: we looked at how many days it rained and realized it was the majority. Of course, machine learning algorithms can get much more complicated than that, but at the end of the day, they are always composed of a set of steps. Our definition of algorithm follows:

> **algorithm**   A procedure, or a set of steps, used to solve a problem or perform a computation. In this book, the goal of an algorithm is to build a model.

In short, a model is what we use to make predictions, and an algorithm is what we use to build the model. Those two definitions are easy to confuse and are often interchanged, but to keep them clear, let's look at a few examples.

Some examples of models that humans use

In this section we focus on a common application of machine learning: spam detection. In the following examples, we will detect spam and non-spam emails. Non-spam emails are also referred to as *ham*.

> **spam and ham**   *Spam* is the common term used for junk or unwanted email, such as chain letters, promotions, and so on. The term comes from a 1972 Monty Python sketch in which every item in the menu of a restaurant contained Spam as an ingredient. Among software developers, the term *ham* is used to refer to non-spam emails.

Example 1: An annoying email friend

In this example, our friend Bob likes to send us email. A lot of his emails are spam, in the form of chain letters. We are starting to get a bit annoyed with him. It is Saturday, and we just got a notification of an email from Bob. Can we guess if this email is spam or ham without looking at it?

To figure this out, we use the remember-formulate-predict method. First, let us **remember**, say, the last 10 emails that we got from Bob. That is our data. We remember that six of them were spam, and the other four were ham. From this information, we can **formulate** the following model:

Model 1: Six out of every 10 emails that Bob sends us are spam.

This rule will be our model. Note, this rule does not need to be true. It could be outrageously wrong. But given our data, it is the best that we can come up with, so we'll live with it. Later in this book, we learn how to evaluate models and improve them when needed.

Now that we have our rule, we can use it to **predict** whether the email is spam. If six out of 10 of Bob's emails are spam, then we can assume that this new email is 60% likely to be spam and 40% likely to be ham. Judging by this rule, it's a little safer to think that the email is spam. Therefore, we predict that the email is spam (figure 1.5).

Again, our prediction may be wrong. We may open the email and realize it is ham. But we have made the prediction *to the best of our knowledge*. This is what machine learning is all about.

You may be thinking, can we do better? We seem to be judging every email from Bob in the same way, but there may be more information that can help us tell the spam and ham emails apart. Let's try to analyze the emails a little more. For example, let's see when Bob sent the emails to see if we find a pattern.

Figure 1.5   A very simple machine learning model

Example 2: A seasonal annoying email friend

Let's look more carefully at the emails that Bob sent us in the previous month. More specifically, we'll look at what day he sent them. Here are the emails with dates and information about being spam or ham:

- Monday: Ham
- Tuesday: Ham
- Saturday: Spam
- Sunday: Spam
- Sunday: Spam
- Wednesday: Ham
- Friday: Ham
- Saturday: Spam
- Tuesday: Ham
- Thursday: Ham

Now things are different. Can you see a pattern? It seems that every email Bob sent during the week is ham, and every email he sent during the weekend is spam. This makes sense—maybe during the week he sends us work email, whereas during the weekend, he has time to send spam and decides to roam free. So, we can **formulate** a more educated rule, or model, as follows:

Model 2: Every email that Bob sends during the week is ham, and those he sends during the weekend are spam.

Now let's look at what day it is today. If it is Sunday and we just got an email from Bob, then we can **predict** with great confidence that the email he sent is spam (figure 1.6). We make this prediction, and without looking, we send the email to the trash and carry on with our day.

Figure 1.6   A slightly more complex machine learning model

Example 3: Things are getting complicated!

Now, let's say we continue with this rule, and one day we see Bob in the street, and he asks, "Why didn't you come to my birthday party?" We have no idea what he is talking about. It turns out last Sunday he sent us an invitation to his birthday party, and we missed it! Why did we miss it? Because he sent it on the weekend, and we assumed that it would be spam. It seems that we need a better model. Let's go back to look at Bob's emails—this is our **remember** step. Let's see if we can find a pattern.

- 1 KB: Ham
- 2 KB: Ham
- 16 KB: Spam
- 20 KB: Spam
- 18 KB: Spam
- 3 KB: Ham
- 5 KB: Ham
- 25 KB: Spam
- 1 KB: Ham
- 3 KB: Ham

What do we see? It seems that the large emails tend to be spam, whereas the smaller ones tend to be ham. This makes sense, because the spam emails frequently have large attachments.

So, we can **formulate** the following rule:

Model 3: Any email of size 10 KB or larger is spam, and any email of size less than 10 KB is ham.

Now that we have formulated our rule, we can make a **prediction**. We look at the email we received today from Bob, and the size is 19 KB. So, we conclude that it is spam (figure 1.7).

Figure 1.7   Another slightly more complex machine learning model

Is *this* the end of the story? Not even close.

But before we keep going, notice that to make our predictions, we used the day of the week and the size of the email. These are examples of *features*. A feature is one of the most important concepts in this book.

> **feature**   Any property or characteristic of the data that the model can use to make predictions

You can imagine that there are many more features that could indicate if an email is spam or ham. Can you think of some more? In the next paragraphs, we'll see a few more features.

Example 4: More?

Our two classifiers were good, because they rule out large emails and emails sent on the weekends. Each one of them uses exactly one of these two features. But what if we wanted a rule that worked with both features? Rules like the following may work:

Model 4: If an email is larger than 10 KB or it is sent on the weekend, then it is classified as spam. Otherwise, it is classified as ham.

Model 5: If the email is sent during the week, then it must be larger than 15 KB to be classified as spam. If it is sent during the weekend, then it must be larger than 5 KB to be classified as spam. Otherwise, it is classified as ham.

Or we can get even more complicated.

Model 6: Consider the number of the day, where Monday is 0, Tuesday is 1, Wednesday is 2, Thursday is 3, Friday is 4, Saturday is 5, and Sunday is 6. If we add the number of the day and the size of the email (in KB), and the result is 12 or more, then the email is classified as spam (figure 1.8). Otherwise, it is classified as ham.

Figure 1.8   An even more complex machine learning model

All of these are valid models. We can keep creating more and more models by adding layers of complexity or by looking at even more features. Now the question is, which is the best model? This is where we start to need the help of a computer.

Some examples of models that machines use

The goal is to make the computer think the way we think, namely, use the remember-formulate-predict framework. In a nutshell, here is what the computer does in each of the steps:

Remember: Look at a huge table of data.

Formulate: Create models by going through many rules and formulas, and check which model fits the data best.

Predict: Use the model to make predictions about future data.

This process is not much different than what we did in the previous section. The great advancement here is that the computer can build models quickly by going through many formulas and combinations of rules until it finds one that fits the existing data well. For example, we can build a spam classifier with features such as the sender, the date and time of day, the number of words, the number of spelling mistakes, and the appearances of certain words such as *buy* or *win*. A model could easily look like the following logical statement:

Model 7:

- If the email has two or more spelling mistakes, then it is classified as spam.

- If it has an attachment larger than 10 KB, it is classified as spam.

- If the sender is not in our contact list, it is classified as spam.

- If it has the words *buy* and *win*, it is classified as spam.

- Otherwise, it is classified as ham.

It could also look like the following formula:

Model 8: If (size) + 10 (number of spelling mistakes) − (number of appearances of the word "mom") + 4 (number of appearances of the word "buy") > 10, then we classify the message as spam (figure 1.9). Otherwise, we classify it as ham.

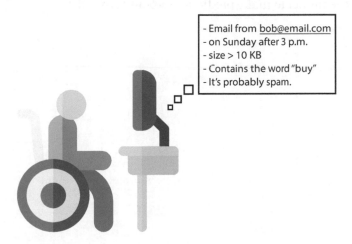

- Email from bob@email.com
- on Sunday after 3 p.m.
- size > 10 KB
- Contains the word "buy"
- It's probably spam.

Figure 1.9   A much more complex machine learning model, found by a computer

Now the question is, which is the best rule? The quick answer is the one that fits the data best, although the real answer is the one that best generalizes to new data. At the end of the day, we may end up with a complicated rule, but the computer can formulate it and use it to make predictions quickly. Our next question is, how do we build the best model? That is exactly what this book is about.

Summary

- Machine learning is easy! Anyone can learn it and use it, regardless of their background. All that is needed is a desire to learn and great ideas to implement!

- Machine learning is tremendously useful, and it is used in most disciplines. From science to technology to social problems and medicine, machine learning is making an impact and will continue doing so.

- Machine learning is common sense, done by a computer. It mimics the ways humans think to make decisions quickly and accurately.

- Just like humans make decisions based on experience, computers can make decisions based on previous data. This is what machine learning is all about.

Machine learning uses the remember-formulate-predict framework, as follows:

- **Remember:** look at the previous data.

- **Formulate:** build a model, or a rule, based on this data.

- **Predict:** use the model to make predictions about future data.

In this chapter

- three different types of machine learning: supervised, unsupervised, and reinforcement learning
- the difference between labeled and unlabeled data
- the difference between regression and classification, and how they are used

As we learned in chapter 1, machine learning is common sense for a computer. Machine learning roughly mimics the process by which humans make decisions based on experience, by making decisions based on previous data. Naturally, programming computers to mimic the human thinking process is challenging, because computers are engineered to store and process numbers, not make decisions. This is the task that machine learning aims to tackle. Machine learning is divided into several branches, depending on the type of decision to be made. In this chapter, we overview some of the most important among these branches.

Machine learning has applications in many fields, such as the following:

- Predicting house prices based on the house's size, number of rooms, and location
- Predicting today's stock market prices based on yesterday's prices and other factors of the market
- Detecting spam and non-spam emails based on the words in the e-mail and the sender
- Recognizing images as faces or animals, based on the pixels in the image
- Processing long text documents and outputting a summary
- Recommending videos or movies to a user (e.g., on YouTube or Netflix)
- Building chatbots that interact with humans and answer questions
- Training self-driving cars to navigate a city by themselves
- Diagnosing patients as sick or healthy
- Segmenting the market into similar groups based on location, acquisitive power, and interests
- Playing games like chess or Go

Try to imagine how we could use machine learning in each of these fields. Notice that some of these applications are different but can be solved in a similar way. For example, predicting housing prices and predicting stock prices can be done using similar techniques. Likewise, predicting whether an email is spam and predicting whether a credit card transaction is legitimate or fraudulent can also be done using similar techniques. What about grouping users of an app based on their similarity? That sounds different from predicting housing prices, but it could be done similarly to grouping newspaper articles by topic. And what about playing chess? That sounds different from all the other previous applications, but it could be like playing Go.

Machine learning models are grouped into different types, according to the way they operate. The main three families of machine learning models are

- *supervised learning,*
- *unsupervised learning,* and
- *reinforcement learning.*

In this chapter, we overview all three. However, in this book, we focus only on supervised learning because it is the most natural one to start learning and arguably the most used right now. Look up the other types in the literature and learn about them, too, because they are all interesting and useful! In the resources in appendix C, you can find some interesting links, including several videos created by the author.

What is the difference between labeled and unlabeled data?

What is data?

We talked about data in chapter 1, but before we go any further, let's first establish a clear definition of what we mean by *data* in this book. Data is simply information. Any time we have a table with information, we have data. Normally, each row in our table is a data point. Say, for example, that we have a dataset of pets. In this case, each row represents a different pet. Each pet in the table is described by certain features of that pet.

And what are features?

In chapter 1, we defined features as the properties or characteristics of the data. If our data is in a table, the features are the columns of the table. In our pet example, the features may be size, name, type, or weight. Features could even be the colors of the pixels in an image of the pet. This is what describes our data. Some features are special, though, and we call them *labels*.

Labels?

This one is a bit less straightforward, because it depends on the context of the problem we are trying to solve. Normally, if we are trying to predict a particular feature based on the other ones, that feature is the label. If we are trying to predict the type of pet (e.g., cat or dog) based on information on that pet, then the label is the type of pet (cat/dog). If we are trying to predict if the pet is sick or healthy based on symptoms and other information, then the label is the state of the pet (sick/healthy). If we are trying to predict the age of the pet, then the label is the age (a number).

Predictions

We have been using the concept of making predictions freely, but let's now pin it down. The goal of a predictive machine learning model is to guess the labels in the data. The guess that the model makes is called a *prediction*.

Now that we know what labels are, we can understand there are two main types of data: *labeled* and *unlabeled* data.

Labeled and unlabeled data

Labeled data is data that comes with labels. Unlabeled data is data that comes with no labels. An example of labeled data is a dataset of emails that comes with a column that records whether the emails are spam or ham, or a column that records whether the email is work related. An example of unlabeled data is a dataset of emails that has no particular column we are interested in predicting.

In figure 2.1, we see three datasets containing images of pets. The first dataset has a column recording the type of pet, and the second dataset has a column specifying the weight of the pet. These two are examples of labeled data. The third dataset consists only of images, with no label, making it unlabeled data.

Figure 2.1   Labeled data is data that comes with a tag, or label. That label can be a type or a number. Unlabeled data is data that comes with no tag. The dataset on the left is labeled, and the label is the type of pet (dog/cat). The dataset in the middle is also labeled, and the label is the weight of the pet (in pounds). The dataset on the right is unlabeled.

Of course, this definition contains some ambiguity, because depending on the problem, we decide whether a particular feature qualifies as a label. Thus, determining if data is labeled or unlabeled, many times, depends on the problem we are trying to solve.

Labeled and unlabeled data yield two different branches of machine learning called *supervised* and *unsupervised* learning, which are defined in the next three sections.

Supervised learning: The branch of machine learning that works with labeled data

We can find supervised learning in some of the most common applications nowadays, including image recognition, various forms of text processing, and recommendation systems. Supervised learning is a type of machine learning that uses labeled data. In short, the goal of a supervised learning model is to predict (guess) the labels.

In the example in figure 2.1, the dataset on the left contains images of dogs and cats, and the labels are "dog" and "cat." For this dataset, the machine learning model would use previous data to predict the label of new data points. This means, if we bring in a new image *without* a label, the model will guess whether the image is of a dog or a cat, thus predicting the label of the data point (figure 2.2).

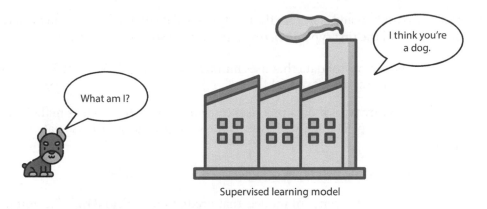

Figure 2.2   A supervised learning model predicts the label of a new data point. In this case, the data point corresponds to a dog, and the supervised learning algorithm is trained to predict that this data point does, indeed, correspond to a dog.

If you recall from chapter 1, the framework we learned for making a decision was remember-formulate-predict. This is precisely how supervised learning works. The model first **remembers** the dataset of dogs and cats. Then it **formulates** a model, or a rule, for what it believes constitutes a dog and a cat. Finally, when a new image comes in, the model makes a **prediction** about what it thinks the label of the image is, namely, a dog or a cat (figure 2.3).

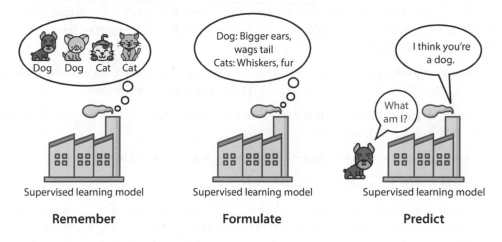

Figure 2.3   A supervised learning model follows the remember-formulate-predict framework from chapter 1. First, it remembers the dataset. Then, it formulates rules for what would constitute a dog and a cat. Finally, it predicts whether a new data point is a dog or a cat.

Now, notice that in figure 2.1, we have two types of labeled datasets. In the dataset in the middle, each data point is labeled with the weight of the animal. In this dataset, the labels are numbers. In the dataset on the left, each data point is labeled with the type of animal (dog or cat). In this dataset, the labels are states. Numbers and states are the two types of data that we'll encounter in supervised learning models. We call the first type *numerical data* and the second type *categorical data.*

numerical data   is any type of data that uses numbers such as 4, 2.35, or −199. Examples of numerical data are prices, sizes, or weights.

categorical data   is any type of data that uses categories, or states, such as male/female or cat/dog/bird. For this type of data, we have a finite set of categories to associate to each of the data points.

This gives rise to the following two types of supervised learning models:

regression models   are the types of models that predict **numerical data**. The output of a regression model is a *number,* such as the weight of the animal.

classification models   are the types of models that predict **categorical data**. The output of a classification model is a *category,* or a *state,* such as the type of animal (cat or dog).

Let's look at two examples of supervised learning models, one regression and one classification.

Model 1: housing prices model (regression). In this model, each data point is a house. The label of each house is its price. Our goal is that when a new house (data point) comes on the market, we would like to predict its label, namely, its price.

Model 2: email spam–detection model (classification). In this model, each data point is an email. The label of each email is either spam or ham. Our goal is that when a new email (data point) comes into our inbox, we would like to predict its label, namely, whether it is spam or ham.

Notice the difference between models 1 and 2.

- The housing prices model is a model that can return a number from many possibilities, such as $100, $250,000, or $3,125,672.33. Thus, it is a *regression* model.

- The spam detection model, on the other hand, can return only two things: spam or ham. Thus, it is a *classification* model.

In the following subsections, we elaborate more on regression and classification.

Regression models predict numbers

As we discussed previously, regression models are those in which the label we want to predict is a number. This number is predicted based on the features. In the housing example, the features can be anything that describes a house, such as the size, the number of rooms, the distance to the closest school, or the crime rate in the neighborhood.

Other places where one can use regression models follow:

- **Stock market:** predicting the price of a certain stock based on other stock prices and other market signals

- **Medicine:** predicting the expected life span of a patient or the expected recovery time, based on symptoms and the medical history of the patient

- **Sales:** predicting the expected amount of money a customer will spend, based on the client's demographics and past purchase behavior
- **Video recommendations:** predicting the expected amount of time a user will watch a video, based on the user's demographics and other videos they have watched

The most common method used for regression is linear regression, which uses linear functions (lines or similar objects) to make our predictions based on the features. We study linear regression in chapter 3. Other popular methods used for regression are decision tree regression, which we learn in chapter 9, and several ensemble methods such as random forests, AdaBoost, gradient boosted trees, and XGBoost, which we learn in chapter 12.

Classification models predict a state

Classification models are those in which the label we want to predict is a state belonging to a finite set of states. The most common classification models predict a "yes" or a "no," but many other models use a larger set of states. The example we saw in figure 2.3 is an example of classification, because it predicts the type of the pet, namely, "cat" or "dog."

In the email spam recognition example, the model predicts the state of the email (namely, spam or ham) from the features of the email. In this case, the features of the email can be the words on it, the number of spelling mistakes, the sender, or anything else that describes the email.

Another common application of classification is image recognition. The most popular image recognition models take as input the pixels in the image, and they output a prediction of what the image depicts. Two of the most famous datasets for image recognition are MNIST and CIFAR-10. MNIST contains approximately 60,000 28-by-28-pixel black-and-white images of handwritten digits which are labelled 0–9. These images come from a combination of sources, including the American Census Bureau and a repository of handwritten digits written by American high school students. The MNIST dataset can be found in the following link: http://yann.lecun.com/exdb/mnist/. The CIFAR-10 dataset contains 60,000 32-by-32-pixel colored images of different things. These images are labeled with 10 different objects (thus the 10 in its name), namely, airplanes, cars, birds, cats, deer, dogs, frogs, horses, ships, and trucks. This database is maintained by the Canadian Institute for Advanced Research (CIFAR), and it can be found in the following link: https://www.cs.toronto.edu/~kriz/cifar.html.

Some additional powerful applications of classification models follow:

- **Sentiment analysis:** predicting whether a movie review is positive or negative, based on the words in the review
- **Website traffic:** predicting whether a user will click a link or not, based on the user's demographics and past interaction with the site
- **Social media:** predicting whether a user will befriend or interact with another user, based on their demographics, history, and friends in common
- **Video recommendations:** predicting whether a user will watch a video, based on the user's demographics and other videos they have watched

The bulk of this book (chapters 5, 6, 8, 9, 10, 11, and 12) covers classification models. In these chapters we learn the perceptrons (chapter 5), logistic classifiers (chapter 6), the naive Bayes algorithm (chapter 8), decision trees (chapter 9), neural networks (chapter 10), support vector machines (chapter 11), and ensemble methods (chapter 12).

Unsupervised learning: The branch of machine learning that works with unlabeled data

Unsupervised learning is also a common type of machine learning. It differs from supervised learning in that the data is unlabeled. In other words, the goal of a machine learning model is to extract as much information as possible from a dataset that has no labels, or targets to predict.

What could such a dataset be, and what could we do with it? In principle, we can do a little less than what we can do with a labeled dataset, because we have no labels to predict. However, we can still extract a lot of information from an unlabeled dataset. For example, let's go back to the cats and dogs example on the rightmost dataset in figure 2.1. This dataset consists of images of cats and dogs, but it has no labels. Therefore, we don't know what type of pet each image represents, so we can't predict if a new image corresponds to a dog or a cat. However, we can do other things, such as determine if two pictures are similar or different. This is something unsupervised learning algorithms do. An unsupervised learning algorithm can group the images based on similarity, even without knowing what each group represents (figure 2.4). If done properly, the algorithm could separate the dog images from the cat images, or even group each of them by breed!

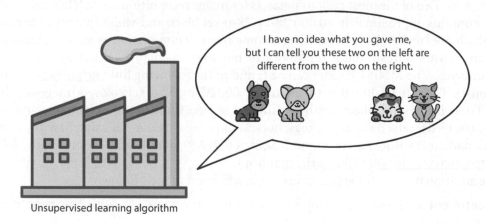

Unsupervised learning algorithm

Figure 2.4   An unsupervised learning algorithm can still extract information from data. For example, it can group similar elements together.

As a matter of fact, even if the labels are there, we can still use unsupervised learning techniques on our data to preprocess it and apply supervised learning methods more effectively.

The main branches of unsupervised learning are clustering, dimensionality reduction, and generative learning.

clustering algorithms   The algorithms that group data into clusters based on similarity

dimensionality reduction algorithms   The algorithms that simplify our data and faithfully describe it with fewer features

generative algorithms   The algorithms that can generate new data points that resemble the existing data

In the following three subsections, we study these three branches in more detail.

Clustering algorithms split a dataset into similar groups

As we stated previously, clustering algorithms are those that split the dataset into similar groups. To illustrate this, let's go back to the two datasets in the section "Supervised learning"—the housing dataset and the spam email dataset—but imagine that they have no labels. This means that the housing dataset has no prices, and the email dataset has no information on the emails being spam or ham.

Let's begin with the housing dataset. What can we do with this dataset? Here is an idea: we could somehow group the houses by similarity. For example, we could group them by location, price, size, or a combination of these factors. This process is called *clustering*. Clustering is a branch of unsupervised machine learning that consists of the tasks that group the elements in our dataset into clusters where all the data points are similar.

Now let's look at the second example, the dataset of emails. Because the dataset is unlabeled, we don't know whether each email is spam or ham. However, we can still apply some clustering to our dataset. A clustering algorithm splits our images into a few different groups based on different features of the email. These features could be the words in the message, the sender, the number and size of the attachments, or the types of links inside the email. After clustering the dataset, a human (or a combination of a human and a supervised learning algorithm) could label these clusters by categories such as "Personal," "Social," and "Promotions."

As an example, let's look at the dataset in table 2.1, which contains nine emails that we would like to cluster. The features of the dataset are the size of the email and the number of recipients.

Table 2.1   A table of emails with their size and number of recipients

Email	Size	Recipients
1	8	1
2	12	1
3	43	1
4	10	2
5	40	2
6	25	5
7	23	6
8	28	6
9	26	7

To the naked eye, it looks like we could group the emails by their number of recipients. This would result in two clusters: one with emails having two or fewer recipients, and one with emails having five or more recipients. We could also try to group them into three groups by size. But you can imagine that as the table gets larger and larger, eyeballing the groups gets harder and harder. What if we plot the data? Let's plot the emails in a graph, where the horizontal axis records the size and the vertical axis records the number of recipients. This gives us the plot in figure 2.5.

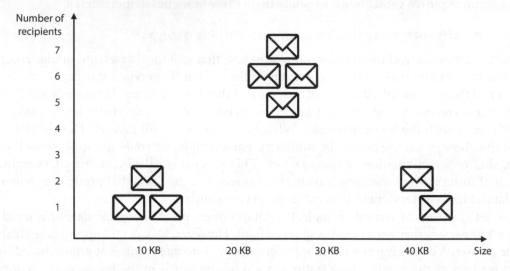

Figure 2.5   A plot of the email dataset. The horizontal axis corresponds to the size of the email and the vertical axis to the number of recipients. We can see three well-defined clusters in this dataset.

In figure 2.5 we can see three well-defined clusters, which are highlighted in figure 2.6.

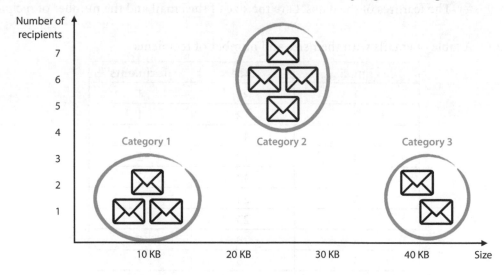

Figure 2.6   We can cluster the emails into three categories based on size and number of recipients.

This last step is what clustering is all about. Of course, for us humans, it's easy to eyeball the three groups once we have the plot. But for a computer, this task is not easy. Furthermore, imagine if our data contained millions of points, with hundreds or thousands of features. With more than three features, it is impossible for humans to see the clusters, because they would be in dimensions that we cannot visualize. Luckily, computers can do this type of clustering for huge datasets with multiple rows and columns.

Other applications of clustering are the following:

- **Market segmentation:** dividing customers into groups based on demographics and previous purchasing behavior to create different marketing strategies for the groups

- **Genetics:** clustering species into groups based on gene similarity

- **Medical imaging:** splitting an image into different parts to study different types of tissue

- **Video recommendations:** dividing users into groups based on demographics and previous videos watched and using this to recommend to a user the videos that other users in their group have watched

More on unsupervised learning models

In the rest of this book, we don't cover unsupervised learning. However, I strongly encourage you to study it on your own. Here are some of the most important clustering algorithms out there. Appendix C lists several more (including some videos of mine) where you can learn these algorithms in detail.

- *K*-means clustering: this algorithm groups points by picking some random centers of mass and moving them closer and closer to the points until they are at the right spots.

- **Hierarchical clustering:** this algorithm starts by grouping the closest points together and continuing in this fashion, until we have some well-defined groups.

- **Density-based spatial clustering (DBSCAN):** this algorithm starts grouping points together in places with high density, while labeling the isolated points as noise.

- **Gaussian mixture models:** this algorithm does not assign a point to one cluster but instead assigns fractions of the point to each of the existing clusters. For example, if there are three clusters, A, B, and C, then the algorithm could determine that 60% of a particular point belongs to group A, 25% to group B, and 15% to group C.

Dimensionality reduction simplifies data without losing too much information

Dimensionality reduction is a useful preprocessing step that we can apply to vastly simplify our data before applying other techniques. As an example, let's go back to the housing dataset. Imagine that the features are the following:

- Size
- Number of bedrooms
- Number of bathrooms

- Crime rate in the neighborhood

- Distance to the closest school

This dataset has five columns of data. What if we wanted to turn the dataset into a simpler one with fewer columns, without losing a lot of information? Let's do this by using common sense. Take a closer look at the five features. Can you see any way to simplify them—perhaps to group them into some smaller and more general categories?

After a careful look, we can see that the first three features are similar, because they are all related to the size of the house. Similarly, the fourth and fifth features are similar to each other, because they are related to the quality of the neighborhood. We could condense the first three features into a big "size" feature, and the fourth and fifth into a big "neighborhood quality" feature. How do we condense the size features? We could forget about rooms and bedrooms and consider only the size, we could add the number of bedrooms and bathrooms, or maybe take some other combination of the three features. We could also condense the area quality features in similar ways. Dimensionality reduction algorithms will find good ways to condense these features, losing as little information as possible and keeping our data as intact as possible while managing to simplify it for easier process and storage (figure 2.7).

Dimensionality reduction

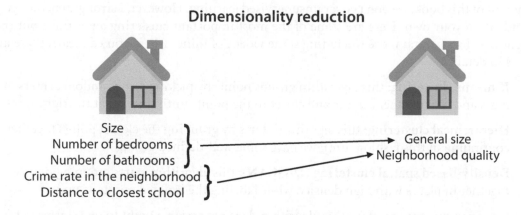

Figure 2.7   Dimensionality reduction algorithms help us simplify our data. On the left, we have a housing dataset with many features. We can use dimensionality reduction to reduce the number of features in the dataset without losing much information and obtain the dataset on the right.

Why is it called dimensionality reduction if all we're doing is reducing the number of columns in our data? The fancy word for the number of columns in a dataset is *dimension*. Think about this: if our data has one column, then each data point is one number. A collection of numbers can be plotted as a collection of points in a line, which has precisely one dimension. If our data has two columns, then each data point is formed by a pair of numbers. We can imagine a collection of pairs of numbers as a collection of points in a city, where the first number is the street number and the second number is the avenue. Addresses on a map are two-dimensional, because they are in a plane. What happens when our data has three columns? In this case, then each data point is formed by three numbers. We can imagine that if every address in our city is a building, then the first and second numbers are the street and avenue, and the third one is the floor in the building. This looks more like a three-dimensional city. We can keep going. What about four numbers? Well, now we can't really visualize it, but if we could, this set of points would look like places in a four-dimensional city, and so on. The best way to imagine a four-dimensional city is by imagining a table with four columns. What about a 100-dimensional city? This would be a table with 100 columns, in which each person has an address that consists of 100 numbers. The mental picture we could have when thinking of higher dimensions is shown in figure 2.8. Therefore, as we went from five dimensions down to two, we reduced our five-dimensional city into a two-dimensional city. This is why it is called dimensionality reduction.

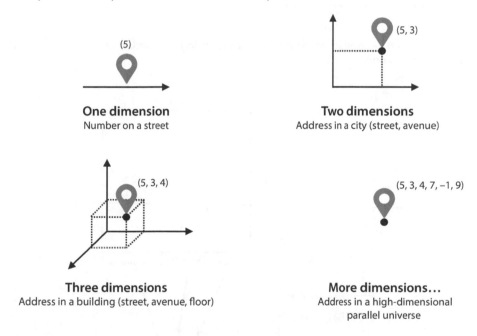

One dimension
Number on a street

Two dimensions
Address in a city (street, avenue)

Three dimensions
Address in a building (street, avenue, floor)

More dimensions...
Address in a high-dimensional
parallel universe

Figure 2.8 How to imagine higher dimensional spaces: One dimension is like a street, in which each house only has one number. Two dimensions is like a flat city, in which each address has two numbers, a street and an avenue. Three dimensions is like a city with buildings, in which each address has three numbers: a street, an avenue, and a floor. Four dimensions is like an imaginary place in which each address has four numbers. We can imagine higher dimensions as another imaginary city in which addresses have as many coordinates as we need.

Other ways of simplifying our data: Matrix factorization and singular value decomposition

It seems that clustering and dimensionality reduction are nothing like each other, but, in reality, they are not so different. If we have a table full of data, each row corresponds to a data point, and each column corresponds to a feature. Therefore, we can use clustering to reduce the number of rows in our dataset and dimensionality reduction to reduce the number of columns, as figures 2.9 and 2.10 illustrate.

Clustering

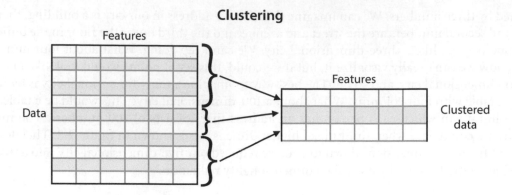

Figure 2.9   Clustering can be used to simplify our data by reducing the number of rows in our dataset by grouping several rows into one.

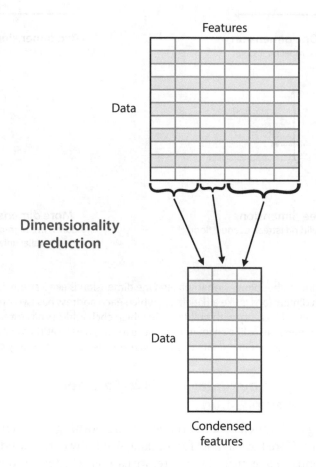

Figure 2.10   Dimensionality reduction can be used to simplify our data by reducing the number of columns in our dataset.

You may be wondering, is there a way that we can reduce both the rows and the columns at the same time? And the answer is yes! Two common ways we can do this are *matrix factorization* and *singular value decomposition*. These two algorithms express a big matrix of data into a product of smaller matrices.

Places like Netflix use matrix factorization extensively to generate recommendations. Imagine a large table where each row corresponds to a user, each column to a movie, and each entry in the matrix is the rating that the user gave the movie. With matrix factorization, one can extract certain features, such as type of movie, actors appearing in the movie, and others, and be able to predict the rating that a user gives a movie, based on these features.

Singular value decomposition is used in image compression. For example, a black-and-white image can be seen as a large table of data, where each entry contains the intensity of the corresponding pixel. Singular value decomposition uses linear algebra techniques to simplify this table of data, thus allowing us to simplify the image and store its simpler version using fewer entries.

Generative machine learning

Generative machine learning is one of the most astonishing fields of machine learning. If you have seen ultra-realistic faces, images, or videos created by computers, then you have seen generative machine learning in action.

The field of generative learning consists of models that, given a dataset, can output new data points that look like samples from that original dataset. These algorithms are forced to learn how the data looks to produce similar data points. For example, if the dataset contains images of faces, then the algorithm will produce realistic-looking faces. Generative algorithms have been able to create tremendously realistic images, paintings, and so on. They have also generated video, music, stories, poetry, and many other wonderful things. The most popular generative algorithm is generative adversarial networks (GANs), developed by Ian Goodfellow and his coauthors. Other useful and popular generative algorithms are variational autoencoders, developed by Kingma and Welling, and restricted Boltzmann machines (RBMs), developed by Geoffrey Hinton.

As you can imagine, generative learning is quite hard. For a human, it is much easier to determine if an image shows a dog than it is to draw a dog. This task is just as hard for computers. Thus, the algorithms in generative learning are complicated, and lots of data and computing power are needed to make them work well. Because this book is on supervised learning, we won't cover generative learning in detail, but in chapter 10, we get an idea of how some of these generative algorithms work, because they tend to use neural networks. Appendix C contains recommendations of resources, including a video by the author, if you'd like to explore this topic further.

What is reinforcement learning?

Reinforcement learning is a different type of machine learning in which no data is given, and we must get the computer to perform a task. Instead of data, the model receives an environment and an agent who is supposed to navigate in this environment. The agent has a goal or a set of goals.

The environment has rewards and punishments that guide the agent to make the right decisions to reach its goal. This all sounds a bit abstract, but let's look at an example.

Example: Grid world

In figure 2.11, we see a grid world with a robot at the bottom-left corner. That is our agent. The goal is to get to the treasure chest in the top right of the grid. In the grid, we can also see a mountain, which means we cannot go through that square, because the robot cannot climb mountains. We also see a dragon, which will attack the robot, should the robot dare to land in its square, which means that part of our goal is to not land over there. This is the game. And to give the robot information about how to proceed, we keep track of a score. The score starts at zero. If the robot gets to the treasure chest, then we gain 100 points. If the robot reaches the dragon, we lose 50 points. And to make sure our robot moves quickly, we can say that for every step the robot makes, we lose 1 point, because the robot loses energy as it walks.

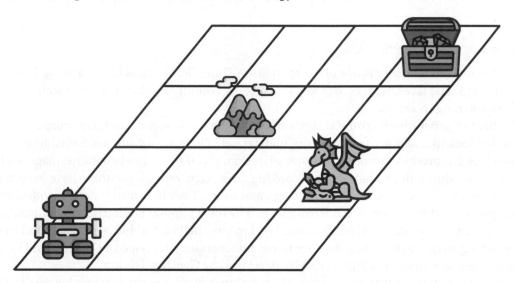

Figure 2.11   A grid world in which our agent is a robot. The goal of the robot is to find the treasure chest, while avoiding the dragon. The mountain represents a place through which the robot can't pass.

The way to train this algorithm, in very rough terms, follows: The robot starts walking around, recording its score and remembering what steps took it there. After some point, it may meet the dragon, losing many points. Therefore, it learns to associate the dragon square and the squares close to it with low scores. At some point it may also hit the treasure chest, and it learns to start associating that square and the squares close to it to high scores. After playing this game for a long time, the robot will have a good idea of how good each square is, and it can take the path following the squares all the way to the treasure chest. Figure 2.12 shows a possible path, although this one is not ideal, because it passes too close to the dragon. Can you think of a better one?

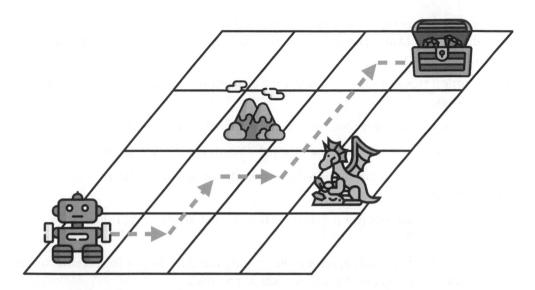

Figure 2.12 Here is a path that the robot could take to find the treasure chest.

Of course, this is a very brief explanation, and there is a lot more to reinforcement learning. Appendix C recommends some resources for further study, including a deep reinforcement learning video.

Reinforcement learning has numerous cutting-edge applications, including the following:

- **Games:** recent advances in teaching computers how to win at games, such as Go or chess, use reinforcement learning. Also, agents have been taught to win at Atari games such as *Breakout* or *Super Mario.*

- **Robotics:** reinforcement learning is used extensively to help robots carry out tasks such as picking up boxes, cleaning a room, or even dancing!

- **Self-driving cars:** reinforcement learning techniques are used to help the car carry out many tasks such as path planning or behaving in particular environments.

Summary

- Several types of machine learning exist, including supervised learning, unsupervised learning, and reinforcement learning.

- Data can be labeled or unlabeled. Labeled data contains a special feature, or label, that we aim to predict. Unlabeled data doesn't contain this feature.

- Supervised learning is used on labeled data and consists of building models that predict the labels for unseen data.

- Unsupervised learning is used on unlabeled data and consists of algorithms that simplify our data without losing a lot of information. Unsupervised learning is often used as a preprocessing step.

- Two common types of supervised learning algorithms are called regression and classification.

  – Regression models are those in which the answer is any number.

  – Classification models are those in which the answer is of a type or a class.

- Two common types of unsupervised learning algorithms are clustering and dimensionality reduction.

  – Clustering is used to group data into similar clusters to extract information or make it easier to handle.

  – Dimensionality reduction is a way to simplify our data, by joining certain similar features and losing as little information as possible.

  – Matrix factorization and singular value decomposition are other algorithms that can simplify our data by reducing both the number of rows and columns.

- Generative machine learning is an innovative type of unsupervised learning, consisting of generating data that is similar to our dataset. Generative models can paint realistic faces, compose music, and write poetry.

- Reinforcement learning is a type of machine learning in which an agent must navigate an environment and reach a goal. It is extensively used in many cutting-edge applications.

Exercises

Exercise 2.1

For each of the following scenarios, state if it is an example of supervised or unsupervised learning. Explain your answers. In cases of ambiguity, pick one, and explain why you picked it.

  a. A recommendation system on a social network that recommends potential friends to a user

  b. A system in a news site that divides the news into topics

  c. The Google autocomplete feature for sentences

  d. A recommendation system on an online retailer that recommends to users what to buy based on their past purchasing history

  e. A system in a credit card company that captures fraudulent transactions

Exercise 2.2

For each of the following applications of machine learning, would you use regression or classification to solve it? Explain your answers. In cases of ambiguity, pick one, and explain why you picked it.

a. An online store predicting how much money a user will spend on their site

b. A voice assistant decoding voice and turning it into text

c. Selling or buying stock from a particular company

d. YouTube recommending a video to a user

Exercise 2.3

Your task is to build a self-driving car. Give at least three examples of machine learning problems that you would have to solve to build it. In each example, explain if you are using supervised/ unsupervised learning, and, if supervised, whether you are using regression or classification. If you are using other types of machine learning, explain which ones, and why.

Drawing a line close to our points: Linear regression | 3

In this chapter

- what is linear regression

- fitting a line through a set of data points

- coding the linear regression algorithm in Python

- using Turi Create to build a linear regression model to predict housing prices in a real dataset

- what is polynomial regression

- fitting a more complex curve to nonlinear data

- discussing examples of linear regression in the real world, such as medical applications and recommender systems

In this chapter, we will learn about linear regression. Linear regression is a powerful and widely used method to estimate values, such as the price of a house, the value of a certain stock, the life expectancy of an individual, or the amount of time a user will watch a video or spend on a website. You may have seen linear regression before as a plethora of complicated formulas including derivatives, systems of equations, and determinants. However, we can also see linear regression in a more graphical and less formulaic way. In this chapter, to understand linear regression, all you need is the ability to visualize points and lines moving around.

Let's say that we have some points that roughly look like they are forming a line, as shown in figure 3.1.

Figure 3.1   Some points that roughly look like they are forming a line

The goal of linear regression is to draw the line that passes as close to these points as possible. What line would you draw that passes close to those points? How about the one shown in figure 3.2?

Think of the points as houses in a town, and our goal is to build a road that goes through the town. We want the line to pass as close as possible to the points because the town's inhabitants all want to live close to the road, and our goal is to please them as much as we can.

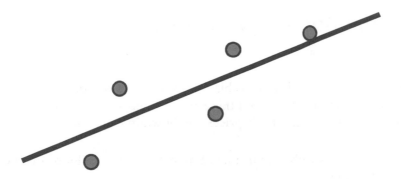

Figure 3.2 A line that passes close to the points

We can also imagine the points as magnets lying bolted to the floor (so they can't move). Now imagine throwing a straight metal rod on top of them. The rod will move around, but because the magnets pull it, it will eventually end up in a position of equilibrium, as close as it can to all the points.

Of course, this can lead to a lot of ambiguity. Do we want a road that goes somewhat close to all the houses, or maybe really close to a few of them and a bit farther from others? Some questions that arise follow:

- What do we mean by "points that roughly look like they are forming a line"?

- What do we mean by "a line that passes really close to the points"?

- How do we find such a line?

- Why is this useful in the real world?

- Why is this machine learning?

In this chapter we answer all these questions, and we build a linear regression model to predict housing prices in a real dataset.

You can find all the code for this chapter in the following GitHub repository: https://github .com/luisguiserrano/manning/tree/master/Chapter_3_Linear_Regression.

The problem: We need to predict the price of a house

Let's say that we are real estate agents in charge of selling a new house. We don't know the price, and we want to infer it by comparing it with other houses. We look at features of the house that could influence the price, such as size, number of rooms, location, crime rate, school quality, and distance to commerce. At the end of the day, we want a formula for all these features that gives us the price of the house, or at least a good estimate for it.

The solution: Building a regression model for housing prices

Let's go with as simple an example as possible. We look at only one of the features—the number of rooms. Our house has four rooms, and there are six houses nearby, with one, two, three, five, six, and seven rooms, respectively. Their prices are shown in table 3.1.

Table 3.1   A table of houses with the number of rooms and prices. House 4 is the one whose price we are trying to infer.

Number of rooms	Price
1	150
2	200
3	250
4	?
5	350
6	400
7	450

What price would you give to house 4, just based on the information on this table? If you said $300, then we made the same guess. You probably saw a pattern and used it to infer the price of the house. What you did in your head was linear regression. Let's study this pattern more. You may have noticed that each time you add a room, $50 is added to the price of the house. More specifically, we can think of the price of a house as a combination of two things: a base price of $100, and an extra charge of $50 for each of the rooms. This can be summarized in a simple formula:

$$\text{Price} = 100 + 50(\text{Number of rooms})$$

What we did here is come up with a model represented by a formula that gives us a *prediction* of the price of the house, based on the *feature*, which is the number of rooms. The price per room is called the *weight* of that corresponding feature, and the base price is called the *bias* of the model. These are all important concepts in machine learning. We learned some of them in chapter 1 and 2, but let's refresh our memory by defining them from the perspective of this problem.

features   The features of a data point are those properties that we use to make our prediction. In this case, the features are the number of rooms in the house, the crime rate, the age of the house, the size, and so on. For our case, we've decided on one feature: the number of rooms in the house.

labels   This is the target that we try to predict from the features. In this case, the label is the price of the house.

model   A machine learning model is a rule, or a formula, which predicts a label from the features. In this case, the model is the equation we found for the price.

prediction   The prediction is the output of the model. If the model says, "I think the house with four rooms is going to cost $300," then the prediction is 300.

weights   In the formula corresponding to the model, each feature is multiplied by a corresponding factor. These factors are the weights. In the previous formula, the only feature is the number of rooms, and its corresponding weight is 50.

bias   As you can see, the formula corresponding to the model has a constant that is not attached to any of the features. This constant is called the bias. In this model, the bias is 100, and it corresponds to the base price of a house.

Now the question is, how did we come up with this formula? Or more specifically, how do we get the computer to come up with this weight and bias? To illustrate this, let's look at a slightly more complicated example. And because this is a machine learning problem, we will approach it using the remember-formulate-predict framework that we learned in chapter 2. More specifically, we'll *remember* the prices of other houses, *formulate* a model for the price, and use this model to *predict* the price of a new house.

The remember step: Looking at the prices of existing houses

To see the process more clearly, let's look at a slightly more complicated dataset, such as the one in table 3.2.

Table 3.2   A slightly more complicated dataset of houses with their number of rooms and their price

Number of rooms	Price
1	155
2	197
3	244
4	?
5	356
6	407
7	448

This dataset is similar to the previous one, except now the prices don't follow a nice pattern, where each price is $50 more than the previous one. However, it's not that far from the original dataset, so we can expect that a similar pattern should approximate these values well.

Normally, the first thing we do when we get a new dataset is to plot it. In figure 3.3, we can see a plot of the points in a coordinate system in which the horizontal axis represents the number of rooms, and the vertical axis represents the price of the house.

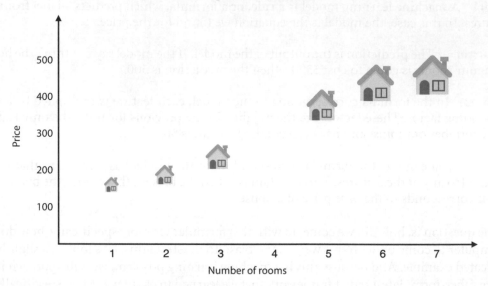

Figure 3.3   Plot of the dataset in table 3.2. The horizontal axis represents the number of rooms, and the vertical axis represents the price of the house.

The formulate step: Formulating a rule that estimates the price of the house

The dataset in table 3.2 is close enough to the one in table 3.1, so for now, we can feel safe using the same formula for the price. The only difference is that now the prices are not exactly what the formula says, and we have a small error. We can write the equation as follows:

$$\text{Price} = 100 + 50(\text{Number of rooms}) + (\text{Small error})$$

If we want to predict prices, we can use this equation. Even though we are not sure we'll get the actual value, we know that we are likely to get close. Now the question is, how did we find this equation? And most important, how does a computer find this equation?

Let's go back to the plot and see what the equation means there. What happens if we look at all the points in which the vertical (y) coordinate is 100 plus 50 times the horizontal (x) coordinate? This set of points forms a line with slope 50 and y-intercept 100. Before we unpack the previous statement, here are the definitions of slope, y-intercept, and the equation of a line. We delve into these in more detail in the "Crash course on slope and y-intercept" section.

slope   The slope of a line is a measure of how steep it is. It is calculated by dividing the rise over the run (i.e., how many units it goes up, divided by how many units it goes to the right). This ratio is constant over the whole line. In a machine learning model, this is the weight of the corresponding feature, and it tells us how much we expect the value of the label to go up, when we increase the value of the feature by one unit. If the line is horizontal, then the slope is zero, and if the line goes down, the slope is negative.

y-intercept   The *y*-intercept of a line is the height at which the line crosses the vertical (*y*-) axis. In a machine learning model, it is the bias and tells us what the label would be in a data point where all the features are precisely zero.

linear equation   This is the equation of a line. It is given by two parameters: the slope and the *y*-intercept. If the slope is m and the *y*-intercept is b, then the equation of the line is $y = mx + b$, and the line is formed by all the points (x,y) that satisfy the equation. In a machine learning model, x is the value of the feature and y is the prediction for the label. The weight and bias of the model are m and b, respectively.

We can now analyze the equation. When we say that the slope of the line is 50—this means that each time we add one room to the house, we estimate that the price of the house will go up by $50. When we say that the *y*-intercept of the line is 100, this means that the estimate for the price of a (hypothetical) house with zero rooms would be the base price of $100. This line is drawn in figure 3.4.

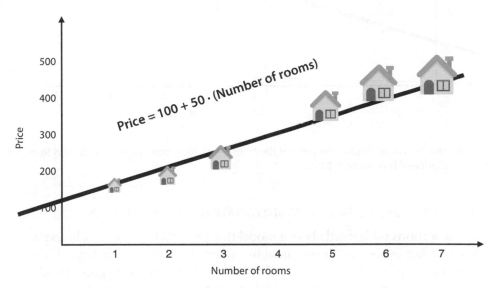

Figure 3.4   The model we formulate is the line that goes as close as possible to all the houses.

Now, of all the possible lines (each with its own equation), why did we pick this one in particular? Because that one passes close to the points. There may be a better one, but at least we know this one is good, as opposed to one that goes nowhere near the points. Now we are back to the original problem, where we have a set of houses, and we want to build a road as close as possible to them.

How do we find this line? We'll look at this later in the chapter. But for now, let's say that we have a crystal ball that, given a bunch of points, finds the line that passes the closest to them.

The predict step: What do we do when a new house comes on the market?

Now, on to using our model to predict the price of the house with four rooms. For this, we plug the number four as the feature in our formula to get the following:

$$\text{Price} = 100 + 50 \cdot 4 = 300$$

Therefore, our model predicts that the house costs $300. This can also be seen graphically by using the line, as illustrated in figure 3.5.

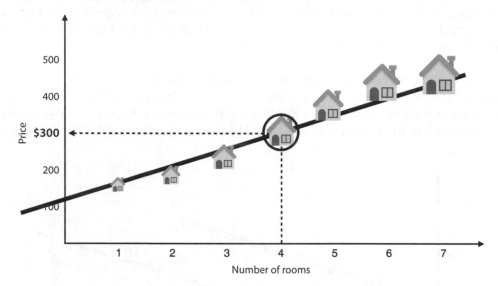

Figure 3.5   Our task is now to predict the price of the house with four rooms. Using the model (line), we deduce that the predicted price of this house is $300.

What if we have more variables? Multivariate linear regression

In the previous sections we learned about a model that predicts the price of a house based on one feature—the number of rooms. We may imagine many other features that could help us predict the price of a house, such as the size, the quality of the schools in the neighborhood, and the age of the house. Can our linear regression model accommodate these other variables? Absolutely. When the only feature is the number of rooms, our model predicts the price as the sum of the feature times their corresponding weight, plus a bias. If we have more features, all we need to do is multiply them by their corresponding weights and add them to the predicted price. Therefore, a model for the price of a house could look like this:

Price = 30(number of rooms) + 1.5(size) + 10(quality of the schools) − 2(age of the house) + 50

In this equation, why are all of the weights positive, except for the one corresponding to the age of the house? The reason is the other three features (number of rooms, size, and quality of the schools) are *positively correlated* to the price of the house. In other words, because houses that are bigger and well located cost more, the higher this feature is, the higher we expect the price of the house to be. However, because we would imagine that older houses tend to be less expensive, the age feature is *negatively correlated* to the price of the house.

What if the weight of a feature is zero? This happens when a feature is irrelevant to the price. For example, imagine a feature that measured the number of neighbors whose last name starts with the letter *A*. This feature is mostly irrelevant to the price of the house, so we would expect that in a reasonable model, the weight corresponding to this feature is either zero or something very close to it.

In a similar way, if a feature has a very high weight (whether negative or positive), we interpret this as the model telling us that that feature is important in determining the price of the house. In the previous model, it seems that the number of rooms is an important feature, because its weight is the largest (in absolute value).

In the section called "Dimensionality reduction simplifies data without losing too much information" in chapter 2, we related the number of columns in a dataset to the dimension in which the dataset lives. Thus, a dataset with two columns can be represented as a set of points in the plane, and a dataset with three columns can be represented as a set of points in three-dimensional space. In such a dataset, a linear regression model corresponds not to a line but to a plane that passes as close as possible to the points. Imagine having many flies flying around in the room in a stationary position, and our task is to try to pass a gigantic cardboard sheet as close as we can to all the flies. This is multivariate linear regression with three variables. The problem becomes hard to visualize for datasets with more columns, but we can always imagine a linear equation with many variables.

In this chapter, we mostly deal with training linear regression models with only one feature, but the procedure is similar with more features. I encourage you to read about it while keeping this fact in the back of your mind, and imagine how you would generalize each of our next statements to a case with several features.

Some questions that arise and some quick answers

OK, your head may be ringing with lots of questions. Let's address some (hopefully all) of them!

1. What happens if the model makes a mistake?

2. How did you come up with the formula that predicts the price? And what would we do if instead of six houses, we had thousands of them?

3. Say we've built this prediction model, and then new houses start appearing in the market. Is there a way to update the model with new information?

This chapter answers all these questions, but here are some quick answers:

1. **What happens if the model makes a mistake?**
   The model is estimating the price of a house, so we expect it to make a small mistake pretty much all the time, because it is very hard to hit the exact price. The training process consists of finding the model that makes the smallest errors at our points.

2. **How did you come up with the formula that predicts the price? And what would we do if instead of six houses, we had thousands of them?**

   Yes, this is the main question we address in this chapter! When we have six houses, the problem of drawing a line that goes close to them is simple, but if we have thousands of houses, this task gets hard. What we do in this chapter is devise an algorithm, or a procedure, for the computer to find a good line.

3. **Say we've built this prediction model, and then new houses start appearing in the market. Is there a way to update the model with new information?**

   Absolutely! We will build the model in a way that it can be easily updated if new data appears. This is always something to look for in machine learning. If we've built our model in such a way that we need to recalculate the entire model every time new data comes in, it won't be very useful.

How to get the computer to draw this line: The linear regression algorithm

Now we get to the main question of this chapter: how do we get a computer to draw a line that passes really close to the points? The way we do this is the same way we do many things in machine learning: step by step. Start with a random line, and figure out a way to improve this line a *little bit* by moving it closer to the points. Repeat this process many times, and voilà, we have the desired line. This process is called the linear regression algorithm.

The procedure may sound silly, but it works really well. Start with a random line. Pick a random point in the dataset, and move the line slightly closer to that one point. Repeat this process many times, always picking a random point in the dataset. The pseudocode for the linear regression algorithm, viewed in this geometric fashion, follows. The illustration is shown in figure 3.6.

Pseudocode for the linear regression algorithm (geometric)

Inputs: A dataset of points in the plane

Outputs: A line that passes close to the points

Procedure:

- Pick a random line.

- Repeat many times:

  - Pick a random data point.

  - Move the line a little closer to that point.

- **Return** the line you've obtained.

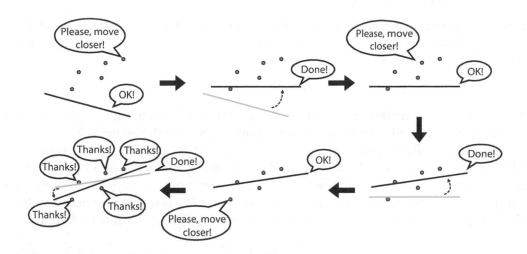

Figure 3.6 An illustration of the linear regression algorithm. We start at the top left with a random line and end in the bottom left with a line that fits the dataset well. At each stage, two things happen: (1) we pick a random point, and (2) the point asks the line to move closer to it. After many iterations, the line will be in a good position. This figure has only three iterations for illustrative purposes, but in real life, many more iterations are needed.

That was the high-level view. To study the process more in detail, we need to delve into the mathematical details. Let's begin by defining some variables.

- p: The price of a house in the dataset
- $\hat{p}$: The predicted price of a house
- r: The number of rooms
- m: The price per room
- b: The base price for a house

Why the hat over the predicted price, $\hat{p}$? Throughout this book, the hat indicates that this is the variable that our model is predicting. In that way, we can tell the actual price of a house in the dataset from its predicted price.

Thus, the equation of a linear regression model that predicts the price as the base price plus the price per room times the number of rooms is

$$\hat{p} = mr + b.$$

This is a formulaic way of saying

Predicted price = (Price per room)(Number of rooms) + Base price of the house.

To get an idea of the linear regression algorithm, imagine that we have a model in which the price per room is \$40 and the base price of the house is \$50. This model predicts the price of a house using the following formula:

$$\hat{p} = 40 \cdot r + 50$$

To illustrate the linear regression algorithm, imagine that in our dataset we have a house with two rooms that costs \$150. This model predicts that the price of the house is $50 + 40 \cdot 2 = 130$. That is not a bad prediction, but it is less than the price of the house. How can we improve the model? It seems like the model's mistake is thinking that the house is too cheap. Maybe the model has a low base price, or maybe it has a low price per room, or maybe both. If we increase both by a small amount, we may get a better estimate. Let's increase the price per room by \$0.50 and the base price by \$1. (I picked these numbers randomly.) The new equation follows:

$$\hat{p} = 40.5 \cdot r + 51$$

The new predicted price for the house is $40.5 \cdot r + 51 = 132$. Because \$132 is closer to \$150, our new model makes a better prediction for this house. Therefore, it is a better model for that data point. We don't know if it is a better model for the other data points, but let's not worry about that for now. The idea of the linear regression algorithm is to repeat the previous process many times. The pseudocode of the linear regression algorithm follows:

Pseudocode for the linear regression algorithm

Inputs: A dataset of points

Outputs: A linear regression model that fits that dataset

Procedure:

- Pick a model with random weights and a random bias.

- Repeat many times:

  - Pick a random data point.

  - Slightly adjust the weights and bias to improve the prediction for that particular data point.

- **Return** the model you've obtained.

You may have a few questions, such as the following:

- By how much should I adjust the weights?

- How many times should I repeat the algorithm? In other words, how do I know when I'm done?

- How do I know that this algorithm works?

We answer all of these questions in this chapter. In the sections "The square trick" and "The absolute trick," we learn some interesting tricks to find good values to adjust the weights. In the sections "The absolute error" and "The square error," we see the error function, which will help us decide when to stop the algorithm. And finally, in the section "Gradient descent," we cover a powerful method called gradient descent, which justifies why this algorithm works. But first, let's start by moving lines in the plane.

Crash course on slope and y-intercept

In the section "The formulate step," we talked about the equation of a line. In this section, we learn how to manipulate this equation to move our line. Recall that the equation of a line has the following two components:

- The slope

- The y-intercept

The slope tells us how steep the line is, and the y-intercept tells us where the line is located. The slope is defined as the rise divided by the run, and the y-intercept tells us where the line crosses the y-axis (the vertical axis). In figure 3.7, we can see both in an example. This line has the following equation:

$$y = 0.5x + 2$$

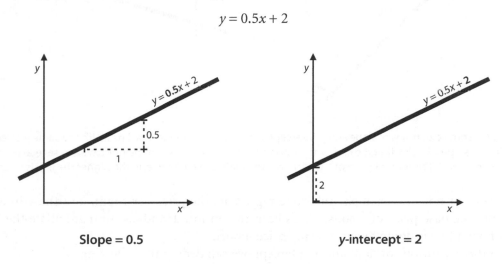

Slope = 0.5   y-intercept = 2

Figure 3.7   The line with equation **y** = 0.5**x** + 2 has slope 0.5 (left) and **y**-intercept 2 (right).

What does this equation mean? It means that the slope is 0.5, and the y-intercept is 2.

When we say that the slope is 0.5, it means that when we walk along this line, for every unit that we move to the right, we are moving 0.5 units up. The slope can be zero if we don't move up at all or negative if we move down. A vertical line has an undefined slope, but luckily, these don't tend to show up in linear regression. Many lines can have the same slope. If I draw any line parallel to the line in figure 3.7, this line will also rise 0.5 units for every unit it moves to the right. This is where the y-intercept comes in. The y-intercept tells us where the line cuts the y-axis. This line cuts the y-axis at height 2, and that is the y-intercept.

In other words, the slope of the line tells us the *direction* in which the line is pointing, and the *y*-intercept tells us the *location* of the line. Notice that by specifying the slope and the *y*-intercept, the line is completely specified. In figure 3.8, we can see different lines with the same *y*-intercept, and different lines with the same slope.

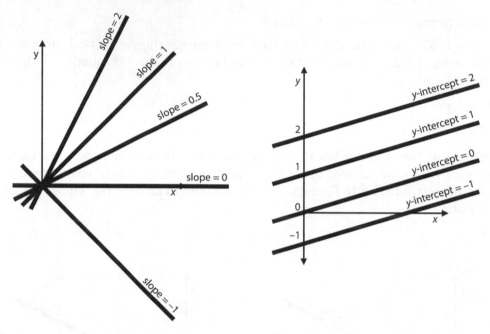

Figure 3.8   Some examples of slope and **y**-intercept. On the left, we see several lines with the same intercept and different slopes. Notice that the higher the slope, the steeper the line. On the right, we see several lines with the same slope and different **y**-intercepts. Notice that the higher the **y**-intercept, the higher the line is located.

In our current housing example, the slope represents the price per room, and the *y*-intercept represents the base price of a house. Let's keep this in mind, and, as we manipulate the lines, think of what this is doing to our housing price model.

From the definitions of slope and *y*-intercept, we can deduce the following:

Changing the slope:

- If we increase the slope of a line, the line will rotate counterclockwise.
- If we decrease the slope of a line, the line will rotate clockwise.

These rotations are on the pivot shown in figure 3.9, namely, the point of intersection of the line and the *y*-axis.

Changing the *y*-intercept:

- If we increase the *y*-intercept of a line, the line is translated upward.
- If we decrease the *y*-intercept of a line, the line is translated downward.

Figure 3.9 illustrates these rotations and translations, which will come in handy when we want to adjust our linear regression models.

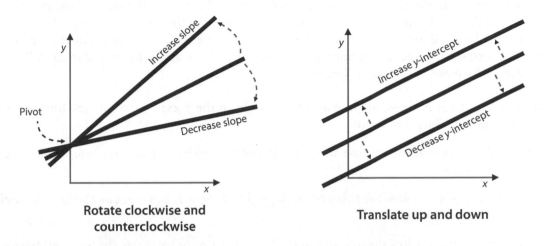

Rotate clockwise and counterclockwise

Translate up and down

Figure 3.9 Left: Increasing the slope rotates the line counterclockwise, whereas decreasing the slope rotates it clockwise. Right: Increasing the **y**-intercept translates the line upward, whereas decreasing the **y**-intercept translates it downward.

As explained earlier, in general, the equation of a line is written as $y = mx + b$, where x and y correspond to the horizontal and vertical coordinates, m corresponds to the slope, and b to the y-intercept. Throughout this chapter, to match the notation, we'll write the equation as $\hat{p} = mr + b$, where $\hat{p}$ corresponds to the predicted price, r to the number of rooms, m (the slope) to the price per room, and b (the y-intercept) to the base price of the house.

A simple trick to move a line closer to a set of points, one point at a time

Recall that the linear regression algorithm consists of repeating a step in which we move a line closer to a point. We can do this using rotations and translations. In this section, we learn a trick called the *simple trick*, which consists of slightly rotating and translating the line in the direction of the point to move it closer (figure 3.10).

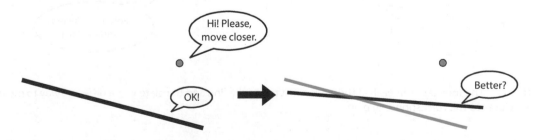

Figure 3.10 Our goal is to rotate and translate the line by a small amount to get closer to the point.

The trick to move the line correctly toward a point is to identify where the point is with respect to the line. If the point is above the line, we need to translate the line up, and if it is below, we need to translate it down. Rotation is a bit harder, but because the pivot is the point of intersection of the line and the y-axis, we can see that if the point is above the line and to the right of the y-axis, or below the line and to the left of the y-axis, we need to rotate the line counterclockwise. In the other two scenarios, we need to rotate the line clockwise. These are summarized in the following four cases, which are illustrated in figure 3.11:

Case 1: If the point is above the line and to the right of the y-axis, we rotate the line counter-clockwise and translate it upward.

Case 2: If the point is above the line and to the left of the y-axis, we rotate the line clockwise and translate it upward.

Case 3: If the point is below the line and to the right of the y-axis, we rotate the line clockwise and translate it downward.

Case 4: If the point is below the line and to the left of the y-axis, we rotate the line counterclockwise and translate it downward.

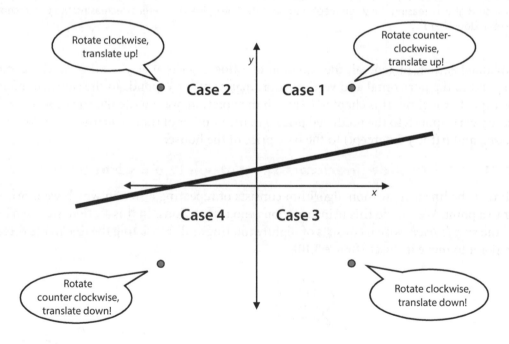

Figure 3.11   The four cases. In each of these we must rotate the line and translate it in a different way to move the line closer to the corresponding point.

Now that we have these four cases, we can write the pseudocode for the simple trick. But first, let's clarify some notation. In this section we've been talking about lines with equation $y = mx + b$, where m is the slope and b is the y-intercept. In the housing example, we used the following similar notation:

- The point with coordinates (r, p) corresponds to a house with r rooms and price p.

- The slope m corresponds to the price per room.

- The y-intercept b corresponds to the base price of the house.

- The prediction $\hat{p} = mr + b$ corresponds to the predicted price of the house.

Pseudocode for the simple trick

Inputs:

- A line with slope m, y-intercept b, and equation $\hat{p} = mr + b$

- A point with coordinates (r, p)

Output:

- A line with equation $\hat{p} = m'r + b$ that is closer to the point

Procedure:

Pick two very small random numbers, and call them η_1 and η_2 (the Greek letter *eta*).

Case 1: If the point is above the line and to the right of the y-axis, we rotate the line counterclockwise and translate it upward:

- Add η_1 to the slope m. Obtain $m' = m + \eta_1$.

- Add η_2 to the y-intercept b. Obtain $b' = b + \eta_2$.

Case 2: If the point is above the line and to the left of the y-axis, we rotate the line clockwise and translate it upward:

- Subtract η_1 from the slope m. Obtain $m' = m - \eta_1$.

- Add η_2 to the y-intercept b. Obtain $b' = b + \eta_2$.

Case 3: If the point is below the line and to the right of the y-axis, we rotate the line clockwise and translate it downward:

- Subtract η_1 from the slope m. Obtain $m' = m - \eta_1$.

- Subtract η_2 from the y-intercept b. Obtain $b' = b - \eta_2$.

Case 4: If the point is below the line and to the left of the y-axis, we rotate the line counterclockwise and translate it downward:

- Add η_1 to the slope m. Obtain $m' = m + \eta_1$.

- Subtract η_2 from the y-intercept b. Obtain $b' = b - \eta_2$.

Return: The line with equation $\hat{p} = m'r + b'$.

Note that for our example, adding or subtracting a small number to the slope means increasing or decreasing the price per room. Similarly, adding or subtracting a small number to the *y*-intercept means increasing or decreasing the base price of the house. Furthermore, because the *x*-coordinate is the number of rooms, this number is never negative. Thus, only cases 1 and 3 matter in our example, which means we can summarize the simple trick in colloquial language as follows:

Simple trick

- If the model gave us a price for the house that is lower than the actual price, add a small random amount to the price per room and to the base price of the house.

- If the model gave us a price for the house that is higher than the actual price, subtract a small random amount from the price per room and the base price of the house.

This trick achieves some success in practice, but it's far from being the best way to move lines. Some questions may arise, such as the following:

- Can we pick better values for η_1 and η_2?

- Can we crunch the four cases into two, or perhaps one?

The answer to both questions is yes, and we'll see how in the following two sections.

The square trick: A much more clever way of moving our line closer to one of the points

In this section, I show you an effective way to move a line closer to a point. I call this the *square trick*. Recall that the simple trick consisted of four cases that were based on the position of the point with respect to the line. The square trick will bring these four cases down to one by finding values with the correct signs (+ or −) to add to the slope and the *y*-intercept for the line to always move closer to the point.

We start with the *y*-intercept. Notice the following two observations:

- **Observation 1:** In the simple trick, when the point is above the line, we add a small amount to the *y*-intercept. When it is below the line, we subtract a small amount.

- **Observation 2:** If a point is above the line, the value $p - \hat{p}$ (the difference between the price and the predicted price) is positive. If it is below the line, this value is negative. This observation is illustrated in figure 3.12.

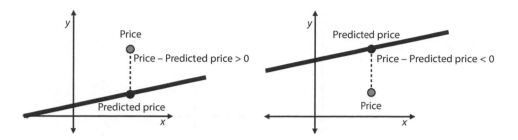

Figure 3.12   Left: When the point is above the line, the price is larger than the predicted price, so the difference is positive. Right: When the point is below the line, the price is smaller than the predicted price, so the difference is negative.

Putting together observation 1 and observation 2, we conclude that if we add the difference $p - \hat{p}$ to the y-intercept, the line will always move toward the point, because this value is positive when the point is above the line and negative when the point is below the line. However, in machine learning, we always want to take small steps. To help us with this, we introduce an important concept in machine learning: the learning rate.

> **learning rate**   A very small number that we pick before training our model. This number helps us make sure our model changes in very small amounts by training. In this book, the learning rate will be denoted by η, the Greek letter *eta*.

Because the learning rate is small, so is the value $\eta(p - \hat{p})$. This is the value we add to the y-intercept to move the line in the direction of the point.

The value we need to add to the slope is similar, yet a bit more complicated. Notice the following two observations:

- **Observation 3:** In the simple trick, when the point is in scenario 1 or 4 (above the line and to the right of the vertical axis, or below the line and to the left of the vertical axis), we rotate the line counterclockwise. Otherwise (scenario 2 or 3), we rotate it clockwise.

- **Observation 4:** If a point (r, p) is to the right of the vertical axis, then r is positive. If the point is to the left of the vertical axis, then r is negative. This observation is illustrated in figure 3.13. Notice that in this example, r will never be negative, because it is the number of rooms. However, in a general example, a feature could be negative.

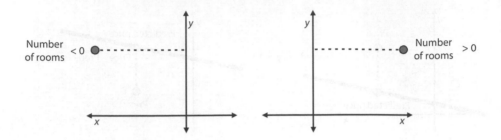

Figure 3.13   Left: When the point is to the left of the **y**-axis, the number of rooms is negative. Right: When the point is to the right of the **y**-axis, the number of rooms is positive.

Consider the value $r(p - \hat{p})$. This value is positive when both r and $p - \hat{p}$ are both positive or both negative. This is precisely what occurs in scenarios 1 and 4. Similarly, $r(p - \hat{p})$ is negative in scenarios 2 and 3. Therefore, due to observation 4, this is the quantity that we need to add to the slope. We want this value to be small, so again, we multiply it by the learning rate and conclude that adding $\eta r(p - \hat{p})$ to the slope will always move the line in the direction of the point.

We can now write the pseudocode for the square trick as follows:

Pseudocode for the square trick

Inputs:

- A line with slope m, y-intercept b, and equation $\hat{p} = mr + b$

- A point with coordinates (r, p)

- A small positive value η (the learning rate)

Output:

- A line with equation $\hat{p} = m'r + b'$ that is closer to the point

Procedure:

- Add $\eta r(p - \hat{p})$ to the slope m. Obtain $m' = m + \eta r(p - \hat{p})$ (this rotates the line).

- Add $\eta(p - \hat{p})$ to the y-intercept b. Obtain $b' = b + \eta(p - \hat{p})$ (this translates the line).

Return: The line with equation $\hat{p} = m'r + b'$

We are now ready to code this algorithm in Python! The code for this section follows:

- **Notebook:** Coding_linear_regression.ipynb

  – https://github.com/luisguiserrano/manning/blob/master/Chapter_3_Linear_Regression/Coding_linear_regression.ipynb

And here is code for the square trick:

```
def square_trick(base_price, price_per_room, num_rooms, price, learning_rate):
    predicted_price = base_price + price_per_room*num_rooms
    base_price += learning_rate*(price-predicted_price)
    price_per_room += learning_rate*num_rooms*(price-predicted_price)
    return price_per_room, base_price
```

Calculates
the prediction

Translates the line

Rotates the line

The absolute trick: Another useful trick to move the line closer to the points

The square trick is effective, but another useful trick, which we call the *absolute trick*, is an intermediate between the simple and the square tricks. In the square trick, we used the two quantities, $p - \hat{p}$ (price − predicted price) and r (number of rooms), to help us bring the four cases down to one. In the absolute trick, we use only r to help us bring the four cases down to two. In other words, here is the absolute trick:

Pseudocode for the absolute trick

Inputs:

- A line with slope m, y-intercept b, and equation $\hat{p} = mr + b$

- A point with coordinates (r, p)

- A small positive value η (the learning rate)

Output:

- A line with equation $\hat{p} = m'r + b'$ that is closer to the point

Procedure:

Case 1: If the point is above the line (i.e., if $p > \hat{p}$):

- Add ηr to the slope m. Obtain $m' = m + \eta r$ (this rotates the line counterclockwise if the point is to the right of the y-axis, and clockwise if it is to the left of the y-axis).

- Add η to the y-intercept b. Obtain $b' = b + \eta$ (this translates the line up).

Case 2: If the point is below the line (i.e., if $p < \hat{p}$):

- Subtract ηr from the slope m. Obtain $m' = m - \eta r$ (this rotates the line clockwise if the point is to the right of the y-axis, and counterclockwise if it is to the left of the y-axis).

- Subtract η from the y-intercept b. Obtain $b' = b - \eta$ (this translates the line down).

Return: The line with equation $\hat{p} = m'r + b'$

Here is the code for the absolute trick:

```
def absolute_trick(base_price, price_per_room, num_rooms, price,
    learning_rate):
    predicted_price = base_price + price_per_room*num_rooms
    if price > predicted_price:
        price_per_room += learning_rate*num_rooms
        base_price += learning_rate
    else:
        price_per_room -= learning_rate*num_rooms
        base_price -= learning_rate
    return price_per_room, base_price
```

I encourage you to verify that the amount added to each of the weights indeed has the correct sign, as we did with the square trick.

The linear regression algorithm: Repeating the absolute or square trick many times to move the line closer to the points

Now that we've done all the hard work, we are ready to develop the linear regression algorithm! This algorithm takes as input a bunch of points and returns a line that fits them well. This algorithm consists of starting with random values for our slope and our *y*-intercept and then repeating the procedure of updating them many times using the absolute or the square trick. Here is the pseudocode:

Pseudocode for the linear regression algorithm

Inputs:

- A dataset of houses with number of rooms and prices

Outputs:

- Model weights: price per room and base price

Procedure:

- Start with random values for the slope and *y*-intercept.

- Repeat many times:

  - Pick a random data point.

  - Update the slope and the *y*-intercept using the absolute or the square trick.

Each iteration of the loop is called an *epoch*, and we set this number at the beginning of our algorithm. The simple trick was mostly used for illustration, but as was mentioned before, it doesn't work very well. In real life, we use the absolute or square trick, which works a lot better. In fact, although both are commonly used, the square trick is more popular. Therefore, we'll use that one for our algorithm, but feel free to use the absolute trick if you prefer.

Here is the code for the linear regression algorithm. Note that we have used the Python `random` package to generate random numbers for our initial values (slope and *y*-intercept) and for selecting our points inside the loop:

```
import random
def linear_regression(features, labels, learning_rate=0.01, epochs = 1000):
    price_per_room = random.random()
    base_price = random.random()
    for epoch in range(epochs):
        i = random.randint(0, len(features)-1)
        num_rooms = features[i]
        price = labels[i]
        price_per_room, base_price = square_trick(base_price,
                                                  price_per_room,
                                                  num_rooms,
                                                  price,
                                                  learning_rate=learning_rate)
    return price_per_room, base_price
```

Imports the random package to generate (pseudo) random numbers

Generates random values for the slope and the y-intercept

Picks a random point on our dataset

Repeats the update step many times

Applies the square trick to move the line closer to our point

The next step is to run this algorithm to build a model that fits our dataset.

Loading our data and plotting it

Throughout this chapter, we load and make plots of our data and models using Matplotlib and NumPy, two very useful Python packages. We use NumPy for storing arrays and carrying out mathematical operations, whereas we use Matplotlib for the plots.

The first thing we do is encode the features and labels of the dataset in table 3.2 as NumPy arrays as follows:

```
import numpy as np
features = np.array([1,2,3,5,6,7])
labels = np.array([155, 197, 244, 356, 407, 448])
```

Next we plot the dataset. In the repository, we have some functions for plotting the code in the file utils.py, which you are invited to take a look at. The plot of the dataset is shown in figure 3.14. Notice that the points do appear close to forming a line.

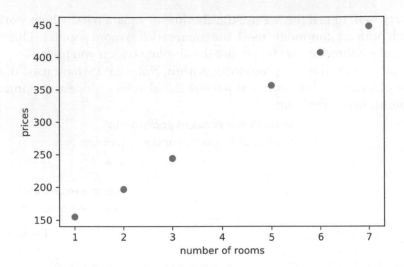

Figure 3.14   The plot of the points in table 3.2

Using the linear regression algorithm in our dataset

Now, let's apply the algorithm to fit a line to these points. The following line of code runs the algorithm with the features, the labels, the learning rate equal to 0.01, and the number of epochs equal to 10,000. The result is the plot shown in figure 3.15.

```
linear_regression(features, labels, learning_rate = 0.01, epochs = 10000)
```

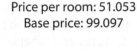

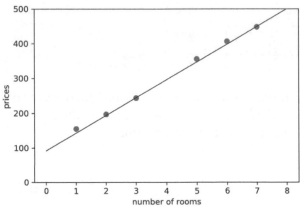

Figure 3.15   The plot of the points in table 3.2 and the line that we obtained with the linear regression algorithm

Figure 3.15 shows the line where the (rounded) price per room is $51.05, and the base price is $99.10. This is not far from the $50 and $100 we eyeballed earlier in the chapter.

To visualize the process, let's look at the progression a bit more. In figure 3.16, you can see a few of the intermediate lines. Notice that the line starts far away from the points. As the algorithm progresses, it moves slowly to fit better and better every time. Notice that at first (in the first 10 epochs), the line moves quickly toward a good solution. After epoch 50, the line is good, but it still doesn't fit the points perfectly. If we let it run for the whole 10,000 epochs, we get a great fit.

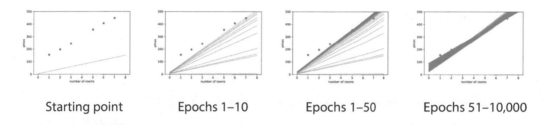

Starting point	Epochs 1–10	Epochs 1–50	Epochs 51–10,000

Figure 3.16 Drawing some of the lines in our algorithm, as we approach a better solution. The first graphic shows the starting point. The second graphic shows the first 10 epochs of the linear regression algorithm. Notice how the line is moving closer to fitting the points. The third graphic shows the first 50 epochs. The fourth graphic shows epochs 51 to 10,000 (the last epoch).

Using the model to make predictions

Now that we have a shiny linear regression model, we can use it to make predictions! Recall from the beginning of the chapter that our goal was to predict the price of a house with four rooms. In the previous section, we ran the algorithm and obtained a slope (price per room) of 51.05 and a y-intercept (base price of the house) of 99.10. Thus, the equation follows:

$$\hat{p} = 51.05r + 99.10$$

The prediction the model makes for a house with $r = 4$ rooms is

$$\hat{p} = 51.05 \cdot 4 + 99.10 = 303.30.$$

Note that $303.30 is not far from the $300 we eyeballed at the beginning of the chapter!

The general linear regression algorithm (optional)

This section is optional, because it focuses mostly on the mathematical details of the more abstract algorithm used for a general dataset. However, I encourage you to read it to get used to the notation that is used in most of the machine learning literature.

In the previous sections, we outlined the linear regression algorithm for our dataset with only one feature. But as you can imagine, in real life, we will be working with datasets with many features. For this, we need a general algorithm. The good news is that the general algorithm is not very different from the specific one that we learned in this chapter. The only difference is that each of the features is updated in the same way that the slope was updated. In the housing example, we had one slope and one y-intercept. In the general case, think of many slopes and still one y-intercept.

The general case will consist of a dataset of m points and n features. Thus, the model has m weights (think of them as the generalization of the slope) and one bias. The notation follows:

- The data points are $x^{(1)}, x^{(2)}, \ldots, x^{(m)}$. Each point is of the form $x^{(i)} = (x_1^{(i)}, x_2^{(i)}, \ldots, x_n^{(i)})$.
- The corresponding labels are $y_1, y_2, \ldots, y_m$.
- The weights of the model are $w_1, w_2, \ldots, w_n$.
- The bias of the model is b.

Pseudocode for the general square trick

Inputs:

- A model with equation $\hat{y} = w_1 x_1 + w_2 x_{2+} + \cdots + w_n x_n + b$
- A point with coordinates (x, y)
- A small positive value η (the learning rate)

Output:

- A model with equation $\hat{y} = w_1' x_1 + w_2' x_2 + \cdots + w_n' x_n + b'$ that is closer to the point

Procedure:

- Add $\eta(y - \hat{y})$ to the y-intercept b. Obtain $b' = b + \eta(y - \hat{y})$.
- For $i = 1, 2, \ldots, n$:
  - Add $\eta x_i(y - \hat{y})$ to the weight w_i. Obtain $w_i' = w_i + \eta x_i(y - \hat{y})$.

Return: The model with equation $\hat{y} = w_1' x_1 + w_2' x_2 + \cdots + w_n' x_n + b'$

The pseudocode of the general linear regression algorithm is the same as the one in the section "The linear regression algorithm," because it consists of iterating over the general square trick, so we'll omit it.

How do we measure our results? The error function

In the previous sections, we developed a direct approach to finding the best line fit. However, many times using a direct approach is difficult to solve problems in machine learning. A more indirect, yet more mechanical, way to do this is using *error functions*. An error function is a metric that tells us how our model is doing. For example, take a look at the two models in figure 3.17. The one on the left is a bad model, whereas the one on the right is a good one. The error function measures this by assigning a large value to the bad model on the left and a small value to the good model on the right. Error functions are also sometimes called *loss functions* or *cost functions* on the literature. In this book, we call them error functions except in some special cases in which the more commonly used name requires otherwise.

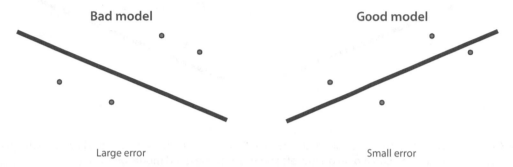

Figure 3.17 Two models, a bad one (on the left) and a good one (on the right). The bad one is assigned a large error, and the good one is assigned a small error.

Now the question is, how do we define a good error function for linear regression models? We have two common ways to do this called the *absolute error* and the *square error*. In short, the absolute error is the sum of vertical distances from the line to the points in the dataset, and the square error is the sum of the squares of these distances.

In the next few sections, we learn about these two error functions in more detail. Then we see how to reduce them using a method called gradient descent. Finally, we plot one of these error functions in our existing example and see how quickly the gradient descent method helps us decrease it.

The absolute error: A metric that tells us how good our model is by adding distances

In this section we look at the absolute error, which is a metric that tells us how good our model is. The absolute error is the sum of the distances between the data points and the line. Why is it called the absolute error? To calculate each of the distances, we take the difference between the label and the predicted label. This difference can be positive or negative depending on whether the point is above or below the line. To turn this difference into a number that is always positive, we take its absolute value.

By definition, a good linear regression model is one where the line is close to the points. What does *close* mean in this case? This is a subjective question, because a line that is close to some of the points may be far from others. In that case, would we rather pick a line that is very close to some of the points and far from some of the others? Or do we try to pick one that is somewhat close to all the points? The absolute error helps us make this decision. The line we pick is the one that minimizes the absolute error, that is, the one for which the sum of vertical distances from each of the points to the line is minimal. In figure 3.18, you can see two lines, and their absolute error is illustrated as the sum of the vertical segments. The line on the left has a large absolute error, whereas the one on the right has a small absolute error. Thus, between these two, we would pick the one on the right.

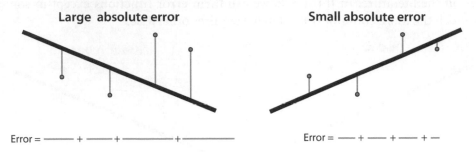

Figure 3.18   The absolute error is the sum of the vertical distances from the points to the line. Note that the absolute error is large for the bad model on the left and small for the good model on the right.

The square error: A metric that tells us how good our model is by adding squares of distances

The square error is very similar to the absolute error, except instead of taking the absolute value of the difference between the label and the predicted label, we take the square. This always turns the number into a positive number, because squaring a number always makes it positive. The process is illustrated in figure 3.19, where the square error is illustrated as the sum of the areas of the squares of the lengths from the points to the line. You can see how the bad model on the left has a large square error, whereas the good model on the right has a small square error.

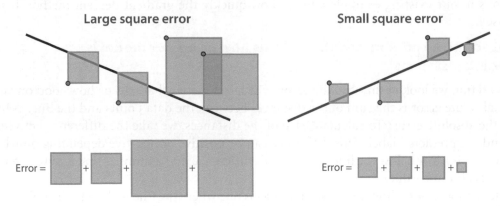

Figure 3.19   The square error is the sum of the squares of the vertical distances from the points to the line. Note that the square error is large for the bad model on the left and small for the good model on the right.

As was mentioned earlier, the square error is used more commonly in practice than the absolute error. Why? A square has a much nicer derivative than an absolute value, which comes in handy during the training process.

Mean absolute and (root) mean square errors are more common in real life

Throughout this chapter we use absolute and square errors for illustration purposes. However, in practice, the *mean absolute error* and the *mean square error* are used much more commonly. These are defined in a similar way, except instead of calculating sums, we calculate averages. Thus, the mean absolute error is the average of the vertical distances from the points to the line, and the mean square error is the average of the squares of these same distances. Why are they more common? Imagine if we'd like to compare the error or a model using two datasets, one with 10 points and one with 1 million points. If the error is a sum of quantities, one for every point, then the error is probably much higher on the dataset of 1 million points, because we are adding many more numbers. If we want to compare them properly, we instead use averages in the calculation of our error to obtain a measure of how far the line is from each point *on average*.

For illustration purposes, another error commonly used is the *root mean square error*, or *RMSE* for short. As the name implies, this is defined as the root of the mean square error. It is used to match the units in the problem and also to give us a better idea of how much error the model makes in a prediction. How so? Imagine the following scenario: if we are trying to predict house prices, then the units of the price and the predicted price are, for example, dollars ($). The units of the square error and the mean square error are dollars squared, which is not a common unit. If we take the square root, then not only do we get the correct unit, but we also get a more accurate idea of roughly by how many dollars the model is off per house. Say, if the root mean square error is $10,000, then we can expect the model to make an error of around $10,000 for any prediction we make.

Gradient descent: How to decrease an error function by slowly descending from a mountain

In this section, I show you how to decrease any of the previous errors using a similar method to the one we would use to slowly descend from a mountain. This process uses derivatives, but here is the great news: you don't need derivatives to understand it. We already used them in the training process in the sections "The square trick" and "The absolute trick" earlier. Every time we "move a small amount in this direction," we are calculating in the background a derivative of the error function and using it to give us a direction in which to move our line. If you love calculus and you want to see the entire derivation of this algorithm using derivatives and gradients, see appendix B.

Let's take a step back and look at linear regression from far away. What is it that we want to do? We want to find the line that best fits our data. We have a metric called the error function, which tells us how far a line is from the data. Thus, if we could just reduce this number as much as possible, we would find the best line fit. This process, common in many areas in mathematics, is called *minimizing functions*, that is, finding the smallest possible value that a function can return. This is where gradient descent comes in: it is a great way to minimize a function.

In this case, the function we are trying to minimize is the error (absolute or square) of our model. A small caveat is that gradient descent doesn't always find the exact minimum value of the function, but it may find something very close to it. The good news is that, in practice, gradient descent is fast and effective at finding points where the function is low.

How does gradient descent work? Gradient descent is the equivalent of descending from a mountain. Let's say we find ourselves on top of a tall mountain called Mount Errorest. We wish to descend, but it is very foggy, and we can see only about one meter away. What do we do? A good method is to look around ourselves and figure out in what direction we can take one single step, in a way that we descend the most. This process is illustrated in figure 3.20.

Figure 3.20   We are on top of Mount Errorest and wish to get to the bottom, but we can't see very far. A way to go down is to look at all the directions in which we can take one step and figure out which one helps us descend the most. Then we are one step closer to the bottom.

When we find this direction, we take one small step, and because that step was taken in the direction of greatest descent, then most likely, we have descended a small amount. All we have to do is repeat this process many times until we (hopefully) reach the bottom. This process is illustrated in figure 3.21.

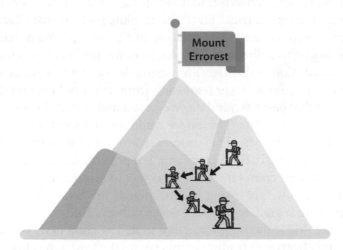

Figure 3.21   The way to descend from the mountain is to take that one small step in the direction that makes us descend the most and to continue doing this for a long time.

Why did I say *hopefully*? Well, this process has many caveats. We could reach the bottom, or we could also reach a valley and then we have nowhere else to move. We won't deal with that now, but we have several techniques to reduce the probability of this happening. In appendix B, "Using gradient descent to train neural networks," some of these techniques are outlined.

A lot of math here that we are sweeping under the rug is explained in more detail in appendix B. But what we did in this chapter was exactly gradient descent. How so? Gradient descent works as follows:

1. Start somewhere on the mountain.

2. Find the best direction to take one small step.

3. Take this small step.

4. Repeat steps 2 and 3 many times.

This may look familiar, because in the section "The linear regression algorithm," after defining the absolute and square tricks, we defined the linear regression algorithm in the following way:

1. Start with any line.

2. Find the best direction to move our line a little bit, using either the absolute or the square trick.

3. Move the line a little bit in this direction.

4. Repeat steps 2 and 3 many times.

The mental picture of this is illustrated in figure 3.22. The only difference is that this error function looks less like a mountain and more like a valley, and our goal is to descend to the lowest point. Each point in this valley corresponds to some model (line) that tries to fit our data. The

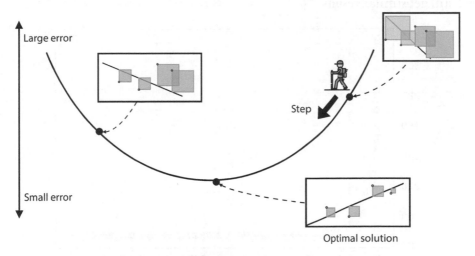

Figure 3.22 Each point on this mountain corresponds to a different model. The points below are good models with a small error, and the points above are bad models with a large error. The goal is to descend from this mountain. The way to descend is by starting somewhere and continuously taking a step that makes us descend. The gradient will help us decide in what direction to take a step that helps us descend the most.

height of the point is the error given by that model. Thus, the bad models are on top, and the good models are on the bottom. We are trying to go as low as possible. Each step takes us from one model to a slightly better model. If we take a step like this many times, we'll eventually get to the best model (or at least, a pretty good one!).

Plotting the error function and knowing when to stop running the algorithm

In this section, we see a plot of the error function for the training that we performed earlier in the section "Using the linear regression algorithm in our dataset." This plot gives us useful information about training this model. In the repository, we have also plotted the root mean square error function (RMSE) defined in the section "Mean absolute and (root) mean square errors ...". The code for calculating the RMSE follows:

```
def rmse(labels, predictions):
    n = len(labels)
    differences = np.subtract(labels, predictions)
    return np.sqrt(1.0/n * (np.dot(differences, differences)))
```

dot product   To code the RMSE function, we used the dot product, which is an easy way to write a sum of products of corresponding terms in two vectors. For example, the dot product of the vectors (1,2,3) and (4,5,6) is $1 \cdot 4 + 2 \cdot 5 + 3 \cdot 6 = 32$. If we calculate the dot product of a vector and itself, we obtain the sum of squares of the entries.

The plot of our error is shown in figure 3.23. Note that it quickly dropped after about 1,000 iterations, and it didn't change much after that. This plot gives us useful information: it tells us that for this model, we can run the training algorithm for only 1,000 or 2,000 iterations instead of 10,000 and still get similar results.

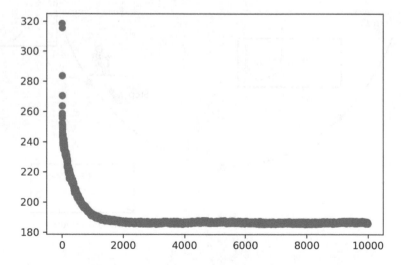

Figure 3.23   The plot of the root mean square error for our running example. Notice how the algorithm succeeded in reducing this error after a little over 1,000 iterations. This means that we don't need to keep running this algorithm for 10,000 iterations, because around 2,000 of them do the job.

In general, the error function gives us good information to decide when to stop running the algorithm. Often, this decision is based on the time and the computational power available to us. However, other useful benchmarks are commonly used in the practice, such as the following:

- When the loss function reaches a certain value that we have predetermined
- When the loss function doesn't decrease by a significant amount during several epochs

Do we train using one point at a time or many?
Stochastic and batch gradient descent

In the section "How to get the computer to draw this line," we trained a linear regression model by repeating a step many times. This step consisted of picking one point and moving the line toward that point. In the section "How do we measure our results," we trained a linear regression model by calculating the error (absolute or squared) and decreasing it using gradient descent. However, this error was calculated on the entire dataset, not on one point at a time. Why is this?

The reality is that we can train models by iterating on one point at a time or on the entire dataset. However, when the datasets are very big, both options may be expensive. We can practice a useful method called *mini-batch learning,* which consists of dividing our data into many mini-batches. In each iteration of the linear regression algorithm, we pick one of the mini-batches and proceed to adjust the weights of the model to reduce the error in that mini-batch. The decision of using one point, a mini-batch of points, or the entire dataset on each iteration gives rise to three general types of gradient descent algorithms. When we use one point at a time, it is called *stochastic gradient descent*. When we use a mini-batch, it is called *mini-batch gradient descent*. When we use the entire dataset, it is called *batch gradient descent*. This process is illustrated in more detail in appendix B, "Using gradient descent to train models."

Real-life application: Using Turi Create to predict housing prices in India

In this section, I show you a real-life application. We'll use linear regression to predict housing prices in Hyderabad, India. The dataset we use comes from Kaggle, a popular site for machine learning competitions. The code for this section follows:

- **Notebook:** House_price_predictions.ipynb
  - https://github.com/luisguiserrano/manning/blob/master/Chapter_3_Linear_Regression/House_price_predictions.ipynb
- **Dataset:** Hyderabad.csv

This dataset has 6,207 rows (one per house) and 39 columns (features). As you can imagine, we won't code the algorithm by hand. Instead, we use Turi Create, a popular and useful package in which many machine learning algorithms are implemented. The main object to store data in

Turi Create is the SFrame. We start by downloading the data into an SFrame, using the following command:

```
data = tc.SFrame('Hyderabad.csv')
```

The table is too big, but you can see the first few rows and columns in table 3.3.

Table 3.3   The first five rows and seven columns of the Hyderabad housing prices dataset

Price	Area	No. of Bedrooms	Resale	MaintenanceStaff	Gymnasium	SwimmingPool
30000000	3340	4	0	1	1	1
7888000	1045	2	0	0	1	1
4866000	1179	2	0	0	1	1
8358000	1675	3	0	0	0	0
6845000	1670	3	0	1	1	1

Training a linear regression model in Turi Create takes only one line of code. We use the function `create` from the package `linear_regression`. In this function, we only need to specify the target (label), which is `Price`, as follows:

```
model = tc.linear_regression.create(data, target='Price')
```

It may take a few moments to train, but after it trains, it outputs some information. One of the fields it outputs is the root mean square error. For this model, the RMSE is in the order of 3,000,000. This is a large RMSE, but it doesn't mean the model makes bad predictions. It may mean that the dataset has many outliers. As you can imagine, the price of a house may depend on many other features that are not in the dataset.

We can use the model to predict the price of a house with an area of 1,000, and three bedrooms as follows:

```
house = tc.SFrame({'Area': [1000], 'No. of Bedrooms':[3]})
model.predict(house)
Output: 2594841
```

The model outputs that the price for a house of size 1,000 and three bedrooms is 2,594,841.

We can also train a model using fewer features. The `create` function allows us to input the features we want to use as an array. The following line of code trains a model called `simple_model` that uses the area to predict the price:

```
simple_model = tc.linear_regression.create(data, features=['Area'],
    target='Price')
```

We can explore the weights of this model with the following line of code:

```
simple_model.coefficients
```

The output gives us the following weights:

- Slope: 9664.97
- *y*-intercept: −6,105,981.01

The intercept is the bias, and the coefficient for area is the slope of the line, when we plot area and price. The plot of the points with the corresponding model is shown in figure 3.24.

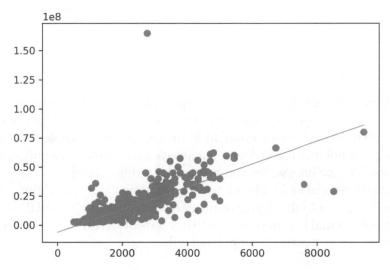

Figure 3.24 The Hyderabad housing prices dataset restricted to area and price. The line is the model we've obtained using only the area feature to predict the price.

We could do a lot more in this dataset, and I invite you to continue exploring. For example, try to explore what features are more important than others by looking at the weights of the model. I encourage you to take a look at the Turi Create documentation (https://apple.github.io/turicreate/docs/api/) for other functions and tricks you can do to improve this model.

What if the data is not in a line? Polynomial regression

In the previous sections, we learned how to find the best line fit for our data, assuming our data closely resembles a line. But what happens if our data doesn't resemble a line? In this section, we learn a powerful extension to linear regression called *polynomial regression*, which helps us deal with cases in which the data is more complex.

A special kind of curved functions: Polynomials

To learn polynomial regression, first we need to learn what polynomials are. *Polynomials* are a class of functions that are helpful when modeling nonlinear data.

We've already seen polynomials, because every line is a polynomial of degree 1. Parabolas are examples of polynomials of degree 2. Formally, a polynomial is a function in one variable that can be expressed as a sum of multiples of powers of this variable. The powers of a variable x are $1, x, x^2, x^3, ...$. Note that the two first are $x^0 = 1$ and $x^1 = x$. Therefore, the following are examples of polynomials:

- $y = 4$

- $y = 3x + 2$

- $y = x^2 - 2x + 5$

- $y = 2x^3 + 8x^2 - 40$

We define the *degree* of the polynomial as the exponent of the highest power in the expression of the polynomial. For example, the polynomial $y = 2x^3 + 8x^2 - 40$ has degree 3, because 3 is the highest exponent that the variable x is raised to. Notice that in the example, the polynomials have degree 0, 1, 2, and 3. A polynomial of degree 0 is always a constant, and a polynomial of degree 1 is a linear equation like the ones we've seen previously in this chapter.

The graph of a polynomial looks a lot like a curve that oscillates several times. The number of times it oscillates is related to the degree of the polynomial. If a polynomial has degree d, then the graph of that polynomial is a curve that oscillates at most $d - 1$ times (for $d > 1$). In figure 3.25 we can see the plots of some examples of polynomials.

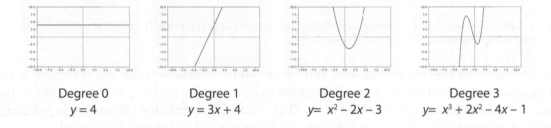

Degree 0	Degree 1	Degree 2	Degree 3
$y = 4$	$y = 3x + 4$	$y = x^2 - 2x - 3$	$y = x^3 + 2x^2 - 4x - 1$

Figure 3.25 Polynomials are functions that help us model our data better. Here are the plots of four polynomials of degrees 0 to 3. Note that the polynomial of degree 0 is a horizontal line, the polynomial of degree 1 is any line, the polynomial of degree 2 is a parabola, and the polynomial of degree 3 is a curve that oscillates twice.

From the plot, notice that polynomials of degree 0 are flat lines. Polynomials of degree 1 are lines with slopes different from 0. Polynomials of degree 2 are quadratics (parabolas). Polynomials of degree 3 look like a curve that oscillates twice (although they could potentially oscillate fewer times). How would the plot of a polynomial of degree 100 look like? For example, the plot of $y = x^{100} - 8x^{62} + 73x^{27} - 4x + 38$? We'd have to plot it to find out, but for sure, we know that it is a curve that oscillates at most 99 times.

Nonlinear data? No problem: Let's try to fit a polynomial curve to it

In this section, we see what happens if our data is not linear (i.e., does not look like it forms a line), and we want to fit a polynomial curve to it. Let's say that our data looks like the left side of figure 3.26. No matter how much we try, we can't really find a good line that fits this data. No problem! If we decide to fit a polynomial of degree 3 (also called a cubic), then we get the curve shown at the right of figure 3.26, which is a much better fit to the data.

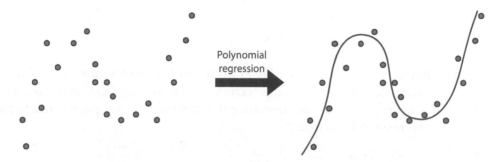

Figure 3.26 Polynomial regression is useful when it comes to modeling nonlinear data. If our data looks like the left part of the figure, it will be hard to find a line that fits it well. However, a curve will fit the data well, as you can see in the right part of the figure. Polynomial regression helps us find this curve.

The process to train a polynomial regression model is similar to the process of training a linear regression model. The only difference is that we need to add more columns to our dataset before we apply linear regression. For example, if we decide to fit a polynomial of degree 3 to the data in figure 3.26, we need to add two columns: one corresponding to the square of the feature and one corresponding to the cube of the feature. If you'd like to study this in more detail, please check out the section "Polynomial regression, testing, and regularization with Turi Create" in chapter 4, in which we learn an example of polynomial regression in a parabolic dataset.

A small caveat with training a polynomial regression model is that we must decide the degree of the polynomial before the training process. How do we decide on this degree? Do we want a line (degree 1), a parabola (degree 2), a cubic (degree 3), or some curve of degree 50? This question is important, and we deal with it in chapter 4, when we learn overfitting, underfitting, and regularization!

Parameters and hyperparameters

Parameters and hyperparameters are some of the most important concepts in machine learning, and in this section, we learn what they are and how to tell them apart.

As we saw in this chapter, regression models are defined by their weights and bias—the *parameters* of the model. However, we can twist many other knobs before training a model, such as the learning rate, the number of epochs, the degree (if considering a polynomial regression model), and many others. These are called *hyperparameters*.

Each machine learning model that we learn in this book has some well-defined parameters and hyperparameters. They tend to be easily confused, so the rule of thumb to tell them apart follows:

- Any quantity that you set *before* the training process is a hyperparameter.
- Any quantity that the model creates or modifies *during* the training process is a parameter.

Applications of regression

The impact of machine learning is measured not only by the power of its algorithms but also by the breadth of useful applications it has. In this section, we see some applications of linear regression in real life. In each of the examples, we outline the problem, learn some features to solve it, and then let linear regression do its magic.

Recommendation systems

Machine learning is used widely to generate good recommendations in some of the most well-known apps, including YouTube, Netflix, Facebook, Spotify, and Amazon. Regression plays a key part in most of these recommender systems. Because regression predicts a quantity, all we have to do to generate good recommendations is figure out what quantity is the best at indicating user interaction or user satisfaction. Following are some more specific examples of this.

Video and music recommendations

One of the ways used to generate video and music recommendations is to predict the amount of time a user will watch a video or listen to a song. For this, we can create a linear regression model where the labels on the data are the amount of minutes that each song is watched by each user. The features can be demographics on the user, such as their age, location, and occupation, but they can also be behavioral, such as other videos or songs they have clicked on or interacted with.

Product recommendations

Stores and ecommerce websites also use linear regression to predict their sales. One way to do this is to predict how much a customer will spend in the store. We can do this using linear regression. The label to predict can be the amount the user spent, and the features can be demographic and behavioral, in a similar way to the video and music recommendations.

Health care

Regression has numerous applications in health care. Depending on what problem we want to solve, predicting the right label is the key. Here are a couple of examples:

- Predicting the life span of a patient, based on their current health conditions
- Predicting the length of a hospital stay, based on current symptoms

Summary

- Regression is an important part of machine learning. It consists of training an algorithm with labeled data and using it to make predictions on future (unlabeled) data.

- Labeled data is data that comes with labels, which in the regression case, are numbers. For example, the numbers could be prices of houses.

- In a dataset, the features are the properties that we use to predict the label. For example, if we want to predict housing prices, the features are anything that describes the house and which could determine the price, such as size, number of rooms, school quality, crime rate, age of the house, and distance to the highway.

- The linear regression method for predicting consists in assigning a weight to each of the features and adding the corresponding weights multiplied by the features, plus a bias.

- Graphically, we can see the linear regression algorithm as trying to pass a line as close as possible to a set of points.

- The way the linear regression algorithm works is by starting with a random line and then slowly moving it closer to each of the points that is misclassified, to attempt to classify them correctly.

- Polynomial regression is a generalization of linear regression, in which we use curves instead of lines to model our data. This is particularly useful when our dataset is nonlinear.

- Regression has numerous applications, including recommendation systems, ecommerce, and health care.

Exercises

Exercise 3.1

A website has trained a linear regression model to predict the amount of minutes that a user will spend on the site. The formula they have obtained is

$$\hat{t} = 0.8d + 0.5m + 0.5y + 0.2a + 1.5$$

where $\hat{t}$ is the predicted time in minutes, and d, m, y, and a are indicator variables (namely, they take only the values 0 or 1) defined as follows:

- d is a variable that indicates if the user is on desktop.

- m is a variable that indicates if the user is on mobile device.

- y is a variable that indicates if the user is young (under 21 years old).

- a is a variable that indicates if the user is an adult (21 years old or older).

Example: If a user is 30 years old and on a desktop, then $d = 1$, $m = 0$, $y = 0$, and $a = 1$.

If a 45-year-old user looks at the website from their phone, what is the expected time they will spend on the site?

Exercise 3.2

Imagine that we trained a linear regression model in a medical dataset. The model predicts the expected life span of a patient. To each of the features in our dataset, the model would assign a weight.

a) For the following quantities, state if you believe the weight attached to this quantity is a positive number, a negative number, or zero. Note: if you believe that the weight is a very small number, whether positive or negative, you can say zero.

1. Number of hours of exercise the patient gets per week

2. Number of cigarettes the patient smokes per week

3. Number of family members with heart problems

4. Number of siblings of the patient

5. Whether or not the patient has been hospitalized

b) The model also has a bias. Do you think the bias is positive, negative, or zero?

Exercise 3.3

The following is a dataset of houses with sizes (in square feet) and prices (in dollars).

	Size (s)	Prize (p)
House 1	100	200
House 2	200	475
House 3	200	400
House 4	250	520
House 5	325	735

Suppose we have trained the model where the prediction for the price of the house based on size is the following:

$$\hat{p} = 2s + 50$$

a. Calculate the predictions that this model makes on the dataset.

b. Calculate the mean absolute error of this model.

c. Calculate the root mean square error of this model.

Exercise 3.4

Our goal is to move the line with equation $\hat{y} = 2x + 3$ closer to the point $(x, y) = (5, 15)$ using the tricks we've learned in this chapter. For the following two problems, use the learning rate $\eta = 0.01$.

a. Apply the absolute trick to modify the line above to be closer to the point.

b. Apply the square trick to modify the line above to be closer to the point.

In this chapter

- what is underfitting and overfitting

- some solutions for avoiding overfitting: testing, the model complexity graph, and regularization

- calculating the complexity of the model using the L1 and L2 norms

- picking the best model in terms of performance and complexity

This chapter is different from most of the chapters in this book, because it doesn't contain a particular machine learning algorithm. Instead, it describes some potential problems that machine learning models may face and effective practical ways to solve them.

Imagine that you have learned some great machine learning algorithms, and you are ready to apply them. You go to work as a data scientist, and your first task is to build a machine learning model for a dataset of customers. You build it and put it in production. However, everything goes wrong, and the model doesn't do a good job of making predictions. What happened?

It turns out that this story is common, because many things can go wrong with our models. Fortunately, we have several techniques to improve them. In this chapter, I show you two problems that happen often when training models: underfitting and overfitting. I then show you some solutions to avoid underfitting and overfitting our models: testing and validation, the model complexity graph, and regularization.

Let's explain underfitting and overfitting with the following analogy. Let's say that we have to study for a test. Several things could go wrong during our study process. Maybe we didn't study enough. There's no way to fix that, and we'll likely perform poorly in our test. What if we studied a lot but in the wrong way. For example, instead of focusing on learning, we decided to memorize the entire textbook word for word. Will we do well in our test? It's likely that we won't, because we simply memorized everything without learning. The best option, of course, would be to study for the exam properly and in a way that enables us to answer new questions that we haven't seen before on the topic.

In machine learning, *underfitting* looks a lot like not having studied enough for an exam. It happens when we try to train a model that is too simple, and it is unable to learn the data. *Overfitting* looks a lot like memorizing the entire textbook instead of studying for the exam. It happens when we try to train a model that is too complex, and it memorizes the data instead of learning it well. A good model, one that neither underfits nor overfits, is one that looks like having studied well for the exam. This corresponds to a good model that learns the data properly and can make good predictions on new data that it hasn't seen.

Another way to think of underfitting and overfitting is when we have a task in hand. We can make two mistakes. We can oversimplify the problem and come up with a solution that is too simple. We can also overcomplicate the problem and come up with a solution that is too complex.

Imagine if our task is to kill Godzilla, as shown in figure 4.1, and we come to battle equipped with nothing but a fly swatter. That is an example of an *oversimplification*. The approach won't go well for us, because we underestimated the problem and came unprepared. This is underfitting: our dataset is complex, and we come to model it equipped with nothing but a simple model. The model will not be able to capture the complexities of the dataset.

In contrast, if our task is to kill a small fly and we use a bazooka to do the job, this is an example of an *overcomplication*. Yes, we may kill the fly, but we'll also destroy everything at hand and put ourselves at risk. We overestimated the problem, and our solution wasn't good. This is overfitting: our data is simple, but we try to fit it to a model that is too complex. The model will be able to fit our data, but it'll memorize it instead of learning it. The first time I learned overfitting, my reaction was, "Well, that's no problem. If I use a model that is too complex, I can still model my data, right?" Correct, but the real problem with overfitting is trying to get the model to make predictions on unseen data. The predictions will likely come out looking horrible, as we see later in this chapter.

Underfitting   **Overfitting**

Figure 4.1 Underfitting and overfitting are two problems that can occur when training our machine learning model. Left: Underfitting happens when we oversimplify the problem at hand, and we try to solve it using a simple solution, such as trying to kill Godzilla using a fly swatter. Right: Overfitting happens when we overcomplicate the solution to a problem and try to solve it with an exceedingly complicated solution, such as trying to kill a fly using a bazooka.

As we saw in the section "Parameters and hyperparameters" in chapter 3, every machine learning model has hyperparameters, which are the knobs that we twist and turn before training the model. Setting the right hyperparameters for our model is of extreme importance. If we set some of them wrong, we are prone to underfit or overfit. The techniques that we cover in this chapter are useful to help us tune the hyperparameters correctly.

To make these concepts clearer, we'll look at an example with a dataset and several different models that are created by changing one particular hyperparameter: the degree of a polynomial.

You can find all the code for this chapter in the following GitHub repository: https://github .com/luisguiserrano/manning/tree/master/Chapter_4_Testing_Overfitting_Underfitting.

An example of underfitting and overfitting using polynomial regression

In this section, we see an example of overfitting and underfitting in the same dataset. Look carefully at the dataset in figure 4.2, and try to fit a polynomial regression model (seen in the section "What if the data is not in a line?" in chapter 3). Let's think of what kind of polynomial would fit this dataset. Would it be a line, a parabola, a cubic, or perhaps a polynomial of degree 100? Recall that the degree of a polynomial is the highest exponent present. For example, the polynomial $2x^{14} + 9x^6 - 3x + 2$ has degree 14.

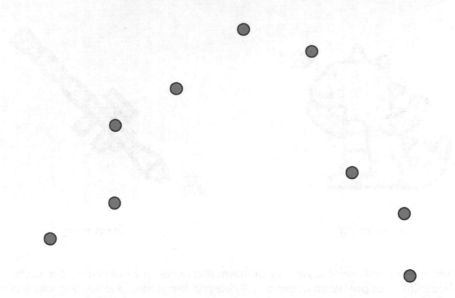

Figure 4.2   In this dataset, we train some models and exhibit training problems such as underfitting and overfitting. If you were to fit a polynomial regression model to this dataset, what type of polynomial would you use: a line, a parabola, or something else?

I think that dataset looks a lot like a parabola that opens downward (a sad face). This is a polynomial of degree 2. However, we are humans, and we eyeballed it. A computer can't do that. A computer needs to try many values for the degree of the polynomial and somehow pick the best one. Let's say the computer will try to fit it with polynomials of degrees 1, 2, and 10. When we fit polynomials of degree 1 (a line), 2 (a quadratic), and 10 (a curve that oscillates at most nine times) to this dataset, we obtain the results shown in figure 4.3.

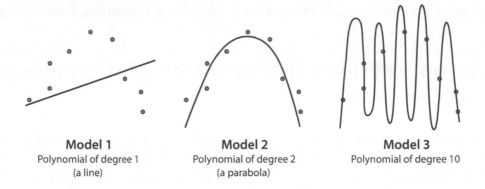

Model 1
Polynomial of degree 1
(a line)

Model 2
Polynomial of degree 2
(a parabola)

Model 3
Polynomial of degree 10

Figure 4.3   Fitting three models to the same dataset. Model 1 is a polynomial of degree 1, which is a line. Model 2 is a polynomial of degree 2, or a quadratic. Model 3 is a polynomial of degree 10. Which one looks like the best fit?

In figure 4.3 we see three models, model 1, model 2, and model 3. Notice that model 1 is too simple, because it is a line trying to fit a quadratic dataset. There is no way we'll find a good line to fit this dataset, because the dataset simply does not look like a line. Therefore, model 1 is a clear example of underfitting. Model 2, in contrast, fits the data pretty well. This model neither overfits nor underfits. Model 3 fits the data extremely well, but it completely misses the point. The data is meant to look like a parabola with a bit of noise, and the model draws a very complicated polynomial of degree 10 that manages to go through each one of the points but doesn't capture the essence of the data. Model 3 is a clear example of overfitting.

To summarize the previous reasoning, here is an observation that we use throughout this chapter, and in many other episodes in this book: very simple models tend to underfit. Very complex models tend to overfit. The goal is to find a model that is neither too simple nor too complex and that captures the essence of our data well.

We're about to get to the challenging part. As humans, we know that the best fit is given by model 2. But what does the computer see? The computer can only calculate error functions. As you may recall from chapter 3, we defined two error functions: absolute error and square error. For visual clarity, in this example we'll use absolute error, which is the average of the sums of the absolute values of the distances from the points to the curve, although the same arguments would work with the square error. For model 1, the points are far from the model, so this error is large. For model 2, these distances are small, so the error is small. However, for model 3, the distances are zero because the points all fall in the actual curve! This means that the computer will think that the perfect model is model 3. This is not good. We need a way to tell the computer that the best model is model 2 and that model 3 is overfitting. How can we do this? I encourage you to put this book down for a few minutes and think of some ideas yourself, because there are several solutions for this problem.

How do we get the computer to pick the right model? By testing

One way to determine if a model overfits is by testing it, and that is what we do in this section. Testing a model consists of picking a small set of the points in the dataset and choosing to use them not for training the model but for testing the model's performance. This set of points is called the *testing set*. The remaining set of points (the majority), which we use for training the model, is called the *training set*. Once we've trained the model on the training set, we use the testing set to evaluate the model. In this way, we make sure that the model is good at generalizing to unseen data, as opposed to memorizing the training set. Going back to the exam analogy, let's imagine training and testing this way. Let's say that the book we are studying for in the exam has 100 questions at the end. We pick 80 of them to train, which means we study them carefully, look up the answers, and learn them. Then we use the remaining 20 questions to test ourselves—we try to answer them without looking at the book, as in an exam setting.

Now let's see how this method looks with our dataset and our models. Notice that the real problem with model 3 is not that it doesn't fit the data; it's that it doesn't generalize well to new data. In other words, if you trained model 3 on that dataset and some new points appeared, would you trust the model to make good predictions with these new points? Probably not, because the model merely memorized the entire dataset without capturing its essence. In this case, the essence of the dataset is that it looks like a parabola that opens downward.

In figure 4.4, we have drawn two white triangles in our dataset, representing the testing set. The training set corresponds to the black circles. Now let's examine this figure in detail and see how these three models perform with both our training and our testing sets. In other words, let's examine the error that the model produces in both datasets. We'll refer to these two errors as the *training error* and the *testing error*.

The top row in figure 4.4 corresponds to the training set and the bottom row to the testing set. To illustrate the error, we have drawn vertical lines from the point to the model. The mean absolute error is precisely the average of the lengths of these lines. Looking at the top row we can see that model 1 has a large training error, model 2 has a small training error, and model 3 has a tiny training error (zero, in fact). Thus, model 3 does the best job on the training set.

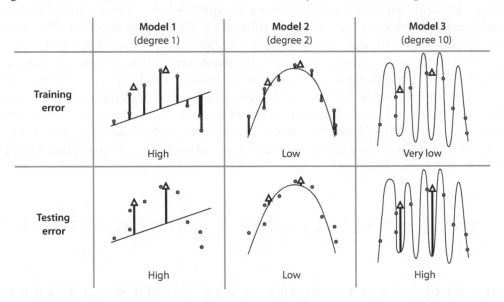

Figure 4.4 We can use this table to decide how complex we want our model. The columns represent the three models of degree 1, 2, and 10. The rows represent the training and the testing error. The solid circles are the training set, and the white triangles are the testing set. The errors at each point can be seen as the vertical lines from the point to the curve. The error of each model is the mean absolute error given by the average of these vertical lengths. Notice that the training error goes down as the complexity of the model increases. However, the testing error goes down and then back up as the complexity increases. From this table, we conclude that out of these three models, the best one is model 2, because it gives us a low testing error.

However, when we get to the testing set, things change. Model 1 still has a large testing error, meaning that this is simply a bad model, underperforming with the training and the testing set: it underfits. Model 2 has a small testing error, which means it is a good model, because it fits both the training and the testing set well. Model 3, however, produces a large testing error. Because it did such a terrible job fitting the testing set, yet such a good job fitting the training set, we conclude that model 3 overfits.

Let's summarize what we have learned so far.

Models can

- Underfit: use a model that is too simple to our dataset.
- Fit the data well: use a model that has the right amount of complexity for our dataset.
- Overfit: use a model that is too complex for our dataset.

In the training set

- The underfit model will do poorly (large training error).
- The good model will do well (small training error).
- The overfit model will do very well (very small training error).

In the testing set

- The underfit model will do poorly (large testing error).
- The good model will do well (small testing error).
- The overfit model will do poorly (large testing error).

Thus, the way to tell whether a model underfits, overfits, or is good, is to look at the training and testing errors. If both errors are high, then it underfits. If both errors are low, then it is a good model. If the training error is low and the testing error is high, then it overfits.

How do we pick the testing set, and how big should it be?

Here's a question. Where did I pull those two new points from? If we are training a model in production where data is always flowing, then we can pick some of the new points as our testing data. But what if we don't have a way to get new points, and all we have is our original dataset of 10 points? When this happens, we just sacrifice some of our data and use it as a test set. How much data? That depends on how much data we have and how well we want the model to do, but in practice, any value from 10% to 20% seems to work well.

Can we use our testing data for training the model? No.

In machine learning, we always need to follow an important rule: when we split our data into training and testing, we should use the training data for training the model, and for absolutely no reason should we touch the testing data while training the model or making decisions on the model's hyperparameters. Failure to do so is likely to result in overfitting, even if it's not noticeable by a human. In many machine learning competitions, teams have submitted models they think are wonderful, only for them to fail miserably when tested on a secret dataset. This can be because the data scientists training the models somehow (perhaps inadvertently) used the testing data to train them. In fact, this rule is so important, we'll make it the golden rule of this book.

golden rule   Thou shalt never use your testing data for training.

Right now, it seems like it's an easy rule to follow, but as we'll see, it's a very easy rule to accidentally break.

As a matter of fact, we already broke the golden rule during this chapter. Can you tell where? I encourage you to go back and find where we broke it. We'll see where in the next section.

Where did we break the golden rule, and how do we fix it? The validation set

In this section, we see where we broke the golden rule and learn a technique called validation, which will come to our rescue.

We broke the golden rule in the section "How do we get the computer to pick the right model." Recall that we had three polynomial regression models: one of degree 1, one of degree 2, and one of degree 10, and we didn't know which one to pick. We used our training data to train the three models, and then we used the testing data to decide which model to pick. We are not supposed to use the testing data to train our model or to make any decisions on the model or its hyperparameters. Once we do this, we are potentially overfitting! We potentially overfit every time we build a model that caters too much to our dataset.

What can we do? The solution is simple: we break our dataset even more. We introduce a new set, the *validation set*, which we then use to make decisions on our dataset. In summary, we break our dataset into the following three sets:

- **Training set:** for training all our models
- **Validation set:** for making decisions on which model to use
- **Testing set:** for checking how well our model did

Thus, in our example, we would have two more points to use for validation, and looking at the validation error should help us decide that the best model to use is model 2. We should use the testing set at the very end, to see how well our model did. If the model is not good, we should throw everything away and start from scratch.

In terms of the sizes of the testing and validation sets, it is common to use a 60-20-20 split or an 80-10-10 split—in other words, 60% training, 20% validation, 20% testing, or 80% training, 10% validation, 10% testing. These numbers are arbitrary, but they tend to work well, because they leave most of the data for training but still allow us to test the model in a big enough set.

A numerical way to decide how complex our model should be: The model complexity graph

In the previous sections, we learned how to use the validation set to help us decide which model was the best among three different ones. In this section, we learn about a graph called the *model complexity graph*, which helps us decide among many more models. Imagine that we have a different and much more complex dataset, and we are trying to build a polynomial regression model to fit it. We want to decide the degree of our model among the numbers between 0 and 10 (inclusive). As we saw in the previous section, the way to decide which model to use is to pick the one that has the smallest validation error.

However, plotting the training and testing errors can give us some valuable information and help us examine trends. In figure 4.5, you can see a plot in which the horizontal axis represents the degree of the polynomial in the model and the vertical axis represents the value of the error. The diamonds represent the training error, and the circles represent the validation error. This is the model complexity graph.

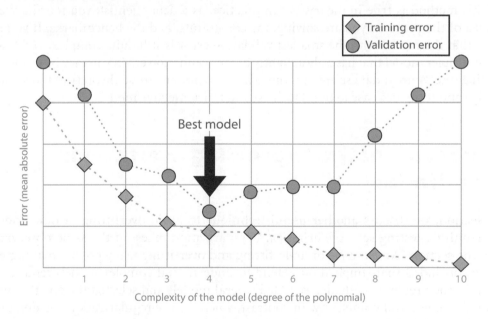

Figure 4.5   The model complexity graph is an effective tool to help us determine the ideal complexity of a model to avoid underfitting and overfitting. In this model complexity graph, the horizontal axis represents the degree of several polynomial regression models, from 0 to 10 (i.e., the complexity of the model). The vertical axis represents the error, which in this case is given by the mean absolute error. Notice that the training error starts large and decreases as we move to the right. This is because the more complex our model is, the better it can fit the training data. The validation error, however, starts large, then decreases, and then increases again—very simple models can't fit our data well (they underfit), whereas very complex models fit our training data but not our validation data because they overfit. A happy point in the middle is where our model neither underfits or overfits, and we can find it using the model complexity graph.

Notice that in the model complexity graph in figure 4.5, the lowest value for the validation error occurs at degree 4, which means that for this dataset, the best-fitting model (among the ones we are considering) is a polynomial regression model of degree 4. Looking at the left of the graph, we can see that when the degree of the polynomial is small, both the training and the validation errors are large, which implies that the models underfit. Looking at the right of the graph, we can see that the training error gets smaller and smaller, but the validation error gets larger and larger, which implies that the models overfit. The sweet spot happens around 4, which is the model we pick.

One benefit of the model complexity graph is that no matter how large our dataset is or how many different models we try, it always looks like two curves: one that always goes down (the training error) and one that goes down and then back up (the validation error). Of course, in a large and complex dataset, these curves may oscillate, and the behavior may be harder to spot. However, the model complexity graph is always a useful tool for data scientists to find a good spot in this graph and decide how complex their models should be to avoid both underfitting and overfitting.

Why do we need such a graph if all we need to do is pick the model with the lowest validation error? This method is true in theory, but in practice, as a data scientist, you may have a much better idea of the problem you are solving, the constraints, and the benchmarks. If you see, for example, that the model with the smallest validation error is still quite complex, and that there is a much simpler model that has only a slightly higher validation error, you may be more inclined to pick that one. A great data scientist is one who can combine these theoretical tools with their knowledge about the use case to build the best and most effective models.

Another alternative to avoiding overfitting: Regularization

In this section, we discuss another useful technique to avoid overfitting in our models that doesn't require a testing set: *regularization*. Regularization relies on the same observation we made in the section "An example of underfitting and overfitting using polynomial regression," where we concluded that simple models tend to underfit and complex models tend to overfit. However, in the previous methods, we tested several models and selected the one that best balanced performance and complexity. In contrast, when we use regularization, we don't need to train several models. We simply train the model once, but during the training, we try to not only improve the model's performance but also reduce its complexity. The key to doing this is to measure both performance and complexity at the same time.

Before we get into the details, let's discuss an analogy for thinking about measuring the performance and complexity of models. Imagine that we have three houses, and all of them have the same problem—the roof is leaking (figure 4.6). Three roofers come, and each fixes one of the houses. The first roofer used a bandage, the second one used roofing shingles, and the third one used titanium. From our intuition, it seems that the best one is roofer 2, because roofer 1 oversimplified the problem (underfitting) and roofer 3 overcomplicated it (overfitting).

Problem: Broken roof

Roofer 1
Solution: Bandage
(Underfitting)

Roofer 2
Solution: Shingles
(Correct)

Roofer 3
Solution: Titanium
(Over!tting)

Figure 4.6 An analogy for underfitting and overfitting. Our problem consists of a broken roof. We have three roofers who can fix it. Roofer 1 comes with a bandage, roofer 2 comes with roofing shingles, and roofer 3 comes with a block of titanium. Roofer 1 oversimplified the problem, so they represent underfitting. Roofer 2 used a good solution. Roofer 3 overcomplicated the solution, so they represent overfitting.

However, we need to make our decisions using numbers, so let's take some measurements. The way to measure the performance of the roofers is by how much water leaked after they fix their roof. They had the following scores:

Performance (in mL of water leaked)

Roofer 1: 1000 mL water

Roofer 2: 1 mL water

Roofer 3: 0 mL water

It seems that roofer 1 had a terrible performance, because the roof was still leaking water. However, between roofers 2 and 3, which one do we pick? Perhaps roofer 3, who had a better performance? The performance measure is not good enough; it correctly removes roofer 1 from the equation, but it erroneously tells us to go with roofer 3, instead of roofer 2. We need a measure of their complexity to help us make the right decision. A good measure of their complexity is how much they charged us to fix the roof, in dollars. The prices were as follows:

Complexity (in price)

Roofer 1: $1

Roofer 2: $100

Roofer 3: $100,000

Now we can tell that roofer 2 is better than roofer 3, because they had the same performance, but roofer 2 charged less. However, roofer 1 was the cheapest one—why on't we go with this one? It seems that what we need is to combine the measures of performance and complexity. We can add the amount of water that the roof leaked and the price, to get the following:

Performance + complexity

Roofer 1: 1001

Roofer 2: 101

Roofer 3: 100,000

Now it is clear that roofer 2 is the best one, which means that optimizing performance and complexity at the same time yields good results that are also as simple as possible. This is what regularization is about: measuring performance and complexity with two different error functions, and adding them to get a more robust error function. This new error function ensures that our model performs well and is not very complex. In the following sections, we get into more details on how to define these two error functions. But before that, let's look at another overfitting example.

Another example of overfitting: Movie recommendations

In this section, we learn a more subtle way in which a model may overfit—this time not related to the degree of the polynomial but on the number of features and the size of the coefficients. Imagine that we have a movie streaming website, and we are trying to build a recommender system. For simplicity, imagine that we have only 10 movies: M1, M2, ..., M10. A new movie, M11, comes out, and we'd like to build a linear regression model to recommend movie 11 based on the previous 10. We have a dataset of 100 users. For each user, we have 10 features, which are the times (in seconds) that the user has watched each of the original 10 movies. If the user hasn't watched a movie, then this amount is 0. The label for each user is the amount of time the user watched movie 11. We want to build a model that fits this dataset. Given that the model is a linear regression model, the equation for the predicted time the user will watch movie 11 is linear, and it will look like the following:

$$\hat{y} = w_1x_1 + w_2x_2 + w_3x_3 + w_4x_4 + w_5x_5 + w_6x_6 + w_7x_7 + w_8x_8 ++ w_9x_9 + w_{10}x_{10} + b,$$

where

- $\hat{y}$ is the amount of time the model predicts that the user will watch movie 11,
- x_i is the amount of time the user watched movie i, for $i = 1, 2, ..., 10$,
- w_i is the weight associated to movie i, and
- b is the bias.

Now let's test our intuition. Out of the following two models (given by their equation), which one (or ones) looks like it may be overfitting?

Model 1: $\hat{y} = 2x_3 + 1.4x_7 - 0.5x_7 + 4$

Model 2: $\hat{y} = 22x_1 - 103x_2 - 14x_3 + 109x_4 - 93x_5 + 203x_6 + 87x_7 - 55x_8 + 378x_9 - 25x_{10} + 8$

If you think like me, model 2 seems a bit complicated, and it may be the one overfitting. The intuition here is that it's unlikely that the time that a user watched movie 2 needs to be multiplied by -103 and then added to other numbers to obtain the prediction. This may fit the data well, but it definitely looks like it's memorizing the data instead of learning it.

Model 1, in contrast, looks much simpler, and it gives us some interesting information. From the fact that most of the coefficients are zero, except those for movies 3, 7, and 9, it tells us that the only three movies that are related to movie 11 are those three movies. Furthermore, from the fact that the coefficients of movies 3 and 7 are positive, the model tells us that if a user watched movie 3 or movie 7, then they are likely to watch movie 11. Because the coefficient of movie 9 is negative, then if the user watched movie 9, they are not likely to watch movie 11.

Our goal is to have a model like model 1 and to avoid models like model 2. But unfortunately, if model 2 produces a smaller error than model 1, then running the linear regression algorithm will select model 2 instead. What can we do? Here is where regularization comes to the rescue. The first thing we need is a measure that tells us that model 2 is much more complex than model 1.

Measuring how complex a model is: L1 and L2 norm

In this section, we learn two ways to measure the complexity of a model. But before this, let's look at models 1 and 2 from the previous section and try to come up with some formula that is low for model 1 and high for model 2.

Notice that a model with more coefficients, or coefficients of higher value, tends to be more complex. Therefore, any formula that matches this will work, such as the following:

- The sum of the absolute values of the coefficients
- The sum of the squares of the coefficients

The first one is called the *L1 norm*, and the second one is called the *L2 norm*. They come from a more general theory of L^P spaces, named after the French mathematician Henri Lebesgue. We use absolute values and squares to get rid of the negative coefficients; otherwise, large negative numbers will cancel out with large positive numbers, and we may end up with a small value for a very complex model.

But before we start calculating the norms, a small technicality: the bias in the models is not included in the L1 and L2 norm. Why? Well, the bias in the model is precisely the number of seconds that we expect a user to watch movie 11 if they haven't watched any of the previous 10 movies. This number is not associated with the complexity of the model; therefore, we leave it alone. The calculation of the L1 norm for models 1 and 2 follows.

Recall that the equations for the models are the following:

Model 1: $\hat{y} = 2x_3 + 1.4x_7 - 0.5x_7 + 8$

Model 2: $\hat{y} = 22x_1 - 103x_2 - 14x_3 + 109x_4 - 93x_5 + 203x_6 + 87x_7 - 55x_8 + 378x_9 - 25x_{10} + 8$

L1 norm:

- **Model 1:** $|2| + |1.4| + |-0.5| = 3.9$
- **Model 2:** $|22| + |-103| + |-14| + |109| + |-93| + |203| + |87| + |-55| + |378| + |-25| = 1{,}089$

L2 norm:

- **Model 1:** $2^2 + 1.4^2 + (-0.5)^2 = 6.21$
- **Model 2:** $22^2 + (-103)^2 + (-14)^2 + 109^2 + (-93)^2 + 203^2 + 87^2 + (-55)^2 + 378^2 + (-25)^2 = 227{,}131$

As expected, both the L1 and L2 norms of model 2 are much larger than the corresponding norms of model 1.

The L1 and L2 norm can also be calculated on polynomials by taking either the sum of absolute values or the sum of squares of the coefficients, except for the constant coefficient. Let's go back to the example at the beginning of this chapter, where our three models were a polynomial of degree 1 (a line), degree 2 (a parabola), and degree 10 (a curve that oscillates 9 times). Imagine that their formulas are the following:

- **Model 1:** $\hat{y} = 2x + 3$
- **Model 2:** $\hat{y} = -x^2 + 6x - 2$
- **Model 3:** $\hat{y} = x^9 + 4x^8 - 9x^7 + 3x^6 - 14x^5 - 2x^4 - 9x^3 + x^2 + 6x + 10$

The L1 and L2 norms are calculated as follows:

L1 norm:

- **Model 1:** $|2| = 2$
- **Model 2:** $|-1| + |6| = 7$
- **Model 3:** $|1| + |4| + |-9| + |3| + |-14| + |-2| + |-9| + |1| + |6| = 49$

L2 norm:

- **Model 1:** $2^2 = 4$
- **Model 2:** $(-1)^2 + 6^2 = 37$
- **Model 3:** $1^2 + 4^2 + (-9)^2 + 3^2 + (-14)^2 + (-2)^2 + (-9)^2 + 1^2 + 6^2 = 425$

Now that we are equipped with two ways to measure the complexity of the models, let's embark into the training process.

Modifying the error function to solve our problem: Lasso regression and ridge regression

Now that we've done most of the heavy lifting, we'll train a linear regression model using regularization. We have two measures for our model: a measure of performance (the error function) and a measure of complexity (the L1 or L2 norm).

Recall that in the roofer analogy, our goal was to find a roofer that provided both good quality and low complexity. We did this by minimizing the sum of two numbers: the measure of quality and the measure of complexity. Regularization consists of applying the same principle to our machine learning model. For this, we have two quantities: the regression error and the regularization term.

regression error A measure of the quality of the model. In this case, it can be the absolute or square errors that we learned in chapter 3.

regularization term A measure of the complexity of the model. It can be the L1 or the L2 norm of the model.

The quantity that we want to minimize to find a good and not too complex model is the modified error, defined as the sum of the two, as shown next:

$$\text{Error} = \text{Regression error} + \text{Regularization term}$$

Regularization is so common that the models themselves have different names based on what norm is used. If we train our regression model using the L1 norm, the model is called *lasso regression*. Lasso stands for "least absolute shrinkage and selection operator." The error function follows:

$$\text{Lasso regression error} = \text{Regression error} + \text{L1 norm}$$

If, instead, we train the model using the L2 norm, it is called *ridge regression*. The name *ridge* comes from the shape of the error function, because adding the L2 norm term to the regression error function turns a sharp corner into a smooth valley when we plot it. The error function follows:

$$\text{Ridge regression error} = \text{Regression error} + \text{L2 norm}$$

Both lasso and ridge regression work well in practice. The decision of which one to use comes down to some preferences that we'll learn about in the upcoming sections. But before we get to that, we need to work out some details to make sure our regularized models work well.

Regulating the amount of performance and complexity in our model: The regularization parameter

Because the process of training the model involves reducing the cost function as much as possible, a model trained with regularization, in principle, should have high performance and low complexity. However, there is some tug-of-war—trying to make the model perform better may make it more complex, whereas trying to reduce the complexity of the model may make it perform worse. Fortunately, most machine learning techniques come with knobs (hyperparameters) for the data scientist to turn and build the best possible models, and regularization is not an exception. In this section, we see how to use a hyperparameter to regulate between performance and complexity.

This hyperparameter is called the *regularization parameter*, and its goal is to determine if the model-training process should emphasize performance or simplicity. The regularization parameter is denoted by λ, the Greek letter *lambda*. We multiply the regularization term by λ, add it to the regression error, and use that result to train our model. The new error becomes the following:

$$\text{Error} = \text{Regression error} + \lambda \text{ Regularization term}$$

Picking a value of 0 for λ cancels out the regularization term, and thus we end up with the same regression model we had in chapter 3. Picking a large value for λ results in a simple model, perhaps of low degree, which may not fit our dataset very well. It is crucial to pick a good value for λ, and for this, validation is a useful technique. It is typical to choose powers of 10, such as 10, 1, 0.1, 0.01, but this choice is somewhat arbitrary. Among these, we select the one that makes our model perform best in our validation set.

Effects of L1 and L2 regularization in the coefficients of the model

In this section, we see crucial differences between L1 and L2 regularization and get some ideas about which one to use in different scenarios. At first glance, they look similar, but the effects they have on the coefficients is interesting, and, depending on what type of model we want, deciding between using L1 and L2 regularization can be critical.

Let's go back to our movie recommendation example, where we are building a regression model to predict the amount of time (in seconds) that a user will watch a movie, given the time that same user has watched 10 different movies. Imagine that we've trained the model, and the equation we get is the following:

Model: $\hat{y} = 22x_1 - 103x_2 - 14x_3 + 109x_4 - 93x_5 + 203x_6 + 87x_7 - 55x_8 + 378x_9 - 25x_{10} + 8$

If we add regularization and train the model again, we end up with a simpler model. The following two properties can be shown mathematically:

- If we use L1 regularization (lasso regression), you end up with a model with fewer coefficients. In other words, L1 regularization turns some of the coefficients into zero. Thus, we may end up with an equation like $\hat{y} = 2x_3 + 1.4x_7 - 0.5x_9 + 8$.

- If we use L2 regularization (ridge regression), we end up with a model with smaller coefficients. In other words, L2 regularization shrinks all the coefficients but rarely turns them into zero. Thus, we may end up with an equation like $\hat{y} = 0.2x_1 - 0.8x_2 - 1.1x_3 + 2.4x_4 - 0.03x_5 + 1.02x_6 + 3.1x_7 - 2x_8 + 2.9x_9 - 0.04x_{10} + 8$.

Thus, depending on what kind of equation we want to get, we can decide between using L1 and L2 regularization.

A quick rule of thumb to use when deciding if we want to use L1 or L2 regularization follows: if we have too many features and we'd like to get rid of most of them, L1 regularization is perfect for that. If we have only few features and believe they are all relevant, then L2 regularization is what we need, because it won't get rid of our useful features.

An example of a problem in which we have many features and L1 regularization can help us is the movie recommendation system we studied in the section "Another example of overfitting: Movie recommendations." In this model, each feature corresponded to one of the movies, and our goal is to find the few movies that were related to the one we're interested in. Thus, we need a model for which most of the coefficients are zero, except for a few of them.

An example in which we should use L2 regularization is the polynomial example at the beginning of the section "An example of underfitting using polynomial regression." For this model, we had only one feature: x. L2 regularization would give us a good polynomial model with small coefficients, which wouldn't oscillate very much and, thus, is less prone to overfitting. In the section "Polynomial regression, testing, and regularization with Turi Create," we will see a polynomial example for which L2 regularization is the right one to use.

The resources corresponding to this chapter (appendix C) point to some places where you can dig deeper into the mathematical reasons why L1 regularization turns coefficients into zero, whereas L2 regularization turns them into small numbers. In the next section, we will learn how to get an intuition for it.

An intuitive way to see regularization

In this section, we learn how the L1 and L2 norms differ in the way they penalize complexity. This section is mostly intuitive and is developed in an example, but if you'd like to see the formal mathematics behind them, please look at appendix B, "Using gradient descent for regularization."

When we try to understand how a machine learning model operates, we should look beyond the error function. An error function says, "This is the error, and if you reduce it, you end up with a good model." But that is like saying, "The secret to succeeding in life is to make as few mistakes as possible." Isn't a positive message better, such as, "These are the things you can do to improve your life," as opposed to "These are the things you should avoid"? Let's see regularization in this way.

In chapter 3, we learned the absolute and the square tricks, which give us a clearer glimpse into regression. At each stage in the training process, we simply pick a point (or several points) and move the line closer to those points. Repeating this process many times will eventually yield a good line fit. We can be more specific and repeat how we defined the linear regression algorithm in chapter 3.

Pseudocode for the linear regression algorithm

Inputs: A dataset of points

Outputs: A linear regression model that fits that dataset

Procedure:

- Pick a model with random weights and a random bias.
- Repeat many times:
  - Pick a random data point.
  - Slightly adjust the weights and bias to improve the prediction for that data point.
- Enjoy your model!

Can we use the same reasoning to understand regularization? Yes, we can.

To simplify things, let's say that we are in the middle of our training, and we want to make the model simpler. We can do this by reducing the coefficients. For simplicity, let's say that our model has three coefficients: 3, 10, and 18. Can we take a small step to decrease these three by a small amount? Of course we can, and here are two methods to do it. Both require a small number, λ, which we'll set to 0.01 for now.

Method 1: Subtract λ from each of the positive parameters, and add λ to each of the negative parameters. If they are zero, leave them alone.

Method 2: Multiply all of them by $1 - \lambda$. Notice that this number is close to 1, because λ is small.

Using method 1, we get the numbers 2.99, 9.99, and 17.99.

Using method 2, we get the numbers 2.97, 9.9, and 17.82.

In this case, λ behaves very much like a learning rate. In fact, it is closely related to the regularization rate (see "Using gradient descent for regularization" in appendix B for details). Notice that in both methods, we are shrinking the size of the coefficients. Now, all we have to do is to repeatedly shrink the coefficients at every stage of the algorithm. In other words, here is how we train the model now:

Inputs: A dataset of points

Outputs: A linear regression model that fits that dataset

Procedure:

- Pick a model with random weights and a random bias.
- Repeat many times:
  - Pick a random data point.
  - Slightly adjust the weights and bias to improve the prediction for that particular data point.
  - **Slightly shrink the coefficients using method 1 or method 2.**
- Enjoy your model!

If we use method 1, we are training the model with L1 regularization, or lasso regression. If we use method 2, we are training it with L2 regularization, or ridge regression. There is a mathematical justification for this, which is described in appendix B, "Using gradient descent for regularization."

In the previous section, we learned that L1 regularization tends to turn many coefficients into 0, whereas L2 regularization tends to decrease them but not turn them into zero. This phenomenon is now easier to see. Let's say that our coefficient is 2, with a regularization parameter of $\lambda = 0.01$. Notice what happens if we use method 1 to shrink our coefficient, and we repeat this process 200 times. We get the following sequence of values:

$$2 \rightarrow 1.99 \rightarrow 1.98 \rightarrow \cdots \rightarrow 0.02 \rightarrow 0.01 \rightarrow 0$$

After 200 epochs of our training, the coefficient becomes 0, and it never changes again. Now let's see what would happen if we apply method 2, again 200 times and with the same learning rate of $\eta = 0.01$. We get the following sequence of values:

$$2 \rightarrow 1.98 \rightarrow 1.9602 \rightarrow \cdots \rightarrow 0.2734 \rightarrow 0.2707 \rightarrow 0.2680$$

Notice that the coefficient decreased dramatically, but it didn't become zero. In fact, no matter how many epochs we run, the coefficient will never become zero. This is because when we multiply a non-negative number by 0.99 many times, the number will never become zero. This is illustrated in figure 4.7.

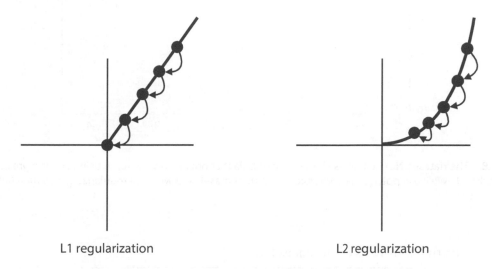

L1 regularization   L2 regularization

Figure 4.7   Both L1 and L2 shrink the size of the coefficient. L1 regularization (left) does it much faster, because it subtracts a fixed amount, so it is likely to eventually become zero. L2 regularization takes much longer, because it multiplies the coefficient by a small factor, so it never reaches zero.

Polynomial regression, testing, and regularization with Turi Create

In this section, we see an example of polynomial regression with regularization in Turi Create. Here is the code for this section:

- **Notebook:**
  - https://github.com/luisguiserrano/manning/blob/master/Chapter_4_Testing_Overfitting_Underfitting/Polynomial_regression_regularization.ipynb

We start with our dataset, which is illustrated in figure 4.8. We can see the curve that best fits this data is a parabola that opens downward (a sad face). Therefore, it is not a problem we can solve with linear regression—we must use polynomial regression. The dataset is stored in an SFrame called `data`, and the first few rows are shown in table 4.1.

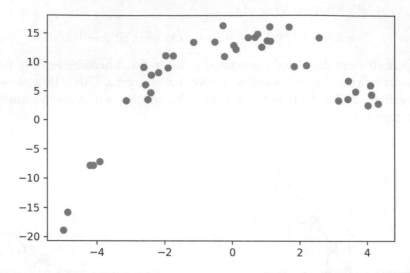

Figure 4.8   The dataset. Notice that its shape is a parabola that opens downward, so using linear regression won't work well. We'll use polynomial regression to fit this dataset, and we'll use regularization to tune our model.

Table 4.1   The first four rows of our dataset

x	y
3.4442185152504816	6.685961311021467
-2.4108324970703663	4.690236225597948
0.11274721368608542	12.205789026637378
-1.9668727392107255	11.133217991032268

The way to do polynomial regression in Turi Create is to add many columns to our dataset, corresponding to the powers of the main feature, and to apply linear regression to this expanded dataset. If the main feature is, say, x, then we add columns with the values of x^2, x^3, x^4, and so on. Thus, our model is finding linear combinations of the powers of x, which are precisely polynomials in x. If the SFrame containing our data is called `data`, we use the following code to add columns for powers up to x^{199}. The first few rows and columns of the resulting dataset appear in table 4.2.

```
for i in range(2,200):
    string = 'x^'+str(i)
    data[string] = data['x'].apply(lambda x:x**i)
```

Table 4.2 The top four rows and the leftmost five columns of our dataset. The column labeled x^k corresponds to the variable x^k, for k = 2, 3, and 4. The dataset has 200 columns.

x	y	x^2	x^3	x^4
3.445	6.686	11.863	40.858	140.722
−2.411	4.690	5.812	−14.012	33.781
0.113	12.206	0.013	0.001	0.000
−1.967	11.133	3.869	−7.609	14.966

Now, we apply linear regression to this large dataset with 200 columns. Notice that a linear regression model in this dataset looks like a linear combination of the variables in the columns. But because each column corresponds to a monomial, then the model obtained looks like a polynomial on the variable *x*.

Before we train any models, we need to split the data into training and testing datasets, using the following line of code:

```
train, test = data.random_split(.8)
```

Now our dataset is split into two datasets, the training set called *train* and the testing set called *test*. In the repository, a random seed is specified, so we always get the same results, although this is not necessary in practice.

The way to use regularization in Turi Create is simple: all we need to do is specify the parameters `l1_penalty` and `l2_penalty` in the `create` method when we train the model. This penalty is precisely the regularization parameter we introduced in the section "Regulating the amount of performance and complexity in our model." A penalty of 0 means we are not using regularization. Thus, we will train three different models with the following parameters:

- No regularization model:
  - `l1_penalty=0`
  - `l2_penalty=0`
- L1 regularization model:
  - `l1_penalty=0.1`
  - `l2_penalty=0`
- L2 regularization model:
  - `l1_penalty=0`
  - `l2_penalty=0.1`

We train the models with the following three lines of code:

```
model_no_reg = tc.linear_regression.create(train, target='y', l1_penalty=0.0,
    l2_penalty=0.0)
model_L1_reg = tc.linear_regression.create(train, target='y', l1_penalty=0.1,
    l2_penalty=0.0)
model_L2_reg = tc.linear_regression.create(train, target='y', l1_penalty=0.0,
    l2_penalty=0.1)
```

The first model uses no regularization, the second one uses L1 regularization with a parameter of 0.1, and the third uses L2 regularization with a parameter of 0.1. The plots of the resulting functions are shown in figure 4.9. Notice that in this figure, the points in the training set are circles, and those in the testing set are triangles.

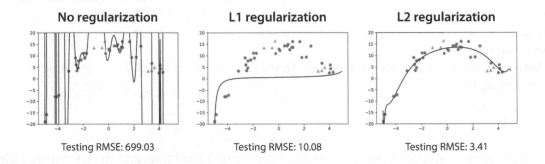

Figure 4.9 Three polynomial regression models for our dataset. The model on the left has no regularization, the model in the middle has L1 regularization with a parameter of 0.1, and the model on the right has L2 regularization with a parameter of 0.1.

Notice that the model with no regularization fits the training points really well, but it's chaotic and doesn't fit the testing points well. The model with L1 regularization does OK with both the training and the testing sets. But the model with L2 regularization does a wonderful job with both the training and the testing sets and also seems to be the one that really captures the shape of the data.

Also note that for the three models, the boundary curve goes a bit crazy on the end points. This is completely understandable, because the endpoints have less data, and it is natural for the model to not know what to do when there's no data. We should always evaluate models by how well they perform inside the boundaries of our dataset, and we should never expect a model to do well outside of those boundaries. Even we humans may not be able to make good predictions outside of the boundaries of the model. For instance, how do you think this curve would look outside of the dataset? Would it continue as parabola that opens downward? Would it oscillate forever like a sine function? If we don't know this, we shouldn't expect the model to know it. Thus, try to ignore the strange behavior at the end points in figure 4.9, and focus on the behavior of the model inside the interval where the data is located.

To find the testing error, we use the following line of code, with the corresponding name of the model. This line of code returns the maximum error and the root mean square error (RMSE).

```
model.predict(test)
```

The testing RMSE for the models follow:

- Model with no regularization: 699.03

- Model with L1 regularization: 10.08

- Model with L2 regularization: 3.41

The model with no regularization had a really large RMSE! Among the other two models, the one with L2 regularization performed much better. Here are two questions to think about:

1. Why did the model with L2 regularization perform better than the one with L1 regularization?

2. Why does the model with L1 regularization look flat, whereas the model with L2 regularization managed to capture the shape of the data?

The two questions have a similar answer, and to find it, we can look at the coefficients of the polynomials. These can be obtained with the following line of code:

```
model.coefficients
```

Each polynomial has 200 coefficients, so we won't display all of them here, but in table 4.3 you can see the first five coefficients for the three models. What do you notice?

Table 4.3   The first five coefficients of the polynomials in our three models. Note that the model with no regularization has large coefficients, the model with L1 regularization has coefficients very close to 0, and the model with L2 regularization has small coefficients.

Coefficient	model_no_reg	model_L1_reg	model_L2_reg
$x^0 = 1$	8.41	0.57	13.24
x^1	15.87	0.07	0.87
x^2	108.87	−0.004	−0.52
x^3	−212.89	0.0002	0.006
x^4	−97.13	−0.0002	−0.02

To interpret table 4.3, we see the predictions for the three models are polynomials of degree 200. The first terms look as follows:

- Model with no regularization: $\hat{y} = 8.41 + 15.87x + 108.87x^2 - 212.89x^3 - 97.13x^4 + \ldots$

- Model with L1 regularization: $\hat{y} = 0.57 + 0.07x - 0.004x^2 + 0.0002x^3 - 0.0002x^4 + \cdots$

- Model with L2 regularization: $\hat{y} = 13.24 + 0.87x - 0.52x^2 + 0.006x^3 - 0.02x^4 + \cdots$

From these polynomials, we see the following:

- For the model with no regularization, all the coefficients are large. This means the polynomial is chaotic and not good for making predictions.

- For the model with L1 regularization, all the coefficients, except for the constant one (the first one), are tiny—almost 0. This means that for the values close to zero, the polynomial looks a lot like the horizontal line with equation $\hat{y} = 0.57$. This is better than the previous model but still not great for making predictions.

- For the model with L2 regularization, the coefficients get smaller as the degree grows but are still not so small. This gives us a decent polynomial for making predictions.

Summary

- When it comes to training models, many problems arise. Two problems that come up quite often are underfitting and overfitting.

- Underfitting occurs when we use a very simple model to fit our dataset. Overfitting occurs when we use an overly complex model to fit our dataset.

- An effective way to tell overfitting and underfitting apart is by using a testing dataset.

- To test a model, we split the data into two sets: a training set and a testing set. The training set is used to train the model, and the testing set is used to evaluate the model.

- The golden rule of machine learning is to never use our testing data for training or making decisions in our models.

- The validation set is another portion of our dataset that we use to make decisions about the hyperparameters in our model.

- A model that underfits will perform poorly in the training set and in the validation set. A model that overfits will perform well in the training set but poorly in the validation set. A good model will perform well on both the training and the validation sets.

- The model complexity graph is used to determine the correct complexity of a model, so that it doesn't underfit or overfit.

- Regularization is a very important technique to reduce overfitting in machine learning models. It consists of adding a measure of complexity (regularization term) to the error function during the training process.

- The L1 and L2 norms are the two most common measures of complexity used in regularization.

- Using the L1 norm leads to L1 regularization, or lasso regression. Using the L2 norm leads to L2 regularization, or ridge regression.

- L1 regularization is recommended when our dataset has numerous features, and we want to turn many of them into zero. L2 regularization is recommended when our dataset has few features, and we want to make them small but not zero.

Exercises

Exercise 4.1

We have trained four models in the same dataset with different hyperparameters. In the following table we have recorded the training and testing errors for each of the models.

Model	Training error	Testing error
1	0.1	1.8
2	0.4	1.2
3	0.6	0.8
4	1.9	2.3

   a. Which model would you select for this dataset?

   b. Which model looks like it's underfitting the data?

   c. Which model looks like it's overfitting the data?

Exercise 4.2

We are given the following dataset:

x	y
1	2
2	2.5
3	6
4	14.5
5	34

We train the polynomial regression model that predicts the value of y as $\hat{y}$, where

$$\hat{y} = 2x^2 - 5x + 4.$$

If the regularization parameter is $\lambda = 0.1$ and the error function we've used to train this dataset is the mean absolute value (MAE), determine the following:

   a. The lasso regression error of our model (using the L1 norm)

   b. The ridge regression error of our model (using the L2 norm)

In this chapter

- what is classification

- sentiment analysis: how to tell if a sentence is happy or sad using machine learning

- how to draw a line that separates points of two colors

- what is a perceptron, and how do we train it

- coding the perceptron algorithm in Python and Turi Create

In this chapter, we learn a branch of machine learning called *classification*. Classification models are similar to regression models, in that their aim is to predict the labels of a dataset based on the features. The difference is that regression models aim to predict a number, whereas classification models aim to predict a state or a category. Classification models are often called *classifiers*, and we'll use the terms interchangeably. Many classifiers predict one of two possible states (often yes/no), although it is possible to build classifiers that predict among a higher number of possible states. The following are popular examples of classifiers:

- A recommendation model that predicts whether a user will watch a certain movie

- An email model that predicts whether an email is spam or ham

- A medical model that predicts whether a patient is sick or healthy

- An image-recognition model that predicts whether an image contains an automobile, a bird, a cat, or a dog

- A voice recognition model that predicts whether the user said a particular command

Classification is a popular area in machine learning, and the bulk of the chapters in this book (chapters 5, 6, 8, 9, 10, 11, and 12) talk about different classification models. In this chapter, we learn the *perceptron* model, also called the *perceptron classifier*, or simply the *perceptron*. A perceptron is similar to a linear regression model, in that it uses a linear combination of the features to make a prediction and is the building block of neural networks (which we learn in chapter 10). Furthermore, the process of training a perceptron is similar to that of training a linear regression model. Just as we did in chapter 3 with the linear regression algorithm, we develop the perceptron algorithm in two ways: using a trick that we can iterate many times, and defining an error function that we can minimize using gradient descent.

The main example of classification models that we learn in this chapter is *sentiment analysis*. In sentiment analysis, the goal of the model is to predict the sentiment of a sentence. In other words, the model predicts whether the sentence is happy or sad. For example, a good sentiment analysis model can predict that the sentence "I feel wonderful!" is a happy sentence, and that the sentence "What an awful day!" is a sad sentence.

Sentiment analysis is used in many practical applications, such as the following:

- When a company analyzes the conversations between customers and technical support, to evaluate the quality of the conversation

- When analyzing the tone of a brand's digital presence, such as comments on social media or reviews related to its products

- When a social platform like Twitter analyzes the overall mood of a certain population after an event

- When an investor uses public sentiment toward a company to predict its stock price

How could we build a sentiment analysis classifier? In other words, how could we build a machine learning model that takes a sentence as an input and, as output, tells us whether the sentence is happy or sad. This model can make mistakes, of course, but the idea is to build it in such a way that it makes as few mistakes as possible. Let's put down the book for a couple of minutes and think of how we would go about building this type of model.

Here is an idea. Happy sentences tend to contain happy words, such as *wonderful, happy,* or *joy,* whereas sad sentences tend to contain sad words, such as *awful, sad,* or *despair.* A classifier can consist of a "happiness" score for every single word in the dictionary. Happy words can be given positive scores, and sad words can be given negative scores. Neutral words such as *the* can be given a score of zero. When we feed a sentence into our classifier, the classifier simply adds the scores of all the words in the sentence. If the result is positive, then the classifier concludes that the sentence is happy. If the result is negative, then the classifier concludes that the sentence is sad. The goal now is to find scores for all the words in the dictionary. For this, we use machine learning.

The type of model we just built is called a *perceptron model*. In this chapter, we learn the formal definition of a perceptron and how to train it by finding the perfect scores for all the words so that our classifier makes as few mistakes as possible.

The process of training a perceptron is called the *perceptron algorithm*, and it is not that different from the linear regression algorithm we learned in chapter 3. Here is the idea of the perceptron algorithm: To train the model, we first need a dataset containing many sentences together with their labels (happy/sad). We start building our classifier by assigning random scores to all the words. Then we go over all the sentences in our dataset several times. For every sentence, we slightly tweak the scores so that the classifier improves the prediction for that sentence. How do we tweak the scores? We do it using a trick called the *perceptron trick*, which we learn in the section "The perception trick." An equivalent way to train perceptron models is to use an error function, just as we did in chapter 3. We then use gradient descent to minimize this function.

However, language is complicated—it has nuances, double entendres, and sarcasm. Wouldn't we lose too much information if we reduce a word to a simple score? The answer is yes—we do lose a lot of information, and we won't be able to create a perfect classifier this way. The good news is that using this method, we can still create a classifier that is correct *most* of the time. Here is a proof that the method we are using can't be correct all the time. The sentences, "I am not sad, I'm happy" and "I am not happy, I am sad" have the same words, yet completely different meanings. Therefore, no matter what scores we give the words, these two sentences will attain the exact same score, and, thus, the classifier will return the same prediction for them. They have different labels, so the classifier must have made a mistake with one of them.

A solution for this problem is to build a classifier that takes the order of the words into account, or even other things such as punctuation or idioms. Some models such as *hidden Markov models* (HMM), *recurrent neural networks* (RNN), or *long short-term memory networks* (LSTM) have had great success with sequential data, but we won't include them in this book. However, if you want to explore these models, in appendix C you can find some very useful references for that.

You can find all the code for this chapter in the following GitHub repository: https://github .com/luisguiserrano/manning/tree/master/Chapter_5_Perceptron_Algorithm.

The problem: We are on an alien planet, and we don't know their language!

Imagine the following scenario: we are astronauts and have just landed on a distant planet where a race of unknown aliens live. We would love to be able to communicate with the aliens, but they speak a strange language that we don't understand. We notice that the aliens have two moods, happy and sad. Our first step in communicating with them is to figure out if they are happy or sad based on what they say. In other words, we want to build a sentiment analysis classifier.

We manage to befriend four aliens, and we start observing their mood and studying what they say. We observe that two of them are happy and two of them are sad. They also keep repeating the same sentence over and over. Their language seems to only have two words: *aack* and *beep*. We form the following dataset with the sentence they say and their mood:

Dataset:

- Alien 1
  - Mood: Happy
  - Sentence: *"Aack, aack, aack!"*
- Alien 2:
  - Mood: Sad
  - Sentence: *"Beep beep!"*
- Alien 3:
  - Mood: Happy
  - Sentence: *"Aack beep aack!"*
- Alien 4:
  - Mood: Sad
  - Sentence: *"Aack beep beep beep!"*

All of a sudden, a fifth alien comes in, and it says, *"Aack beep aack aack!"* We can't really tell the mood of this alien. From what we know, how should we predict for the mood of the alien (figure 5.1)?

We predict that this alien is happy because, even though we don't know the language, the word *aack* seems to appear more in happy sentences, whereas the word *beep* seems to appear more in sad sentences. Perhaps *aack* means something positive, such as "joy" or "happiness," whereas *beep* may mean something sad, such as "despair" or "sadness."

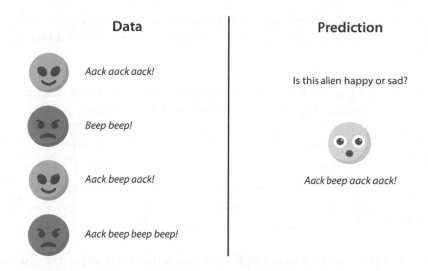

Figure 5.1 Our dataset of aliens. We have recorded their mood (happy or sad) and the sentence they keep repeating. Now a fifth alien comes in, saying a different sentence. Do we predict that this alien is happy or sad?

This observation gives rise to our first sentiment analysis classifier. This classifier makes a prediction in the following way: it counts the number of appearances of the words *aack* and *beep*. If the number of appearances of *aack* is larger than that of *beep*, then the classifier predicts that the sentence is happy. If it is smaller, then the classifier predicts that the sentence is sad. What happens when both words appear the same number of times? We have no basis to tell, so let's say that by default, the prediction is that the sentence is happy. In practice, these types of edge cases don't happen often, so they won't create a big problem for us.

The classifier we just built is a perceptron (also called linear classifier). We can write it in terms of scores, or weights, in the following way:

Sentiment analysis classifier

Given a sentence, assign the following scores to the words:

Scores:

- *Aack*: 1 point
- *Beep*: –1 points

Rule:

Calculate the score of the sentence by adding the scores of all the words on it as follows:

- If the score is positive or zero, predict that the sentence is happy.
- If the score is negative, predict that the sentence is sad.

In most situations, it is useful to plot our data, because sometimes nice patterns become visible. In table 5.1, we have our four aliens, as well as the number of times each said the words *aack* and *beep*, and their mood.

Table 5.1   Our dataset of aliens, the sentences they said, and their mood. We have broken each sentence down to its number of appearances of the words aack and beep.

Sentence	*Aack*	*Beep*	Mood
Aack aack aack!	3	0	Happy
Beep beep!	0	2	Sad
Aack beep aack!	2	1	Happy
Aack beep beep beep!	1	3	Sad

The plot consists of two axes, the horizontal (*x*) axis and the vertical (*y*) axis. In the horizontal axis, we record the number of appearances of *aack*, and in the vertical axis, the appearances of *beep*. This plot can be seen in figure 5.2.

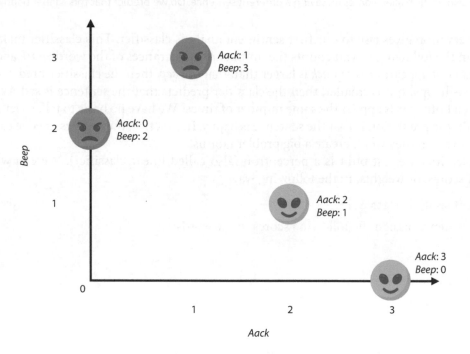

Figure 5.2   A plot of the dataset of aliens. In the horizontal axis we plot the number of appearances of the word *aack*, and in the vertical axis, the appearances of the word *beep*.

Note that in the plot in figure 5.2, the happy aliens are located on the bottom right, whereas the sad aliens are in the top left. This is because the bottom right is the area where the sentences have more appearances of *aack* than *beep*, and the top left area is the opposite. In fact, a line formed by all the sentences with the same number of appearances of *aack* and *beep* divides these two regions, as shown in figure 5.3. This line has the following equation:

$$\#aack = \#beep$$

Or equivalently, this equation:

$$\#aack - \#beep = 0$$

Throughout this chapter, we'll use the variables x with different subscripts to indicate the number of appearances of a word in a sentence. In this case, x_{aack} is the number of times the word *aack* appears, and x_{beep} is the number of times the word *beep* appears.

Using this notation, the equation of the classifier becomes $x_{aack} - x_{beep} = 0$, or equivalently, $x_{aack} = x_{beep}$. This is the equation of a line in the plane. If it doesn't appear so, think of the equation of the line $y = x$, except instead of x, we have x_{aack}, and instead of y, we have x_{beep}. Why not use x and y instead like we've done since high school? I would love to, but unfortunately we need the y for something else (the prediction) later. Thus, let's think of the x_{aack}-axis as the horizontal axis and the x_{beep}-axis as the vertical axis. Together with this equation, we have two important areas, which we call the *positive zone* and the *negative zone*. They are defined as follows:

Positive zone: The area on the plane for which $x_{aack} - x_{beep} \geq 0$. This corresponds to the sentences in which the word *aack* appears at least as many times as the word *beep*.

Negative zone: The area on the plane for which $x_{aack} - x_{beep} < 0$. This corresponds to the sentences in which the word *aack* appears fewer times than the word *beep*.

The classifier we created predicts that every sentence in the positive zone is happy and every sentence in the negative zone is sad. Therefore, our goal is to find the classifier that can put as many happy sentences as possible in the positive area and as many sad sentences as possible in the negative area. For this small example, our classifier achieves this job to perfection. This is not always the case, but the perceptron algorithm will help us find a classifier that will perform this job really well.

In figure 5.3, we can see the line that corresponds to the classifier and the positive and negative zones. If you compare figures 5.2 and 5.3, you can see that the current classifier is good, because all the happy sentences are in the positive zone and all the sad sentences are in the negative zone.

Now that we've built a simple sentiment analysis perceptron classifier, let's look at a slightly more complex example.

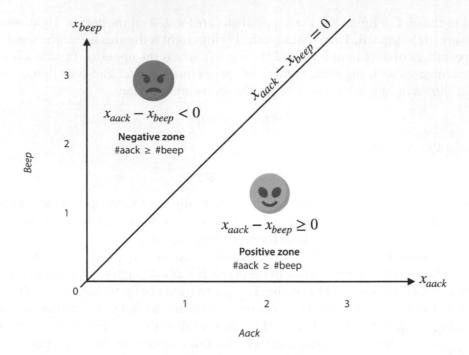

Figure 5.3   The classifier is the diagonal line that splits the happy and the sad points. The equation of this line is $x_{aack} = x_{beep}$ (or equivalently, $x_{aack} - x_{beep} = 0$), because the line corresponds to all the points where the horizontal and the vertical coordinates are equal. The happy zone is the zone in which the number of appearances of *aack* is greater than or equal to the number of appearances of *beep*, and the sad zone is the zone in which the number of appearances of *aack* is less than that of *beep*.

A slightly more complicated planet

In this section, we see a more complicated example, which introduces a new aspect of the perceptron: the bias. After we can communicate with the aliens on the first planet, we are sent on a mission to a second planet, where the aliens have a slightly more complicated language. Our goal is still the same: to create a sentiment analysis classifier in their language. The language in the new planet has two words: *crack* and *doink*. The dataset is shown in table 5.2.

Building a classifier for this dataset seems to be a bit harder than for the previous dataset. First of all, should we assign positive or negative scores to the words *crack* and *doink*? Let's take a pen and paper and try coming up with a classifier that can correctly separate the happy and sad sentences in this dataset. Looking at the plot of this dataset in figure 5.4 may be helpful.

Table 5.2 The new dataset of alien words. Again, we've recorded each sentence, the number of appearances of each word in that sentence, and the mood of the alien.

Sentence	Crack	Doink	Mood
Crack!	1	0	Sad
Doink doink!	0	2	Sad
Crack doink!	1	1	Sad
Crack doink crack!	2	1	Sad
Doink crack doink doink!	1	3	Happy
Crack doink doink crack!	2	2	Happy
Doink doink crack crack crack!	3	2	Happy
Crack doink doink crack doink!	2	3	Happy

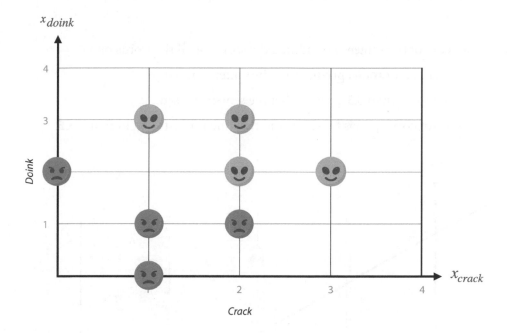

Figure 5.4 The plot of the new dataset of aliens. Notice that the happy ones tend to be above and to the right, and the sad ones below and to the left.

The idea for this classifier is to count the number of words in a sentence. Notice that the sentences with one, two, or three words are all sad, and the sentences with four and five words are happy. That is the classifier! It classifies sentences with three words or fewer as sad, and the sentences with four words or more as happy. We can again write this in a more mathematical way.

Sentiment analysis classifier

Given a sentence, assign the following scores to the words:

Scores:

- *Crack*: one point
- *Doink*: one point

Rule:

Calculate the score of the sentence by adding the scores of all the words on it.

- If the score is four or more, predict that the sentence is happy.
- If the score is three or less, predict that the sentence is sad.

To make it simpler, let's slightly change the rule by using a cutoff of 3.5.

Rule:

Calculate the score of the sentence by adding the scores of all the words on it.

- If the score is 3.5 or more, predict that the sentence is happy.
- If the score is less than 3.5, predict that the sentence is sad.

This classifier again corresponds to a line, and that line is illustrated in figure 5.5.

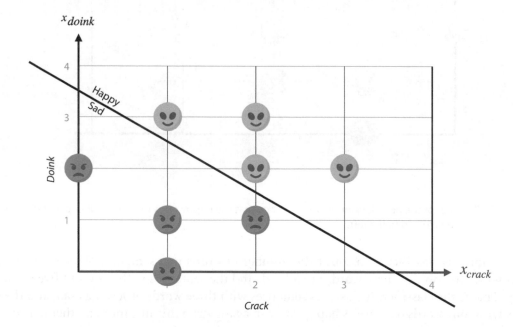

Figure 5.5   The classifier for the new dataset of aliens. It is again a line that splits the happy and the sad aliens.

In the previous example, we concluded that the word *aack* was a happy word, and the word *beep* was a sad one. What happens in this example? It seems that both words *crack* and *doink* are happy, because their scores are both positive. Why, then, is the sentence "*Crack doink*" a sad sentence? It doesn't have enough words. The aliens on this planet have a distinctive personality. The aliens that don't speak much are sad, and those who speak a lot are happy. The way we can interpret it is that the aliens on this planet are inherently sad, but they can get out of the sadness by talking a lot.

Another important element in this classifier is the cutoff, or threshold, of 3.5. This threshold is used by the classifier to make the prediction, because sentences with scores higher than or equal to the threshold are classified as happy, and sentences with scores lower than the threshold are classified as sad. However, thresholds are not common, and instead we use the notion of a *bias*. The bias is the negative of the threshold, and we add it to the score. This way, the classifier can calculate the score and return a prediction of happy if the score is nonnegative, or sad if it is negative. As a final change in notation, we'll call the scores of the words *weights*. Our classifier can be expressed as follows:

Sentiment analysis classifier

Given a sentence, assign the following weights and bias to the words:

Weights:

- *Crack*: one point
- *Doink*: one point

Bias: –3.5 points

Rule:

Calculate the score of the sentence by adding the weights of all the words on it and the bias.

- If the score is greater than or equal to zero, predict that the sentence is happy.
- If the score is less than zero, predict that the sentence is sad.

The equation of the score of the classifier, and also of the line in figure 5.5, follows:

$$\#crack + \#doink - 3.5 = 0$$

Notice that defining a perceptron classifier with a threshold of 3.5 and with a bias of –3.5 is the same thing, because the following two equations are equivalent:

- $\#crack + \#doink \geq 3.5$
- $\#crack + \#doink - 3.5 \geq 0$

We can use a similar notation as in the previous section, where x_{crack} is the number of appearances of the word *crack* and x_{doink} is the number of appearances of the word *doink*. Thus, the equation of the line in figure 3.5 can be written as

$$x_{crack} + x_{doink} - 3.5 = 0.$$

This line also divides the plane into positive and negative zones, defined as follows:

Positive zone: the area on the plane for which $x_{crack} + x_{doink} - 3.5 \geq 0$

Negative zone: the area on the plane for which $x_{crack} + x_{doink} - 3.5 < 0$

Does our classifier need to be correct all the time? No

In the previous two examples, we built a classifier that was correct all the time. In other words, the classifier classified the two happy sentences as happy and the two sad sentences as sad. This is not something one finds often in practice, especially in datasets with many points. However, the goal of the classifier is to classify the points as best as possible. In figure 5.6, we can see a dataset with 17 points (eight happy and nine sad) that is impossible to perfectly split into two using a single line. However, the line in the picture does a good job, only classifying three points incorrectly.

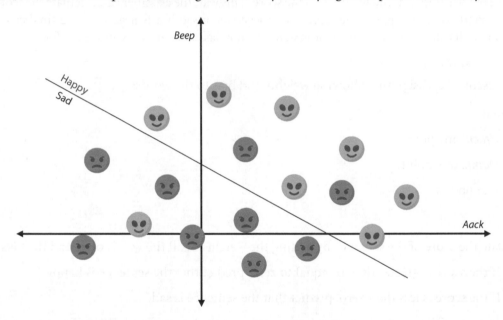

Figure 5.6   This line splits the dataset well. Note that it makes only three mistakes: two on the happy zone and one on the sad zone.

A more general classifier and a slightly different way to define lines

In this section, we get a more general view of the perceptron classifier. For a moment, let's call our words 1 and 2, and the variables keeping track of their appearances x_1 and x_2. The equations of the two previous classifiers follow:

- $x_1 - x_2 = 0$
- $x_1 + x_2 - 3.5 = 0$

The general form of the equation of a perceptron classifier is $ax_1 + bx_2 + c = 0$, where a is the score of the word 1, b the score of the word 2, and c is the bias. This equation corresponds to a line that splits the plane into two zones as follows:

Positive zone: the zone on the plane for which $ax_1 + bx_2 + c \geq 0$

Negative zone: the zone on the plane for which $ax_1 + bx_2 + c < 0$

For example, if the word 1 has a score of 4, the word 2 has a score of –2.5, and the bias is 1.8, then the equation of this classifier is

$$4x_1 - 2.5x_2 + 1.8 = 0,$$

and the positive and negative zones are those where $4x_1 - 2.5x_2 + 1.8 \geq 0$ and $4x_1 - 2.5x_2 + 1.8 < 0$, respectively.

> **aside: Equations of lines and zones in the plane**   In chapter 3, we defined lines using the equation $y = mx + b$ on a plane where the axes are x and y. In this chapter, we define them with the equation $ax_1 + bx_2 + c = 0$ on a plane where the axes are x_1 and x_2. How are they different? They are both perfectly valid ways to define a line. However, whereas the first equation is useful for linear regression models, the second equation is useful for perceptron models (and, in general, for other classification algorithms, such as logistic regression, neural networks, and support vector machines, that we'll see in chapters 6, 10, and 11, respectively). Why is this equation better for perceptron models? Some advantages follow:
>
> * The equation $ax_1 + bx_2 + c = 0$ not only defines a line but also clearly defines the two zones, positive and negative. If we wanted to have the same line, except with the positive and negative regions flipped, we would consider the equation $-ax_1 - bx_2 - c = 0$.
>
> * Using the equation $ax_1 + bx_2 + c = 0$, we can draw vertical lines, because the equation of a vertical line is $x = c$ or $1x_1 + 0x_2 - c = 0$. Although vertical lines don't often show up in linear regression models, they do show up in classification models.

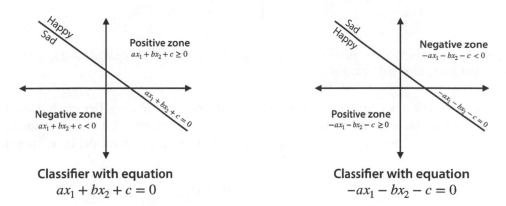

Figure 5.7   A classifier is defined by a line with the equation $ax_1 + bx_2 + c = 0$, a positive zone, and a negative zone. If we want to flip the positive and negative zones, all we need to do is negate the weights and the bias. On the left we have the classifier with equation $ax_1 + bx_2 + c = 0$. On the right, the classifier with flipped zones and the equation $-ax_1 - bx_2 - c = 0$.

The step function and activation functions: A condensed way to get predictions

In this section, we learn a mathematical shortcut to obtain the predictions. Before learning this, however, we need to turn all our data into numbers. Notice that the labels in our dataset are "happy" and "sad." We record these as 1 and 0, respectively.

Both perceptron classifiers that we've built in this chapter have been defined using an if statement. Namely, the classifier predicts "happy" or "sad" based on the total score of the sentence; if this score is positive or zero, the classifier predicts "happy," and if it is negative, the classifier predicts "sad." We have a more direct way to turn the score into a prediction: using the *step function*.

step function   The function that returns a 1 if the output is nonnegative and a 0 if the output is negative. In other words, if the input is x, then

- $step(x) = 1$ if $x \geq 0$
- $step(x) = 0$ if $x < 0$

Figure 5.8 shows the graph of the step function.

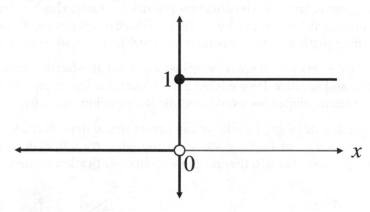

Figure 5.8   The step function is useful in the study of perceptron models. The output of the step function is 0 when the input is negative and 1 otherwise.

With the step function, we can express the output of the perceptron classifier easily. In our dataset, we use the variable y to refer to the labels, just as we did in chapter 3. The prediction that the model makes for the label is denoted $\hat{y}$. The output of the perceptron model is written in condensed form as

$$\hat{y} = step(ax_1 + bx_2 + c).$$

The step function is a specific case of an *activation function*. The activation function is an important concept in machine learning, especially in deep learning and will appear again in chapters 6 and 10. The formal definition of an activation function will come later, because its full power is used in building neural networks. But for now, we can think of the activation function as a function we can use to turn the scores into a prediction.

What happens if I have more than two words? General definition of the perceptron classifier

In the two alien examples at the beginning of this section, we built perceptron classifiers for languages with two words. But we can build classifiers with as many words as we want. For example, if we had a language with three words, say, *aack*, *beep*, and *crack*, the classifier would make predictions according to the following formula:

$$\hat{y} = step(ax_{aack} + bx_{beep} + cx_{crack} + d),$$

where *a*, *b*, and *c* are the weights of the words *aack*, *beep*, and *crack*, respectively, and *d* is the bias.

As we saw, the sentiment analysis perceptron classifiers for languages with two words can be expressed as a line in the plane that splits the happy and the sad points. Sentiment analysis classifiers for languages with three words can also be represented geometrically. We can imagine the points as living in three-dimensional space. In this case, each of the axes corresponds to each of the words *aack*, *beep*, and *crack*, and a sentence corresponds to a point in space for which its three coordinates are the number of appearances of the three words. Figure 5.9 illustrates an example in which the sentence containing *aack* five times, *beep* eight times, and *crack* three times, corresponds to the point with coordinates (5, 8, 3).

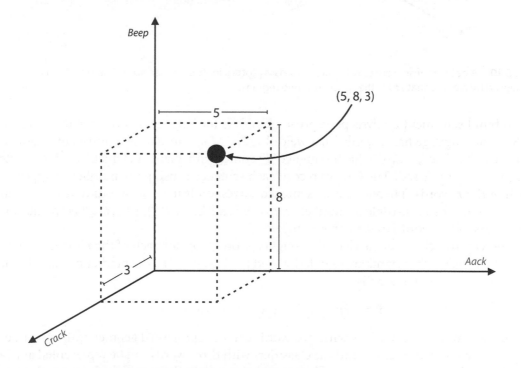

Figure 5.9   A sentence with three words can be plotted as a point in space. In this case, a sentence with the word *aack* five times, *beep* eight times, and *crack* three times is plotted in the point with coordinates (5,8,3).

The way to separate these points is using a plane. The equation with a plane is precisely $ax_{aack} + bx_{beep} + cx_{crack} + d$, and this plane is illustrated in figure 5.10.

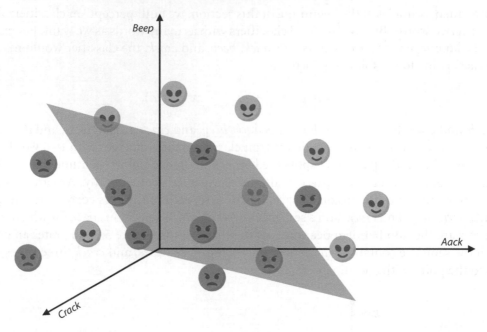

Figure 5.10   A dataset of sentences with three words is plotted in three dimensions. The classifier is represented by a plane that splits the space into two regions.

We can build sentiment analysis perceptron classifiers for languages with as many words as we can. Say our language has n words, that we call $1, 2, \ldots, n$. Our dataset consists of m sentences, which we call $x^{(1)}, x^{(2)}, \ldots, x^{(m)}$. Each sentence $x^{(1)}$ comes with a label y_i, which is 1 if the sentence is happy and 0 if it is sad. The way we record each sentence is using the number of appearances of each of the n words. Therefore, each sentence corresponds to a row in our dataset and can be seen as a vector, or an n-tuple of numbers $x^{(i)} = (x_1^{(i)}, x_2^{(i)}, \ldots, x_n^{(i)})$, where $x_j^{(i)}$ is the number of appearances of the word j in the i-th sentence.

   The perceptron classifier consists of n weights (scores), one for each of the n words in our language, and a bias. The weights are denoted w_i and the bias b. Thus, the prediction that the classifier makes for the sentence $x^{(i)}$ is

$$\hat{y}_i = \text{step}(w_1 x_1^{(i)} + w_2 x_2^{(i)} + \cdots + w_n x_n^{(i)} + b).$$

In the same way as the classifiers with two words can be represented geometrically as a line that cuts the plane into two regions, and the classifiers with three words can be represented as a plane that cuts the three-dimensional space into two regions, classifiers with n words can also be represented geometrically. Unfortunately, we need n-dimensions to see them. Humans can see only three dimensions, so we may have to imagine an $(n-1)$-dimensional plane (called a *hyperplane*) cutting the n-dimensional space into two regions.

However, the fact that we can't imagine them geometrically doesn't mean we can't have a good idea of how they work. Imagine if our classifier is built on the English language. Every single word gets a weight assigned. That is equivalent to going through the dictionary and assigning a happiness score to each of the words. The result could look something like this:

Weights (scores):

- A: 0.1 points

- Aardvark: 0.2 points

- Aargh: −4 points

- …

- Joy: 10 points

- …

- Suffering: −8.5 points

- ...

- Zygote: 0.4 points

Bias:

- −2.3 points

If those were the weights and bias of the classifier, to predict whether a sentence is happy or sad, we add the scores of all the words on it (with repetitions). If the result is higher than or equal to 2.3 (the negative of the bias), the sentence is predicted as happy; otherwise, it is predicted as sad.

Furthermore, this notation works for any example, not only sentiment analysis. If we have a different problem with different data points, features, and labels, we can encode it using the same variables. For example, if we have a medical application where we are trying to predict whether a patient is sick or healthy using n weights and a bias, we can still call the labels y, the features x_i, the weights w_i, and the bias b.

The bias, the *y*-intercept, and the inherent mood of a quiet alien

So far we have a good idea of what the weights of the classifier mean. Words with positive weights are happy, and words with negative words are sad. Words with very small weights (whether positive or negative) are more neutral words. However, what does the bias mean?

In chapter 3, we specified that the bias in a regression model for house prices was the base price of a house. In other words, it is the predicted price of a hypothetical house with zero rooms (a studio?). In the perceptron model, the bias can be interpreted as the score of the empty sentence. In other words, if an alien says absolutely nothing, is this alien happy or sad? If a sentence has no words, its score is precisely the bias. Thus, if the bias is positive, the alien that says nothing is happy, and if the bias is negative, that same alien is sad.

Geometrically, the difference between a positive and negative bias lies in the location of the origin (the point with coordinates (0,0)) with respect to the classifier. This is because the point with coordinates (0,0) corresponds to the sentence with no words. In classifiers with a positive bias, the origin lies in the positive zone, whereas in classifiers with a negative bias, the origin lies in the negative zone, as illustrated in figure 5.11.

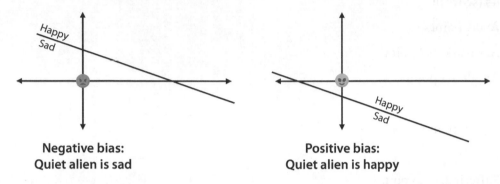

Negative bias:
Quiet alien is sad

Positive bias:
Quiet alien is happy

Figure 5.11   Left: the classifier has a negative bias, or a positive *threshold* (*y*-intercept). This means that the alien that doesn't say anything falls in the sad zone and is classified as sad. Right: The classifier has a positive bias, or a negative threshold. This means that the alien that doesn't say anything falls in the happy zone and is classified as happy.

Can we think of sentiment analysis datasets in which the bias is positive or negative? What about the following two examples:

Example 1 (positive bias): a dataset of online reviews of a product

Imagine a dataset in which we record all the reviews of a particular product on Amazon. Some of them are positive, and some of them are negative, according to the number of stars they receive. What do you think the score would be for an empty review? From my experience, bad reviews tend to contain lots of words, because the customer is upset, and they describe their negative experience. However, many of the positive reviews are empty—the customer simply gives a good score, without the need to explain why they enjoyed the product. Therefore, this classifier probably has a positive bias.

Example 2 (negative bias): a dataset of conversations with friends

Imagine that we record all our conversations with friends and classify them as happy or sad conversations. If one day we bump into a friend, and our friend says absolutely nothing, we imagine that they are mad at us or that they are very upset. Therefore, the empty sentence is classified as sad. This means that this classifier probably has a negative bias.

How do we determine whether a classifier is good or bad? The error function

Now that we have defined what a perceptron classifier is, our next goal is to understand how to train it—in other words, how do we find the perceptron classifier that best fits our data? But before learning how to train perceptrons, we need to learn an important concept: how to evaluate them. More specifically, in this section we learn a useful error function that will tell us whether a perceptron classifier fits our data well. In the same way that the absolute and square errors worked for linear regression in chapter 3, this new error function will be large for classifiers that don't fit the data well and small for those that fit the data well.

How to compare classifiers? The error function

In this section, we learn how to build an effective error function that helps us determine how good a particular perceptron classifier is. First, let's test our intuition. Figure 5.12 shows two different perceptron classifiers on the same dataset. The classifiers are represented as a line with two well-defined sides, happy and sad. Clearly, the one on the left is a bad classifier, and the one on the right is good. Can we come up with a measure of how good they are? In other words, can we assign a number to each one of them, in a way that the one on the left is assigned a high number and the one on the right a low number?

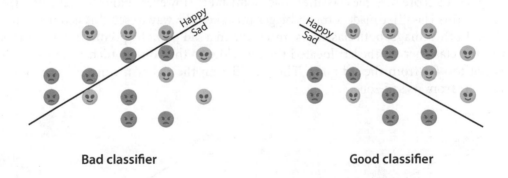

Bad classifier   **Good classifier**

Figure 5.12 Left: a bad classifier, which doesn't really split the points well. Right: a good classifier. Can we think of an error function that assigns a high number to the bad classifier and a low number to the good one?

Next, we see different answers to this question, all with some pros and cons. One of them (spoiler: the third one) is the one we use to train perceptrons.

Error function 1: Number of errors

The simplest way to evaluate a classifier is by counting the number of mistakes it makes—in other words, by counting the number of points that it classifies incorrectly.

In this case, the classifier on the left has an error of 8, because it erroneously predicts four happy points as sad, and four sad points as happy. The good classifier has an error of 3, because it erroneously predicts one happy point as sad, and two sad points as happy. This is illustrated in figure 5.13.

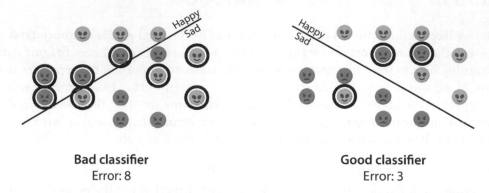

Bad classifier
Error: 8

Good classifier
Error: 3

Figure 5.13   We evaluate the two classifiers by counting the number of points that each one of them misclassifies. The classifier on the left misclassifies eight points, whereas the classifier on the right misclassifies three points. Thus, we conclude that the classifier on the right is a better one for our dataset.

This is a good error function, but it's not a great error function. Why? It tells us when there is an error, but it doesn't measure the gravity of the error. For example, if a sentence is sad, and the classifier gave it a score of 1, the classifier made a mistake. However, if another classifier gave it a score of 100, this classifier made a much bigger mistake. The way to see this geometrically is in figure 5.14. In this image, both classifiers misclassified a sad point by predicting that it is happy. However, the classifier on the left located the line close to the point, which means that the sad point is not too far from the sad zone. The classifier on the right, in contrast, has located the point very far from its sad zone.

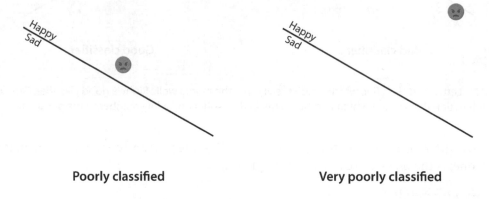

Poorly classified

Very poorly classified

Figure 5.14   The two classifiers misclassify the point. However, the classifier on the right made a much bigger mistake than the classifier on the left. The point on the left is not far from the boundary, and thus, it is not very far from the sad zone. However, the point on the right is very far from the sad zone. Ideally, we would like an error function that assigns a higher error to the classifier in the right than to the classifier in the left.

Why do we care about measuring how bad an error is? Wouldn't it be enough to count them? Recall what we did in chapter 3 with the linear regression algorithm. More specifically, recall the section "Gradient descent," where we used gradient descent to reduce this error. The way to reduce an error is by decreasing it in small amounts, until we reach a point where the error is small. In the linear regression algorithm, we wiggled the line small amounts and picked the direction in which the error decreased the most. If our error is calculated by counting the number of misclassified points, then this error will take only integer values. If we wiggle the line a small amount, the error may not decrease at all, and we don't know in which direction to move. The goal of gradient descent is to minimize a function by taking small steps in the direction in which the function decreases the most. If the function takes only integer values, this is equivalent to trying to descend from an Aztec staircase. When we are at a flat step, we don't know what step to take, because the function doesn't decrease in any direction. This is illustrated in figure 5.15.

Figure 5.15   Performing gradient descent to minimize an error function is like descending from a mountain by taking small steps. However, for us to do that, the error function must not be flat (like the one on the right), because in a flat error function, taking a small step will not decrease the error. A good error function is like the one on the left, in which we can easily see the direction we must use to take a step to slightly decrease the error function.

We need a function that measures the magnitude of an error and that assigns a higher error to misclassified points that are far from the boundary than to those that are close to it.

Error function 2: Distance

A way to tell the two classifiers apart in figure 5.16 is by considering the perpendicular distance from the point to the line. Notice that for the classifier on the left, this distance is small, whereas for the classifier on the right, the distance is large.

This error function is much more effective. What this error function does follows:

- Points that are correctly classified produce an error of 0.

- Points that are misclassified produce an error equal to the distance from that point to the line.

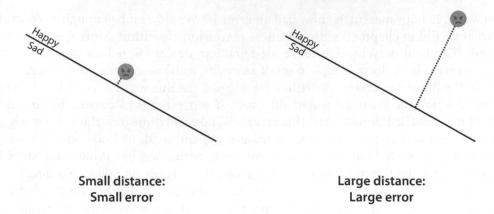

Figure 5.16   An effective way to measure how bad a classifier misclassifies a point is by measuring the perpendicular distance from the point to the line. For the classifier on the left, this distance is small, whereas for the classifier on the right, the distance is large.

Let's go back to the two classifiers we had at the beginning of this section. The way we calculate the total error is by adding the errors corresponding to all the data points, as illustrated in figure 5.17. This means that we look only at the misclassified points and add the perpendicular distances from these points to the line. Notice that the bad classifier has a large error, and the good classifier has a small error.

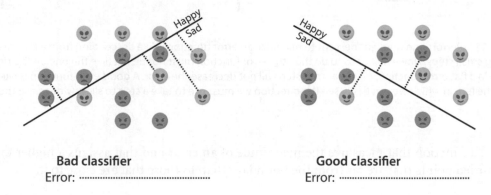

Figure 5.17   To calculate the total error of a classifier, we add up all the errors, which are the perpendicular distances from the misclassified points. The error is large for the classifier on the left and small for the classifier on the right. Thus, we conclude that the classifier on the right is better.

This is *almost* the error function we will use. Why don't we use this one? Because the distance from a point to a line is a complicated formula. It contains a square root, because we calculate it using the Pythagorean theorem. Square roots have complicated derivatives, which adds unnecessary complexity the moment we apply the gradient descent algorithm. We don't need to undertake this complication, because we can instead create an error function that is easier to calculate yet still manages to capture the essence of an error function: returning an error for points that are misclassified and varying the magnitude based on how far the misclassified point is from the boundary.

Error function 3: Score

In this section, we see how to build the standard error function for perceptrons, which we call the *perceptron error function*. First, let's summarize the properties we want in an error function as follows:

- The error function of a correctly classified point is 0.
- The error function of an incorrectly classified point is a positive number.
  - For misclassified points close to the boundary, the error function is small.
  - For misclassified points far from the boundary, the error function is large.
- It is given by a simple formula.

Recall that the classifier predicts a label of 1 for points in the positive zone and a label of 0 for points in the negative zone. Therefore, a misclassified point is either a point with label 0 in the positive zone, or a point with label 1 in the negative zone.

To build the perceptron error function, we use the score. In particular, we use the following properties of the score:

Properties of the score:

1. The points in the boundary have a score of 0.
2. The points in the positive zone have positive scores.
3. The points in the negative zone have negative scores.
4. The points close to the boundary have scores of low magnitude (i.e., positive or negative scores of low absolute value).
5. The points far from the boundary have scores of high magnitude (i.e., positive or negative scores of high absolute value).

For a misclassified point, the perceptron error wants to assign a value that is proportional to its distance to the boundary. Therefore, the error for misclassified points that are far from the boundary must be high, and the error for misclassified points that are close to the boundary must be low. Looking at properties 4 and 5, we can see that the absolute value of the score is always high for points far from the boundary and low for points close to the boundary. Thus, we define the error as the absolute value of the score for misclassified points.

More specifically, consider the classifier that assigns weights of a and b to the words *aack* and *beep*, and has a bias of c. This classifier makes the prediction $\hat{y} = step(ax_{aack} + bx_{beep} + c)$ to the sentence with x_{aack} appearances of the word *aack* and x_{beep} appearances of the word *beep*. The perceptron error is defined as follows:

Perceptron error for a sentence

- If the sentence is correctly classified, the error is 0.
- If the sentence is misclassified, the error is $|x_{aack} + bx_{beep} + c|$.

In the general scenario, where the notation is defined as in the section "What happens if I have more than two words?," the following is the definition of the perceptron error:

Perceptron error for a point (general)

- If the point is correctly classified, the error is 0.
- If the point is misclassified, the error is $|w_1 x_1 + w_2 x_2 + \cdots + w_n x_n + b|$.

The mean perceptron error: A way to calculate the error of an entire dataset

To calculate the perceptron error for an entire dataset, we take the average of all the errors corresponding to all the points. We can also take the sum if we choose, although in this chapter we choose the average and call it the *mean perceptron error*.

To illustrate the mean perceptron error, let's look at an example.

Example

Consider the dataset made of four sentences, two labeled happy and two labeled sad, illustrated in table 5.3.

Table 5.3   The new dataset of aliens. Again, we've recorded each sentence, the number of appearances of each word in that sentence, and the mood of the alien.

Sentence	*Aack*	*Beep*	Label (mood)
Aack	1	0	Sad
Beep	0	1	Happy
Aack beep beep beep	1	3	Happy
Aack beep beep aack aack	3	2	Sad

We'll compare the following two classifiers on this dataset:

Classifier 1

Weights:

- *Aack*: $a = 1$
- *Beep*: $b = 2$

Bias: $c = -4$

Score of a sentence: $1x_{aack} + 2x_{beep} - 4$

Prediction: $\hat{y} = step(1x_{aack} + 2x_{beep} - 4)$

Classifier 2

Weights:

- *Aack*: $a = -1$
- *Beep*: $b = 1$

Bias: $c = 0$

Score of a sentence: $-x_{aack} + x_{beep}$

Prediction: $\hat{y} = step(-x_{aack} + x_{beep})$

The points and the classifiers can be seen in figure 5.18. At first glance, which one looks like a better classifier? It appears classifier 2 is better, because it classifies every point correctly, whereas classifier 1 makes two mistakes. Now let's calculate the errors and make sure that classifier 1 has a higher error than classifier 2.

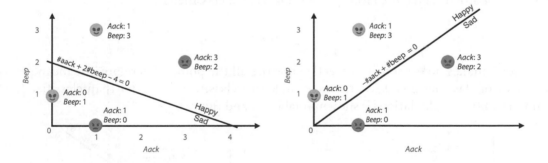

Figure 5.18 On the left we have classifier 1, and on the right we have classifier 2.

The predictions for both classifiers are calculated in table 5.4.

Table 5.4 Our dataset of four sentences with their labels. For each of the two classifiers, we have the score and the prediction.

Sentence (x_{aack}, x_{beep})	Label y	Classifier 1 score $1x_{aack} + 2x_{beep} - 4$	Classifier 1 prediction $step(1x_{aack} + 2x_{beep} - 4)$	Classifier 1 error	Classifier 2 score $-x_{aack} + 2x_{beep}$	Classifier 2 prediction $step(-x_{aack} + 2x_{beep})$	Classifier 2 error
(1,0)	Sad (0)	−3	0 (correct)	0	−1	0 (correct)	0
(0,1)	Happy (1)	-2	0 (incorrect)	2	1	1 (correct)	0
(1,3)	Happy (1)	3	1 (correct)	3	2	1 (correct)	0
(3,2)	Sad (0)	3	1 (incorrect)	0	−1	0 (correct)	0
Mean perceptron error				1.25			0

Now on to calculate the errors. Note that classifier 1 misclassified only sentences 2 and 4. Sentence 2 is happy, but it is misclassified as sad, and sentence 4 is sad, but it is misclassified as happy. The error of sentence 2 is the absolute value of the score, or $|{-2}| = 2$. The error of sentence 4 is the absolute value of the score, or $|3| = 3$. The other two sentences have an error of 0, because they are correctly classified. Thus, the mean perceptron error of classifier 1 is

$$\frac{1}{4}(0 + 2 + 0 + 3) = 1.25.$$

Classifier 2 makes no errors—it correctly classifies all the points. Therefore, the mean perceptron error of classifier 2 is 0. We then conclude that classifier 2 is better than classifier 1. The summary of these calculations is shown in table 5.4 and figure 5.19.

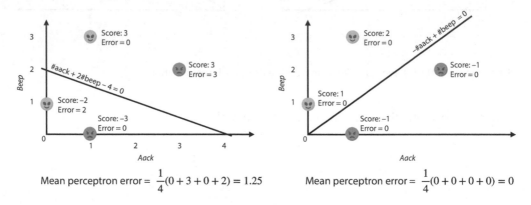

Figure 5.19 Classifier 1 has an error of 1.25, whereas classifier 2 has an error of 0. Thus, we conclude that classifier 2 is better than classifier 1.

Now that we know how to compare classifiers, let's move on to finding the best one of them, or at least a pretty good one.

How to find a good classifier? The perceptron algorithm

To build a good perceptron classifier, we'll follow a similar approach as the one we followed with linear regression in chapter 3. The process is called the *perceptron algorithm*, and it consists of starting with a random perceptron classifier and slowly improving it until we have a good one. The main steps of the perceptron algorithm follow:

1. Start with a random perceptron classifier.

2. Slightly improve the classifier. (Repeat many times.)

3. Measure the perceptron error to decide when to stop running the loop.

We start by developing the step inside the loop, a technique used to slightly improve a perceptron classifier called *the perceptron trick*. It is similar to the square and absolute tricks we learned in the sections "The square trick" and "The absolute trick" in chapter 3.

The perceptron trick: A way to slightly improve the perceptron

The perceptron trick is a tiny step that helps us go from a perceptron classifier to a slightly better perceptron classifier. However, we'll start by describing a slightly less ambitious step. Just as we did in chapter 3, we'll first focus on one point and try to improve the classifier for that one point.

There are two ways to see the perceptron step, although both are equivalent. The first way is the geometric way, where we think of the classifier as a line.

Pseudocode for the perceptron trick (geometric)

- **Case 1:** If the point is correctly classified, leave the line as it is.

- **Case 2:** If the point is incorrectly classified, move the line a little closer to the point.

Why does this work? Let's think about it. If the point is misclassified, it means it is on the wrong side of the line. Moving the line closer to it may not put it on the right side, but at least it gets it closer to the line and, thus, closer to the correct side of the line. We repeat this process many times, so it is imaginable that one day we'll be able to move the line past the point, thus correctly classifying it. This process is illustrated in figure 5.20.

We also have an algebraic way to see the perceptron trick.

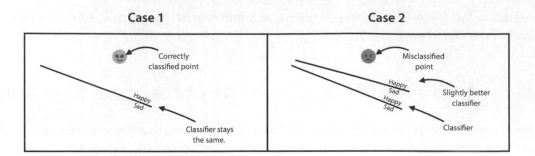

Figure 5.20   Case 1 (left): A point that is correctly classified tells the line to stay where it is. Case 2 (right): A point that is misclassified tells the line to move closer toward it.

Pseudocode for the perceptron trick (algebraic)

- **Case 1:** If the point is correctly classified, leave the classifier as it is.

- **Case 2:** If the point is incorrectly classified, that means it produces a positive error. Adjust the weights and the bias a small amount so that this error slightly decreases.

The geometric way is an easier way to visualize this trick, but the algebraic way is an easier way to develop it, so we'll look at it the algebraic way. First, let's use our intuition. Imagine that we have a classifier for the entire English language. We try this classifier on the sentence "I am sad," and it predicts that the sentence is happy. This is clearly wrong. Where could we have gone wrong? If the prediction is that the sentence is happy, then the sentence must have received a positive score. This sentence shouldn't receive a positive score—it should receive a negative score to be classified as sad. The score is calculated as the sum of the scores of its words *I*, *am*, and *sad*, plus the bias. We need to decrease this score, to make the sentence slightly sadder. It is OK if we decrease it only a little bit, and the score is still positive. Our hope is that running this process many times will one day turn the score into negative and correctly classify our sentence. The way to decrease the score is by decreasing all its parts, namely, the weights of the words *I*, *am*, and *sad* and the bias. By how much should we decrease them? We decrease them by an amount equal to the learning rate that we learned in the section "The square trick" in chapter 3.

Similarly, if our classifier misclassifies the sentence "I am happy" as a sad sentence, then our procedure is to slightly increase the weights of the words *I*, *am*, and *happy* and the bias by an amount equal to the learning rate.

Let's illustrate this with a numerical example. In this example, we use a learning rate of $\eta = 0.01$. Imagine that we have the same classifier that we had in the previous section, namely, the one with the following weights and bias. We'll call it the bad classifier, because our goal is to improve it.

Bad classifier

Weights:

- *Aack*: $a = 1$

- *Beep*: $b = 2$

Bias: $c = -4$

Prediction: $\hat{y} = step(x_{aack} + 2x_{beep} - 4)$

The following sentence is misclassified by the model, and we'll use it to improve the weights:

Sentence 1: "Beep aack aack beep beep beep beep."

Label: Sad (0)

For this sentence, the number of appearances of *aack* is $x_{aack} = 2$, and the number of appearances of *beep* is $x_{beep} = 5$. Thus, the score is $1 \cdot x_{aack} + 2 \cdot x_{beep} - 4 = 1 \cdot 2 + 2 \cdot 5 - 4 = 8$, and the prediction is $\hat{y} = step(8) = 1$.

The sentence should have had a negative score, to be classified as sad. However, the classifier gave it a score of 8, which is positive. We need to decrease this score. One way to decrease it is to subtract the learning rate to the weight of *aack* to the weight of *beep* and to the bias, thus obtaining new weights, which we call $a' = 0.99$, $b' = 1.99$, and a new bias $c' = 4.01$. However, think about this: the word *beep* appeared many more times than the word *aack*. In some way, *beep* is more crucial to the score of the sentence than *aack*. We should probably decrease the weight of *beep* more than the score of *aack*. Let's decrease the weight of each word by the learning rate times the number of times the word appears in the sentence. In other words:

- The word *aack* appears twice, so we'll reduce its weight by two times the learning rate, or 0.02. We obtain a new weight $a' = 1 - 2 \cdot 0.01 = 0.98$.

- The word *beep* appears five times, so we'll reduce its weight by five times the learning rate, or 0.05. We obtain a new weight $b' = 2 - 5 \cdot 0.01 = 1.95$.

- The bias adds to the score only once, so we reduce the bias by the learning rate, or 0.01. We obtain a new bias $c' = -4 - 0.01 = -4.01$.

> **aside** Instead of subtracting the learning rate from each weight, we subtracted the learning rate times the number of appearances of the word in the sentence. The true reason for this is calculus. In other words, when we develop the gradient descent method, the derivative of the error function forces us to do this. This process is detailed in appendix B, section "Using gradient descent to train classification models."

The new improved classifier follows:

Improved classifier 1

Weights:

- *Aack*: $a' = 0.98$

- *Beep*: $b' = 1.95$

Bias: $c' = -4.01$

Prediction: $\hat{y} = step(0.98x_{aack} + 1.95x_{beep} - 4.01)$

Let's verify the errors of both classifiers. Recall that the error is the absolute value of the score. Thus, the bad classifier produces an error of $|1 \cdot x_{aack} + 2 \cdot x_{beep} - 4| = |1 \cdot 2 + 2 \cdot 5 - 4| = 8$. The improved classifier produces an error of $|0.98 \cdot x_{aack} + 1.95 \cdot x_{beep} - 4.01| = |0.98 \cdot 2 + 1.95 \cdot 5 - 4.01|$ = 7.7. That is a smaller error, so we have indeed improved the classifier for that point!

The case we just developed consists of a misclassified point with a negative label. What happens if the misclassified point has a positive label? The procedure is the same, except instead of subtracting an amount from the weights, we add it. Let's go back to the bad classifier and consider the following sentence:

Sentence 2: "Aack aack."

Label: Happy

The prediction for this sentence is $\hat{y} = step(x_{aack} + 2x_{beep} - 4) = step(2 + 2 \cdot 0 - 4) = step(-2) = 0$. Because the prediction is sad, the sentence is misclassified. The score of this sentence is –2, and to classify this sentence as happy, we need the classifier to give it a positive score. The perceptron trick will increase this score of –2 by increasing the weights of the words and the bias as follows:

- The word *aack* appears twice, so we'll increase its weight by two times the learning rate, or 0.02. We obtain a new weight $a' = 1 + 2 \cdot 0.01 = 1.02$.

- The word *beep* appears zero times, so we won't increase its weight, because this word is irrelevant to the sentence.

- The bias adds to the score only once, so we increase the bias by the learning rate, or 0.01. We obtain a new bias $c' = -4 + 0.01 = -3.99$.

Thus, our new improved classifier follows:

Improved classifier 2

Weights:

- *Aack*: $a' = 1.02$

- *Beep*: $b' = 2$

Bias: $c' = -3.99$

Prediction: $\hat{y} = step(1.02x_{aack} + 2x_{beep} - 3.99)$

Now let's verify the errors. Because the bad classifier gave the sentence a score of –2, then the error is $|-2| = 2$. The second classifier gave the sentence a score of $1.02x_{aack} + 2x_{beep} - 3.99 = 1.02 \cdot 2 + 2 \cdot 0 - 3.99 = -1.95$, and an error of 1.95. Thus, the improved classifier has a smaller error on that point than the bad classifier, which is exactly what we were expecting.

Let's summarize these two cases and obtain the pseudocode for the perceptron trick.

Pseudocode for the perceptron trick

Inputs:

- A perceptron with weights a, b, and bias c
- A point with coordinates (x_1, x_2) and label y
- A small positive value η (the learning rate)

Output:

- A perceptron with new weights a', b', and bias c'

Procedure:

- The prediction the perceptron makes at the point is $\hat{y} = step(ax_1 + bx_2 + c)$.
- **Case 1:** If $\hat{y} = y$:
  - **Return** the original perceptron with weights a, b, and bias c.
- **Case 2:** If $\hat{y} = 1$ and $y = 0$:
  - **Return** the perceptron with the following weights and bias:
    - $a' = a - \eta x_1$
    - $b' = b - \eta x_2$
    - $c' = c - \eta x_1$.
- **Case 3:** If $\hat{y} = 0$ and $y = 1$:
  - **Return** the perceptron with the following weights and bias:
    - $a' = a + \eta x_1$
    - $b' = b - \eta x_2$
    - $c' = c + \eta x_1$.

If the perceptron correctly classifies the point, the output perceptron is the same as the input, and both of them produce an error of 0. If the perceptron misclassifies the point, the output perceptron produces a smaller error than the input perceptron.

The following is a slick trick to condense the pseudocode. Note that the quantity $y - \hat{y}$ is 0, -1, and $+1$ for the three cases in the perceptron trick. Thus, we can summarize it as follows:

Pseudocode for the perceptron trick

Inputs:

- A perceptron with weights a, b, and bias c
- A point with coordinates (x_1, x_2) and label y
- A small value η (the learning rate)

Output:

- A perceptron with new weights a', b', and bias c'

Procedure:

- The prediction the perceptron makes at the point is $\hat{y} = step(ax_1 + bx_2 + c)$.
- **Return** the perceptron with the following weights and bias:
  - $a' = a + \eta(y - \hat{y})x_1$
  - $b' = b + \eta(y - \hat{y})x_2$
  - $c' = c + \eta(y - \hat{y})$

Repeating the perceptron trick many times: The perceptron algorithm

In this section, we learn the *perceptron algorithm*, which is used to train a perceptron classifier on a dataset. Recall that the perceptron trick allows us to slightly improve a perceptron to make a better prediction on one point. The perceptron algorithm consists of starting with a random classifier and continuously improving it, using the perceptron trick many times.

As we've seen in this chapter, we can study this problem in two ways: geometrically and algebraically. Geometrically, the dataset is given by points in the plane colored with two colors, and the classifier is a line that tries to split these points. Figure 5.21 contains a dataset of happy and sad sentences just like the ones we saw at the beginning of this chapter. The first step of the algorithm is to draw a random line. It's clear that the line in figure 5.21 does not represent a great perceptron classifier, because it doesn't do a good job of splitting the happy and the sad sentences.

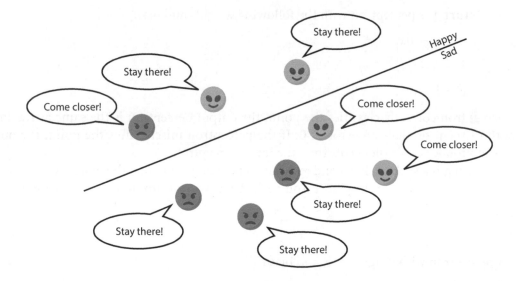

Figure 5.21   Each point tells the classifier what to do to make life better for itself. The points that are correctly classified tell the line to stay still. The points that are misclassified tell the line to move slightly toward them.

The next step in the perceptron algorithm consists of picking one point at random, such as the one in figure 5.22. If the point is correctly classified, the line is left alone. If it is misclassified, then the line gets moved slightly closer to the point, thus making the line a better fit for that point. It may become a worse fit for other points, but that doesn't matter for now.

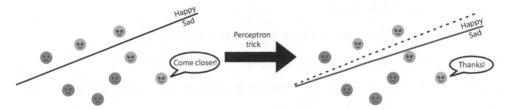

Figure 5.22 If we apply the perceptron trick to a classifier and a misclassified point, the classifier moves slightly toward the point.

It is imaginable that if we were to repeat this process many times, eventually we will get to a good solution. This procedure doesn't always get us to the best solution. But in practice, this method often reaches to a good solution as shown in figure 5.23. We call this the *perceptron algorithm*.

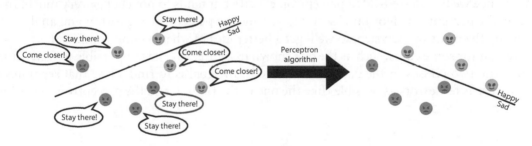

Figure 5.23 If we apply the perceptron trick many times, each time picking a random point, we can imagine that we'll obtain a classifier that classifies most points correctly.

The number of times we run the algorithm is the number of epochs. Therefore, this algorithm has two hyperparameters: the number of epochs, and the learning rate. The pseudocode of the perceptron algorithm follows:

Pseudocode for the perceptron algorithm

Inputs:

- A dataset of points, labeled 1 and 0
- A number of epochs, n
- A learning rate η

Output:

- A perceptron classifier consisting of a set of weights and a bias that fits the dataset

Procedure:

- Start with random values for the weights and bias of the perceptron classifier.
- Repeat many times:
  - Pick a random data point.
  - Update the weights and the bias using the perceptron trick.

Return: The perceptron classifier with the updated weights and bias.

How long should we run the loop? In other words, how many epochs should we use? Several criteria to help us make that decision follow:

- Run the loop a fixed number of times, which could be based on our computing power, or the amount of time we have.
- Run the loop until the error is lower than a certain threshold we set beforehand.
- Run the loop until the error doesn't change significantly for a certain number of epochs.

Normally, if we have the computing power, it's OK to run it many more times than needed, because once we have a well-fitted perceptron classifier, it tends to not change very much. In the "Coding the perceptron algorithm" section, we code the perceptron algorithm and analyze it by measuring the error in each step, so we'll get a better idea of when to stop running it.

Note that for some cases, such as the one shown in figure 5.24, it is impossible to find a line to separate the two classes in the dataset. That is OK: the goal is to find a line that separates the dataset with as few errors as possible (like the one in the figure), and the perceptron algorithm is good at this.

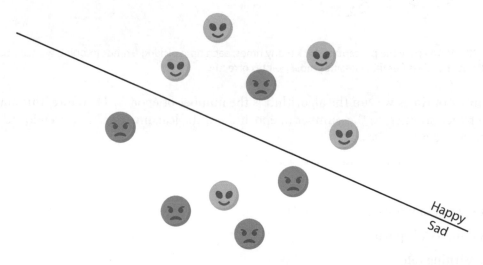

Figure 5.24   A dataset with two classes that are impossible to separate with a line. The perceptron algorithm is then trained to find a line that separates them as best as possible.

Gradient descent

You may notice that the process for training this model looks very familiar. In fact, it is similar to what we did in chapter 3 with linear regression. Recall that the purpose of linear regression is to fit a line as close as possible to a set of points. In chapter 3, we trained our linear regression model by starting with a random line and taking small steps to get closer and closer to the points. We then used the analogy of descending from a mountain (Mount Errorest) by taking small steps toward the bottom. The height at each point in the mountain is the mean perceptron error function, which we defined as the absolute error, or the square error. Therefore, descending from the mountain is equivalent to minimizing the error, which is equivalent to finding the best line fit. We called this process gradient descent, because the gradient is precisely the vector that points in the direction of largest growth (so its negative points in the direction of largest decrease), and taking a step in this direction will get us to descend the most.

In this chapter, the same thing happens. Our problem is a little different because we don't want to fit a line as close as possible to a set of points. Instead, we want to draw a line that separates two sets of points in the best possible way. The perceptron algorithm is the process that starts with random line, and it slowly moves it step by step to build a better separator. The analogy of descending from a mountain also works here. The only difference is that in this mountain, the height at each point is the mean perceptron error that we learned in the section "How to compare classifiers? The error function."

Stochastic and batch gradient descent

The way we developed the perceptron algorithm in this section is by repeatedly taking one point at a time and adjusting the perceptron (line) to be a better fit for that point. This is called an epoch. However, just as we did with linear regression in section "Do we train using one point at a time or many?" in chapter 3, the better approach is to take a batch of points at a time and adjust the perceptron to be a better fit for those points in one step. The extreme case is to take all the points in the set at a time and adjust the perceptron to fit all of them better in one step. In section "Do we train using one point at a time or many?" in chapter 3, we call these approaches *stochastic*, *mini-batch*, and *batch gradient descent*. In this section, we use the formal perceptron algorithm using mini-batch gradient descent. The mathematical details appear in appendix B, section "Using gradient descent to train classification models," where the perceptron algorithm is described in full generality using mini-batch gradient descent.

Coding the perceptron algorithm

Now that we have developed the perceptron algorithm for our sentiment analysis application, in this section we write the code for it. First we'll write the code from scratch to fit our original dataset, and then we'll use Turi Create. In real life, we always use a package and have little need to code our own algorithms. However, it's good to code some of the algorithms at least once—think of it as doing long division. Although we usually don't do long division without using a calculator, it's good we had to in high school, because now when we do it using a calculator, we know what's happening in the background. The code for this section follows, and the dataset we use is shown in table 5.5:

- • **Notebook:** Coding_perceptron_algorithm.ipynb
  - – https://github.com/luisguiserrano/manning/blob/master/Chapter_5_Perceptron_Algorithm/Coding_perceptron_algorithm.ipynb

Table 5.5 A dataset of aliens, the times they said each of the words, and their mood.

Aack	Beep	Happy/Sad
1	0	0
0	2	0
1	1	0
1	2	0
1	3	1
2	2	1
2	3	1
3	2	1

Let's begin by defining our dataset as a NumPy array. The features correspond to two numbers corresponding to the appearances of *aack* and *beep*. The labels are 1 for the happy sentences and 0 for the sad ones.

```
import numpy as np
features = np.array([[1,0],[0,2],[1,1],[1,2],[1,3],[2,2],[2,3],[3,2]])
labels = np.array([0,0,0,0,1,1,1,1])
```

This gives us the plot in figure 5.25. In this figure, the happy sentences are triangles, and the sad ones are squares.

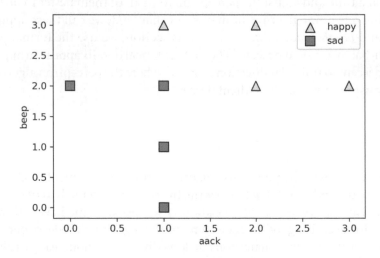

Figure 5.25 The plot of our dataset. Triangles are happy aliens, and squares are sad aliens.

Coding the perceptron trick

In this section, we code the perceptron trick. We'll code it using stochastic gradient descent (one point at a time), but we could also code it using either mini-batch or batch gradient descent. We start by coding the score function and the prediction. Both functions receive the same input, which is the weights of the model, the bias, and the features of one data point. The score function returns the score that the model gives to that data point, and the prediction function returns a 1 if the score is greater than or equal to zero and a 0 if the score is less than zero. For this function we use the dot product defined in the section "Plotting the error function and knowing when to stop running the algorithm" in chapter 3.

Calculates the dot product between the weights and the features, adds the bias, and applies the step function

```
def score(weights, bias, features):
    return np.dot(features, weights) + bias
```

To write the prediction function, we first write the step function. The prediction is the step function of the score.

```
def step(x):
    if x >= 0:
        return 1
    else:
        return 0

def prediction(weights, bias, features):
    return step(score(weights, bias, features))
```

Looks at the score, and if it is positive or zero, returns 1; if it is negative, returns 0

Next, we code the error function for one point. Recall that the error is zero if the point is correctly classified and the absolute value of the score if the point is misclassified. This function takes as input the weights and bias of the model and the features and label of the data point.

```
def error(weights, bias, features, label):
    pred = prediction(weights, bias, features)
    if pred == label:
        return 0
    else:
        return np.abs(score(weights, bias, features))
```

If the prediction is equal to the label, then the point is well classified, which means the error is zero.

If the prediction is different from the label, then the point is misclassified, which means the error is equal to the absolute value of the score.

We now write a function for the mean perceptron error. This function calculates the average of the errors of all the points in our dataset.

```
def mean_perceptron_error(weights, bias, features, labels):
    total_error = 0
    for i in range(len(features)):
```

Loops through our data, and for each point, adds the error at that point, then returns this error

```
        total_error += error(weights, bias, features[i], labels[i])
    return total_error/len(features)
```

The sum of errors is divided by the number of points to get the mean perceptron error.

Now that we have the error function, we can go ahead and code the perceptron trick. We'll code the condensed version of the algorithm found at the end of the section "The perceptron trick." However, in the notebook, you can find it coded in both ways, the first one using an if statement that checks whether the point is well classified.

```
def perceptron_trick(weights, bias, features, label, learning_rate = 0.01):
    pred = prediction(weights, bias, features)
    for i in range(len(weights)):
        weights[i] += (label-pred)*features[i]*learning_rate
    bias += (label-pred)*learning_rate
    return weights, bias
```

Updates the weights and biases using the perceptron trick

Coding the perceptron algorithm

Now that we have the perceptron trick, we can code the perceptron algorithm. Recall that the perceptron algorithm consists of starting with a random perceptron classifier and repeating the perceptron trick many times (as many as the number of epochs). To track the performance of the algorithm, we'll also keep track of the mean perceptron error at each epoch. As inputs, we have the data (features and labels), the learning rate, which we default to 0.01, and the number of epochs, which we default to 200. The code for the perceptron algorithm follows:

Repeats the process as many times as the number of epochs

Initializes the weights to 1 and the bias to 0. Feel free to initialize them to small random numbers if you prefer.

```
def perceptron_algorithm(features, labels, learning_rate = 0.01,
    epochs = 200):
    weights = [1.0 for i in range(len(features[0]))]
    bias = 0.0
    errors = []
    for epoch in range(epochs):
        error = mean_perceptron_error(weights, bias, features, labels)
        errors.append(error)
        i = random.randint(0, len(features)-1)
        weights, bias = perceptron_trick(weights, bias, features[i], labels[i])
    return weights, bias, errors
```

An array to store the errors

Calculates the mean perceptron error and stores it

Picks a random point in our dataset

Applies the perceptron algorithm to update the weights and the bias of our model based on that point

Now let's run the algorithm on our dataset!

```
perceptron_algorithm(features, labels)
Output: ([0.6299999999999997, 0.17999999999999938], -1.0400000000000007)
```

The output shows that the weights and bias we obtained are the following:

- Weight of *aack*: 0.63
- Weight of *beep*: 0.18
- Bias: −1.04

We could have a different answer, because of the randomness in our choice of points inside the algorithm. For the code in the repository to always return the same answer, the random seed is set to zero.

Figure 5.26 shows two plots: on the left is the line fit, and on the right is the error function. The line corresponding to the resulting perceptron is the thick line, which classifies every point correctly. The thinner lines are the lines corresponding to the perceptrons obtained after each of the 200 epochs. Notice how at each epoch, the line becomes a better fit for the points. The error decreases (mostly) as we increase the number of epochs, until it reaches zero at around epoch 140, meaning that every point is correctly classified.

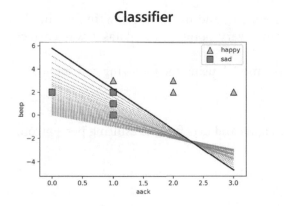
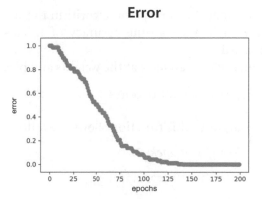

Figure 5.26 Left: The plot of our resulting classifier. Notice that it classifies each point correctly. Right: The error plot. Notice that the more epochs we run the perceptron algorithm for, the lower the error gets.

That is the code for the perceptron algorithm! As I mentioned before, in practice, we don't normally code algorithms by hand, but we use a package, such as Turi Create or Scikit-Learn. This is what we cover in the next section.

Coding the perceptron algorithm using Turi Create

In this section, we learn to code the perceptron algorithm in Turi Create. The code is in the same notebook as the previous exercise. Our first task is to import Turi Create and create an SFrame with our data from a dictionary as follows:

```
import turicreate as tc

datadict = {'aack': features[:,0], 'beep':features[:,1], 'prediction': labels}
data = tc.SFrame(datadict)
```

Next, we create and train our perceptron classifier, using the `logistic_classifier` object and the `create` method, as shown in the next code. The inputs are the dataset and the name of the column containing the labels (target).

```
perceptron = tc.logistic_classifier.create(data, target='prediction')
```

Output:

```
+-----------+----------+--------------+-------------------+
| Iteration | Passes   | Elapsed Time | Training Accuracy |
+-----------+----------+--------------+-------------------+
| 1         | 2        | 1.003120     | 1.000000          |
| 2         | 3        | 1.004235     | 1.000000          |
| 3         | 4        | 1.004840     | 1.000000          |
| 4         | 5        | 1.005574     | 1.000000          |
+-----------+----------+--------------+-------------------+
SUCCESS: Optimal solution found.
```

Notice that the perceptron algorithm ran for four epochs, and in the last one (in fact, in all of them), it had a training accuracy of 1. This means every point in the dataset was correctly classified.

Finally, we can look at the weights and bias of the model, using the following command:

```
perceptron.coefficients
```

The output of this function shows the following weights and bias for the resulting perceptron:

- Weight of *aack*: 2.70

- Weight of *beep*: 2.46

- Bias: −8.96

These are different results from what we obtained by hand, but both perceptrons work well in the dataset.

Applications of the perceptron algorithm

The perceptron algorithm has many applications in real life. Virtually every time we need to answer a question with yes or no, where the answer is predicted from previous data, the perceptron algorithm can help us. Here are some examples of real-life applications of the perceptron algorithm.

Spam email filters

In a similar way as we predicted whether a sentence is happy or sad based on the words in the sentence, we can predict whether an email is spam or not spam based on the words in the email. We can also use other features, such as the following:

- Length of the email
- Size of attachments
- Number of senders
- Whether any of our contacts is a sender

Currently, the perceptron algorithm (and its more advanced counterparts, logistic regression and neural networks) and other classification models are used as a part of spam classification pipelines by most of the biggest email providers, with great results.

We can also categorize emails using classification algorithms like the perceptron algorithm. Classifying email into personal, subscriptions, and promotions is the exact same problem. Even coming up with potential responses to an email is also a classification problem, except now the labels that we use are responses to emails.

Recommendation Systems

In many recommendation systems, recommending a video, movie, song, or product to a user boils down to a yes or no answer. In these cases, the question can be any of the following:

- Will the user click on the video/movie we're recommending?
- Will the user watch the entire video/movie we're recommending?
- Will the user listen to the song we're recommending?
- Will the user buy the product we're recommending?

The features can be anything, from demographic (age, gender, location of the user), to behavioral (what videos did the user watch, what songs did they hear, what products did they buy?). You can imagine that the user vector would be a long one! For this, large computing power and very clever implementations of the algorithms are needed.

Companies such as Netflix, YouTube, and Amazon, among many others, use the perceptron algorithm or similar, more advanced classification models in their recommendation systems.

Health care

Many medical models also use classification algorithms such as the perceptron algorithm to answer questions such as the following:

- Does the patient suffer from a particular illness?
- Will a certain treatment work for a patient?

The features for these models will normally be the symptoms the patient is suffering and their medical history. For these types of algorithms, one needs very high levels of performance.

Recommending the wrong treatment for a patient is much more serious than recommending a video that a user won't watch. For this type of analysis, refer to chapter 7, where we talk about accuracy and other ways to evaluate classification models.

Computer vision

Classification algorithms such as the perceptron algorithm are widely used in computer vision, more specifically, in image recognition. Imagine that we have a picture, and we want to teach the computer to tell whether the picture contains a dog. This is a classification model in which the features are the pixels of the image.

The perceptron algorithm has decent performance in curated image datasets such as MNIST, which is a dataset of handwritten digits. However, for more complicated images, it doesn't do very well. For these, one uses models that consist of a combination of many perceptrons. These models are aptly called multilayer perceptrons, or neural networks, and we learn about them in detail in chapter 10.

Summary

- Classification is an important part of machine learning. It is similar to regression in that it consists of training an algorithm with labeled data and using it to make predictions on future (unlabeled) data. The difference from regression is that in classification, the predictions are categories, such as yes/no, spam/ham, and so on.

- Perceptron classifiers work by assigning a weight to each of the features and a bias. The score of a data point is calculated as the sum of products of the weights and features, plus the bias. If the score is greater than or equal to zero, the classifier predicts a yes. Otherwise, it predicts a no.

- For sentiment analysis, a perceptron consists of a score for each of the words in the dictionary, together with a bias. Happy words normally end up with a positive score, and sad words with a negative score. Neutral words such as *the* likely end up with a score close to zero.

- The bias helps us decide if the empty sentence is happy or sad. If the bias is positive, then the empty sentence is happy, and if it is negative, then the empty sentence is sad.

- Graphically, we can see a perceptron as a line trying to separate two classes of points, which can be seen as points of two different colors. In higher dimensions, a perceptron is a hyperplane separating points.

- The perceptron algorithm works by starting with a random line and then slowly moving it to separate the points well. In every iteration, it picks a random point. If the point is correctly classified, the line doesn't move. If it is misclassified, then the line moves a little bit closer to the point to pass over it and classify it correctly.

- The perceptron algorithm has numerous applications, including spam email detection, recommendation systems, e-commerce, and health care.

Exercises

Exercise 5.1

The following is a dataset of patients who have tested positive or negative for COVID-19. Their symptoms are cough (C), fever (F), difficulty breathing (B), and tiredness (T).

	Cough (C)	Fever (F)	Difficulty breathing (B)	Tiredness (T)	Diagnosis (D)
Patient 1		X	X	X	Sick
Patient 2	X	X		X	Sick
Patient 3	X		X	X	Sick
Patient 4	X	X	X		Sick
Patient 5	X			X	Healthy
Patient 6		X	X		Healthy
Patient 7		X			Healthy
Patient 8				X	Healthy

Build a perceptron model that classifies this dataset.

hint You can use the perceptron algorithm, but you may be able to eyeball a good perceptron model that works.

Exercise 5.2

Consider the perceptron model that assigns to the point (x_1, x_2) the prediction $\hat{y} = step(2x_1 + 3x_2 - 4)$. This model has as a boundary line with equation $2x_1 + 3x_2 - 4 = 0$. We have the point $p = (1, 1)$ with label 0.

a. Verify that the point p is misclassified by the model.

b. Calculate the perceptron error that the model produces at the point p.

c. Use the perceptron trick to obtain a new model that still misclassifies p but produces a smaller error. You can use $\eta = 0.01$ as the learning rate.

d. Find the prediction given by the new model at the point p, and verify that the perceptron error obtained is smaller than the original.

Exercise 5.3

Perceptrons are particularly useful for building logical gates such as AND and OR.

a. Build a perceptron that models the AND gate. In other words, build a perceptron to fit the following dataset (where x_1, x_2 are the features and y is the label):

x_1	x_2	y
0	0	0
0	1	0
1	0	0
1	1	1

b. Similarly, build a perceptron that models the OR gate, given by the following dataset:

x_1	x_2	y
0	0	0
0	1	1
1	0	1
1	1	1

c. Show that there is no perceptron that models the XOR gate, given by the following dataset:

x_1	x_2	y
0	0	0
0	1	1
1	0	1
1	1	0

A continuous approach to splitting points: Logistic classifiers | 6

In this chapter

- the difference between hard assignments and soft assignments in classification models

- the sigmoid function, a continuous activation function

- discrete perceptrons vs. continuous perceptrons, also called logistic classifiers

- the logistic regression algorithm for classifying data

- coding the logistic regression algorithm in Python

- using the logistic classifier in Turi Create to analyze the sentiment of movie reviews

- using the softmax function to build classifiers for more than two classes

In the previous chapter, we built a classifier that determined if a sentence was happy or sad. But as we can imagine, some sentences are happier than others. For example, the sentence "I'm good" and the sentence "Today was the most wonderful day in my life!" are both happy, yet the second is much happier than the first. Wouldn't it be nice to have a classifier that not only predicts if sentences are happy or sad but that gives a rating for how happy sentences are—say, a classifier that tells us that the first sentence is 60% happy and the second one is 95% happy? In this chapter, we define the *logistic classifier*, which does precisely that. This classifier assigns a score from 0 to 1 to each sentence, in a way that the happier a sentence is, the higher the score it receives.

In a nutshell, a logistic classifier is a type of model that works just like a perceptron classifier, except instead of returning a yes or no answer, it returns a number between 0 and 1. In this case, the goal is to assign scores close to 0 to the saddest sentences, scores close to 1 to the happiest sentences, and scores close to 0.5 to neutral sentences. This threshold of 0.5 is common in practice, though arbitrary. In chapter 7, we'll see how to adjust it to optimize our model, but for this chapter we use 0.5.

This chapter relies on chapter 5, because the algorithms we develop here are similar, aside from some technical differences. Making sure you understand chapter 5 well will help you understand the material in this chapter. In chapter 5, we described the perceptron algorithm using an error function that tells us how good a perceptron classifier is and an iterative step that turns a classifier into a slightly better classifier. In this chapter, we learn the logistic regression algorithm, which works in a similar way. The main differences follow:

- The step function is replaced by a new activation function, which returns values between 0 and 1.

- The perceptron error function is replaced by a new error function, which is based on a probability calculation.

- The perceptron trick is replaced by a new trick, which improves the classifier based on this new error function.

aside In this chapter we carry out a lot of numerical computations. If you follow the equations, you might find that your calculations differ from those in the book by a small amount. The book rounds the numbers at the very end of the equation, not in between steps. This, however, should have very little effect on the final results.

At the end of the chapter, we apply our knowledge to a real-life dataset of movie reviews on the popular site IMDB (www.imdb.com). We use a logistic classifier to predict whether movie reviews are positive or negative.

The code for this chapter is available in the following GitHub repository: https://github.com/luisguiserrano/manning/tree/master/Chapter_6_Logistic_Regression.

Logistic classifiers: A continuous version of perceptron classifiers

In chapter 5, we covered the perceptron, which is a type of classifier that uses the features of our data to make a prediction. The prediction can be 1 or 0. This is called a *discrete perceptron*, because it returns an answer from a discrete set (the set containing 0 and 1). In this chapter, we learn *continuous perceptrons*, which return an answer that can be any number in the interval between 0 and 1. A more common name for continuous perceptrons is *logistic classifiers*. The output of a logistic classifier can be interpreted as a score, and the goal of the logistic classifier is to assign scores as close as possible to the label of the points—points with label 0 should get scores close to 0, and points with label 1 should get scores close to 1.

We can visualize continuous perceptrons similar to discrete perceptrons: with a line (or high-dimensional plane) that separates two classes of data. The only difference is that the discrete perceptron predicts that everything to one side of the line has label 1 and to the other side has label 0, whereas the continuous perceptron assigns a value from 0 to 1 to all the points based on their position with respect to the line. Every point on the line gets a value of 0.5. This value means the model can't decide if the sentence is happy or sad. For example, in the ongoing sentiment analysis example, the sentence "Today is Tuesday" is neither happy nor sad, so the model would assign it a score close to 0.5. Points in the positive zone get scores larger than 0.5, where the points even farther away from the 0.5 line in the positive direction get values closer to 1. Points in the negative zone get scores smaller than 0.5, where, again, the points farther from the line get values closer to 0. No point gets a value of 1 or 0 (unless we consider points at infinity), as shown in figure 6.1.

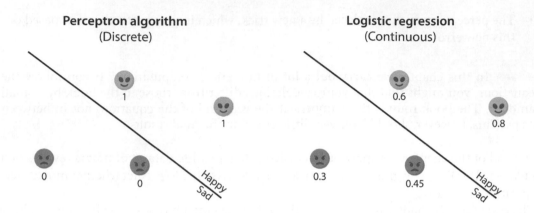

Figure 6.1   Left: The perceptron algorithm trains a discrete perceptron, where the predictions are 0 (happy) and 1 (sad). Right: The logistic regression algorithm trains a continuous perceptron, where the predictions are numbers between 0 and 1 which indicate the predicted level of happiness.

Why do we call this *classification* instead of *regression*, given that the logistic classifier is not outputting a state per se but a number? The reason is, after scoring the points, we can classify them into two classes, namely, those points with a score of 0.5 or higher and those points with a score lower than 0.5. Graphically, the two classes are separated by the boundary line, just like with the perceptron classifier. However, the algorithm we use to train logistic classifiers is called the *logistic regression algorithm*. This notation is a bit peculiar, but we'll keep it as it is to match the literature.

A probability approach to classification: The sigmoid function

How do we slightly modify the perceptron models from the previous section to get a score for each sentence, as opposed to a simple "happy" or "sad"? Recall how we made the predictions in the perceptron models. We scored each sentence by separately scoring each word and adding the scores, plus the bias. If the score was positive, we predicted that the sentence was happy, and if it was negative, we predicted that the sentence was sad. In other words, what we did was apply the step function to the score. The step function returns a 1 if the score was nonnegative and a 0 if it was negative.

Now we do something similar. We take a function that receives the score as the input and outputs a number between 0 and 1. The number is close to 1 if the score is positive and close to zero if the score is negative. If the score is zero, then the output is 0.5. Imagine if you could take the entire number line and crunch it into the interval between 0 and 1. It would look like the function in figure 6.2.

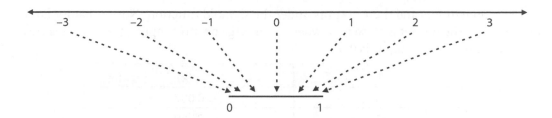

Figure 6.2 The sigmoid function sends the entire number line to the interval (0,1).

Many functions can help us here, and in this case, we use one called the *sigmoid*, denoted with the Greek letter *sigma* (σ). The formula for the sigmoid follows:

$$\sigma(x) = \frac{1}{1+e^{-x}}$$

What really matters here is not the formula but what the function does, which is crunching the real number line into the interval (0,1). In figure 6.3, we can see a comparison of the graphs of the step and the sigmoid functions.

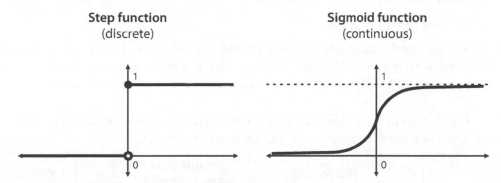

Figure 6.3 Left: The step function used to build discrete perceptrons. It outputs a value of 0 for any negative input and a value of 1 for any input that is positive or zero. It has a discontinuity at zero. Right: The sigmoid function used to build continuous perceptrons. It outputs values less than 0.5 for negative inputs and values greater than 0.5 for positive inputs. At zero, it outputs 0.5. It is continuous and differentiable everywhere.

The sigmoid function is, in general, better than the step function for several reasons. Having continuous predictions gives us more information than discrete predictions. In addition, when we get into the calculus, the sigmoid function has a much nicer derivative than the step function. The step function has a derivative of zero, with the exception of the origin, where it is undefined. In table 6.1, we calculate some values of the sigmoid function to make sure the function does what we want it to.

Table 6.1   Some inputs and their outputs under the sigmoid function. Notice that for large negative inputs, the output is close to 0, whereas for large positive inputs, the output is close to 1. For the input 0, the output is 0.5.

x	$\sigma(x)$
−5	0.007
−1	0.269
0	0.5
1	0.731
5	0.993

The prediction of a logistic classifier is obtained by applying the sigmoid function to the score, and it returns a number between 0 and 1, which, as was mentioned earlier, can be interpreted in our example as the probability that the sentence is happy.

In chapter 5, we defined an error function for a perceptron, called the perceptron error. We used this perceptron error to iteratively build a perceptron classifier. In this chapter, we follow the same procedure. The error of a continuous perceptron is slightly different from the one of a discrete predictor, but they still have similarities.

The dataset and the predictions

In this chapter, we use the same use case as in chapter 5, in which we have a dataset of sentences in alien language with the labels "happy" and "sad," denoted by 1 and 0, respectively. The dataset for this chapter is slightly different than that in chapter 5, and it is shown in table 6.2.

Table 6.2   The dataset of sentences with their happy/sad labels. The coordinates are the number of appearances of the words aack and beep in the sentence.

	Words	**Coordinates (#aack, #beep)**	**Label**
Sentence 1	*Aack beep beep aack aack.*	(3,2)	Sad (0)
Sentence 2	*Beep aack beep.*	(1,2)	Happy (1)
Sentence 3	*Beep!*	(0,1)	Happy (1)
Sentence 4	*Aack aack.*	(2,0)	Sad (0)

The model we use has the following weights and bias:

Logistic Classifier 1

- Weight of *Aack*: $a = 1$
- Weight of *Beep*: $b = 2$
- Bias: $c = -4$

We use the same notation as in chapter 5, where the variables x_{aack} and x_{beep} keep track of the appearances of *aack* and *beep*, respectively. A perceptron classifier would predict according to the formula $\hat{y} = step(ax_{aack} + bx_{beep} + c)$, but because this is a logistic classifier, it uses the sigmoid function instead of the step function. Thus, its prediction is $\hat{y} = \sigma(ax_{aack} + bx_{beep} + c)$. In this case, the prediction follows:

Prediction: $\hat{y} = \sigma(1 \cdot x_{aack} + 2 \cdot x_{beep} - 4)$

Therefore, the classifier makes the following predictions on our dataset:

- **Sentence 1:** $\hat{y} = \sigma(3 + 2 \cdot 2 - 4) = \sigma(3) = 0.953$.

- **Sentence 2:** $\hat{y} = \sigma(1 + 2 \cdot 2 - 4) = \sigma(1) = 0.731$.

- **Sentence 3:** $\hat{y} = \sigma(0 + 2 \cdot 1 - 4) = \sigma(-2) = 0.119$.

- **Sentence 4:** $\hat{y} = \sigma(2 + 2 \cdot 0 - 4) = \sigma(-2) = 0.119$.

The boundary between the "happy" and "sad" classes is the line with equation $x_{aack} + 2x_{beep} - 4 = 0$, depicted in figure 6.4.

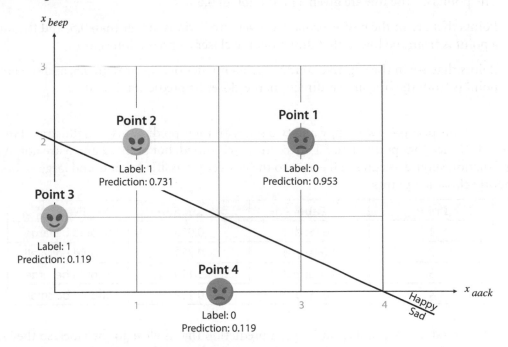

Figure 6.4 The plot of the dataset in table 6.2 with predictions. Notice that points 2 and 4 are correctly classified, but points 1 and 3 are misclassified.

This line splits the plane into positive (happy) and negative (sad) zones. The positive zone is formed by the points with prediction higher than or equal to 0.5, and the negative zone is formed by those with prediction less than 0.5.

The error functions: Absolute, square, and log loss

In this section, we build three error functions for a logistic classifier. What properties would you like a good error function to have? Some examples follow:

- If a point is correctly classified, the error is a small number.

- If a point is incorrectly classified, the error is a large number.

- The error of a classifier for a set of points is the sum (or average) of the errors at all the points.

Many functions satisfy these properties, and we will see three of them; the absolute error, the square error, and the log loss. In table 6.3, we have the labels and predictions for the four points corresponding to the sentences in our dataset with the following characteristics:

- The points on the line are given a prediction of 0.5.

- Points that are in the positive zone are given predictions higher than 0.5, and the farther a point is from the line in that direction, the closer its prediction is to 1.

- Points that are in the negative zone are given predictions lower than 0.5, and the farther a point is from the line in that direction, the closer its prediction is to 0.

Table 6.3 Four points—two happy and two sad with their predictions—as illustrated in figure 6.4. Notice that points 1 and 4 are correctly classified, but points 2 and 3 are not. A good error function should assign small errors to the correctly classified points and large errors to the poorly classified points.

Point	Label	Prediction	Error?
1	0 (Sad)	0.953	Should be large
2	1 (Happy)	0.731	Should be small
3	1 (Happy)	0.119	Should be large
4	0 (Sad)	0.119	Should be small

Notice that in table 6.3, points 2 and 4 get a prediction that is close to the label, so they should have small errors. In contrast, points 1 and 3 get a prediction that is far from the label, so they should have large errors. Three error functions that have this particular property follow:

Error function 1: Absolute error

The *absolute error* is similar to the absolute error we defined for linear regression in chapter 3. It is the absolute value of the difference between the prediction and the label. As we can see, it is large when the prediction is far from the label and small when they are close.

Error function 2: Square error

Again, just like in linear regression, we also have the *square error*. This is the square of the difference between the prediction and the label, and it works for the same reason that the absolute error works.

Before we proceed, let's calculate the absolute and square error for the points in table 6.4. Notice that points 2 and 4 (correctly classified) have small errors, and points 1 and 3 (incorrectly classified) have larger errors.

Table 6.4   We have attached the absolute error and the square error for the points in table 6.3. Notice that as we desired, points 2 and 4 have small errors, and points 1 and 3 have larger errors.

Point	Label	Predicted label	Absolute Error	Square Error
1	0 (Sad)	0.953	0.953	0.908
2	1 (Happy)	0.731	0.269	0.072
3	1 (Happy)	0.119	0.881	0.776
4	0 (Sad)	0.119	0.119	0.014

The absolute and the square errors may remind you of the error functions used in regression. However, in classification, they are not so widely used. The most popular is the next one we see. Why is it more popular? The math (derivatives) works much nicer with the next function. Also, these errors are all pretty small. In fact, they are all smaller than 1, no matter how poorly classified the point is. The reason is that the difference (or the square of the difference) between two numbers that are between 0 and 1 is at most 1. To properly train models, we need error functions that take larger values than that. Thankfully, a third error function can do that for us.

Error function 3: log loss

The *log loss* is the most widely used error function for continuous perceptrons. Most of the error functions in this book have the word *error* in their name, but this one instead has the word *loss* in its name. The *log* part in the name comes from a natural logarithm that we use in the formula. However, the real soul of the log loss is probability.

The outputs of a continuous perceptron are numbers between 0 and 1, so they can be considered probabilities. The model assigns a probability to every data point, and that is the probability that the point is happy. From this, we can infer the probability that the point is sad, which is 1 minus the probability of being happy. For example, if the prediction is 0.75, that means the model believes the point is happy with a probability of 0.75 and sad with a probability of 0.25.

Now, here is the main observation. The goal of the model is to assign high probabilities to the happy points (those with label 1) and low probabilities to the sad points (those with label 0). Notice that the probability that a point is sad is 1 minus the probability that the point is happy. Thus, for each point, let's calculate the probability that the model gives to its label. For the points in our dataset, the corresponding probabilities follow:

- **Point 1:**
  - Label = 0 (sad)
  - Prediction (probability of being happy) = 0.953
  - Probability of being its label: $1 - 0.953 = \mathbf{0.047}$
- **Point 2:**
  - Label = 1 (happy)
  - Prediction (probability of being happy) = 0.731
  - Probability of being its label: **0.731**
- **Point 3:**
  - Label = 1 (happy)
  - Prediction (probability of being happy) = 0.119
  - Probability of being its label: **0.119**
- **Point 4:**
  - Label = 0 (sad)
  - Prediction (probability of being happy) = 0.119
  - Probability of being its label: $1 - 0.119 = \mathbf{0.881}$

Notice that points 2 and 4 are the points that are well classified, and the model assigns a high probability that they are their own label. In contrast, points 1 and 3 are poorly classified, and the model assigns a low probability that they are their own label.

The logistic classifier, in contrast with the perceptron classifier, doesn't give definite answers. The perceptron classifier would say, "I am 100% sure that this point is happy," whereas the logistic classifier says, "Your point has a 73% probability of being happy and 27% of being sad." Although the goal of the perceptron classifier is to be correct as many times as possible, the goal of the logistic classifier is to assign to each point the highest possible probability of having the correct label. This classifier assigns the probabilities 0.047, 0.731, 0.119, and 0.881 to the four labels. Ideally, we'd like these numbers to be higher. How do we measure these four numbers? One way would be to add them or average them. But because they are probabilities, the natural approach is to multiply them. When events are independent, the probability of them occurring simultaneously is the product of their probabilities. If we assume that the four predictions are independent, then the probability that this model assigns to the labels "sad, happy, happy, sad" is the product of the four numbers, which is $0.047 \cdot 0.731 \cdot 0.119 \cdot 0.881 = 0.004$. This is a very small probability. Our hope would be that a model that fits this dataset better would result in a higher probability.

That probability we just calculated seems like a good measure for our model, but it has some problems. For instance, it is a product of many small numbers. Products of many small numbers tend to be tiny. Imagine if our dataset had one million points. The probability would be a product of one million numbers, all between 0 and 1. This number may be so small that a computer may not be able to represent it. Also, manipulating a product of one million numbers is extremely difficult. Is there any way that we could perhaps turn it into something easier to manipulate, like a sum?

Luckily for us, we have a convenient way to turn products into sums—using the logarithms. For this entire book, all we need to know about the logarithm is that it turns products into sums. More specifically, the logarithm of a product of two numbers is the sum of the logarithms of the numbers, as shown next:

$$ln(a \cdot b) = ln(a) + ln(b)$$

We can use logarithms in base 2, 10, or e. In this chapter, we use the natural logarithm, which is on base e. However, the same results can be obtained if we were to use the logarithm in any other base.

If we apply the natural logarithm to our product of probabilities, we obtain

$$ln(0.047 \cdot 0.731 \cdot 0.119 \cdot 0.881) = ln(0.047) + ln(0.731) + ln(0.119) + ln(0.881) = -5.616.$$

One small detail. Notice that the result is a negative number. In fact, this will always be the case, because the logarithm of a number between 0 and 1 is always negative. Thus, if we take the negative logarithm of the product of probabilities, it is always a positive number.

The log loss is defined as the negative logarithm of the product of probabilities, which is also the sum of the negative logarithms of the probabilities. Furthermore, each of the summands is the log loss at that point. In table 6.5, you can see the calculation of the log loss for each of the points. By adding the log losses of all the points, we obtain a total log loss of 5.616.

Table 6.5 Calculation of the log loss for the points in our dataset. Notice that points that are well classified (2 and 4) have a small log loss, whereas points that are poorly classified (1 and 3) have a large log loss.

Point	Label	Predicted label	Probability of being its label	Log loss
1	0 (Sad)	0.953	0.047	$-ln(0.047) = 3.049$
2	1 (Happy)	0.731	0.731	$-ln(0.731) = 0.313$
3	1 (Happy)	0.119	0.119	$-ln(0.119) = 2.127$
4	0 (Sad)	0.119	0.881	$-ln(0.881) = 0.127$

Notice that, indeed, the well-classified points (2 and 4) have a small log loss, and the poorly classified points have a large log loss. The reason is that if a number x is close to 0, $-ln(x)$ is a large number, but if x is close to 1, then $-ln(x)$ is a small number.

To summarize, the steps for calculating the log loss follow:

- For each point, we calculate the probability that the classifier gives its label.
  - For the happy points, this probability is the score.
  - For the sad points, this probability is 1 minus the score.

- We multiply all these probabilities to obtain the total probability that the classifier has given to these labels.

- We apply the natural logarithm to that total probability.

- The logarithm of a product is the sum of the logarithms of the factors, so we obtain a sum of logarithms, one for each point.

- We notice that all the terms are negative, because the logarithm of a number less than 1 is a negative number. Thus, we multiply everything by –1 to get a sum of positive numbers.

- This sum is our log loss.

The log loss is closely related to the concept of *cross-entropy*, which is a way to measure similarity between two probability distributions. More details about cross-entropy are available in the references in appendix C.

Formula for the log loss

The log loss for a point can be condensed into a nice formula. Recall that the log loss is the negative logarithm of the probability that the point is its label (happy or sad). The prediction the model gives to each point is $\hat{y}$, and that is the probability that the point is happy. Thus, the probability that the point is sad, according to the model, is $1 - \hat{y}$. Therefore, we can write the log loss as follows:

- If the label is 0: $log\ loss = -ln(1 - \hat{y})$

- If the label is 1: $log\ loss = -ln(\hat{y})$

Because the label is y, the previous if statement can be condensed into the following formula:

$$log\ loss = -y\ ln(\hat{y}) - (1 - y)\ ln(1 - \hat{y})$$

The previous formula works because if the label is 0, the first summand is 0, and if the label is 1, the second summand is 0. We use the term *log loss* when we refer to the log loss of a point or of a whole dataset. The log loss of a dataset is the sum of the log losses at every point.

Comparing classifiers using the log loss

Now that we have settled on an error function for logistic classifiers, the log loss, we can use it to compare two classifiers. Recall that the classifier we've been using in this chapter is defined by the following weights and bias:

Logistic Classifier 1

- Weight of *Aack*: $a = 1$

- Weight of *Beep*: $b = 2$

- Bias: $c = -4$

In this section, we compare it with the following logistic classifier:

Logistic Classifier 2

- Weight of *Aack*: $a = -1$
- Weight of *Beep*: $b = 1$
- Bias: $c = 0$

The predictions that each classifier makes follow:

- **Classifier 1:** $\hat{y} = \sigma(x_{aack} + 2x_{beep} - 4)$
- **Classifier 2:** $\hat{y} = \sigma(-x_{aack} + x_{beep})$

The predictions of both classifiers are recorded in table 6.6, and the plot of the dataset and the two boundary lines are shown in figure 6.5.

Table 6.6 Calculation of the log loss for the points in our dataset. Notice that the predictions made by classifier 2 are much closer to the labels of the points than the predictions made by classifier 1. Thus, classifier 2 is a better classifier.

Point	Label	Classifier 1 prediction	Classifier 2 prediction
1	0 (Sad)	0.953	0.269
2	1 (Happy)	0.731	0.731
3	1 (Happy)	0.119	0.731
4	0 (Sad)	0.881	0.119

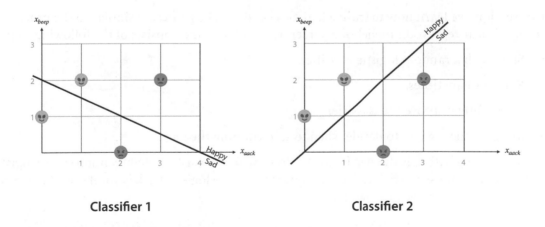

Classifier 1   Classifier 2

Figure 6.5 Left: A bad classifier that makes two mistakes. Right: A good classifier that classifies all four points correctly.

From the results in table 6.6 and figure 6.5, it is clear that classifier 2 is much better than classifier 1. For instance, in figure 6.5, we can see that classifier 2 correctly located the two happy sentences in the positive zone and the two sad sentences in the negative zone. Next, we compare the log losses. Recall that the log loss for classifier 1 was 5.616. We should obtain a smaller log loss for classifier 2, because this is the better classifier.

According to the formula $log\ loss = -y\ ln(\hat{y}) - (1 - y)\ ln(1 - \hat{y})$, the log loss for classifier 2 at each of the points in our dataset follows:

- **Point 1:** $y = 0$, $\hat{y} = 0.269$:
  - $log\ loss = ln(1 - 0.269) = 0.313$
- **Point 2:** $y = 1$, $\hat{y} = 0.731$:
  - $log\ loss = ln(0.731) = 0.313$
- **Point 3:** $y = 1$, $\hat{y} = 0.731$:
  - $log\ loss = ln(0.731) = 0.313$
- **Point 4:** $y = 0$, $\hat{y} = 0.119$:
  - $log\ loss = ln(1 - 0.119) = 0.127$

The total log loss for the dataset is the sum of these four, which is 1.067. Notice that this is much smaller than 5.616, confirming that classifier 2 is indeed much better than classifier 1.

How to find a good logistic classifier? The logistic regression algorithm

In this section, we learn how to train a logistic classifier. The process is similar to the process of training a linear regression model or a perceptron classifier and consists of the following steps:

- Start with a random logistic classifier.
- Repeat many times:
  - Slightly improve the classifier.
- Measure the log loss to decide when to stop running the loop.

The key to the algorithm is the step inside the loop, which consists of slightly improving a logistic classifier. This step uses a trick called the *logistic trick*. The logistic trick is similar to the perceptron trick, as we see in the next section.

The logistic trick: A way to slightly improve the continuous perceptron

Recall from chapter 5 that the perceptron trick consists of starting with a random classifier, successively picking a random point, and applying the perceptron trick. It had the following two cases:

- **Case 1:** If the point is correctly classified, leave the line as it is.
- **Case 2:** If the point is incorrectly classified, move the line a little closer to the point.

The logistic trick (illustrated in figure 6.6) is similar to the perceptron trick. The only thing that changes is that when the point is well classified, we move the line *away* from the point. It has the following two cases:

- **Case 1:** If the point is correctly classified, slightly move the line away from the point.

- **Case 2:** If the point is incorrectly classified, slightly move the line closer to the point.

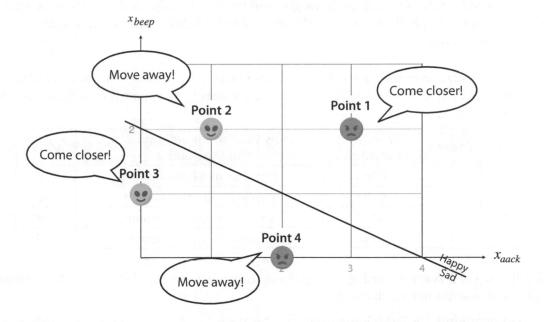

Figure 6.6 In the logistic regression algorithm, every point has a say. Points that are correctly classified tell the line to move farther away, to be deeper in the correct zone. Points that are incorrectly classified tell the line to come closer, in hopes of one day being on the correct side of the line.

Why do we move the line away from a correctly classified point? If the point is well classified, it means it is in the correct zone with respect to the line. If we move the line farther away, we move the point even deeper into the correct zone. Because the prediction is based on how far the point is from the boundary line, for points in the positive (happy) zone, the prediction increases if the point is farther from the line. Similarly, for points in the negative (sad) zone, the prediction decreases if the point is farther from the line. Thus, if the label of the point is 1, we are increasing the prediction (making it even closer to 1), and if the label of the point is 0, we are decreasing the prediction (making it even closer to 0).

For example, look at classifier 1 and the first sentence in our dataset. Recall that the classifier has weights $a = 1$, $b = 2$, and bias $c = -4$. The sentence corresponds to a point of coordinates $(x_{aack}, x_{beep}) = (3,2)$, and label $y = 0$. The prediction we obtained for this point was $\hat{y} = \sigma(3 + 2 \cdot 2 - 4) = \sigma(3) = 0.953$. The prediction is quite far from the label, so the error is high: in fact, in table 6.5, we calculated it to be 3.049. The error that this classifier made was to think that this sentence is happier than it is. Thus, to tune the weights to ensure that the classifier reduces the prediction for this sentence, we should drastically decrease the weights *a*, *b*, and the bias *c*.

Using the same logic, we can analyze how to tune the weights to improve the classification for the other points. For the second sentence in the dataset, the label is $y = 1$ and the prediction is 0.731. This is a good prediction, but if we want to improve it, we should slightly increase the weights and the bias. For the third sentence, because the label is $y = 1$ and the prediction is $\hat{y} = 0.119$, we should drastically increase the weights and the bias. Finally, for the fourth sentence, the label is $y = 0$ and the prediction is $\hat{y} = 0.119$, so we should slightly decrease the weights and the bias. These are summarized in table 6.7.

Table 6.7   Calculation of the log loss for the points in our dataset. Notice that points that are well classified (2 and 4) have a small log loss, whereas points that are poorly classified (1 and 3) have a large log loss.

Point	Label y	Classifier 1 prediction y	How to tune the weights *a, b,* and the bias *c*	$y - \hat{y}$
1	0	0.953	Decrease by a large amount	−0.953
2	1	0.731	Increase by a small amount	0.269
3	1	0.119	Increase by a large amount	0.881
4	0	0.119	Decrease by a small amount	−0.119

The following observations can help us figure out the perfect amount that we want to add to the weights and bias to improve the predictions:

- **Observation 1:** the last column of table 6.7 has the value of the label minus the prediction. Notice the similarities between the two rightmost columns in this table. This hints that the amount we should update the weights and the bias should be a multiple of $y - \hat{y}$.

- **Observation 2:** imagine a sentence in which the word *aack* appears 10 times and *beep* appears once. If we are to add (or subtract) a value to the weights of these two words, it makes sense to think that the weight of *aack* should be updated by a larger amount, because this word is more crucial to the overall score of the sentence. Thus, the amount we should update the weight of *aack* should be multiplied by x_{aack}, and the amount we should update the weight of *beep* should be multiplied by x_{beep}.

- **Observation 3:** the amount that we update the weights and biases should also be multiplied by the learning rate η because we want to make sure that this number is small.

Putting the three observations together, we conclude that the following is a good set of updated weights:

- $a' = a + \eta(y - \hat{y})x_1$
- $b' = b + \eta(y - \hat{y})x_2$
- $c' = c + \eta(y - \hat{y})$

Thus, the pseudocode for the logistic trick follows. Notice how similar it is to the pseudocode for the perceptron trick we learned at the end of the section "The perceptron trick" in chapter 5.

Pseudocode for the logistic trick

Inputs:

- A logistic classifier with weights a, b, and bias c
- A point with coordinates (x_1, x_2) and label y
- A small value η (the learning rate)

Output:

- A perceptron with new weights a', b', and bias c' which is at least as good as the input perceptron for that point

Procedure:

- The prediction the perceptron makes at the point is $\hat{y} = \sigma(ax_1 + bx_2 + c)$.

Return:

- The perceptron with the following weights and bias:
    - $a' = a + \eta(y - \hat{y})x_1$
    - $b' = b + \eta(y - \hat{y})x_2$
    - $c' = c + \eta(y - \hat{y})$

The way we updated the weights and bias in the logistic trick is no coincidence. It comes from applying the gradient descent algorithm to reduce the log loss. The mathematical details are described in appendix B, section "Using gradient descent to train classification models."

To verify that the logistic trick works in our case, let's apply it to the current dataset. In fact, we'll apply the trick to each of the four points separately, to see how much each one of them would modify the weights and bias of the model. Finally, we'll compare the log loss at that point before and after the update and verify that it has indeed been reduced. For the following calculations, we use a learning rate of $\eta = 0.05$.

Updating the classifier using each of the sentences

Using the first sentence:

- Initial weights and bias: $a = 1$, $b = 2$, $c = -4$
- Label: $y = 0$
- Prediction: 0.953
- Initial log loss: $-0 \cdot ln(0.953) - 1\ ln(1 - 0.953) = 3.049$
- Coordinates of the point: $x_{aack} = 3$, $x_{beep} = 2$
- Learning rate: $\eta = 0.01$

- Updated weights and bias:
    - $a' = 1 + 0.05 \cdot (0 - 0.953) \cdot 3 = 0.857$
    - $b' = 2 + 0.05 \cdot (0 - 0.953) \cdot 2 = 1.905$
    - $c' = -4 + 0.05 \cdot (0 - 0.953) = -4.048$
- Updated prediction: $\hat{y} = \sigma(0.857 \cdot 3 + 1.905 \cdot 2 - 4.048 = 0.912$. (Notice that the prediction decreased, so it is now closer to the label 0.)
- Final log loss: $-0 \cdot ln(0.912) - 1\, ln(1 - 0.912) = 2.426$. (Note that the error decreased from 3.049 to 2.426.)

The calculations for the other three points are shown in table 6.8. Notice that in the table, the updated prediction is always closer to the label than the initial prediction, and the final log loss is always smaller than the initial log loss. This means that no matter which point we use for the logistic trick, we'll be improving the model for that point and decreasing the final log loss.

Table 6.8 Calculations of the predictions, log loss, updated weights, and updated predictions for all the points.

Point	Coordinates	Label	Initial prediction	Initial log loss	Updated weights:	Updated prediction	Final log loss
1	(3,2)	0	0.953	3.049	$a' = 0.857$ $b' = 1.905$ $c' = -4.048$	0.912	2.426
2	(1,2)	1	0.731	0.313	$a' = 1.013$ $b' = 2.027$ $c' = -3.987$	0.747	0.292
3	(0,1)	1	0.119	2.127	$a' = 1$ $b' = 2.044$ $c' = -3.956$	0.129	2.050
4	(2,0)	0	0.119	0.127	$a' = 0.988$ $b' = 2$ $c' = -4.006$	0.127	0.123

At the beginning of this section, we discussed that the logistic trick can also be visualized geometrically as moving the boundary line with respect to the point. More specifically, the line is moved closer to the point if the point is misclassified and farther from the point if the point is correctly classified. We can verify this by plotting the original classifier and the modified classifier in the four cases in table 6.8. In figure 6.7, you can see the four plots. In each of them, the solid line is the original classifier, and the dotted line is the classifier obtained by applying the logistic trick, using the highlighted point. Notice that points 2 and 4, which are correctly classified, push the line away, whereas points 1 and 3, which are misclassified, move the line closer to them.

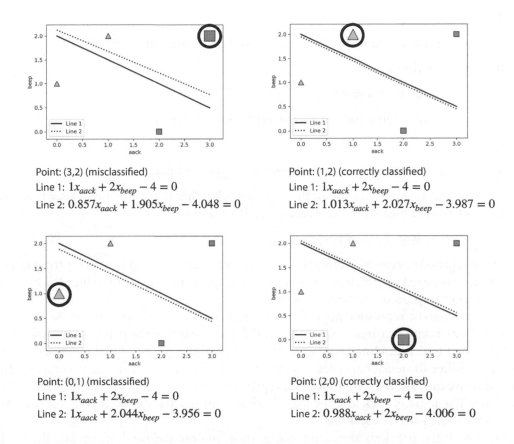

Point: (3,2) (misclassified)
Line 1: $1x_{aack} + 2x_{beep} - 4 = 0$
Line 2: $0.857x_{aack} + 1.905x_{beep} - 4.048 = 0$

Point: (1,2) (correctly classified)
Line 1: $1x_{aack} + 2x_{beep} - 4 = 0$
Line 2: $1.013x_{aack} + 2.027x_{beep} - 3.987 = 0$

Point: (0,1) (misclassified)
Line 1: $1x_{aack} + 2x_{beep} - 4 = 0$
Line 2: $1x_{aack} + 2.044x_{beep} - 3.956 = 0$

Point: (2,0) (correctly classified)
Line 1: $1x_{aack} + 2x_{beep} - 4 = 0$
Line 2: $0.988x_{aack} + 2x_{beep} - 4.006 = 0$

Figure 6.7 The logistic trick applied to each of the four data points. Notice that for correctly classified points, the line moves away from the point, whereas for misclassified points, the line moves closer to the point.

Repeating the logistic trick many times: The logistic regression algorithm

The logistic regression algorithm is what we use to train a logistic classifier. In the same way that the perceptron algorithm consists of repeating the perceptron trick many times, the logistic regression algorithm consists of repeating the logistic trick many times. The pseudocode follows:

Pseudocode for the logistic regression algorithm

Inputs:

- A dataset of points, labeled 1 and 0
- A number of epochs, n
- A learning rate η

Output:

- A logistic classifier consisting of a set of weights and a bias, which fits the dataset

Procedure:

- Start with random values for the weights and bias of the logistic classifier.

- Repeat many times:

  - Pick a random data point.

  - Update the weights and the bias using the logistic trick.

Return:

- The perceptron classifier with the updated weights and bias

As we saw previously, each iteration of the logistic trick either moves the line closer to a misclassified point or farther away from a correctly classified point.

Stochastic, mini-batch, and batch gradient descent

The logistic regression algorithm, together with linear regression and the perceptron, is another algorithm that is based on gradient descent. If we use gradient descent to reduce the log loss, the gradient descent step becomes the logistic trick.

The general logistic regression algorithm works not only for datasets with two features but for datasets with as many features as we want. In this case, just like the perceptron algorithm, the boundary won't look like a line, but it would look like a higher-dimensional hyperplane splitting points in a higher dimensional space. However, we don't need to visualize this higher-dimensional space; we only need to build a logistic regression classifier with as many weights as features in our data. The logistic trick and the logistic algorithm update the weights in a similar way to what we did in the previous sections.

Just like with the previous algorithms we learned, in practice, we don't update the model by picking one point at a time. Instead, we use mini-batch gradient descent—we take a batch of points and update the model to fit those points better. For the fully general logistic regression algorithm and a thorough mathematical derivation of the logistic trick using gradient descent, please refer to appendix B, section "Using gradient descent to train classification models."

Coding the logistic regression algorithm

In this section, we see how to code the logistic regression algorithm by hand. The code for this section follows:

- **Notebook:** Coding_logistic_regression.ipynb

  - https://github.com/luisguiserrano/manning/blob/master/Chapter_6_Logistic_Regression/Coding_logistic_regression.ipynb

We'll test our code in the same dataset that we used in chapter 5. The dataset is shown in table 6.9.

Table 6.9   The dataset that we will fit with a logistic classifier

Aack x_1	Beep x_2	Label y
1	0	0
0	2	0
1	1	0
1	2	0
1	3	1
2	2	1
2	3	1
3	2	1

The code for loading our small dataset follows, and the plot of the dataset is shown in figure 6.8:

```
import numpy as np
features = np.array([[1,0],[0,2],[1,1],[1,2],[1,3],[2,2],[2,3],[3,2]])
labels = np.array([0,0,0,0,1,1,1,1])
```

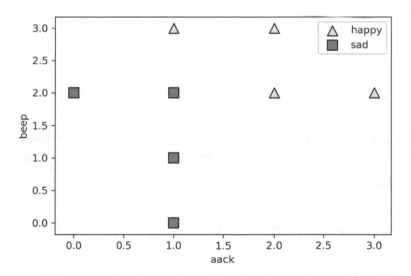

Figure 6.8   The plot of our dataset, where the happy sentences are represented by triangles and the sad sentences by squares.

Coding the logistic regression algorithm by hand

In this section, we see how to code the logistic trick and the logistic regression algorithm by hand. More generally, we'll code the logistic regression algorithm for a dataset with n weights. The notation we use follows:

- Features: $x_1, x_2, \ldots, x_n$
- Label: y
- Weights: $w_1, w_2, \ldots, w_n$
- Bias: b

The score for a particular sentence is the sigmoid of the sum of the weight of each word (w_i) times the number of times that appears (x_i), plus the bias (b). Notice that we use the summation notation for

$$\sum_{i=1}^{n} a_i = a_1 + a_2 + \cdots + a_n .$$

- Prediction: $\hat{y} = \sigma(w_1 x_1 + w_2 x_2 + \cdots + w_n x_n + b) = \sigma(\sum_{i=1}^{n} w_i x_i + b)$.

For our current problem, we'll refer to x_{aack} and x_{beep} as x_1 and x_2, respectively. Their corresponding weights are w_1 and w_1, and the bias is b.

We start by coding the sigmoid function, the score, and the prediction. Recall that the formula for the sigmoid function is

$$\sigma(x) = \frac{1}{1 + e^{-x}}.$$

```
def sigmoid(x):
    return np.exp(x)/(1+np.exp(x))
```

For the score function, we use the dot product between the features and the weights. Recall that the dot product between vectors $(x_1, x_2, \ldots, x_n)$ and $(w_1, w_2, \ldots, w_n)$ is $w_1 x_1 + w_2 x_2 + \ldots + w_n x_n$.

```
def score(weights, bias, features):
    return np.dot(weights, features) + bias
```

Finally, recall that the prediction is the sigmoid activation function applied to the score.

```
def prediction(weights, bias, features):
    return sigmoid(score(weights, bias, features))
```

Now that we have the prediction, we can proceed to the log loss. Recall that the formula for the log loss is

$$log\ loss = -y\ ln(\hat{y}) - (1 - y)\ ln(1 - y).$$

Let's code that formula as follows:

```
def log_loss(weights, bias, features, label):
    pred = prediction(weights, bias, features)
    return -label*np.log(pred) - (1-label)*np.log(1-pred)
```

We need the log loss over the whole dataset, so we can add over all the data points as shown here:

```
def total_log_loss(weights, bias, features, labels):
    total_error = 0
    for i in range(len(features)):
        total_error += log_loss(weights, bias, features[i], labels[i])
    return total_error
```

Now we are ready to code the logistic regression trick, and the logistic regression algorithm. In more than two variables, recall that the logistic regression step for the i-th weight is the following formula, where η is the learning rate:

- $w_i \rightarrow w_i + \eta(y - \hat{y})x_i$ for $i = 1, 2, \ldots, n$
- $b \rightarrow b + \eta(y - \hat{y})$ for $i = 1, 2, \ldots, n$.

```
def logistic_trick(weights, bias, features, label, learning_rate = 0.01):
    pred = prediction(weights, bias, features)
    for i in range(len(weights)):
        weights[i] += (label-pred)*features[i]*learning_rate
        bias += (label-pred)*learning_rate
    return weights, bias

def logistic_regression_algorithm(features, labels, learning_rate = 0.01,
    epochs = 1000):
    utils.plot_points(features, labels)
    weights = [1.0 for i in range(len(features[0]))]
    bias = 0.0
    errors = []
    for i in range(epochs):
        errors.append(total_log_loss(weights, bias, features, labels))
        j = random.randint(0, len(features)-1)
        weights, bias = logistic_trick(weights, bias, features[j], labels[j])
    return weights, bias
```

Now we can run the logistic regression algorithm to build a logistic classifier that fits our dataset as follows:

```
logistic_regression_algorithm(features, labels)
([0.46999999999999953, 0.09999999999999937], -0.680000000000004)
```

The classifier we obtain has the following weights and biases:

- $w_1 = 0.47$
- $w_2 = 0.10$
- $b = -0.68$

The plot of the classifier (together with a plot of the previous classifiers at each of the epochs) is depicted in figure 6.9.

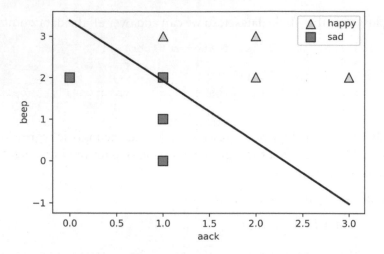

Figure 6.9   The boundary of the resulting logistic classifier

In figure 6.10, we can see the plot of the classifiers corresponding to all the epochs (left) and the plot of the log loss (right). On the plot of the intermediate classifiers (Figure 6.10, left), the final one corresponds to the dark line. Notice from the log loss plot that, as we run the algorithm for more epochs, the log loss decreases drastically, which is exactly what we want. Furthermore, the log loss is never zero, even though all the points are correctly classified. This is because for any point, no matter how well classified, the log loss is never zero. Contrast this to figure 5.26 in chapter 5, where the perceptron loss indeed reaches a value of zero when every point is correctly classified.

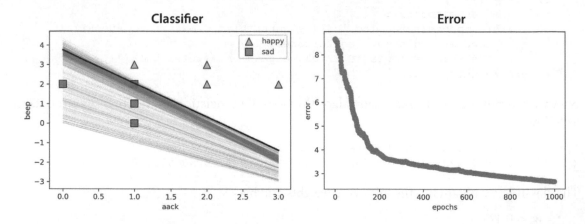

Figure 6.10   Left: A plot of all the intermediate steps of the logistic regression algorithm. Notice that we start with a bad classifier and slowly move toward a good one (the thick line). Right: The error plot. Notice that the more epochs we run the logistic regression algorithm, the lower the error gets.

Real-life application: Classifying IMDB reviews with Turi Create

In this section, we see a real-life application of the logistic classifier in sentiment analysis. We use Turi Create to build a model that analyzes movie reviews on the popular IMDB site. The code for this section follows:

- **Notebook:** Sentiment_analysis_IMDB.ipynb
  - https://github.com/luisguiserrano/manning/blob/master/Chapter_6_Logistic_Regression/Sentiment_analysis_IMDB.ipynb
- **Dataset:** IMDB_Dataset.csv

First, we import Turi Create, download the dataset, and convert it into an SFrame, which we call `movies`, as follows:

```
import turicreate as tc
movies = tc.SFrame('IMDB Dataset.csv')
```

The first five rows of the dataset appear in table 6.10.

Table 6.10 The first five rows of the IMDB dataset. The Review column has the text of the review, and the Sentiment column has the sentiment of the review, which can be positive or negative.

Review	Sentiment
One of the other reviewers has mentioned...	Positive
A wonderful little production...	Positive
I thought this was a wonderful day to spend...	Positive
Basically, there's a family where a little...	Negative
Petter Mattei's "Love in the time of money" is a...	Positive

The dataset has two columns, one with the review, as a string, and one with the sentiment, as positive or negative. First, we need to process the string, because each of the words needs to be a different feature. The Turi Create built-in function `count_words` in the `text_analytics` package is useful for this task, because it turns a sentence into a dictionary with the word counts. For example, the sentence "to be or not to be" is turned into the dictionary {'to':2, 'be':2, 'or':1, 'not':1}. We add a new column called `words` containing this dictionary as follows:

```
movies['words'] = tc.text_analytics.count_words(movies['review'])
```

The first few rows of our dataset with the new column are shown in table 6.11.

Table 6.11   The Words column is a dictionary where each word in the review is recorded together with its number of appearances. This is the column of features for our logistic classifier.

Review	Sentiment	Words
One of the other reviewers has mentioned...	Positive	{'if': 1.0, 'viewing': 1.0, 'comfortable': 1.0, ...
A wonderful little production...	Positive	{'done': 1.0, 'every': 1.0, 'decorating': 1.0, ...
I thought this was a wonderful day to spend...	Positive	{'see': 1.0, 'go': 1.0, 'great': 1.0, 'superm ...
Basically, there's a family where a little...	Negative	{'them': 1.0, 'ignore': 1.0, 'dialogs': 1.0, ...
Peter Mattei's *Love in the Time of Money* is a...	Positive	{'work': 1.0, 'his': 1.0, 'for': 1.0, 'anxiously': ...

We are ready to train our model! For this, we use the function `create` in the `logistic_classifier` package, in which we specify the target (label) to be the `sentiment` column and the features to be the `words` column. Note that the target is expressed as a string with the name of the column containing the label, but the features are expressed as an array of strings with the names of the columns containing each of the features (in case we need to specify several columns), as shown here:

```
model = tc.logistic_classifier.create(movies, features=['words'],
    target='sentiment')
```

Now that we've trained our model, we can look at the weights of the words, with the `coefficients` command. The table we obtain has several columns, but the ones we care about are `index` and `value`, which show the words and their weights. The top five follow:

- (intercept): 0.065

- if: −0.018

- viewing: 0.089

- comfortable: 0.517

- become: 0.106

The first one, called intercept, is the bias. Because the bias of the model is positive, the empty review is positive, as we learned in chapter 5, in the section "The bias, the y-intercept, and the inherent mood of a quiet alien." This makes sense, because users who rate movies negatively tend to leave a review, whereas many users who rate movies positively don't leave any review. The other words are neutral, so their weights don't mean very much, but let's explore the weights of some words, such as *wonderful, horrible,* and *the,* as shown next:

- wonderful: 1.043

- horrible: −1.075

- the: 0.0005

As we see, the weight of the word *wonderful* is positive, the weight of the word *horrible* is negative, and the weight of the word *the* is small. This makes sense: *wonderful* is a positive word, *horrible* is a negative word, and *the* is a neutral word.

As a last step, let's find the most positive and negative reviews. For this, we use the model to make predictions for all the movies. These predictions will be stored in a new column called `predictions`, using the following command:

```
movies['prediction'] = model.predict(movies, output_type='probability')
```

Let's find the most positive and most negative movies, according to the model. We do this by sorting the array, as follows:

Most positive review:

```
movies.sort('predictions')[-1]
```

Output: "It seems to me that a lot of people don't know that *Blade* is actually a superhero movie on par with *X-Men*…"

Most negative review:

```
movies.sort('predictions')[0]
```

Output: "Even duller, if possible, than the original…"

We could do a lot more to improve this model. For example, some text manipulation techniques, such as removing punctuation and capitalization, or removing stop words (such as *the, and, of, it*), tend to give us better results. But it's great to see that with a few lines of code, we can build our own sentiment analysis classifier!

Classifying into multiple classes: The softmax function

So far we have seen continuous perceptrons classify two classes, happy and sad. But what if we have more classes? At the end of chapter 5, we discussed that classifying between more than two classes is hard for a discrete perceptron. However, this is easy to do with a logistic classifier.

Imagine an image dataset with three labels: "dog", "cat", and "bird". The way to build a classifier that predicts one of these three labels for every image is to build three classifiers, one for each one of the labels. When a new image comes in, we evaluate it with each of the three classifiers. The classifier corresponding to each animal returns a probability that the image is the corresponding animal. We then classify the image as the animal from the classifier that returned the highest probability.

This, however, is not the ideal way to do it, because this classifier returns a discrete answer, such as "dog," "cat," or "bird." What if we wanted a classifier that returns probabilities for the three animals? Say, an answer could be of the form "10% dog, 85% cat, and 5% bird." The way we do this is using the softmax function.

The softmax function works as follows: recall that a logistic classifier makes a prediction using a two-step process—first it calculates a score, and then it applies the sigmoid function to this score. Let's forget about the sigmoid function and output the score instead. Now imagine that the three classifiers returned the following scores:

- Dog classifier: 3

- Cat classifier: 2

- Bird classifier: −1

How do we turn these scores into probabilities? Well, here's an idea: we can normalize. This means dividing all these numbers by their sum, which is five, to get them to add to one. When we do this, we get the probabilities 3/5 for dog, 2/5 for cat, and −1/5 for bird. This works, but it's not ideal, because the probability of the image being a bird is a negative number. Probabilities must always be positive, so we need to try something different.

What we need is a function that is always positive and that is also increasing. Exponential functions work great for this. Any exponential function, such as 2^x, 3^x, or 10^x, would do the job. By default, we use the function e^x, which has wonderful mathematical properties (e.g., the derivative of e^x is also e^x). We apply this function to the scores, to get the following values:

- Dog classifier: $e^3 = 20.085$

- Cat classifier: $e^2 = 7.389$

- Bird classifier: $e^{-1} = 0.368$

Now, we do what we did before—we normalize, or divide by the sum of these numbers for them to add to one. The sum is $20.085 + 7.389 + 0.368 = 27.842$, so we get the following:

- Probability of dog: $20.085/27.842 = 0.721$

- Probability of cat: $7.389/27.842 = 0.265$

- Probability of bird: $0.368/27.842 = 0.013$

These are the three probabilities given by our three classifiers. The function we used was the softmax, and the general version follows: if we have n classifiers that output the n scores $a_1, a_2, \ldots, a_n$, the probabilities obtained are $p_1, p_2, \ldots, p_n$, where

$$p_i = \frac{e^{a_i}}{e^{a_1} + e^{a_2} + \cdots + e^{a_n}}.$$

This formula is known as the softmax function.

What would happen if we use the softmax function for only two classes? We obtain the sigmoid function. Why not convince yourself of this as an exercise?

Summary

- Continuous perceptrons, or logistic classifiers, are similar to perceptron classifiers, except instead of making a discrete prediction such as 0 or 1, they predict any number between 0 and 1.

- Logistic classifiers are more useful than discrete perceptrons, because they give us more information. Aside from telling us which class the classifier predicts, they also give us a probability. A good logistic classifier would assign low probabilities to points with label 0 and high probabilities to points with label 1.

- The log loss is an error function for logistic classifiers. It is calculated separately for every point as the negative of the natural logarithm of the probability that the classifier assigns to its label.

- The total log loss of a classifier on a dataset is the sum of the log loss at every point.

- The logistic trick takes a labeled data point and a boundary line. If the point is incorrectly classified, the line is moved closer to the point, and if it is correctly classified, the line is moved farther from the point. This is more useful than the perceptron trick, because the perceptron trick doesn't move the line if the point is correctly classified.

- The logistic regression algorithm is used to fit a logistic classifier to a labeled dataset. It consists of starting with a logistic classifier with random weights and continuously picking a random point and applying the logistic trick to obtain a slightly better classifier.

- When we have several classes to predict, we can build several linear classifiers and combine them using the softmax function.

Exercises

Exercise 6.1

A dentist has trained a logistic classifier on a dataset of patients to predict if they have a decayed tooth. The model has determined that the probability that a patient has a decayed tooth is

$$\sigma(d + 0.5c - 0.8),$$

where

- d is a variable that indicates whether the patient has had another decayed tooth in the past, and

- c is a variable that indicates whether the patient eats candy.

For example, if a patient eats candy, then $c = 1$, and if they don't, then $c = 0$. What is the probability that a patient that eats candy and was treated for a decayed tooth last year has a decayed tooth today?

Exercise 6.2

Consider the logistic classifier that assigns to the point (x_1, x_2) the prediction $\hat{y} = \sigma(2x_1 + 3x_2 - 4)$, and the point $p = (1, 1)$ with label 0.

a. Calculate the prediction $\hat{y}$ that the model gives to the point p.

b. Calculate the log loss that the model produces at the point p.

c. Use the logistic trick to obtain a new model that produces a smaller log loss. You can use $\eta = 0.1$ as the learning rate.

d. Find the prediction given by the new model at the point p, and verify that the log loss obtained is smaller than the original.

Exercise 6.3

Using the model in the statement of exercise 6.2, find a point for which the prediction is 0.8.

hint   First find the score that will give a prediction of 0.8, and recall that the prediction is $\hat{y} = \sigma(\text{score})$.

In this chapter

- types of errors a model can make: false positives and false negatives

- putting these errors in a table: the confusion matrix

- what are accuracy, recall, precision, F-score, sensitivity, and specificity, and how are they used to evaluate models

- what is the ROC curve, and how does it keep track of sensitivity and specificity at the same time

This chapter is slightly different from the previous two—it doesn't focus on building classification models; instead, it focuses on evaluating them. For a machine learning professional, being able to evaluate the performance of different models is as important as being able to train them. We seldom train a single model on a dataset; we train several different models and select the one that performs best. We also need to make sure models are of good quality before putting them in production. The quality of a model is not always trivial to measure, and in this chapter, we learn several techniques to evaluate our classification models. In chapter 4, we learned how to evaluate regression models, so we can think of this chapter as its analog but with classification models.

The simplest way to measure the performance of a classification model is by calculating its accuracy. However, we'll see that accuracy doesn't paint the whole picture, because some models exhibit great accuracy but are not good models anyway. To fix this, we'll define some useful metrics, such as precision and recall. Then we'll combine them into a new, more powerful metric called the F-score. These metrics are widely used by data scientists to evaluate their models. However, in other disciplines, such as medicine, other similar metrics are used, such as sensitivity and specificity. Using these last two metrics, we'll be able to build a curve called the receiver operating characteristic (ROC) curve. The ROC curve is a simple plot that gives us great insights into our models.

Accuracy: How often is my model correct?

In this section, we discuss accuracy, the simplest and most common measure of classification models. The accuracy of a model is the percentage of times that a model is correct. In other words, it is the ratio between the number of correctly predicted data points and the total number of data points. For example, if we evaluate a model on a test dataset of 1,000 samples, and the model predicted the correct label of the samples 875 times, then this model has an accuracy of $875/1000 = 0.875$, or 87.5%.

Accuracy is the most common way to evaluate a classification model, and we should always use it. However, sometimes accuracy doesn't fully describe the performance of the model, as we'll see shortly. Let's begin by looking at two examples that we'll study throughout this chapter.

Two examples of models: Coronavirus and spam email

In this chapter, we use our metrics to evaluate several models on two datasets. The first dataset is a medical dataset of patients, where some of them have been diagnosed with coronavirus. The second dataset is a dataset of emails that have been labeled as spam or not spam. As we learned in chapter 1, *spam* is the term used for junk email, and *ham* is the term used for email that is not spam. In chapter 8, we'll study a dataset like this in much more detail, when we learn the naive Bayes algorithm. In this chapter, we aren't building models. Instead, we use the models as black boxes and evaluate them based on how many of the data points they predict correctly or incorrectly. Both datasets are completely imaginary.

Medical dataset: A set of patients diagnosed with coronavirus

Our first dataset is a medical dataset with 1,000 patients. Out of them, 10 have been diagnosed with coronavirus, and the remaining 990 have been diagnosed as healthy. Thus, the labels in this dataset are "sick" or "healthy," corresponding to the diagnosis. The goal of a model would be to predict the diagnosis based on the features of each patient.

Email dataset: A set of emails labeled spam or ham

Our second dataset is a dataset of 100 emails. Out of them, 40 are spam, and the remaining 60 are ham. The labels in this dataset are "spam" and "ham," and the goal of a model would be to predict the label based on the features of the email.

A super effective yet super useless model

Accuracy is a very useful metric, but does it paint the whole picture of the model? It doesn't, and we'll illustrate this with an example. For now, let's focus on the coronavirus dataset. We'll come back to the email dataset in the next section.

Suppose a data scientist tells us the following: "I have developed a test for coronavirus that takes 10 seconds to run, doesn't require any examinations, and has an accuracy of 99%!" Should we be excited or skeptical? We'd probably be skeptical. Why? We'll soon see that calculating a model's accuracy sometimes isn't enough. Our model may have an accuracy of 99% and yet be completely useless.

Can we think of a completely useless model that predicts coronavirus in our dataset, yet is correct 99% of the time? Recall that our dataset contains 1,000 patients, and out of those, 10 have coronavirus. Feel free to put this book down for a moment and think of how to build a model that detects coronavirus and that is correct 99% of the time for this dataset.

It could be a model like this: simply diagnose every patient as healthy. That's a simple model, but it's still a model; it's the model that predicts everything as one class.

What is the accuracy of this model? Well, out of 1,000 tries, it's incorrect 10 times and correct 990 times. This gives an accuracy of 99%, just like we promised. However, the model equates to telling everyone that they are healthy in the middle of a global pandemic, which is terrible!

What is the problem with our model, then? The problem is that errors are not created equal, and some mistakes are much more expensive than others, as we'll see in the next section.

How to fix the accuracy problem? Defining different types of errors and how to measure them

In the previous section, we built a useless model that had great accuracy. In this section, we study what went wrong. Namely, we study what the problem was with calculating accuracy in that model, and we introduce some slightly different metrics that will give us better evaluations of this model.

The first thing we need to study is types of errors. In the next section, we see that some errors are more critical than others. Then in the sections "Storing the correctly and incorrectly classified points in a table" to "Recall, precision, or F-scores," we learn different metrics that are more equipped to catch these critical errors than accuracy.

False positives and false negatives: Which one is worse?

In many cases, the total number of errors doesn't tell us everything about the model's performance, and we need to dig in deeper and identify certain types of errors in different ways. In this section, we see two types of errors. What are the two types of errors that the coronavirus model can make? It can diagnose a healthy person as sick or a sick person as healthy. In our model, we label the sick patients as positive, by convention. The two error types are called false positives and negatives, as follows:

- **False positive:** a healthy person who is incorrectly diagnosed as sick
- **False negative:** a sick person who is incorrectly diagnosed as healthy

In the general setting, a false positive is a data point that has a negative label, but the model falsely classifies it as positive. A false negative is a data point that has a positive label, but the model falsely classified it as negative. Naturally, the cases that are correctly diagnosed also have names, as follows:

- **True positive:** a sick person who is diagnosed as sick
- **True negative:** a healthy person who is diagnosed as healthy

In the general setting, a true positive is a data point that has a positive label that is correctly classified as positive, and a true negative is one with a negative label that is correctly classified as negative.

Now, let's look at the email dataset. Let's say we have a model that predicts whether each email is spam or ham. We consider the positives to be the spam emails. Therefore, our two types of errors follow:

- **False positive:** a ham email that is incorrectly classified as spam
- **False negative:** a spam email that is incorrectly classified as ham

And the correctly classified emails are the following:

- **True positive:** a spam email that is correctly classified as spam
- **True negative:** a ham email that is correctly classified as ham

Figure 7.1 shows a graphical representation of the models, in which the vertical line is the boundary, the zone to the left of the line is the negative zone, and the zone to the right is the positive zone. The triangles are the points with positive labels, and the circles are the points with negative labels. The four quantities defined above are the following:

- Triangle to the right of the line: true positive
- Triangle to the left of the line: false negative
- Circle to the right of the line: false positive
- Circle to the left of the line: true negative

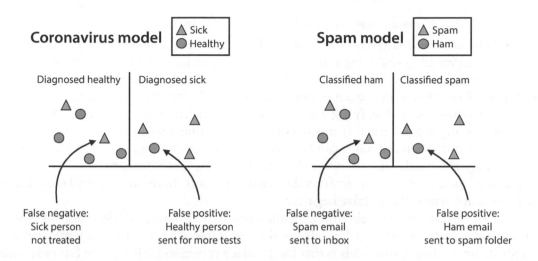

Figure 7.1 Examples of two models that are widely used in real life and that we'll use throughout this chapter. On the left, a coronavirus model where the people are diagnosed as healthy or sick. On the right, a spam-detection model where the emails are classified as spam or ham. For each model, we have highlighted some of their errors and separated them as false positives and false negatives.

Notice that both models in figure 7.1 produce the following quantities:

- Three true positives
- Four true negatives
- One false positive
- Two false negatives

To see the difference between the coronavirus model and the spam model, we need to analyze which one is worse between the false positives and the false negatives. Let's do this for each model separately.

Analyzing false positives and negatives in the coronavirus model

Let's stop and think. In the coronavirus model, which one sounds like a worse mistake: a false positive or a false negative? In other words, what is worse: to incorrectly diagnose a healthy patient as sick, or a sick patient as healthy? Let's say that when we diagnose a patient as healthy, we send them home with no treatment, and that when we diagnose a patient as sick, we send them for more tests. Incorrectly diagnosing a healthy person may be a small nuisance, because it means a healthy person will have to stay for extra tests. However, incorrectly diagnosing a sick person means that a sick person won't get treatment, their condition may worsen, and they may potentially infect many others. Thus, **in the coronavirus model, a false negative is much worse than a false positive.**

Analyzing false positives and negatives in the spam email model

Now we'll do the same analysis on the spam model. In this case, let's say that if our spam classifier classifies an email as spam, then this email is automatically deleted. If it classifies it as ham, then the email is sent to our inbox. Which one sounds like a worse mistake: a false positive or a false negative? In other words, what is worse, to incorrectly classify a ham email as spam and delete it, or to incorrectly classify a spam email as ham and send it to the inbox? I think we can agree that deleting a good email is much worse than sending a spam email to the inbox. The occasional spam email in our inbox can be annoying, but a deleted ham email can be a complete disaster! Imagine the sadness we would feel in our heart if our grandma sent us a very kind email telling us she baked cookies, and our filter deleted it. Therefore, **in the spam email model, a false positive is much worse than a false negative**.

This is where the two models differ. In the coronavirus model, a false negative is worse, whereas in the spam email model, a false positive is worse. The problem with measuring the accuracy in any of these two models is that the accuracy considers both types of errors as equally serious and doesn't tell them apart.

In the section "A super effective yet super useless model," we had an example of a model that diagnosed every patient as healthy. This model made only 10 errors among 1,000 patients. However, all those 10 were false negatives, which is terrible. If those 10 were false positives instead, the model would be much better.

In the following sections, we'll devise two new metrics, similar to accuracy. The first metric helps us deal with models in which false negatives are worse, and the second one helps us deal with models in which false positives are worse.

Storing the correctly and incorrectly classified points in a table: The confusion matrix

In the previous subsection, we learned about false positives, false negatives, true positives, and true negatives. To keep track of these four entities, we put them together in a table aptly named *the confusion matrix*. For binary classification models (models that predict two classes), the confusion matrix has two rows and two columns. In the rows we write the true labels (in the medical example, this is the condition of the person, sick or healthy), and in the columns we write the predicted labels (the diagnosis of the person, sick or healthy). The general confusion matrix is illustrated in table 7.1, and specific ones for examples of models in these two datasets are shown in tables 7.2 to 7.5. This is called a confusion matrix because it makes it easy to see if the model is confusing two classes, namely the positive (sick) and the negative (healthy).

Table 7.1   The confusion matrix helps us count how many times each class is predicted correctly and how many times each class is confused with a different class. In this matrix, the rows represent the label, and the columns represent the prediction. The elements in the diagonal are classified correctly, and the elements off the diagonal are not.

Person's condition	Predicted positive	Predicted negative
Positive	Number of true positives	Number of false negatives
Negative	Number of false positives	Number of true negatives

For our existing model (the one that diagnoses every patient as healthy), which from now on we call coronavirus model 1, the confusion matrix is illustrated in table 7.2.

Table 7.2   The confusion matrix of our coronavirus model helps us dig into our model and tell the two types of errors apart. This model makes 10 false negative errors (a sick person diagnosed healthy) and zero false positive errors (a healthy person diagnosed sick). Notice that the model creates too many false negatives, which are the worst type of error in this case, which implies that this model is not very good.

Coronavirus model 1	Diagnosed sick (predicted positive)	Diagnosed healthy (predicted negative)
Sick (positive)	0 (number of true positives)	10 (number of false negatives)
Healthy (negative)	0 (number of false positives)	990 (number of true negatives)

For problems with more classes, we have a larger confusion matrix. For example, if our model classifies images into aardvarks, birds, cats, and dogs, then our confusion matrix is a four-by-four matrix, where along the rows we have the true labels (the type of animal), and along the columns we have the predicted labels (the type of animal that the model predicted). This confusion matrix also has the property that the correctly classified points are counted in the diagonal, and the incorrectly classified are counted off the diagonal.

Recall: Among the positive examples, how many did we correctly classify?

Now that we know the two types of errors, in this section, we learn a metric that will give coronavirus model 1 a much lower score. We have established that the problem with this model is that it gives us too many false negatives, namely, that it diagnoses too many sick people as healthy.

Let's assume, for a moment, that we don't mind false positives at all. Say that if the model diagnoses a healthy person as sick, the person may need to take an extra test or quarantine for a little longer, but this is no problem at all. Naturally, this is not the case; false positives are also expensive, but for now, let's pretend that they're not. In this case, we need a metric that replaces accuracy and that places importance on finding positive cases and cares less about mistakenly classifying negative cases.

To find this metric, we need to evaluate what our goal is. If we want to cure coronavirus, then what we really want is the following: out of all the sick people in the world, we want to find them all. It doesn't matter if we accidentally find others who aren't sick, as long as we find all the sick ones. This is the key. This new metric, called *recall*, measures precisely that: out of the sick people, how many did our model diagnose correctly?

In more general lingo, recall finds the proportion of correct predictions among the data points with a positive label. This is the number of true positives, divided by the total number of positives. Coronavirus model 1 has a total of 0 true positives among 10 positives, so its recall is 0/10 = 0. Another way to put it is as the number of true positives divided by the sum of true positives and false negatives, as shown here:

$$Recall = \frac{True\ positives}{True\ positives + False\ negatives}$$

In contrast, let's say we had a second model called coronavirus model 2. The confusion matrix of this model is shown in table 7.3. This second model made more mistakes than the first model—it made 50 total mistakes as opposed to only 10. The accuracy of the second model is 950/1000 = 0.95, or 95%. In terms of accuracy, the second model is not as good as the first model.

However, the second model correctly diagnosed eight out of the 10 sick people and 942 out of the 1,000 people. In other words, it has two false negatives and 48 false positives.

Table 7.3   The confusion matrix of our second coronavirus model

Coronavirus model 2	Diagnosed sick	Diagnosed healthy
Sick	8 (true positives)	2 (false negatives)
Healthy	48 (false positives)	942 (true negatives)

The recall of this model is the number of true positives (eight sick people correctly diagnosed) divided by the total number of positives (10 sick people), which is 8/10 = 0.8, or 80%. In terms of recall, the second model is much better. Let's summarize these calculations for clarity as follows:

Coronavirus Model 1:

True positives (sick patients diagnosed sick and sent for more tests) = 0

False negatives (sick patients diagnosed healthy and sent home) = 10

Recall = 0/10 = 0%

Coronavirus Model 2:

True positives (sick patients diagnosed sick and sent for more tests) = 8

False negatives (sick patients diagnosed healthy and sent home) = 2

Recall = 8/10 = 80%

Models like the coronavirus model, in which false negatives are much more expensive than false positives, are *high recall models.*

Now that we have a better metric, could we fool this metric in the same way we fooled accuracy? In other words, can we build a model that has total recall? Well, get ready for a surprise, because we can. If we build a model that diagnoses every patient as sick, this model has a 100% recall. However, this model is terrible, too, because although it has zero false negatives, it has too many false positives to make it a good model. It seems that we still need more metrics to be able to evaluate our models properly.

Precision: Among the examples we classified as positive, how many did we correctly classify?

In the previous section we learned recall, a metric that measures how well our model did with false negatives. That metric worked well for the coronavirus model—we've seen that this model can't afford to have too many false negatives. In this section, we learn about a similar metric, *precision*, which measures how well our model does with false positives. We'll use this metric to evaluate the spam email model, because this model can't afford to have too many false positives.

Just as we did with recall, to come up with a metric, we first need to define our goal. We want a spam filter that doesn't delete any ham emails. If instead of deleting emails, it sends them to a spam box. Then we need to look into that spam box and hope that we do not see a single ham email. Thus, our metric should measure precisely that: Among the emails in our spam box, how many were actually spam? In other words, out of the emails that are predicted to be spam, how many of them are actually spam? This is our metric, and we call it *precision*.

More formally, precision considers only the data points that have been labeled positive, and among those, how many are true positives. Because the data points that are predicted positive are the union of the true positives and the false positives, the formula is the following:

$$Precision = \frac{True\ positives}{True\ positives + False\ positives}$$

Remember that in our dataset of 100 emails, 40 are spam and 60 are ham. Say we trained the following two models called spam model 1 and spam model 2. Their confusion matrices are shown in tables 7.4 and 7.5.

Table 7.4   The confusion matrix of our first spam model

Spam model 1	Predicted spam	Predicted ham
Spam	30 (true positives)	10 (false negatives)
Ham	5 (false positives)	55 (true negatives)

Table 7.5   The confusion matrix of our second spam model

Spam model 2	Predicted spam	Predicted ham
Spam	35 (true positives)	5 (false negatives)
Ham	10 (false positives)	50 (true negatives)

In terms of accuracy, it seems that both models are just as good—they both make correct predictions 85% of the time (85 correct out of 100 emails). However, at first glance, it seems that the first model is better than the second one, because the first model deletes only five ham emails, and the second one deletes 10 of them. Now let's calculate the precision as follows:

Spam Model 1:

- True positives (spam emails deleted) = 30

- False positives (ham emails deleted) = 5

- Precision = 30/35 = 85.7%

Spam Model 2:

- True positives (spam emails deleted) = 35

- False positives (ham emails deleted) = 10

- Precision = 35/45 = 77.7%

Just as we thought: precision gave a higher score to the first model than to the second model. We conclude that models like the spam model, in which false positives are much more expensive than false negatives, are *high precision models*. And why is the first model better than the second one? The second model deleted 10 good (ham) emails, but the first model deleted only five of them. The second model may have cleaned up more spam than the first one, but that doesn't make up for the five ham emails it deleted.

Now, in the same way we tricked accuracy and recall, we can also trick precision. Consider the following spam filter: a spam filter that never detects any spam. What is the precision of this model? This is complicated, because there are zero spam emails deleted (zero true positives) and zero ham emails deleted (zero false positives). We won't attempt to divide zero over zero, because this book would burst into flames, but by convention, a model that makes no false positive mistakes has a precision of 100%. But, of course, a spam filter that does nothing is not a good spam filter.

This goes to show that no matter how good our metrics are, they can always be fooled. That doesn't mean they don't work. Accuracy, precision, and recall are useful tools in a data scientist's toolbox. It is up to us to decide which ones are good for our model, by deciding what errors are more expensive than others. Always be careful to not fall into the trap of thinking that a model is good before evaluating it with different metrics.

Combining recall and precision as a way to optimize both: The F-score

In this section, we discuss the F-score, a metric that combines both recall and precision. In the previous sections, we saw two examples, the coronavirus model and the spam model, in which either false negatives or false positives were more important. However, in real life, both are important, even if they are important to different degrees. For example, we may want a model that doesn't misdiagnose any sick person but that also doesn't misdiagnose too many healthy people, because misdiagnosing a healthy person may involve unnecessary and painful testing, or even an unnecessary surgery, which could affect their health negatively. In the same way, we may want a model that doesn't delete any of our good emails. But to be a good spam filter, it still needs to catch a lot of spam; otherwise, it's useless. The F-score has a parameter β accompanying it, so the more common term is F_β-score. When $\beta = 1$, it is called the F_1-score.

Calculating the F-score

Our goal is to find a metric that gives us some number between the recall and the precision. The first thing that comes to mind is the average between recall and precision. Would this work? It would, but it's not the one we pick, for one fundamental reason. A good model is one that has good recall and good precision. If a model has, say, recall of 50% and precision of 100%, the average is 75%. This is a good score, but the model may not be, because a recall of 50% is not very good. We need a metric that behaves like the average but that is closer to the minimum value of the two.

A quantity that is like the average of two numbers is called the *harmonic mean*. Whereas the average of two numbers a and b is $(a + b)/2$, their harmonic mean is $2ab/(a + b)$. The harmonic mean has this property: it is always smaller than or equal to the average. If the numbers a and b are equal, one can quickly check that their harmonic mean is equal to both of them, just like the average. But in other cases, the harmonic mean is smaller. Let's look at an example: If $a = 1$ and $b = 9$, their average is 5. The harmonic mean is $\dfrac{2 \cdot 1 \cdot 9}{1+9} = 1.8$.

The F_1-score is defined as the harmonic mean between the precision and the recall, as follows:

$$F_1 = \frac{2PR}{P+R}$$

If both numbers are high, the F_1-score is high. However, if one of them is low, the F_1-score will be low. The purpose of the F_1-score is to measure if both recall and precision are high and to ring a bell when one of these two scores is low.

Calculating the F_β-score

In the previous subsection, we learned about the F_1-score, a score that combines recall and precision, for the purpose of evaluating a model. However, sometimes we want more recall than precision, or vice versa. Thus, when we combine the two scores, we may want to give one of them more weight. This means that sometimes we may want a model that cares both about false positives and false negatives but assigns more weight to one of them. For example, the coronavirus model cares much more about false negatives, because people's lives may depend on a correct identification of the virus, but it still doesn't want to create too many false positives, because we may not want to spend excessive resources retesting healthy people. The spam model cares much more about false positives, because we really wouldn't want to delete good emails but still doesn't want to create too many false negatives, because we wouldn't want our inbox cluttered with spam messages.

This is where F_β-score comes into play. The formula for the F_β-score may look complicated at first, but once we look at it carefully, it does exactly what we want. The F_β-score uses a parameter called β (the Greek letter *beta*), which can take any positive value. The point of β is to act as a dial that we turn to emphasize precision or recall. More specifically, if we slide the β dial to zero, we get full precision; if we slide it to infinity, we get full recall. In general, the lower the value of β, the more we emphasize precision, and the higher the value of β, the more we emphasize recall. The F_β-score is defined as follows (where precision is P and recall is R):

$$F_\beta = \frac{(1+\beta^2)PR}{\beta^2 P + R}$$

Let's analyze this formula carefully by looking at some values for β.

Case 1: $\beta = 1$

When β is equal to 1, the F_β-score becomes the following:

$$F_1 = \frac{(1+1^2)PR}{1^2 P + R}$$

This is the same as the F_1-score that considers recall and precision equally.

Case 2: $\beta = 10$

When β is equal to 10, the F_β-score becomes the following:

$$F_{10} = \frac{(1+10^2)PR}{10^2 P + R}$$

This can be written as

$$\frac{101PR}{100P + R}.$$

This is similar to the F_1-score, except notice how it gives much more importance to R than to P. To see this, notice that the limit as β tends to ∞ of the F_β-score is R. Therefore, when we want a score between recall and precision that gives more weight to recall, we pick a value of β that is larger than 1. The larger the value, the more emphasis we put on the recall and less on the precision.

Case 3: $\beta = 0.1$

When β is equal to 0.1, the F_β-score becomes the following:

$$F_{0.1} = \frac{(1+0.1^2)PR}{0.1^2 P + R}$$

Just like before, we can write this as

$$\frac{1.01PR}{0.01P + R}.$$

This is similar to the formula from case 2, except this one gives P a lot more importance. Therefore, when we want a score between recall and precision that gives more weight to precision, we pick a value of β that is smaller than 1. The smaller the value, the more emphasis we put on the precision and less on the recall. In the limits, we say that a value of $\beta = 0$ gives us the precision, and a value of $\beta = \infty$ gives us the recall.

Recall, precision, or F-scores: Which one should we use?

Now, how do we put recall and precision into practice? When we have a model, is it a high recall or a high precision model? Do we use the F-score? If so, which value of β should we pick? The answers to these questions are up to us, the data scientists. It is important for us to know the problem we are trying to solve very well to decide which error, between a false positive and a false negative, is more expensive.

In the previous two examples, we can see that because the coronavirus model needs to focus more on recall than on precision, we should pick a large value of β, say, for example, 2. In contrast, the spam model needs to focus more on precision than on recall, so we should pick a small value of β, say, 0.5. For more practice analyzing models and estimating what values of β to use, see exercise 7.4 at the end of the chapter.

A useful tool to evaluate our model: The receiver operating characteristic (ROC) curve

In the section "How to fix the accuracy problem?," we learned how to evaluate a model using metrics such as precision, recall, and the F-score. We also learned that one of the main challenges of evaluating a model lies in the fact that more than one type of error exists and different types of errors have different levels of importance. We learned two types of errors: false positives and false negatives. In some models, false negatives are much more expensive than false positives, and in some models, it's the opposite.

In this section, I teach you a useful technique to evaluate a model based on its performance on false positives and negatives at the same time. Furthermore, this method has an important feature: a dial that allows us to gradually switch between a model that performs well on false positives and one that performs well on false negatives. This technique is based on a curve called the *receiver operating characteristic (ROC) curve*.

Before we learn the ROC curve, we need to introduce two new metrics called specificity and sensitivity. Actually, only one of them is new. The other one, we've seen before.

Sensitivity and specificity: Two new ways to evaluate our model

In the section "How to fix the accuracy problem?," we defined recall and precision as our metrics and found that they were useful tools to measure our model both for false negatives and for false positives. However, in this section, we use two different, yet very similar, metrics: *sensitivity* and *specificity*. These have a similar use to the previous ones, but they are more useful for us when we have to build the ROC curve. Furthermore, although precision and recall are more widely used by data scientists, sensitivity and specificity are more common in the medical field. Sensitivity and specificity are defined as follows:

Sensitivity (true positive rate): the capacity of the test to identify the positively labeled points. This is the ratio between the number of true positives and the total number of positives. (Note: this is the same as recall).

$$Sensitivity = \frac{True\ positives}{True\ positives + False\ negatives}$$

Specificity (true negative rate): the capacity of the test to identify the negatively labeled points. This is the ratio between the number of true negatives and the total number of negatives.

$$Specificity = \frac{True\ negatives}{True\ negatives + False\ positives}$$

As I mentioned, sensitivity is the same as recall. However, specificity is not the same as precision (each nomenclature is popular in different disciplines, and for that reason, we use them both here). We see this more in detail in the section "Recall is sensitivity, but precision and specificity are different."

In the coronavirus model, the sensitivity is the proportion of sick people that the model has correctly diagnosed, among all the sick people. The specificity is the proportion of healthy people the model has correctly diagnosed, among the healthy people. We are more concerned about correctly diagnosing sick people, so we need the coronavirus model to have *high sensitivity.*

In the spam-detection model, the sensitivity is the proportion of spam messages we correctly deleted, among all the spam messages. The specificity is the proportion of ham emails we correctly sent to the inbox, among all the ham emails. Because we are more concerned about correctly detecting the ham emails, we need the spam detection model to have *high specificity.*

To clarify the previous concepts, let's look at them in the graphical example we are working on. Namely, let's calculate the specificity and sensitivity for our two models in figure 7.2 (which is the same as figure 7.1).

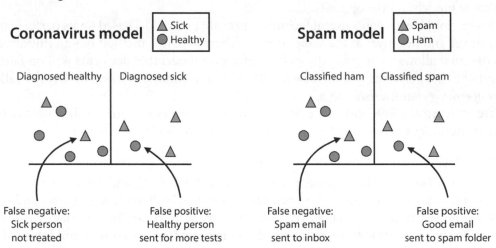

Figure 7.2   On the left, a coronavirus model where the people are diagnosed as healthy or sick; on the right, a spam detection model where the emails are classified as spam or ham

As we saw previously, these two models produce the following quantities:

- Three true positives
- Four true negatives
- One false positive
- Two false negatives

Now let's calculate the specificity and sensitivity of these models.

Calculating the sensitivity

In this case, we calculate sensitivity as follows: among the positive points, how many did the model classify correctly? This is equivalent to asking: among the triangles, how many are located to the right of the line? There are five triangles, and the model classified three of them correctly to the right of the line, so the sensitivity is 3/5, which equals 0.6, or 60%.

Calculating the specificity

We calculate specificity as follows: among the negative points, how many did the model classify correctly? This is equivalent to asking: among the circles, how many are located to the left of the line? There are five circles, and the model classified four of them correctly to the left of the line, so the specificity is 4/5, which equals 0.8, or 80%.

The receiver operating characteristic (ROC) curve: A way to optimize sensitivity and specificity in a model

In this section, we see how to draw the receiver operating characteristic (ROC) curve, which will give us a lot of information about the model. In short, what we'll do is slowly modify the model and record the sensitivity and specificity of the model at each time step.

The first and only assumption we need to make about our model is that it returns the prediction as a continuous value, namely, as a probability. This is true about models such as logistic classifiers, where the prediction is not a class, such as positive/negative, but a value between 0 and 1, such as 0.7. What we normally do with this value is pick a threshold, such as 0.5, and classify every point that receives a prediction higher than or equal to the threshold as positive and every other point as negative. However, this threshold can be any value—it need not be 0.5. Our procedure consists in varying this threshold from 0 all the way to 1 and recording the sensitivity and specificity of the model at each threshold value.

Let's look at an example. We calculate the sensitivity and specificity for three different thresholds: 0.2, 0.5, and 0.8. In figure 7.3, we can see how many points are to the left and right of the line for each one of these thresholds. Let's study them in detail. Remember that sensitivity is the ratio of true positives over all positives, and specificity is the ratio of true negatives over all negatives. Also remember that for each one of these, there are five total positives and five total negatives.

Threshold = 0.2

Number of true positives: 4

Sensitivity: $\frac{4}{5}$

Number of true negatives: 3

Specificity: $\frac{3}{5}$

Threshold = 0.5

Number of true positives: 3

Sensitivity: $\frac{3}{5}$

Number of true negatives: 4

Specificity: $\frac{4}{5}$

Threshold = 0.2

Number of true positives: 2

Sensitivity: $\frac{2}{5}$

Number of true negatives: 5

Specificity: $\frac{5}{5} = 1$

Note that a low threshold leads to many positive predictions. Therefore, we will have few false negatives, implying a high sensitivity score, and many false positives, implying a low specificity score. Similarly, a high threshold implies a low sensitivity score and a high specificity score. As we move the threshold from low to high, the sensitivity decreases, and the specificity increases. This is an important point that we'll touch on later in this chapter, when we get to the point of deciding the best threshold for our model.

Now we are ready to build the ROC curve. First, we consider a threshold of 0 and slowly increase the value of this threshold by small intervals, until it reaches 1. For every increment in threshold, we pass over exactly one point. The values of the thresholds are not important—what is important is that at every step, we pass over exactly one point (this is possible because all the points give us different scores, but it's not a requirement in general). Thus, we'll refer to the steps as 0, 1, 2,..., 10. In your head, you should imagine the vertical line in figure 7.3 starting at 0 and moving slowly from left to right, sweeping one point at a time, until reaching 1. These steps are recorded in table 7.6, together with the number of true positives and negatives, sensitivity, and specificity at each step.

One thing to notice is that in the first step (step 0), the line is at threshold 0. This means every point is classified as positive by the model. All the positive points are also classified as positive, so every positive is a true positive. This means that at timestep 0, the sensitivity is $\frac{5}{5} = 1$. But because every negative point is classified as positive, there are no true negatives, so the specificity is $\frac{0}{5} = 0$. Similarly, at the last step (step 10), the threshold is 1, and we can check that because every point is classified as negative, the sensitivity is now 0 and the specificity is 1. For clarity, the three models in figure 7.3 are highlighted in table 7.6 as timesteps 4, 6, and 8, respectively.

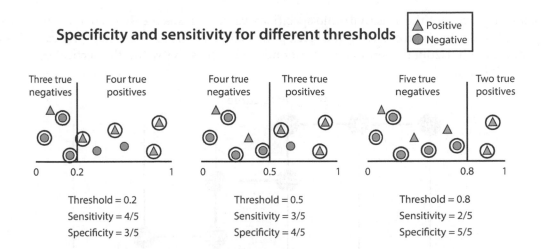

Figure 7.3 The effects of moving the threshold on the sensitivity and the specificity. On the left, we have a model with a low threshold; in the middle, we have one with a medium threshold; and on the right, we have one with a high threshold. For each of the models, there are five positive and five negative points. Each model is represented by the vertical line. The model predicts that the points to the right of the line are positive and those to the left are negative. For each of the models, we've counted the number of true positives and true negatives, that is, the number of positive and negative points that have been correctly predicted. We have used those to calculate the sensitivity and the specificity. Note that as we increase the threshold (i.e., as we move the vertical line from left to right), the sensitivity goes down and the specificity goes up.

Table 7.6   All the timesteps in the process of increasing our threshold, which is an important step in building our ROC curve. At each timestep, we record the number of true positives and true negatives. We then calculate the specificity of the model by dividing the number of true positives by the total number of positives. As a final step, we calculate the specificity by dividing the number of true negatives by the total number of negatives.

Step	True positives	Sensitivity	True negatives	Specificity
0	5	1	0	0
1	**5**	**1**	**1**	**0.2**
2	4	0.8	1	0.2
3	4	0.8	2	0.4
4	**4**	**0.8**	**3**	**0.6**
5	3	0.6	3	0.6
6	**3**	**0.6**	**4**	**0.8**
7	2	0.4	4	0.8
8	**2**	**0.4**	**5**	**1**
9	1	0.2	5	1
10	0	0	5	1

As a last step, we plot the sensitivity and specificity values. This is the ROC curve, which we see in figure 7.4. In this figure, each of the black points corresponds to a timestep (indicated inside the point), the horizontal coordinate corresponds to the sensitivity, and the vertical coordinate to the specificity.

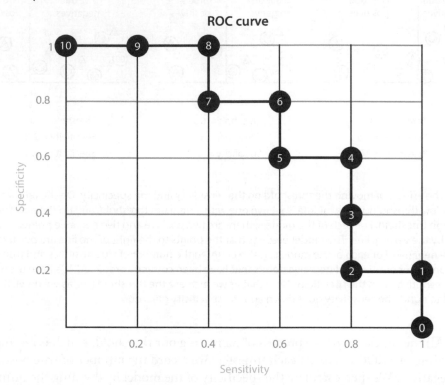

Figure 7.4   Here we can see the ROC curve corresponding to our ongoing example, which gives us a great deal of information on our model. The highlighted dots correspond to the timesteps obtained by moving our threshold from 0 to 1, and each dot is labeled by the timestep. On the horizontal axis we record the sensitivity of the model at each timestep, and on the vertical axis we record the specificity.

A metric that tells us how good our model is: The AUC (area under the curve)

As we've seen before in this book, evaluating a machine learning model is a highly important task, and in this section, we discuss how to use the ROC curve to evaluate a model. For this, we've done all the work already—all that is left is to calculate the area under the curve, or AUC. At the top of figure 7.5, we can see three models, in which the prediction is given by the horizontal axis (from 0 to 1). On the bottom, you can see the three corresponding ROC curves. Each one of the squares has size 0.2 times 0.2. The number of squares under each curve are 13, 18, and 25, which amounts to areas under the curve of 0.52, 0.72, and 1.

Note that the best a model can do is an AUC of 1, which corresponds to the model on the right. The worst a model can do is an AUC of 0.5, because this means the model is as good as random guessing. This corresponds to the model on the left. The model in the middle is our original model, with an AUC of 0.72.

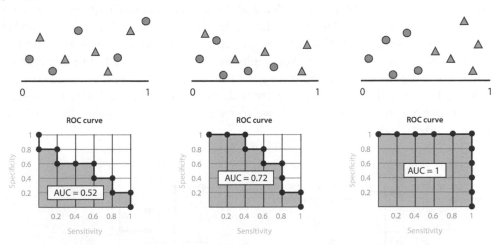

Figure 7.5   In this figure, we can see that AUC, or area under the curve, is a good metric to determine how good a model is. The higher the AUC, the better the model. On the left, we have a bad model with an AUC of 0.52. In the middle, we have a good model with an AUC of 0.72. On the right, we have a great model with an AUC of 1.

What about a model with an AUC of zero? Well, this is tricky. A model with an AUC of zero would correspond to a model that classifies every point wrong. Is this a bad model? It's actually a very good model, because all we have to do to fix it is to flip all the positive and negative predictions and get a perfect model. It's the same effect as having a person that lies every single time they get a true-or-false question. All we have to do to get them to tell the truth is to flip all their answers. This means the worst we can have in a binary classification model is an AUC of 0.5, because this corresponds to a person who lies 50% of the time. They give us no information because we never know if they are telling the truth or lying! Incidentally, if we have a model with an AUC less than 0.5, we can flip the positive and negative predictions and obtain a model with an AUC larger than 0.5.

How to make decisions using the ROC curve

The ROC is a powerful graphic that gives us a lot of information about our model. In this section, we learn how we can use it to improve our model. In short, we use the ROC to tweak the threshold in a model and apply it to pick the best model for our use case.

At the beginning of this chapter, we introduced two models, the coronavirus model and the spam-detection model. These models were very different because, as we saw, the coronavirus model requires high sensitivity, whereas the spam-detection model requires high specificity. Every model requires some amount of sensitivity and specificity based on the problem we are to solve. Let's say we are in the following situation: we are training a model that is supposed to have high sensitivity, and we get a model with low sensitivity and high specificity. Is there any way we can trade off some specificity and gain some sensitivity?

The answer is yes! We can trade off specificity and sensitivity by moving the threshold. Recall that when we first defined the ROC curve, we noticed that the lower the threshold, the higher sensitivity and lower specificity in the model, and the higher the threshold, the lower sensitivity and higher specificity in the model. When the vertical line corresponding to the threshold is at the very left, every point is predicted to be positive, so all the positives are true positives, whereas when the vertical line is at the very right, every point is predicted to be negative, so all the negatives are true negatives. As we move the line to the right, we lose some true positives and gain some true negatives, thus the sensitivity decreases and the specificity increases. Notice that as the threshold moves from 0 to 1, we move up and to the left in the ROC curve, as figure 7.6 illustrates.

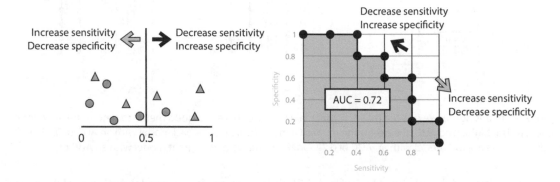

Figure 7.6   The threshold of the model has a lot to do with the sensitivity and the specificity, and this relationship will help us pick the perfect threshold for our model. On the left, we have our model and, on the right, the corresponding ROC curve. As we increase or decrease the threshold, we change the sensitivity and specificity of the model, and this change is illustrated by moving in the ROC curve.

Why does this happen? The threshold tells us where we draw the line on classifying a point. For example, in the coronavirus model, the threshold tells us where we draw the line on a person being sent for more tests or sent home. A model with a low threshold is a model that sends people for extra tests if they so much as show mild symptoms. A model with a high threshold is one that needs the people to show strong symptoms to send them for more tests. Because we want to catch all the sick people, we want a low threshold for this model, which means we want a model with high sensitivity. For clarity, in figure 7.7, we can see the three thresholds used previously, as well as the points where they correspond in the curve.

If we want our model to have high sensitivity, we just push the threshold to the left (i.e., decrease it) until we get to a point in the curve that has as much sensitivity as we want. Note that the model may lose some specificity, and that's the price we pay. In contrast, if we want higher specificity, we push the threshold to the right (i.e., increase it) until we get to a point in the curve that has as much specificity as we want. Again, we lose some sensitivity during this process. The curve tells us exactly how much of one we gain and lose, so as data scientists, this is a great tool to help us decide the best threshold for our model. In figure 7.8, we can see a more general example with a bigger dataset.

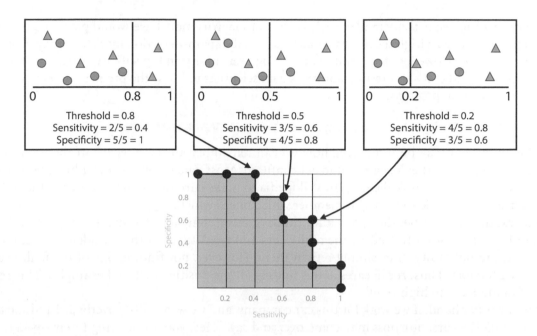

Figure 7.7   The parallel between the threshold of the model and its ROC. The model on the left has a high threshold, low sensitivity, and high specificity. The model in the middle has medium values for threshold, sensitivity, and specificity. The model on the right has a low threshold, high sensitivity, and low specificity.

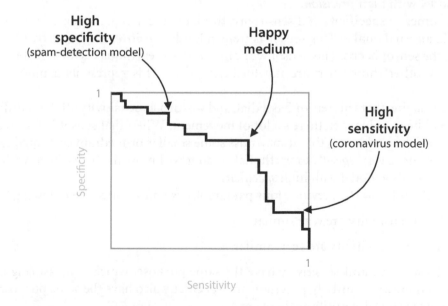

Figure 7.8   In this more general scenario, we can see an ROC curve and three points on it corresponding to three different thresholds. If we want to pick a threshold that gives us high specificity, we pick the one on the left. For a model with high sensitivity, we pick the one on the right. If we want a model that has a good amount of both sensitivity and specificity, we pick the one in the middle.

If we need a high sensitivity model, such as the coronavirus model, we would pick the point on the right. If we need a high specificity model, such as the spam-detection model, we may pick the point on the left. However, if we want relatively high sensitivity and specificity, we may go for the point in the middle. It's our responsibility as data scientists to know the problem well enough to make this decision properly.

Recall is sensitivity, but precision and specificity are different

At this point you may be wondering how we can remember all these terms off the top of our head. The answer is, they're hard not to get confused. Most data scientists (including the author) often need to quickly look them up in Wikipedia to make sure they're not confusing them. We could use a mnemonic to help us remember which one is which.

For example, when we think of recall, think of a car company that made a car with a fatal design flaw. They need to find all the faulty cars and *recall* them. If they accidentally get more cars that are not faulty, they simply return them. However, not finding one of the faulty cars would be terrible. Thus, recall cares about finding all the positively labeled examples. This represents a model with high *recall*.

On the other hand, if we work for this car company, and we went a little overboard and started recalling *all* the cars, our boss may come over and say, "Hey, you are sending too many cars to fix, and we are running out of resources. Can you please be more selective and send me *precisely* those that are faulty?" Then we need to add precision to the model and try to find only the ones that are faulty, even if we accidentally miss some of the faulty ones (hopefully not!). This represents a model with high *precision*.

When it comes to specificity and sensitivity, think of an earthquake sensor that beeps every time there is an earthquake. This sensor is tremendously *sensitive*. If a butterfly sneezes in the next house, the sensor beeps. This sensor will capture all the earthquakes for sure, but it will also capture many other things that are not an earthquake. This represents a model with high *sensitivity*.

Now, let's imagine that this sensor has a dial, and we turn its sensitivity all the way down. Now the sensor will beep only when there's a lot of movement. When that sensor beeps, we *know* it's an earthquake. The problem is that it may miss some smaller or medium earthquakes. In other words, this sensor is very *specific* to earthquakes, so it will most likely not beep with anything else. This represents a model with high *specificity*.

If we go back and read the previous four paragraphs, we may notice the following two things:

- Recall and sensitivity are very similar.

- Precision and specificity are very similar.

At the very least, recall and sensitivity have the same purpose, which is measuring how many false negatives there are. Similarly, precision and specificity also have the same purpose, which is measuring how many false positives there are.

It turns out that recall and sensitivity are *exactly* the same thing. However, precision and specificity are not the same thing. Although they don't measure the same, they both punish models with a high number of false positives. How to remember all these metrics? A graphical heuristic can help us remember recall, precision, sensitivity, and specificity. In figure 7.9, we see a confusion matrix with the four quantities: true positives, true negatives, false positives, and false negatives. If we focus on the top row (the positively labeled examples), we can calculate recall by dividing the number in the left column by the sum of the numbers in both columns. If we focus on the leftmost column (the examples that are predicted as positive), we can calculate precision by dividing the number on the top row by the sum of the numbers in both rows. If we focus on the bottom row (the negatively labeled examples), we can calculate specificity by dividing the number on the right column by the sum of the numbers on both columns. In other words

- Recall and sensitivity correspond to the top row.

- Precision corresponds to the left column.

- Specificity corresponds to the bottom row.

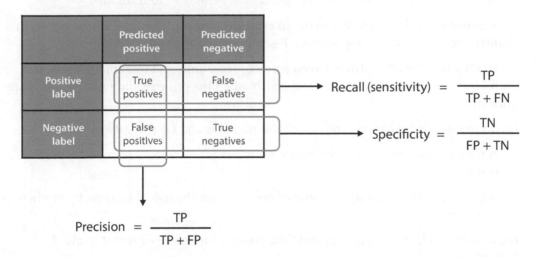

Figure 7.9 The top row of the confusion matrix gives us recall and sensitivity: the ratio between the number of true positives and the sum of true positives and false negatives. The leftmost column gives us precision: the ratio between the number of true positives and the sum of true positives and false positives. The bottom row gives us specificity: the ratio between the number of false positives and the sum of false positives and true negatives.

To wrap up, these quantities are the following in both of our models:

Medical model:

- **Recall and sensitivity:** among the sick people (positives), how many were correctly diagnosed as sick?

- **Precision:** among the people diagnosed as sick, how many were actually sick?

- **Specificity:** among the healthy people (negatives), how many were correctly diagnosed as healthy?

Email model:

- **Recall and sensitivity:** among the spam emails (positives), how many were correctly deleted?

- **Precision:** among the deleted emails, how many were actually spam?

- **Specificity:** among the ham emails (negatives), how many were correctly sent to the inbox?

Summary

- Being able to evaluate a model is as important as being able to train one.

- We can use several important metrics to evaluate a model. The ones we learned in this chapter are accuracy, recall, precision, F-score, specificity, and sensitivity.

- Accuracy calculates the ratio between correct predictions and total predictions. It is useful but can fail in certain cases, especially when the positive and negative labels are unbalanced.

- Errors are divided into two categories: false positives and false negatives.

  - A false positive is a negatively labeled point, which the model incorrectly predicts as positive.

  - A false negative is a positively labeled point, which the model incorrectly predicts as negative.

- For some models, false negatives and false positives are given different levels of importance.

- Recall and precision are useful metrics to evaluate models, especially when the models give false negatives and false positives different levels of importance.

  - Recall measures how many of the positive points were correctly predicted by the model. Recall is low when the model creates many false negatives. For this reason, recall is a useful metric in models in which we don't want many false negatives, such as models for medical diagnosis.

  - Precision measures how many of the points that the model predicted as positive are actually positive. Precision is low when the model creates many false positives. For this reason, precision is a useful metric in models in which we don't want many false positives, such as spam email models.

- F_1-score is a useful metric that combines recall and precision. It returns a value in between recall and precision but which is closer to the smaller of the two.

- F_β-score is a variation of F_1-score, in which one can adjust the parameter β to give either precision or recall a higher importance. Higher values of β give recall more importance, and lower values of β give precision more importance. F_β-score is particularly useful to evaluate models in which either precision or recall is more important than the other one, but we still care about both metrics.

- Sensitivity and specificity are two useful metrics that help us evaluate models. They are highly used in medical fields.

  - Sensitivity, or true positive ratio, measures how many of the positive points were correctly predicted by the model. Sensitivity is low when the model creates many false negatives. For this reason, sensitivity is a useful metric to use in medical models where we don't want to accidentally leave many healthy patients without treatment.

  - Specificity, or true negative ratio, measures how many of the negative points were correctly predicted by the model. Specificity is low when the model creates many false positives. For this reason, specificity is a useful metric in medical models where we don't want to accidentally treat or do further invasive tests on patients who are healthy.

- Recall and sensitivity are the exact same thing. However, precision and specificity are not the same thing. Precision makes sure that most of the predicted positives are truly positive, and specificity checks that most of the true negatives have been detected.

- As we increase the threshold in a model, we decrease its sensitivity and increase its specificity.

- The ROC, or receiver operating characteristic curve, is a useful graph that helps us keep track of the sensitivity and specificity of the model for each different value of the threshold.

- The ROC also helps us determine how good a model is, using the area under the curve, or AUC. The closer the AUC is to 1, the better the model. The closer the AUC is to 0.5, the worse the model.

- By looking at the ROC curve, we can make decisions on what threshold to use to give us good values for both the sensitivity and the specificity, depending on how much of each our model expects. This makes the ROC curve one of the most popular and useful ways to evaluate and improve a model.

Exercises

Exercise 7.1

A video site has established that a particular user likes animal videos and absolutely nothing else. In the next figure, we can see the recommendations that this user got when logging in to the site.

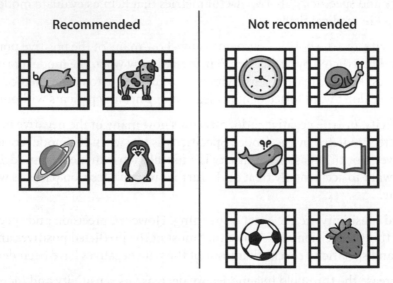

If this is all the data we have on the model, answer the following questions:

a. What is the accuracy of the model?

b. What is the recall of the model?

c. What is the precision of the model?

d. What is the F_1-score of the model?

e. Would you say that this is a good recommendation model?

Exercise 7.2

Find the sensitivity and specificity of the medical model with the following confusion matrix:

	Predicted sick	Predicted healthy
Sick	120	22
Healthy	63	795

Exercise 7.3

For the following models, determine which error is worse, a false positive or a false negative. Based on that, determine which of the two metrics, precision or recall, we should emphasize on when evaluating each of the models.

1. A movie-recommendation system that predicts whether a user will watch a movie

2. An image-detection model used in self-driving cars that detects whether an image contains a pedestrian

3. A voice assistant at home that predicts whether the user gave it an order

Exercise 7.4

We are given the following models:

1. A self-driving car model for detecting a pedestrian based on the image from the car's camera

2. A medical model for diagnosing a deadly illness based on the patient's symptoms

3. A recommendation system for movies based on the user's previous movies watched

4. A voice assistant that determines whether the user needs assistance given the voice command

5. A spam-detection model that determines whether an email is spam based on the words in the email

We are given the task of evaluating these models using F_β-scores. However, we haven't been given the values of β to use. What value of β would you use to evaluate each of the models?

Using probability to its maximum: The naive Bayes model | 8

In this chapter

- what is Bayes theorem

- dependent and independent events

- the prior and posterior probabilities

- calculating conditional probabilities based on events

- using the naive Bayes model to predict whether an email is spam or ham, based on the words in the email

- coding the naive Bayes algorithm in Python

Naive Bayes is an important machine learning model used for classification. The naive Bayes model is a purely probabilistic model, which means the prediction is a number between 0 and 1, indicating the probability that a label is positive. The main component of the naive Bayes model is Bayes' theorem.

Bayes' theorem plays a fundamental role in probability and statistics, because it helps calculate probabilities. It is based on the premise that the more information we gather about an event, the better estimate of the probability we can make. For example, let's say we want to find the probability that it will snow today. If we have no information of where we are and what time of the year it is, we can only come up with a vague estimate. However, if we are given information, we can make a better estimate of the probability. Imagine that I tell you that I am thinking of a type of animal, and I would like you to guess it. What is the probability that the animal I'm thinking of is a dog? Given that you don't know any information, the probability is quite small. However, if I tell you that the animal I'm thinking of is a house pet, the probability increases quite a bit. However, if I now tell you that the animal I'm thinking of has wings, the probability is now zero. Each time I tell you a new piece of information, your estimate for the probability that it's a dog becomes more and more accurate. Bayes' theorem is a way to formalize this type of logic and put it into formulas.

More specifically, Bayes' theorem answers the question, "What is the probability of Y given that X occurred?" which is called a *conditional probability*. As you can imagine, answering this type of question is useful in machine learning, because if we can answer the question, "What is the probability that *the label is positive* given *the features*?" we have a classification model. For example, we can build a sentiment analysis model (just like we did in chapter 6) by answering the question, "What is the probability that *this sentence is happy* given *the words that it contains*?" However, when we have too many features (in this case, words), the computation of the probability using Bayes' theorem gets very complicated. This is where the naive Bayes algorithm comes to our rescue. The naive Bayes algorithm uses a slick simplification of this calculation to help us build our desired classification model, called the *naive Bayes model*. It's called *naive* Bayes because to simplify the calculations, we make a slightly naive assumption that is not necessarily true. However, this assumption helps us come up with a good estimate of the probability.

In this chapter, we see Bayes theorem used with some real-life examples. We start by studying an interesting and slightly surprising medical example. Then we dive deep into the naive Bayes model by applying it to a common problem in machine learning: spam classification. We finalize by coding the algorithm in Python and using it to make predictions in a real spam email dataset.

All the code for this chapter is available at this GitHub repository: https://github.com/luisguiserrano/manning/tree/master/Chapter_8_Naive_Bayes.

Sick or healthy? A story with Bayes' theorem as the hero

Consider the following scenario. Your (slightly hypochondriac) friend calls you, and the following conversation unfolds:

You: Hello!

Friend: Hi. I have some terrible news!

You: Oh no, what is it?

Friend: I heard about this terrible and rare disease, and I went to the doctor to be tested for it. The doctor said she would administer a very accurate test. Then today, she called me and told me that I tested positive! I must have the disease!

Oh no! What should you say to your friend? First of all, let's calm him down, and try to figure out if it is likely that he has the disease.

You: First, let's calm down. Mistakes happen in medicine. Let's try to see how likely it is that you actually have the disease. How accurate did the doctor say the test was?

Friend: She said it was 99% accurate. That means I'm 99% likely to have the disease!

You: Wait, let's look at *all* the numbers. How likely is it to have the disease, regardless of the test? How many people have the disease?

Friend: I was reading online, and it says that on average, one out of every 10,000 people have the disease.

You: OK, let me get a piece of paper (*puts friend on hold*).

Let's stop for a quiz.

quiz In what range do you think is the probability that your friend has the disease, given that he has tested positive?

a. 0–20%

b. 20–40%

c. 40–60%

d. 60–80%

e. 80–100%

Let's calculate this probability. To summarize, we have the following two pieces of information:

- The test is correct 99% of the time. To be more exact (we checked with the doctor to confirm this), on average, out of every 100 healthy people, the test correctly diagnoses 99 of them, and out of every 100 sick people, the test correctly diagnoses 99 of them. Therefore, both on healthy and sick people, the test has an accuracy of 99%.

- On average, 1 out of every 10,000 people has the disease.

Let's do some rough calculations to see what the probability would be. These are summarized in the confusion matrix shown in figure 8.1. For reference, we can pick a random group of one million people. On average, one out of every 10,000 people are sick, so we expect 100 of these people to have the disease and 999,900 to be healthy.

First, let's run the test on the 100 sick ones. Because the test is correct 99% of the time, we expect 99 of these 100 people to be correctly diagnosed as sick—that is, 99 sick people who test positive.

Now, let's run the test on the 999,900 healthy ones. The test makes mistakes 1% of the time, so we expect 1% of these 999,900 healthy people to be misdiagnosed as sick. That is 9,999 healthy people who test positive.

This means that the total number of people who tested positive is 99 + 9,999 = 10,098. Out of these, only 99 are sick. Therefore, the probability that your friend is sick, given that he tested positive, is $\frac{99}{10,098} = 0.0098$, or 0.98%. That is less than 1%! So we can get back to our friend.

You: Don't worry, based on the numbers you gave me, the probability that you have the disease given that you tested positive is less than 1%!

Friend: Oh, my God, really? That's such a relief, thank you!

You: Don't thank me, thank math (*winks eye*).

Let's summarize our calculation. These are our facts:

- **Fact 1:** Out of every 10,000 people, one has the disease.

- **Fact 2:** Out of every 100 sick people who take the test, 99 test positive, and one tests negative.

- **Fact 3:** Out of every 100 healthy people who take the test, 99 test negative, and one tests positive.

We pick a sample population of one million people, which is broken down in figure 8.1, as follows:

- According to fact 1, we expect 100 people in our sample population to have the disease, and 999,900 to be healthy.

- According to fact 2, out of the 100 sick people, 99 tested positive and one tested negative.

- According to fact 3, out of the 999,900 healthy people, 9,999 tested positive and 989,901 tested negative

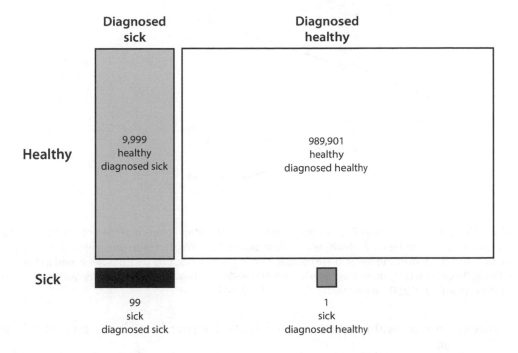

Figure 8.1 Among our 1,000,000 patients, only 100 of them are sick (bottom row). Among the 10,098 diagnosed as sick (left column), only 99 of them are actually sick. The remaining 9,999 are healthy, yet were misdiagnosed as sick. Therefore, if our friend was diagnosed as sick, he has a much higher chance to be among the 9,999 healthy (top left) than to be among the 99 sick (bottom left).

Because our friend tested positive, he must be in the left column of figure 8.1. This column has 9,999 healthy people who were misdiagnosed as sick and 99 sick people who were correctly diagnosed. The probability that your friend is sick is $\frac{99}{99+9,999} = 0.0098$, which is less than 1%.

This is a bit surprising, if the test is correct 99% of the time, why on earth is it so wrong? Well, the test is not bad if it's wrong only 1% of the time. But because one person out of every 10,000 is sick with the disease, that means a person is sick 0.01% of the time. What is more likely, to be among the 1% of the population that got misdiagnosed or to be among the 0.01% of the population that is sick? The 1%, although a small group, is much larger than the 0.01%. The test has a problem; it has an error rate much larger than the rate of being sick. We have a similar problem in the section "Two examples of models: Coronavirus and spam email" in chapter 7—we can't rely on accuracy to measure this model.

A way to look at this is using treelike diagrams. In our diagram, we start with a root at the left, which branches out into two possibilities: that your friend is sick or healthy. Each of these two possibilities branches out into two more possibilities: that your friend gets diagnosed as healthy or diagnosed as sick. The tree is illustrated in figure 8.2, together with the count of patients in each branch.

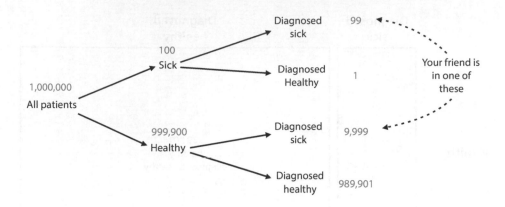

Figure 8.2   The tree of possibilities. Each patient can be sick or healthy. For each of the possibilities, the patient can be diagnosed as sick or healthy, which gives us four possibilities. We start with one million patients: 100 of them are sick, and the remaining 999,900 are healthy. Out of the 100 sick, one gets misdiagnosed as healthy, and the remaining 99 get correctly diagnosed as sick. Out of the 999,900 healthy patients, 9,999 get misdiagnosed as sick, and the remaining 989,901 are correctly diagnosed as healthy.

From figure 8.2, we can again see that the probability that your friend is sick given that he tested positive is $\frac{99}{99 + 9,999} = 0.0098$, given that he can only be in the first and third groups at the right.

Prelude to Bayes' theorem: The prior, the event, and the posterior

We now have all the tools to state Bayes' theorem. The main goal of Bayes' theorem is calculating a probability. At the beginning, with no information in our hands, we can calculate only an initial probability, which we call the *prior*. Then, an event happens, which gives us information. After this information, we have a much better estimate of the probability we want to calculate. We call this better estimate the *posterior*. The prior, event, and posterior, are illustrated in figure 8.3.

prior   The initial probability

event   Something that occurs, which gives us information

posterior   The final (and more accurate) probability that we calculate using the prior probability and the event

An example follows. Imagine that we want to find out the probability that it will rain today. If we don't know anything, we can come up with only a rough estimate for the probability, which is the prior. If we look around and find out that we are in the Amazon rain forest (the event), then we can come up with a much more exact estimate. In fact, if we are in the Amazon rain forest, it will probably rain today. This new estimate is the posterior.

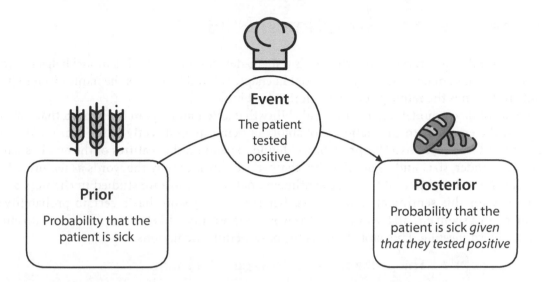

Figure 8.3   The prior, the event, and the posterior. The prior is the "raw" probability, namely, the probability we calculate when we know very little. The event is the information that we obtain, which will help us refine our calculation of the probability. The posterior is the "cooked" probability, or the much more accurate probability that we calculate when we have more information.

In our ongoing medical example, we need to calculate the probability that a patient is sick. The prior, the event, and the posterior follow:

- **Prior:** Initially, this probability is 1/10,000, because we don't have any other information, other than the fact that one out of every 10,000 patients is sick. This 1/10,000, or 0.0001, is the prior.

- **Event:** All of a sudden, new information comes to light. In this case, the patient took a test and tested positive.

- **Posterior:** After coming out positive, we recalculate the probability that the patient is sick, and that comes out to be 0.0098. This is the posterior.

Bayes' theorem is one of the most important building blocks of probability and of machine learning. It is so important that several fields are named after it, such as *Bayesian learning*, *Bayesian statistics*, and *Bayesian analysis*. In this chapter, we learn Bayes' theorem and an important classification model derived from it: the naive Bayes model. In a nutshell, the naive Bayes model does what most classification models do, which is predict a label out of a set of features. The model returns the answer in the form of a probability, which is calculated using Bayes' theorem.

Use case: Spam-detection model

The use case that we study in this chapter is a spam-detection model. This model helps us separate spam from ham emails. As we discussed in chapters 1 and 7, spam is the name given to junk email, and ham is the name given to email that isn't junk.

The naive Bayes model outputs the probability that an email is spam or ham. In that way, we can send the emails with the highest probability of being spam directly to the spam folder and keep the rest in our inbox. This probability should depend on the features of the email, such as its words, sender, size, and so on. For this chapter, we consider only the words as features. This example is not that different from the sentiment analysis example we studied in chapters 5 and 6. The key for this sentiment analysis classifier is that each word has a certain probability of appearing in a spam email. For example, the word *lottery* is more likely to appear in a spam email than the word *meeting*. This probability is the basis of our calculations.

Finding the prior: The probability that any email is spam

What is the probability that an email is spam? That is a hard question, but let's try to make a rough estimate, which we call the prior. We look at our current inbox and count how many emails are spam and ham. Imagine that in 100 emails, 20 are spam and 80 are ham. Thus, 20% of the emails are spam. If we want to make a decent estimate, we can say that *to the best of our knowledge*, the probability that a new email is spam is 0.2. This is the prior probability. The calculation is illustrated in figure 8.4, where the spam emails are colored dark gray and the ham emails white.

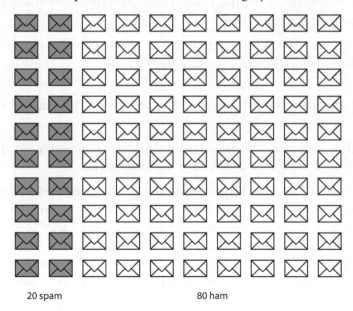

20 spam   80 ham

Probability of spam: 0.2

Figure 8.4   We have a dataset with 100 emails, 20 of which are spam. An estimate for the probability that an email is spam is 0.2. This is the prior probability.

Finding the posterior: The probability that an email is spam, knowing that it contains a particular word

Of course, not all emails are created equally. We'd like to come up with a more educated guess for the probability, using the properties of the email. We can use many properties, such as sender, size, or words in the email. For this application, we use only the words in the email. However, I encourage you to go through the example thinking how this could be used with other properties.

Let's say that we find a particular word, say, the word *lottery*, which tends to appear more often in spam emails than in ham emails. That word represents our event. Among the spam emails, the word *lottery* appears in 15 of them, whereas it appears in only 5 of the ham emails. Therefore, among the 20 emails containing the word *lottery*, 15 of them are spam, and 5 of them are ham. Thus, the probability that an email containing the word *lottery* is spam, is precisely $\frac{15}{20} = 0.75$.

That is the posterior probability. The process of calculating this probability is illustrated in figure 8.5.

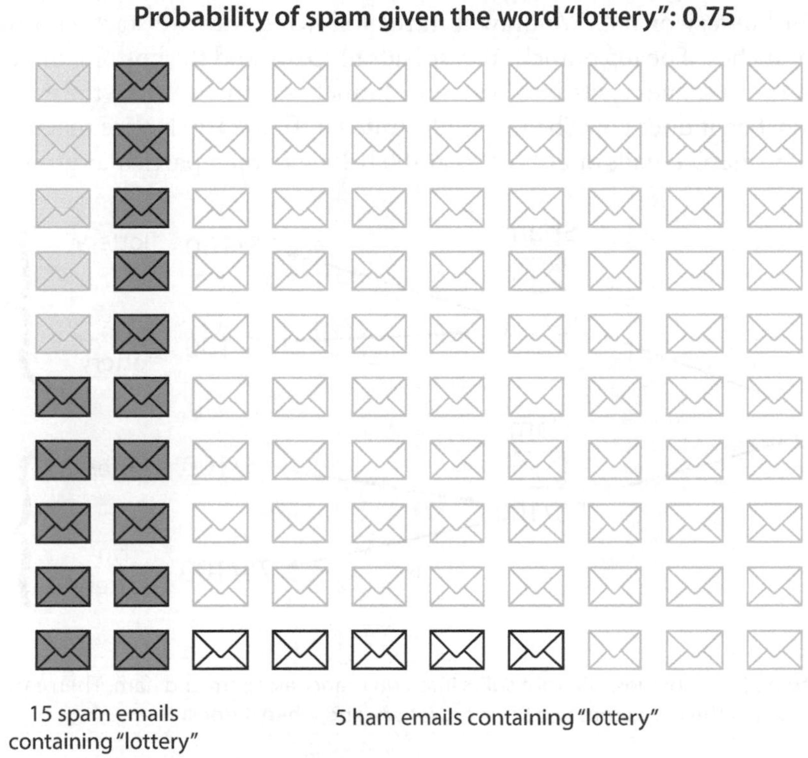

Probability of spam given the word "lottery": 0.75

15 spam emails containing "lottery"

5 ham emails containing "lottery"

Figure 8.5 We have removed (grayed out) the emails that don't contain the word *lottery*. All of a sudden, our probabilities change. Among the emails that contain the word *lottery*, there are 15 spam emails and 5 ham emails, so the probability that an email containing the word *lottery* is spam, is $\frac{15}{20} = 0.75$.

There we have it: we've calculated the probability that an email is spam given that it contains the word *lottery*. To summarize:

- The **prior** probability is 0.2. This is the probability that an email is spam, knowing nothing about the email.

- The **event** is that the email contains the word *lottery*. This helps us make a better estimate of the probability.

- The **posterior** probability is 0.75. This is the probability that the email is spam, *given that* it contains the word *lottery*.

In this example, we calculated the probability by counting emails and dividing. This is mostly done for pedagogical purposes, but in real life, we can use a shortcut to calculate this probability using a formula. This formula is called Bayes' theorem, and we see it next.

What the math just happened? Turning ratios into probabilities

One way to visualize the previous example is with a tree of all four possibilities, just as we did with the medical example in figure 8.2. The possibilities are that the email is spam or ham, and that it contains the word *lottery* or not. We draw it in the following way: we start with the root, which splits into two branches. The top branch corresponds to spam, and the bottom branch corresponds to ham. Each of the branches splits into two more branches, namely, when the email contains the word *lottery* and when it does not. The tree is illustrated in figure 8.6. Notice that in this tree, we've also indicated how many emails out of the total 100 belong to each particular group.

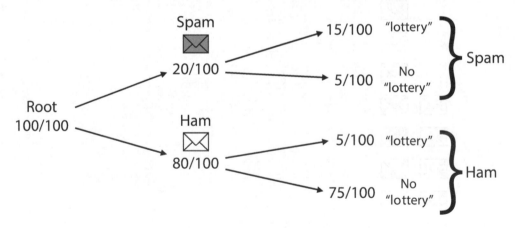

Figure 8.6   The tree of possibilities. The root splits into two branches: spam and ham. Then each of these splits into two branches: when the email contains the word *lottery*, and when it doesn't.

Once we have this tree, and we want to calculate the probability that an email is spam *given that* it contains the word *lottery*, we simply remove all the branches in which the emails don't contain the word *lottery*. This is illustrated in figure 8.7.

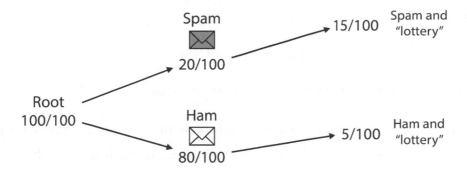

Figure 8.7 From the previous tree, we have removed the two branches where the emails don't contain the word *lottery*. Out of the original 100 emails, we have 20 left that contain *lottery*. Because of these 20 emails, 15 are spam, we conclude that the probability that an email is spam given that it contains the word *lottery* is 0.75.

Now, we have 20 emails, and of them, 15 are spam and 5 are ham. Thus, the probability that an email is spam given that it contains the word *lottery* is $\dfrac{15}{20} = 0.75$.

But we've already done that, so what is the benefit of the diagram? Aside from making things simpler, the benefit is that normally, the information we have is based on probabilities, and not on the number of emails. Many times, we don't know how many emails are spam or ham. All we know is the following:

- The probability that an email is spam is $\dfrac{1}{5} = 0.2$.

- The probability that a spam email contains the word *lottery* is $\dfrac{3}{4} = 0.75$.

- The probability that a ham email contains the word *lottery* is $\dfrac{1}{16} = 0.0625$.

- **Question:** What is the probability that an email that contains the word *lottery* is spam?

First, let's check if this is enough information. Do we know the probability that an email is ham? Well, we know that the probability that it is spam is $\dfrac{1}{5} = 0.2$. The *only* other possibility is that an email is ham, so it must be the complement, or $\dfrac{4}{5} = 0.8$. This is an important rule—the rule of complementary probabilities.

rule of complementary probabilities For an event E, the complement of the event E, denoted E^c, is the event opposite to E. The probability of E^c is 1 minus the probability of E, namely,

$$P\left(E^c\right) = 1 - P\left(E\right).$$

Therefore, we have the following:

- $P(spam) = \dfrac{1}{5} = 0.2$: the probability of an email being spam

- $P(ham) = \dfrac{4}{5} = 0.8$: the probability of an email being ham

Now let's look at the other information. The probability that a spam email contains the word *lottery* is $\dfrac{3}{4} = 0.75$. This can be read as, the probability that an email contains the word *lottery* *given that* it is spam, is 0.75. This is a conditional probability, where the condition is that the email is spam. We denote condition by a vertical bar, so this can be written as $P('lottery' \mid spam)$. The complement of this is $P(no\ 'lottery' \mid spam)$, namely, the probability that a spam email does *not* contain the word *lottery*. This probability is $1 - P('lottery' \mid spam)$. This way, we can calculate other probabilities as follows:

- $P('lottery' \mid spam) = \dfrac{3}{4} = 0.75$: the probability that a spam email contains the word *lottery*.

- $P(no\ 'lottery' \mid spam) = \dfrac{1}{4} = 0.25$: the probability that a spam email does not contain the word *lottery*.

- $P('lottery' \mid ham) = \dfrac{1}{16} = 0.0625$: the probability that a ham email contains the word *lottery*.

- $P(no\ 'lottery' \mid ham) = \dfrac{15}{16} = 0.9375$: the probability that a ham email does not contain the word *lottery*.

The next thing we do is find the probabilities of two events happening *at the same time*. More specifically, we want the following four probabilities:

- The probability that an email is spam *and* contains the word *lottery*

- The probability that an email is spam *and* does not contain the word *lottery*

- The probability that an email is ham *and* contains the word *lottery*

- The probability that an email is ham *and* does not contain the word *lottery*

These events are called *intersections* of events and denoted with the symbol ∩. Thus, we need to find the following probabilities:

- $P('lottery' \cap spam)$

- $P(no\ 'lottery' \cap spam)$

- $P(\text{'lottery'} \cap ham)$

- $P(\text{no 'lottery'} \cap ham)$

Let's look at some numbers. We know that $\frac{1}{5}$, or 20 out of 100, of emails are spam. Out of those 20, $\frac{3}{4}$ of them contain the word *lottery*. At the end, we multiply these two numbers, $\frac{1}{5}$ times $\frac{3}{4}$, to obtain $\frac{3}{20}$, which is the same as $\frac{15}{100}$, the proportion of emails that are spam and contain the word *lottery*. What we did was the following: we multiplied the probability that an email is spam *times* the probability that a spam email contains the word *lottery*, to obtain the probability that an email is spam *and* contains the word *lottery*. The probability that a spam email contains the word *lottery* is precisely the conditional probability, or the probability that an email contains the word *lottery given that* it is a spam email. This gives rise to the multiplication rule for probabilities.

> **Product rule of probabilities**   For events E and F, the probability of their intersection is the product of the conditional probability of F given E, times the probability of F, namely, $P(E \cap F) = P(E \mid F) \cap P(F)$.

Now we can calculate these probabilities as follows:

- $P(\text{'lottery'} \cap spam) = P(\text{'lottery'} \mid spam) \cap P(spam) = \frac{3}{4} \cdot \frac{1}{5} = \frac{3}{20} = 0.15$

- $P(\text{no 'lottery'} \cap spam) = P(\text{no 'lottery'} \mid spam) \cap P(spam) = \frac{1}{4} \cdot \frac{1}{5} = \frac{1}{20} = 0.05$

- $P(\text{no 'lottery'} \cap ham) = P(\text{no 'lottery'} \mid ham) \cap P(ham) = \frac{1}{16} \cdot \frac{4}{5} = \frac{1}{20} = 0.05$

- $P(\text{no 'lottery'} \cap ham) = P(\text{no 'lottery'} \mid ham) \cdot P(ham) = \frac{15}{16} \cdot \frac{4}{5} = \frac{15}{20} = 0.75$

These probabilities are summarized in figure 8.8. Notice that the product of the probabilities on the edges are the probabilities at the right. Furthermore, notice that the sum of all these four probabilities is one, because they encompass all the possible scenarios.

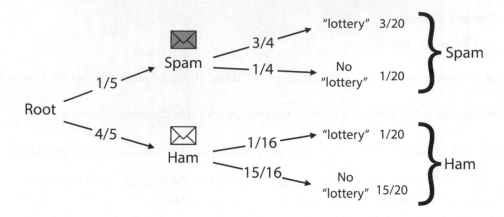

Figure 8.8   The same tree from figure 8.6, but now with probabilities. From the root, two branches emerge, one for spam emails and one for ham emails. In each one, we record the corresponding probability. Each branch again splits into two leaves: one for emails containing the word *lottery*, and one for emails not containing it. In each branch we record the corresponding probability. Notice that the product of these probabilities is the probability at the right of each leaf. For example, for the top leaf, $1/5 \cdot 3/4 = 3/20 = 0.15$.

We're almost done. We want to find $P(spam \mid \textit{'lottery'})$, which is the probability that an email is spam *given that* it contains the word *lottery*. Among the four events we just studied, in only two of them does the word *lottery* appear. Thus, we need to consider only those, namely:

- $P(\textit{'lottery'} \cap spam) = \dfrac{3}{20} = 0.15$

- $P(\textit{'lottery'} \cap ham) = \dfrac{1}{20} = 0.05$

In other words, we need to consider only the two branches shown in figure 8.9—the first and the third, namely, those in which the email contains the word *lottery*.

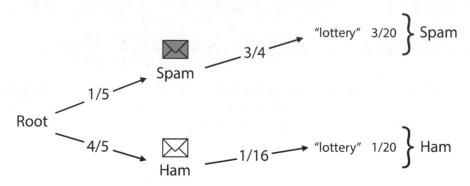

Figure 8.9   From the tree in figure 8.8, we have removed the two branches where the emails don't contain the word *lottery*.

The first one is the probability that an email is spam, and the second one is the probability that the email is ham. These two probabilities don't add to one. However, because we now live in a world in which the email contains the word *lottery*, then these two are the only possible scenarios. Thus, their probabilities *should* add to 1. Furthermore, they should still have the same relative ratio with respect to each other. The way to fix this is to normalize—to find two numbers that are in the same relative ratio with respect to each other as $\frac{3}{20}$ and $\frac{1}{20}$ but that add to one.

The way to find these is to divide both by the sum. In this case, the numbers become $\frac{3/20}{3/20 + 1/20}$ and $\frac{1/20}{3/20 + 1/20}$. These simplify to $\frac{3}{4}$ and $\frac{1}{4}$, which are the desired probabilities. Thus, we conclude the following:

- $P(spam \mid 'lottery') = \frac{3}{4} = 0.75$

- $P(ham \mid 'lottery') = \frac{1}{4} = 0.25$

This is exactly what we figured out when we counted the emails. To wrap up this information, we need a formula. We had two probabilities: the probability that an email is spam *and* contains the word *lottery*, and the probability that an email is spam *and* does not contain the word *lottery*. To get them to add to one, we normalized them. This is the same thing as dividing each one of them by their sum. In math terms, we did the following:

$$P(spam \mid 'lottery') = \frac{P('lottery' \cap spam)}{P('lottery' \cap spam) + P('lottery' \cap ham)}$$

If we remember what these two probabilities were, using the product rule, we get the following:

$$P(spam \mid 'lottery') = \frac{P('lottery' \mid spam) \cdot P(spam)}{P('lottery' \mid spam) \cdot P(spam) + P('lottery' \mid ham) \cdot P(ham)}$$

To verify, we plug in the numbers to get:

$$P(spam \mid 'lottery') = \frac{\frac{1}{5} \cdot \frac{3}{4}}{\frac{1}{5} \cdot \frac{3}{4} + \frac{4}{5} \cdot \frac{1}{16}} = \frac{\frac{3}{20}}{\frac{3}{20} + \frac{1}{20}} = \frac{\frac{3}{20}}{\frac{4}{20}} = \frac{3}{4} = 0.75$$

This is the formula for Bayes' theorem! More formally:

Bayes theorem   For events E and F,

$$P(E \mid F) = \frac{P(F \mid E) \cdot P(E)}{P(F)}.$$

Because the event F can be broken down into the two disjoint events $F \cap E$ and $F \cap E^c$, then

$$P(E \mid F) = \frac{P(F \mid E) \cdot P(E)}{P(F \mid E) \cdot P(E) + P(F \mid E^c) \cdot P(E^c)}.$$

What about two words? The naive Bayes algorithm

In the previous section we calculated the probability that an email is spam given that it contains the keyword *lottery*. However, the dictionary contains many more words, and we'd like to calculate the probability that an email is spam given that it contains several words. As you can imagine, the calculations get more complicated, but in this section, we learn a trick that helps us estimate this probability.

In general, the trick helps us calculate a posterior probability based on two events instead of one (and it easily generalizes to more than two events). It is based on the premise that when events are independent, the probability of both occurring at the same time is the product of their probabilities. Events are not always independent, but assuming they are sometimes helps us make good approximations. For example, imagine the following scenario: there is an island with 1,000 people. Half of the inhabitants (500) are women, and one-tenth of the inhabitants (100) have brown eyes. How many of the inhabitants do you think are women with brown eyes? If all we know is this information, we can't find out unless we count them in person. However, if we assume that gender and eye color are independent, then we can estimate that half of one tenth of the population consists of women with brown eyes. That is $\frac{1}{2} \cdot \frac{1}{10} = \frac{1}{20}$ of the population. Because the total population is 1,000 people, our estimate for the number of women with brown eyes is $1000 \cdot \frac{1}{20} = 50$ people. Maybe we go to the island and find out that that's not the case, but *to the best of our knowledge*, 50 is a good estimate. One may say that our assumption about the independence of gender and eye color was *naive*, and maybe it was, but it was the best estimate we could come up with given the information we had.

The rule we used in the previous example is the product rule for independent probabilities, which states the following:

product rule for independent probabilities   If two events E and F are independent, namely, the occurrence of one doesn't influence in any way the occurrence of the other one, then the probability of both happening (the intersection of the events) is the product of the probabilities of each of the events. In other words,

$$P(E \cap F) = P(E) \cdot P(F).$$

Back to the email example. After we figured out the probability that an email is spam given that it contains the word *lottery*, we noticed that another word, *sale*, also tends to appear a lot in spam email. We'd like to figure out the probability that an email is spam given that it contains both *lottery* and *sale*. We begin by counting how many spam and ham emails contain the word *sale* and find that it appears in 6 of the 20 spam emails and 4 of the 80 ham emails. Thus, the probabilities are the following (illustrated in figure 8.10):

- $P('sale' \mid spam) = \dfrac{6}{20} = 0.3$

- $P('sale' \mid ham) = \dfrac{4}{80} = 0.05$

Probability of spam given the word "sale": 0.6

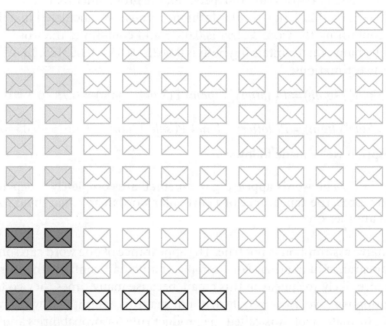

6 spam emails
containing "sale"

4 ham emails containing "sale"

Figure 8.10 In a similar calculation as for the word *lottery*, we look at the emails containing the word *sale*. Among these (not grayed-out) emails, there are six spam and four ham.

One can use Bayes' theorem again to conclude that the probability that an email is spam given that it contains the word *sale* is 0.6, and I encourage you to go through the calculations yourself. However, the more important question is: what is the probability that an email is spam given that it contains the words *lottery* and *sale* at the same time? Before we do this, let's find the probability that an email contains the words *lottery* and *sale* given that it is spam. This should be easy: we go through all our emails and find how many of the spam emails have the words *lottery* and *sale*.

However, we may run into the problem that there are no emails with the words *lottery* and *sale*. We have only 100 emails, and when we are trying to find two words on them, we may not have enough to be able to properly estimate a probability. What can we do? One possible solution is to collect more data, until we have so many emails that it's likely that the two words appear in some of them. However, the case may be that we can't collect any more data, so we have to work with what we have. This is where the naive assumption will help us.

Let's try to estimate this probability in the same way that we estimated the number of women with brown eyes on the island at the beginning of this section. We know that the probability that the word *lottery* appears in a spam email is 0.75, from the previous section. From earlier in this section, the probability that *sale* appears in a spam email is 0.3. Thus, if we naively assume that the appearances of these two words are independent, the probability that both words appear in a spam email is $0.75 \cdot 0.3 = 0.225$. In a similar fashion, because we calculated that the probabilities of a ham email containing the word *lottery* is 0.0625 and containing the word *sale* is 0.05, then the probability of a ham email containing both is $0.0625 \cdot 0.05 = 0.003125$. In other words, we've done the following estimations:

- $P('lottery', 'sale' \mid spam) = P('lottery' \mid spam) \, P('sale' \mid spam) = 0.75 \cdot 0.3 = 0.225$

- $P('lottery', 'sale' \mid ham) = P('lottery' \mid ham) \, P('sale' \mid ham) = 0.0625 \cdot 0.05 = 0.003125$

The naive assumption we've made follows:

naive assumption   The words appearing in an email are completely independent of each other. In other words, the appearance of a particular word in an email in no way affects the appearance of another one.

Most likely, the naive assumption is not true. The appearance of one word can sometimes heavily influence the appearance of another. For example, if an email contains the word *salt*, then the word *pepper* is more likely to appear in this email, because many times they go together. This is why our assumption is naive. However, it turns out that this assumption works well in practice, and it simplifies our math a lot. It is called the product rule for probabilities and is illustrated in figure 8.11.

Now that we have estimates for the probabilities, we proceed to find the expected number of spam and ham emails that contain the words *lottery* and *sale*.

- Because there are 20 spam emails, and the probability that a spam email contains both words is 0.225, the expected number of spam emails containing both words is $20 \cdot 0.225 = 4.5$.

- Similarly, there are 80 ham emails, and the probability that a ham email contains both words is 0.00325, so the expected number of ham emails containing both words is $80 \cdot 0.00325 = 0.25$.

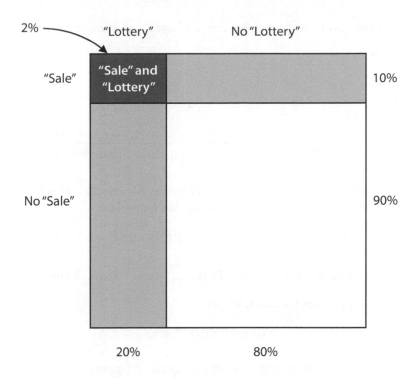

Figure 8.11 Say 20% of the emails contain the word *lottery*, and 10% of the emails contain the word *sale*. We make the naive assumption that these two words are independent of each other. Under this assumption, the percentage of emails that contain both words can be estimated as 2%, namely, the product of 20% and 10%.

The previous calculations imply that if we restrict our dataset to only emails that contain both the words *lottery* and *sale*, we expect 4.5 of them to be spam and 0.25 to be ham. Thus, if we were to pick one at random among these, what is the probability that we pick one that is spam? This may look harder with nonintegers than with integers, but if we look at figure 8.12, this may be more clear. We have 4.5 spam emails and 0.25 ham emails (this is exactly one-fourth of an email). If we throw a dart and it falls in one of the emails, what's the probability that it landed on a spam email? Well, the total number of emails (or the total area, if you'd like to imagine it that way) is 4.5 + 0.25 = 4.75. Because 4.5 are spam, the probability that the dart landed on spam is 4.5/4.75 = 0.9474. This means that an email with the words *lottery* and *sale* has a 94.74% probability of being spam. That is quite high!

4.5 spam emails
containing "lottery" and "sale"

0.25 ham emails
containing "lottery" and "sale"

Figure 8.12 We have 4.5 spam emails and 0.25 ham emails. We throw a dart, and it hits one of the emails. What is the probability that it hit a spam email? The answer is 94.74%.

What we did here, using probability, was employing Bayes' theorem, except with the events

- $E = lottery \cap sale$

- $F = spam$

to get the formula

$$P(spam \,|lottery \cap sale) = \frac{P(lottery \cap sale \,|spam) \cdot P\left(spam\right)}{P(lottery \cap sale \,|spam) \cdot P\left(spam\right) + P(lottery \cap sale \,|ham) \cdot P\left(ham\right)}.$$

Then we (naively) assumed that the appearances of the words *lottery* and *sale* were independent among spam (and ham) emails, to get the following two formulas:

$$P(lottery \cap sale \,|\, spam) = P(lottery \,|\, spam) \cdot P(sale \,|\, spam)$$

$$P(lottery \cap sale \,|\, ham) = P(lottery \,|\, ham) \cdot P(sale \,|\, ham)$$

Plugging them into the previous formula, we get

$$P(spam \,|lottery \cap sale)$$

$$= \frac{P(lottery \,|spam) \cdot P(sale \,|spam) \cdot P\left(spam\right)}{P(lottery \,|spam) \cdot P(sale \,|spam) \cdot P\left(spam\right) + P(lottery \,|ham) \cdot P(sale \,|ham) \cdot P\left(ham\right)}.$$

Finally, plugging in the following values:

- $P(lottery \,|\, spam) = \dfrac{3}{4}$

- $P(sale \,|\, spam) = \dfrac{3}{10}$

- $P(spam) = \dfrac{1}{5}$

- $P(lottery \,|\, ham) = \dfrac{1}{16}$

- $P(sale \,|\, ham) = \dfrac{1}{20}$

- $P(ham) = \dfrac{4}{5}$

we get

$$P(spam \,|lottery \cap sale) = \frac{\dfrac{3}{4} \cdot \dfrac{3}{10} \cdot \dfrac{1}{5}}{\dfrac{3}{4} \cdot \dfrac{3}{10} \cdot \dfrac{1}{5} + \dfrac{1}{16} \cdot \dfrac{1}{20} \cdot \dfrac{4}{5}} = 0.9474.$$

What about more than two words?

In the general case, the email has n words $x_1, x_2, \ldots, x_n$. Bayes' theorem states that the probability of an email being spam given that it contains the words $x_1, x_2, \ldots, x_n$ is

$$P\big(spam \,|\, x_1, x_2, \ldots, x_n\big) = \frac{P(x_1, x_2, \ldots, x_n \,|\, spam) \; P\big(spam\big)}{P(x_1, x_2, \ldots, x_n \,|\, spam) P\big(spam\big) + \; P(x_1, x_2, \ldots, x_n \,|\, ham) \; P\big(ham\big)}.$$

In the previous equation we removed the intersection sign and replaced it with a comma. The naive assumption is that the appearances of all these words are independent. Therefore,

$$P(x_1, x_2, \ldots, x_n \,|\, spam) = P(x_1 \,|\, spam) \, P(x_2 \,|\, spam) \cdots P(x_n \,|\, spam)$$

and

$$P(x_1, x_2, \ldots, x_n \,|\, ham) = P(x_1 \,|\, ham) \, P(x_2 \,|\, ham) \cdots P(x_n \,|\, ham).$$

Putting together the last three equations, we get

$$P\big(spam \,|\, x_1, x_2, \ldots, x_n\big)$$

$$= \frac{P(x_1 \,|\, spam) P(x_2 \,|\, spam) \ldots P(x_n \,|\, spam) P\big(spam\big)}{P(x_1 \,|\, spam) P(x_2 \,|\, spam) \ldots P(x_n \,|\, spam) P\big(spam\big) + P(x_1 \,|\, ham) P(x_2 \,|\, ham) \ldots P(x_n \,|\, ham) P\big(ham\big)}.$$

Each of these quantities on the right-hand side is easy to estimate as a ratio between numbers of emails. For example, $P(x_i \,|\, spam)$ is the ratio between the number of spam emails that contain the word x_i and the total number of spam emails.

As a small example, let's say that the email contains the words *lottery*, *sale*, and *mom*. We examine the word *mom* and notice that it occurs in only one out of the 20 spam emails and in 10 out of the 80 ham emails. Therefore, $P('mom' \,|\, spam) = \dfrac{1}{20}$ and $P('mom' \,|\, ham) = \dfrac{1}{8}$. Using the same probabilities for the words *lottery* and *sale* as in the previous section, we get the following:

$$P(spam \,|\, 'lottery', 'sale', 'mom')$$

$$= \frac{P('lottery' \,|\, spam) P('sale' \,|\, spam) P('mom' \,|\, spam) P\big(spam\big)}{P('lottery' \,|\, spam) P('sale' \,|\, spam) P('mom' \,|\, spam) P\big(spam\big) + P('lottery' \,|\, ham) P('sale' \,|\, ham) P('mom' \,|\, ham) P\big(ham\big)}$$

$$= \frac{\dfrac{3}{4} \cdot \dfrac{3}{10} \cdot \dfrac{1}{20} \cdot \dfrac{1}{5}}{\dfrac{3}{4} \cdot \dfrac{3}{10} \cdot \dfrac{1}{20} \cdot \dfrac{1}{5} + \dfrac{1}{16} \cdot \dfrac{1}{20} \cdot \dfrac{1}{8} \cdot \dfrac{4}{5}}$$

$$= 0.8780$$

Notice that adding the word *mom* into the equation reduced the probability of spam from 94.74% to 87.80%, which makes sense, because this word is more likely to appear in ham emails than in spam emails.

Building a spam-detection model with real data

Now that we have developed the algorithm, let's roll up our sleeves and code the naive Bayes algorithm. Several packages such as Scikit-Learn have great implementations of this algorithm, and I encourage you to look at them. However, we'll code it by hand. The dataset we use is from Kaggle, and for a link to download it, please check the resources for this chapter in appendix C. Here is the code for this section:

- **Notebook:** Coding_naive_Bayes.ipynb
    - https://github.com/luisguiserrano/manning/blob/master/Chapter_8_Naive_Bayes/Coding_naive_Bayes.ipynb
- **Dataset:** emails.csv

For this example, we'll introduce a useful package for handling large datasets called Pandas (to learn more about it, please check out the section "Using Pandas to load the dataset" in chapter 13). The main object used to store datasets in pandas is the DataFrame. To load our data into a Pandas DataFrame, we use the following command:

```
import pandas
emails = pandas.read_csv('emails.csv')
```

In table 8.1, you can see the first five rows of the dataset.

This dataset has two columns. The first column is the text of the email (together with its subject line), in string format. The second column tells us if the email is spam (1) or ham (0). First we need to do some data preprocessing.

Table 8.1 The first five rows of our email dataset. The Text column shows the text in each email, and the Spam column shows a 1 if the email is spam and a 0 if the email is ham. Notice that the first five emails are all spam.

Text	Spam
Subject: naturally irresistible your corporate...	1
Subject: the stock trading gunslinger fanny i...	1
Subject: unbelievable new homes made easy im ...	1
Subject: 4 color printing special request add...	1
Subject: do not have money, get software cds ...	1

Data preprocessing

Let's start by turning the text string into a list of words. We do this using the following function, which uses the `lower()` function to turn all the words into lowercase and the `split()` function to turn the words into a list. We check only whether each word appears in the email, regardless of how many times it appears, so we turn it into a set and then into a list.

```
def process_email(text):
    text = text.lower()
    return list(set(text.split()))
```

Now we use the `apply()` function to apply this change to the entire column. We call the new column `emails['words']`.

```
emails['words'] = emails['text'].apply(process_email)
```

The first five rows of the modified email dataset are shown in table 8.2.

Table 8.2 The email dataset with a new column called Words, which contains a list of the words in the email (without repetition) and subject line

Text	Spam	Words
Subject: naturally irresistible your corporate...	1	[letsyou, all, do, but, list, is, information,...
Subject: the stock trading gunslinger fanny i...	1	[not, like, duane, trading, libretto, attainde...
Subject: unbelievable new homes made easy im ...	1	[im, have, $, take, foward, all, limited, subj...
Subject: 4 color printing special request add...	1	[color, azusa, pdf, printable, 8102, subject:,...
Subject: do not have money, get software cds ...	1	[get, not, have, all, do, subject:, be, by, me...

Finding the priors

Let's first find the probability that an email is spam (the prior). For this, we calculate the number of emails that are spam and divide it by the total number of emails. Notice that the number of emails that are spam is the sum of entries in the Spam column. The following line will do the job:

```
sum(emails['spam'])/len(emails)
0.2388268156424581
```

We deduce that the prior probability that the email is spam is around 0.24. This is the probability that an email is spam if we don't know anything about the email. Likewise, the prior probability that an email is ham is around 0.76.

Finding the posteriors with Bayes' theorem

We need to find the probabilities that spam (and ham) emails contain a certain word. We do this for all words at the same time. The following function creates a dictionary called model, which records each word, together with the number of appearances of the word in spam emails and in ham emails:

```
model = {}

for index, email in emails.iterrows():
    for word in email['words']:
        if word not in model:
            model[word] = {'spam': 1, 'ham': 1}
        if word in model:
            if email['spam']:
                model[word]['spam'] += 1
            else:
                model[word]['ham'] += 1
```

Note that the counts are initialized at 1, so in reality, we are recording one more appearance of the email as spam and ham. We use this small hack to avoid having zero counts, because we don't want to accidentally divide by zero. Now let's examine some rows of the dictionary as follows:

```
model['lottery']
{'ham': 1, 'spam': 9}

model['sale']
{'ham': 42, 'spam': 39}
```

This means that the word *lottery* appears in 1 ham email and 9 spam emails, whereas the word *sale* appears in 42 ham emails and 39 spam emails. Although this dictionary doesn't contain any probabilities, these can be deduced by dividing the first entry by the sum of both entries. Thus, if an email contains the word *lottery*, the probability of it being spam is $\frac{9}{9+1} = 0.9$, and if it contains the word *sale*, the probability of it being spam is $\frac{39}{39+42} = 0.48$.

Implementing the naive Bayes algorithm

The input of the algorithm is the email. It goes through all the words in the email, and for each word, it calculates the probabilities that a spam email contains it and that a ham email contains it. These probabilities are calculated using the dictionary we defined in the previous section. Then we multiply these probabilities (the naive assumption) and apply Bayes' theorem to find the probability that an email is spam given that it contains the words on this particular email. The code to make a prediction using this model follows:

```
def predict_naive_bayes(email):
    total = len(emails)          ←———  Calculates the total number of emails,
    num_spam = sum(emails['spam'])      spam emails, and ham emails
    num_ham = total - num_spam
    email = email.lower()         ←———  Processes each email by turning it
    words = set(email.split())          into a list of its words in lowercase
    spams = [1.0]
    hams = [1.0]                         For each word, computes the conditional
    for word in words:                   probability that an email containing that
        if word in model:                word is spam (or ham), as a ratio
            spams.append(model[word]['spam']/num_spam*total)   ←———
            hams.append(model[word]['ham']/num_ham*total)
    prod_spams = np.long(np.prod(spams)*num_spam)   ←———
    prod_hams = np.long(np.prod(hams)*num_ham)
    return prod_spams/(prod_spams + prod_hams)   multiplies all the previous
                                                 probabilities times the prior
                                                 probability of the email being spam,
Normalizes these two probabilities to            and calls this prod_spams. Does a
get them to add to one (using Bayes'             similar process for prod_hams.
theorem) and returns the result
```

You may note that in the previous code, we used another small hack. Every probability is multiplied by the total number of emails in the dataset. This won't affect our calculations because this factor appears in the numerator and the denominator. However, it does ensure that our products of probabilities are not too small for Python to handle.

Now that we have built the model, let's test it by making predictions on some emails as follows:

```
predict_naive_bayes('Hi mom how are you')
0.12554358867163865
```

```
predict_naive_bayes('meet me at the lobby of the hotel at nine am')
0.00006964603508395
```

```
predict_naive_bayes('buy cheap lottery easy money now')
0.9999734722659664
```

```
predict_naive_bayes('asdfgh')
0.2388268156424581
```

It seems to work well. Emails like 'hi mom how are you' get a low probability (about 0.12) of being spam, and emails like 'buy cheap lottery easy money now' get a very high probability (over 0.99) of being spam. Notice that the last email, which doesn't contain any of the words in the dictionary, gets a probability of 0.2388, which is precisely the prior.

Further work

This was a quick implementation of the naive Bayes algorithm. But for larger datasets, and larger emails, we should use a package. Packages like Scikit-Learn offer great implementations of the naive Bayes algorithm, with many parameters to play with. Explore this and other packages, and use the naive Bayes algorithm on all types of datasets!

Summary

- Bayes' theorem is a technique widely used in probability, statistics, and machine learning.

- Bayes' theorem consists of calculating a posterior probability, based on a prior probability and an event.

- The prior probability is a basic calculation of a probability, given very little information.

- Bayes' theorem uses the event to make a much better estimate of the probability in question.

- The naive Bayes algorithm is used when one wants to combine a prior probability together with several events.

- The word *naive* comes from the fact that we are making a naive assumption, namely, that the events in question are all independent.

Exercises

Exercise 8.1

For each pair of events A and B, determine if they are independent or dependent. For (a) to (d), provide mathematical justification. For (e) and (f) provide verbal justification.

Throwing three fair coins:

    a.   A: First one falls on heads. B: Third one falls on tails.

    b.   A: First one falls on heads. B: There is an odd number of heads among the three throws.

Rolling two dice:

    c.   A: First one shows a 1. B: Second one shows a 2.

    d.   A: First one shows a 3. B: Second one shows a higher value than the first one.

For the following, provide a verbal justification. Assume that for this problem, we live in a place with seasons.

    e. A: It's raining outside. B: It's Monday.

    f. A: It's raining outside. B: It's June.

Exercise 8.2

There is an office where we have to go regularly for some paperwork. This office has two clerks, Aisha and Beto. We know that Aisha works there three days a week, and Beto works the other two. However, the schedules change every week, so we never know which three days Aisha is there, and which two days Beto is there.

    a. If we show up on a random day to the office, what is the probability that Aisha is the clerk?

We look from outside and notice that the clerk is wearing a red sweater, although we can't tell who the clerk is. We've been going to that office a lot, so we know that Beto tends to wear red more often than Aisha. In fact, Aisha wears red one day out of three (one-third of the time), and Beto wears red one day out of two (half of the time).

    b. What is the probability that Aisha is the clerk, knowing that the clerk is wearing red today?

Exercise 8.3

The following is a dataset of patients who have tested positive or negative for COVID-19. Their symptoms are cough (C), fever (F), difficulty breathing (B), and tiredness (T).

	Cough (C)	Fever (F)	Difficulty breathing (B)	Tiredness (T)	Diagnosis
Patient 1		X	X	X	Sick
Patient 2	X	X		X	Sick
Patient 3	X		X	X	Sick
Patient 4	X	X	X		Sick
Patient 5	X			X	Healthy
Patient 6		X	X		Healthy
Patient 7		X			Healthy
Patient 8				X	Healthy

The goal of this exercise is to build a naive Bayes model that predicts the diagnosis from the symptoms. Use the naive Bayes algorithm to find the following probabilities:

note   For the following questions, the symptoms that are not mentioned are completely unknown to us. For example, if we know that the patient has a cough, but nothing is said about their fever, it does not mean the patient doesn't have a fever.

a. The probability that a patient is sick given that the patient has a cough

b. The probability that a patient is sick given that the patient is not tired

c. The probability that a patient is sick given that the patient has a cough and a fever

d. The probability that a patient is sick given that the patient has a cough and a fever, but no difficulty breathing

Splitting data by asking questions: Decision trees

In this chapter

- what is a decision tree

- using decision trees for classification and regression

- building an app-recommendation system using users' information

- accuracy, Gini index, and entropy, and their role in building decision trees

- using Scikit-Learn to train a decision tree on a university admissions dataset

In this chapter, we cover decision trees. Decision trees are powerful classification and regression models, which also give us a great deal of information about our dataset. Just like the previous models we've learned in this book, decision trees are trained with labeled data, where the labels that we want to predict can be classes (for classification) or values (for regression). For most of this chapter, we focus on decision trees for classification, but near the end of the chapter, we describe decision trees for regression. However, the structure and training process of both types of tree is similar. In this chapter, we develop several use cases, including an app-recommendation system and a model for predicting admissions at a university.

Decision trees follow an intuitive process to make predictions—one that very much resembles human reasoning. Consider the following scenario: we want to decide whether we should wear a jacket today. What does the decision process look like? We may look outside and check if it's raining. If it's raining, then we definitely wear a jacket. If it's not, then maybe we check the temperature. If it is hot, then we don't wear a jacket, but if it is cold, then we wear a jacket. In figure 9.1, we can see a graph of this decision process, where the decisions are made by traversing the tree from top to bottom.

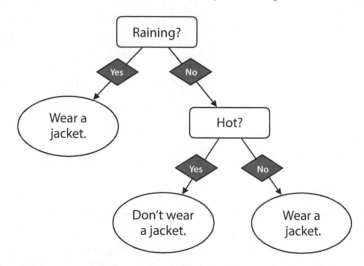

Figure 9.1   A decision tree used to decide whether we want to wear a jacket or not on a given day. We make the decision by traversing the tree down and taking the branch corresponding to each correct answer.

Our decision process looks like a tree, except it is upside down. The tree is formed of vertices, called *nodes*, and edges. On the very top, we can see the *root node*, from which two branches emanate. Each of the nodes has either two or zero branches (edges) emanating from them, and for this reason, we call it a *binary tree*. The nodes that have two branches emanating from them are called *decision nodes*, and the nodes with no branches emanating from them are called *leaf nodes*, or *leaves*. This arrangement of nodes, leaves, and edges is what we call a decision tree. Trees are natural objects in computer science, because computers break every process into a sequence of binary operations.

The simplest possible decision tree, called a *decision stump*, is formed by a single decision node (the root node) and two leaves. This represents a single yes-or-no question, based on which we immediately make a decision.

   The depth of a decision tree is the number of levels underneath the root node. Another way to measure it is by the length of the longest path from the root node to a leaf, where a path is measured by the number of edges it contains. The tree in figure 9.1 has a depth of 2. A decision stump has a depth of 1.

   Here is a summary of the definitions we've learned so far:

decision tree   A machine learning model based on yes-or-no questions and represented by a binary tree. The tree has a root node, decision nodes, leaf nodes, and branches.

root node   The topmost node of the tree. It contains the first yes-or-no question. For convenience, we refer to it as the *root*.

decision node   Each yes-or-no question in our model is represented by a decision node, with two branches emanating from it (one for the "yes" answer, and one for the "no" answer).

leaf node   A node that has no branches emanating from it. These represent the decisions we make after traversing the tree. For convenience, we refer to them as *leaves*.

branch   The two edges emanating from each decision node, corresponding to the "yes" and "no" answers to the question in the node. In this chapter, by convention, the branch to the left corresponds to "yes" and the branch to the right to "no."

depth   The number of levels in the decision tree. Alternatively, it is the number of branches on the longest path from the root node to a leaf node.

Throughout this chapter, nodes are drawn as rectangles with rounded edges, the answers in the branches as diamonds, and leaves as ovals. Figure 9.2 shows how a decision tree looks in general.

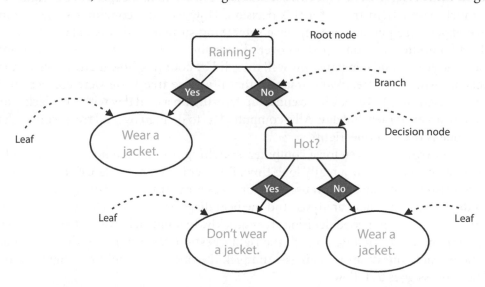

Figure 9.2   A regular decision tree with a root node, decision nodes, branches, and leaves. Note that each decision node contains a yes-or-no question. From each possible answer, one branch emanates, which can lead to another decision node or a leaf. This tree has a depth of 2, because the longest path from a leaf to the root goes through two branches.

How did we build this tree? Why were those the questions we asked? We could have also checked if it was Monday, if we saw a red car outside, or if we were hungry, and built the following decision tree:

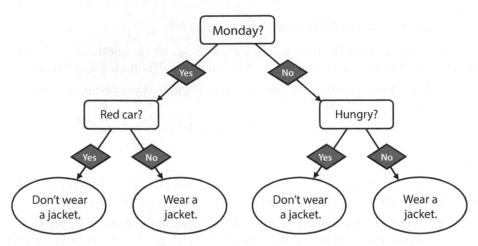

Figure 9.3   A second (maybe not as good) decision tree we could use to decide whether we want to wear a jacket on a given day

Which tree do we think is better when it comes to deciding whether or not to wear a jacket: tree 1 (figure 9.1) or tree 2 (figure 9.3)? Well, as humans, we have enough experience to figure out that tree 1 is much better than tree 2 for this decision. How would a computer know? Computers don't have experience per se, but they have something similar, which is data. If we wanted to think like a computer, we could just go over all possible trees, try each one of them for some time—say, one year—and compare how well they did by counting how many times we made the right decision using each tree. We'd imagine that if we use tree 1, we were correct most days, whereas if we used tree 2, we may have ended up freezing on a cold day without a jacket or wearing a jacket on an extremely hot day. All a computer has to do is go over all trees, collect data, and find which one is the best one, right?

Almost! Unfortunately, even for a computer, searching over all the possible trees to find the most effective one would take a really long time. But luckily, we have algorithms that make this search much faster, and thus, we can use decision trees for many wonderful applications, including spam detection, sentiment analysis, and medical diagnosis. In this chapter, we'll go over an algorithm for constructing good decision trees quickly. In a nutshell, we build the tree one node at a time, starting from the top. To pick the right question corresponding to each node, we go over all the possible questions we can ask and pick the one that is right the highest number of times. The process goes as follows:

Picking a good first question

We need to pick a good first question for the root of our tree. What would be a good question that helps us decide whether to wear a jacket on a given day? Initially, it can be anything. Let's say we come up with five candidates for our first question:

1. Is it raining?

2. Is it cold outside?

3. Am I hungry?

4. Is there a red car outside?

5. Is it Monday?

Out of these five questions, which one seems like the best one to help us decide whether we should wear a jacket? Our intuition says that the last three questions are useless to help us decide. Let's say that from experience, we've noticed that among the first two, the first one is more useful. We use that question to start building our tree. So far, we have a simple decision tree, or a decision stump, consisting of that single question, as illustrated in Figure 9.4.

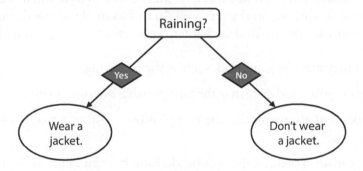

Figure 9.4   A simple decision tree (decision stump) that consists of only the question, "Is it raining?" If the answer is yes, the decision we make is to wear a jacket.

Can we do better? Imagine that we start noticing that when it rains, wearing a jacket is always the correct decision. However, there are days on which it doesn't rain, and not wearing a jacket is not the correct decision. This is where question 2 comes to our rescue. We use that question to help us in the following way: after we check that it is not raining, *then* we check the temperature, and if it is cold, we decide to wear a jacket. This turns the left leaf of the tree into a node, with two leaves emanating from it, as shown in figure 9.5.

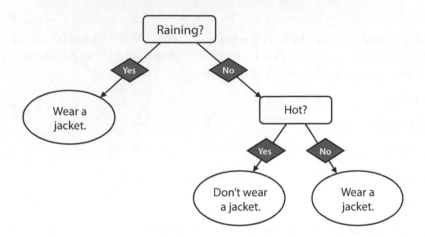

Figure 9.5   A slightly more complicated decision tree than the one in figure 9.4, where we have picked one leaf and split it into two further leaves. This is the same tree as in figure 9.1.

Now we have our decision tree. Can we do better? Maybe we can if we add more nodes and leaves to our tree. But for now, this one works very well. In this example, we made our decisions using our intuition and our experience. In this chapter, we learn an algorithm that builds these trees solely based on data.

Many questions may arise in your head, such as the following:

1. How exactly do you decide which is the best possible question to ask?

2. Does the process of always picking the best possible question actually get us to build *the* best decision tree?

3. Why don't we instead build all the possible decision trees and pick the best one from there?

4. Will we code this algorithm?

5. Where can we find decision trees in real life?

6. We can see how decision trees work for classification, but how do they work for regression?

This chapter answers all of these questions, but here are some quick answers:

1. **How exactly do you decide which is the best possible question to ask?**

   We have several ways to do this. The simplest one is using accuracy, which means: which question helps me be correct more often? However, in this chapter, we also learn other methods, such as Gini index or entropy.

2. **Does the process of always picking the best possible question actually get us to build *the* best decision tree?**

   Actually, this process does not guarantee that we get the best possible tree. This is what we call a *greedy algorithm*. Greedy algorithms work as follows: at every point, the algorithm makes the best possible available move. They tend to work well, but it's not always the case that making the best possible move at each timestep gets you to the best overall outcome. There may be times in which asking a weaker question groups our data in a way that we end up with a better tree at the end of the day. However, the algorithms for building decision trees tend to work very well and very quickly, so we'll live with this. Look at the algorithms that we see in this chapter, and try to figure out ways to improve them by removing the greedy property!

3. Why don't we instead build all the possible decision trees and pick the best one from there?

The number of possible decision trees is very large, especially if our dataset has many features. Going through all of them would be very slow. Here, finding each node requires only a linear search across the features and not across all the possible trees, which makes it much faster.

4. Will we code this algorithm?

This algorithm can be coded by hand. However, we'll see that because it is recursive, the coding can get a bit tedious. Thus, we'll use a useful package called Scikit-Learn to build decision trees with real data.

5. Where can we find decision trees in real life?

In many places! They are used extensively in machine learning, not only because they work very well but also because they give us a lot of information on our data. Some places in which decision trees are used are in recommendation systems (to recommend videos, movies, apps, products to buy, etc.), in spam classification (to decide whether or not an email is spam), in sentiment analysis (to decide whether a sentence is happy or sad), and in biology (to decide whether or not a patient is sick or to help identify certain hierarchies in species or in types of genomes).

6. We can see how decision trees work for classification, but how do they work for regression?

A regression decision tree looks exactly like a classification decision tree, except for the leaves. In a classification decision tree, the leaves have classes, such as yes and no. In a regression decision tree, the leaves have values, such as 4, 8.2, or –199. The prediction our model makes is given by the leaf at which we arrived when traversing the tree in a downward fashion.

The first use case that we'll study in this chapter is a popular application in machine learning, and one of my favorites: recommendation systems.

The code for this chapter is available in this GitHub repository: https://github.com/luisguiserrano/manning/tree/master/Chapter_9_Decision_Trees.

The problem: We need to recommend apps to users according to what they are likely to download

Recommendation systems are one of the most common and exciting applications in machine learning. Ever wonder how Netflix recommends movies, YouTube guesses which videos you may watch, or Amazon shows you products you might be interested in buying? These are all examples of recommendation systems. One simple and interesting way to see recommendation problems is to consider them classification problems. Let's start with an easy example: our very own app-recommendation system using decision trees.

Let's say we want to build a system that recommends to users which app to download among the following options. We have the following three apps in our store (figure 9.6):

- **Atom Count:** an app that counts the number of atoms in your body
- **Beehive Finder:** an app that maps your location and finds the closest beehives
- **Check Mate Mate:** an app for finding Australian chess players

Atom Count   Beehive Finder   Check Mate Mate

Figure 9.6   The three apps we are recommending: Atom Count, an app for counting the number of atoms in your body; Beehive Finder, an app for locating the nearest beehives to your location; and Check Mate Mate, an app for finding Australian chess players in your area

The training data is a table with the platform used by the user (iPhone or Android), their age, and the app they have downloaded (in real life there are many more platforms, but for simplicity we'll assume that these are the only two options). Our table contains six people, as shown in table 9.1.

Table 9.1   A dataset with users of an app store. For each customer, we record their platform, age, and the app they downloaded.

Platform	Age	App
iPhone	15	Atom Count
iPhone	25	Check Mate Mate
Android	32	Beehive Finder
iPhone	35	Check Mate Mate
Android	12	Atom Count
Android	14	Atom Count

Given this table, which app would you recommend to each of the following three customers?

- **Customer 1:** a 13-year-old iPhone user
- **Customer 2:** a 28-year-old iPhone user
- **Customer 3:** a 34-year-old Android user

What we should do follows:

Customer 1: a 13-year-old iPhone user. To this customer, we should recommend Atom Count, because it seems (looking at the three customers in their teens) that young people tend to download Atom Count.

Customer 2: a 28-year-old iPhone user. To this customer, we should recommend Check Mate Mate, because looking at the two iPhone users in the dataset (aged 25 and 35), they both downloaded Check Mate Mate.

Customer 3: a 34-year-old Android user. To this customer, we should recommend Beehive Finder, because there is one Android user in the dataset who is 32 years old, and they downloaded Beehive Finder.

However, going customer by customer seems like a tedious job. Next, we'll build a decision tree to take care of all customers at once.

The solution: Building an app-recommendation system

In this section, we see how to build an app-recommendation system using decision trees. In a nutshell, the algorithm to build a decision tree follows:

1. Figure out which of the data is the most useful to decide which app to recommend.

2. This feature splits the data into two smaller datasets.

3. Repeat processes 1 and 2 for each of the two smaller datasets.

In other words, what we do is decide which of the two features (platform or age) is more successful at determining which app the users will download and pick this one as our root of the decision tree. Then, we iterate over the branches, always picking the most determining feature for the data in that branch, thus building our decision tree.

First step to build the model: Asking the best question

The first step to build our model is to figure out the most useful feature: in other words, the most useful question to ask. First, let's simplify our data a little bit. Let's call everyone under 20 years old "Young" and everyone 20 or older "Adult" (don't worry—we'll go back to the original dataset soon, in the section "Splitting the data using continuous features, such as age"). Our modified dataset is shown in table 9.2.

Table 9.2   A simplified version of the dataset in table 9.1, where the age column has been simplified to two categories, "young" and "adult"

Platform	Age	App
iPhone	Young	Atom Count
iPhone	Adult	Check Mate Mate
Android	Adult	Beehive Finder
iPhone	Adult	Check Mate Mate
Android	Young	Atom Count
Android	Young	Atom Count

The building blocks of decision trees are questions of the form "Does the user use an iPhone?" or "Is the user young?" We need one of these to use as our root of the tree. Which one should we pick? We should pick the one that best determines the app they downloaded. To decide which question is better at this, let's compare them.

First question: Does the user use an iPhone or Android?

This question splits the users into two groups, the iPhone users and Android users. Each group has three users in it. But we need to keep track of which app each user downloaded. A quick look at table 9.2 helps us notice the following:

- Of the iPhone users, one downloaded Atom Count and two downloaded Check Mate Mate.
- Of the Android users, two downloaded Atom Count and one downloaded Beehive Finder.

The resulting decision stump is shown in figure 9.7.

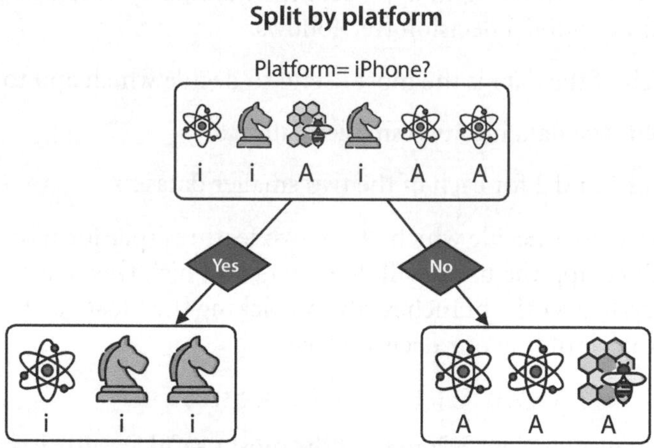

Figure 9.7   If we split our users by platform, we get this split: the iPhone users are on the left, and the Android users on the right. Of the iPhone users, one downloaded Atom Count and two downloaded Check Mate Mate. Of the Android users, two downloaded Atom Count and one downloaded Beehive Finder.

Now let's see what happens if we split them by age.

Second question: Is the user young or adult?

This question splits the users into two groups, the young and the adult. Again, each group has three users in it. A quick look at table 9.2 helps us notice what each user downloaded, as follows:

- The young users all downloaded Atom Count.

- Of the adult users, two downloaded Atom Count and one downloaded Beehive Finder.

The resulting decision stump is shown in figure 9.8.

Split by age

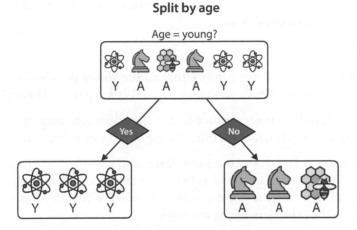

Figure 9.8 If we split our users by age, we get this split: the young are on the left, and the adults on the right. Out of the young users, all three downloaded Atom Count. Out of the adult users, one downloaded Beehive Finder and two downloaded Check Mate Mate.

From looking at figures 9.7 and 9.8, which one looks like a better split? It seems that the second one (based on age) is better, because it has picked up on the fact that all three young people downloaded Atom Count. But we need the computer to figure out that age is a better feature, so we'll give it some numbers to compare. In this section, we learn three ways to compare these two splits: accuracy, Gini impurity, and entropy. Let's start with the first one: accuracy.

Accuracy: How often is our model correct?

We learned about accuracy in chapter 7, but here is a small recap. Accuracy is the fraction of correctly classified data points over the total number of data points.

Suppose that we are allowed only one question, and with that one question, we must determine which app to recommend to our users. We have the following two classifiers:

- **Classifier 1:** asks the question "What platform do you use?" and from there, determines what app to recommend

- **Classifier 2:** asks the question "What is your age?" and from there, determines what app to recommend

Let's look more carefully at the classifiers. The key observation follows: if we must recommend an app by asking only one question, our best bet is to look at all the people who answered with the same answer and recommend the most common app among them.

Classifier 1: What platform do you use?

- If the answer is "iPhone," then we notice that of the iPhone users, the majority downloaded Check Mate Mate. Therefore, we recommend Check Mate Mate to all the iPhone users. We are correct **two times out of three**.

- If the answer is "Android," then we notice that of the Android users, the majority downloaded Atom Count, so that is the one we recommend to all the Android users. We are correct **two times out of three**.

Classifier 2: What is your age?

- If the answer is "young," then we notice that all the young people downloaded Atom Count, so that is the recommendation we make. We are correct **three times out of three**.

- If the answer is "adult," then we notice that of the adults, the majority downloaded Check Mate Mate, so we recommend that one. We are correct **two times out of three**.

Notice that classifier 1 is correct **four times out of six**, and classifier 2 is correct **five times out of six.** Therefore, for this dataset, classifier 2 is better. In figure 9.9, you can see the two classifiers with their accuracy. Notice that the questions are reworded so that they have yes-or-no answers, which doesn't change the classifiers or the outcome.

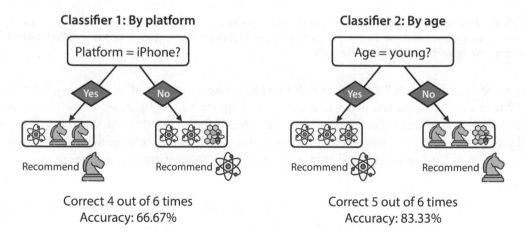

Figure 9.9 Classifier 1 uses platform, and classifier 2 uses age. To make the prediction at each leaf, each classifier picks the most common label among the samples in that leaf. Classifier 1 is correct four out of six times, and classifier 2 is correct five out of six times. Therefore, based on accuracy, classifier 2 is better.

Gini impurity index: How diverse is my dataset?

The *Gini impurity index,* or *Gini index,* is another way we can compare the platform and age splits. The Gini index is a measure of diversity in a dataset. In other words, if we have a set in which all the elements are similar, this set has a low Gini index, and if all the elements are different, it has a large Gini index. For clarity, consider the following two sets of 10 colored balls (where any two balls of the same color are indistinguishable):

- **Set 1:** eight red balls, two blue balls
- **Set 2:** four red balls, three blue balls, two yellow balls, one green ball

Set 1 looks more pure than set 2, because set 1 contains mostly red balls and a couple of blue ones, whereas set 2 has many different colors. Next, we devise a measure of impurity that assigns a low value to set 1 and a high value to set 2. This measure of impurity relies on probability. Consider the following question:

If we pick two random elements of the set, what is the probability that they have a different color? The two elements don't need to be distinct; we are allowed to pick the same element twice.

For set 1, this probability is low, because the balls in the set have similar colors. For set 2, this probability is high, because the set is diverse, and if we pick two balls, they're likely to be of different colors. Let's calculate these probabilities. First, notice that by the law of complementary probabilities (see the section "What the math just happened?" in chapter 8), the probability that we pick two balls of different colors is 1 minus the probability that we pick two balls of the same color:

$$P(\text{picking two balls of different color}) = 1 - P(\text{picking two balls of the same color})$$

Now let's calculate the probability that we pick two balls of the same color. Consider a general set, where the balls have n colors. Let's call them color 1, color 2, all the way up to color n. Because the two balls must be of one of the n colors, the probability of picking two balls of the same color is the sum of probabilities of picking two balls of each of the n colors:

$$P(\text{picking two balls of the same color}) = P(\text{both balls are color 1}) +$$
$$P(\text{both balls are color 2}) + \ldots + P(\text{both balls are color } n)$$

What we used here is the sum rule for disjoint probabilities, that states the following:

sum rule for disjoint probabilities If two events E and F are disjoint, namely, they never occur at the same time, then the probability of either one of them happening (the union of the events) is the sum of the probabilities of each of the events. In other words,

$$P(E \cup F) = P(E) + P(F)$$

Now, let's calculate the probability that two balls have the same color, for each of the colors. Notice that we're picking each ball completely independently from the others. Therefore, by the product rule for independent probabilities (section "What the math just happened?" in chapter 8), the probability that both balls have color 1 is the square of the probability that we pick one ball and it is of color 1. In general, if p_i is the probability that we pick a random ball and it is of color i, then

$$P(\text{both balls are color } i) = p_i^2.$$

Putting all these formulas together (figure 9.10), we get that

$$P(\text{picking two balls of different colors}) = 1 - p_1^2 - p_2^2 - \cdots - p_n^2.$$

This last formula is the Gini index of the set.

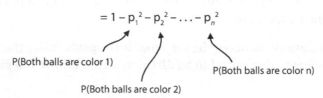

Gini impurity Index = P(picking two balls of different colors)

= 1 − P(picking two balls of the same color)

= 1 − p$_1$² − p$_2$² − ... − p$_n$²

P(Both balls are color 1)

P(Both balls are color 2)

P(Both balls are color n)

Figure 9.10   Summary of the calculation of the Gini impurity index

Finally, the probability that we pick a random ball of color i is the number of balls of color i divided by the total number of balls. This leads to the formal definition of the Gini index.

> **gini impurity index**   In a set with m elements and n classes, with a_i elements belonging to the i-th class, the Gini impurity index is
>
> $$Gini = 1 - p_1^2 - p_2^2 - \cdots - p_n^2,$$
>
> where $p_i = \dfrac{a_i}{m}$. This can be interpreted as the probability that if we pick two random elements

out of the set, they belong to different classes.

Now we can calculate the Gini index for both of our sets. For clarity, the calculation of the Gini index for set 1 is illustrated in figure 9.11 (with red and blue replaced by black and white).

Set 1: {red, red, red, red, red, red, red, red, blue, blue} (eight red balls, two blue balls)

$$\text{Gini impurity index} = 1 - \left(\frac{8}{10}\right)^2 - \left(\frac{2}{10}\right)^2 = 1 - \frac{68}{100} = 0.32$$

Set 2: {red, red, red, red, blue, blue, blue, yellow, yellow, green}

$$\text{Gini impurity index} = 1 - \left(\frac{4}{10}\right)^2 - \left(\frac{3}{10}\right)^2 - \left(\frac{2}{10}\right)^2 - \left(\frac{1}{10}\right)^2 = 1 - \frac{30}{100} = 0.7$$

Notice that, indeed, the Gini index of set 1 is larger than that of set 2.

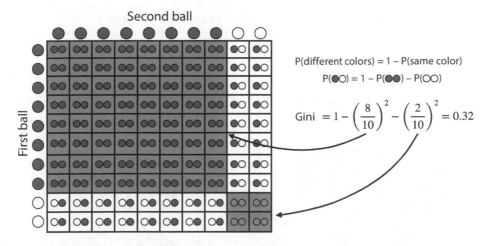

Figure 9.11 The calculation of the Gini index for the set with eight black balls and two white balls. Note that if the total area of the square is 1, the probability of picking two black balls is 0.8^2, and the probability of picking two white balls is 0.2^2 (these two are represented by the shaded squares). Thus, the probability of picking two balls of a different color is the remaining area, which is $1 - 0.8^2 - 0.2^2 = 0.32$. That is the Gini index.

How do we use the Gini index to decide which of the two ways to split the data (age or platform) is better? Clearly, if we can split the data into two purer datasets, we have performed a better split. Thus, let's calculate the Gini index of the set of labels of each of the leaves. Looking at figure 9.12, here are the labels of the leaves (where we abbreviate each app by the first letter in its name):

Classifier 1 (by platform):

- Left leaf (iPhone): {A, C, C}
- Right leaf (Android): {A, A, B}

Classifier 2 (by age):

- Left leaf (young): {A, A, A}
- Right leaf (adult): {B, C, C}

The Gini indices of the sets {A, C, C}, {A, A, B}, and {B, C, C} are all the same: $1 - \left(\dfrac{2}{3}\right)^2 - \left(\dfrac{1}{3}\right)^2 = 0.444$.

The Gini index of the set {A, A, A} is $1 - \left(\dfrac{3}{3}\right)^2 = 0$. In general, the Gini index of a pure set is always 0. To measure the purity of the split, we average the Gini indices of the two leaves. Therefore, we have the following calculations:

Classifier 1 (by platform):

$$\text{Average Gini index} = \frac{1}{2}(0.444+0.444) = 0.444$$

Classifier 2 (by age):

$$\text{Average Gini index} = \frac{1}{2}(0.444+0) = 0.222$$

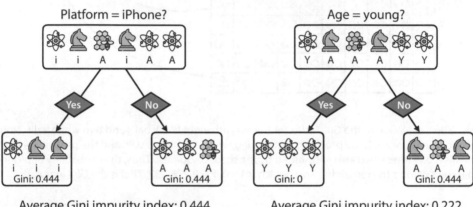

Figure 9.12   The two ways to split the dataset, by platform and age, and their Gini index calculations. Notice that splitting the dataset by age gives us two smaller datasets with a lower average Gini index. Therefore, we choose to split the dataset by age.

We conclude that the second split is better, because it has a lower average Gini index.

aside   The Gini impurity index should not be confused with the Gini coefficient. The Gini coefficient is used in statistics to calculate the income or wealth inequality in countries. In this book, whenever we talk about the Gini index, we are referring to the Gini impurity index.

Entropy: Another measure of diversity with strong applications in information theory

In this section, we learn another measure of homogeneity in a set—its entropy—which is based on the physical concept of entropy and is highly important in probability and information theory. To understand entropy, we look at a slightly strange probability question. Consider the same two sets of colored balls as in the previous section, but think of the colors as an ordered set.

- **Set 1:** {red, red, red, red, red, red, red, red, blue, blue} (eight red balls, two blue balls)
- **Set 2:** {red, red, red, red, blue, blue, blue, yellow, yellow, green} (four red balls, three blue balls, two yellow balls, one green ball)

Now, consider the following scenario: we have set 1 inside a bag, and we start picking balls out of this bag and immediately return each ball we just picked back to the bag. We record the colors of the balls we picked. If we do this 10 times, imagine that we get the following sequence:

- Red, red, red, blue, red, blue, blue, red, red, red

Here is the main question that defines entropy:

What is the probability that, by following the procedure described in the previous paragraph, we get the exact sequence that defines set 1, which is {red, red, red, red, red, red, red, red, blue, blue}?

This probability is not very large, because we must be really lucky to get this sequence. Let's calculate it. We have eight red balls and two blue balls, so the probability that we get a red ball is $\frac{8}{10}$, and the probability that we get a blue ball is $\frac{2}{10}$. Because all the draws are independent, the probability that we get the desired sequence is

$$P(r, r, r, r, r, r, r, r, b, b) = \frac{8}{10} \cdot \frac{8}{10} \cdot \frac{8}{10} \cdot \frac{8}{10} \cdot \frac{8}{10} \cdot \frac{8}{10} \cdot \frac{8}{10} \cdot \frac{8}{10} \cdot \frac{2}{10} \cdot \frac{2}{10}$$

$$= \left(\frac{8}{10}\right)^8 \left(\frac{2}{10}\right)^2 = 0.0067108864.$$

This is tiny, but can you imagine the corresponding probability for set 2? For set 2, we are picking balls out of a bag with four red balls, three blue balls, two yellow balls, and one green ball and hoping to obtain the following sequence:

- Red, red, red, red, blue, blue, blue, yellow, yellow, green.

This is nearly impossible, because we have many colors and not many balls of each color. This probability, which is calculated in a similar way, is

$$P(r, r, r, r, b, b, b, y, y, g) = \frac{4}{10} \cdot \frac{4}{10} \cdot \frac{4}{10} \cdot \frac{4}{10} \cdot \frac{3}{10} \cdot \frac{3}{10} \cdot \frac{3}{10} \cdot \frac{2}{10} \cdot \frac{2}{10} \cdot \frac{1}{10}$$

$$= \left(\frac{4}{10}\right)^4 \left(\frac{3}{10}\right)^3 \left(\frac{2}{10}\right)^2 \left(\frac{1}{10}\right)^1 = 0.0000027648.$$

The more diverse the set, the more unlikely we'll be able to get the original sequence by picking one ball at a time. In contrast, the most pure set, in which all balls are of the same color, is easy to obtain this way. For example, if our original set has 10 red balls, each time we pick a random ball, the ball is red. Thus, the probability of getting the sequence {red, red, red, red, red, red, red, red, red, red} is 1.

These numbers are very small for most cases—and this is with only 10 elements. Imagine if our dataset had one million elements. We would be dealing with tremendously small numbers. When we have to deal with really small numbers, using logarithms is the best method, because they provide a convenient way to write small numbers. For instance, 0.000000000000001 is equal to 10^{-15}, so its logarithm in base 10 is –15, which is a much nicer number to work with.

The entropy is defined as follows: we start with the probability that we recover the initial sequence by picking elements in our set, one at a time, with repetition. Then we take the logarithm, and divide by the total number of elements in the set. Because decision trees deal with binary decisions, we'll be using logarithms in base 2. The reason we took the negative of the logarithm is because logarithms of very small numbers are all negative, so we multiply by –1 to turn it into a positive number. Because we took a negative, the more diverse the set, the higher the entropy.

Now we can calculate the entropies of both sets and expand them using the following two identities:

- $log(ab) = log(a) + log(b)$

- $log(a^c) = c\, log(a)$

Set 1: {red, red, red, red, red, red, red, red, blue, blue} (eight red balls, two blue balls)

$$Entropy = -\frac{1}{10}\log_2\left[\left(\frac{8}{10}\right)^8\left(\frac{2}{10}\right)^2\right] = -\frac{8}{10}\log_2\left(\frac{8}{10}\right) - \frac{2}{10}\log_2\left(\frac{2}{10}\right) = 0.722$$

Set 2: {red, red, red, red, blue, blue, blue, yellow, yellow, green}

$$Entropy = -\frac{1}{10}\log_2\left[\left(\frac{4}{10}\right)^4\left(\frac{3}{10}\right)^3\left(\frac{2}{10}\right)^2\left(\frac{1}{10}\right)^1\right]$$

$$= -\frac{4}{10}\log_2\left(\frac{4}{10}\right) - \frac{3}{10}\log_2\left(\frac{3}{10}\right) - \frac{2}{10}\log_2\left(\frac{2}{10}\right) - \frac{1}{10}\log_2\left(\frac{1}{10}\right) = 1.846$$

Notice that the entropy of set 2 is larger than the entropy of set 1, which implies that set 2 is more diverse than set 1. The following is the formal definition of entropy:

entropy   In a set with m elements and n classes, with a_i elements belonging to the i-th class, the entropy is

$$Entropy = -p_1\, log_2(p_1) - p_2\, log_2(p_2) - \cdots - p_n\, log_2(p_n),$$

$$where\ p_i = \frac{a_i}{m}.$$

We can use entropy to decide which of the two ways to split the data (platform or age) is better in the same way as we did with the Gini index. The rule of thumb is that if we can split the data into two datasets with less combined entropy, we have performed a better split. Thus, let's calculate the entropy of the set of labels of each of the leaves. Again, looking at figure 9.12, here are the labels of the leaves (where we abbreviate each app by the first letter in its name):

Classifier 1 (by platform):
Left leaf: {A, C, C}
Right leaf: {A, A, B}

Classifier 2 (by age):
Left leaf: {A, A, A}
Right leaf: {B, C, C}

The entropies of the sets {A, C, C}, {A, A, B}, and {B, C, C} are all the same: $-\frac{2}{3}\log_2\left(\frac{2}{3}\right) - \frac{1}{3}\log_2\left(\frac{1}{3}\right)$

$= 0.918$. The entropy of the set {A, A, A} is $-\log\left(\frac{3}{3}\right) = -\log_2(1) = 0$. In general, the entropy of a

set in which all elements are the same is always 0. To measure the purity of the split, we average the entropy of the sets of labels of the two leaves, as follows (illustrated in figure 9.13):

Classifier 1 (by platform):

Average entropy $= \frac{1}{2}(0.918 + 0.918) = 0.918$

Classifier 2 (by age):

Average entropy $= \frac{1}{2}(0.918+0) = 0.459$

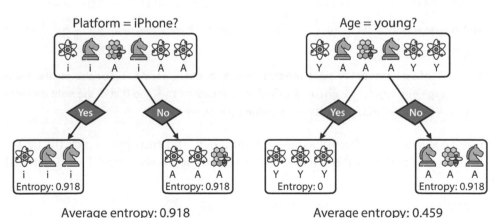

Figure 9.13 The two ways to split the dataset, by platform and age, and their entropy calculations. Notice that splitting the dataset by age gives us two smaller datasets with a lower average entropy. Therefore, we again choose to split the dataset by age.

Thus, again we conclude that the second split is better, because it has a lower average entropy.

Entropy is a tremendously important concept in probability and statistics, because it has strong connections with information theory, mostly thanks to the work of Claude Shannon. In fact, an important concept called *information gain* is precisely the change in entropy. To learn more on the topic, please see appendix C for a video and a blog post which covers this topic in much more detail.

Classes of different sizes? No problem: We can take weighted averages

In the previous sections we learned how to perform the best possible split by minimizing average Gini impurity index or entropy. However, imagine that you have a dataset with eight data points (which when training the decision tree, we also refer to as samples), and you split it into two datasets of sizes six and two. As you may imagine, the larger dataset should count for more in the calculations of Gini impurity index or entropy. Therefore, instead of considering the average, we consider the weighted average, where at each leaf, we assign the proportion of points corresponding to that leaf. Thus, in this case, we would weigh the first Gini impurity index (or entropy) by 6/8, and the second one by 2/8. Figure 9.14 shows an example of a weighted average Gini impurity index and a weighted average entropy for a sample split.

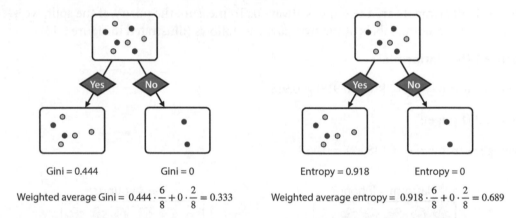

Weighted average Gini = $0.444 \cdot \dfrac{6}{8} + 0 \cdot \dfrac{2}{8} = 0.333$ Weighted average entropy = $0.918 \cdot \dfrac{6}{8} + 0 \cdot \dfrac{2}{8} = 0.689$

Figure 9.14 A split of a dataset of size eight into two datasets of sizes six and two. To calculate the average Gini index and the average entropy, we weight the index of the left dataset by $\frac{6}{8}$ and that of the right dataset by $\frac{2}{8}$. This results in a weighted Gini index of 0.333 and a weighted entropy of 0.689.

Now that we've learned three ways (accuracy, Gini index, and entropy) to pick the best split, all we need to do is iterate this process many times to build the decision tree! This is detailed in the next section.

Second step to build the model: Iterating

In the previous section, we learned how to split the data in the best possible way using one of the features. That is the bulk of the training process of a decision tree. All that is left to finish building our decision tree is to iterate on this step many times. In this section we learn how to do this.

Using the three methods, accuracy, Gini index, and entropy, we decided that the best split was made using the "age" feature. Once we make this split, our dataset is divided into two datasets. The split into these two datasets, with their accuracy, Gini index, and entropy, is illustrated in figure 9.15.

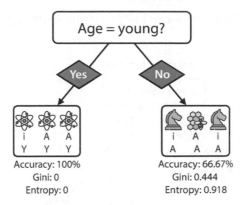

Figure 9.15 When we split our dataset by age, we get two datasets. The one on the left has three users who downloaded Atom Count, and the one on the right has one user who downloaded Beehive Count and two who downloaded Check Mate Mate.

Notice that the dataset on the left is pure—all the labels are the same, its accuracy is 100%, and its Gini index and entropy are both 0. There's nothing more we can do to split this dataset or to improve the classifications. Thus, this node becomes a leaf node, and when we get to that leaf, we return the prediction "Atom Count."

The dataset on the right can still be divided, because it has two labels: "Beehive Count" and "Check Mate Mate." We've used the age feature already, so let's try using the platform feature. It turns out that we're in luck, because the Android user downloaded Beehive Count, and the two iPhone users downloaded Check Mate Mate. Therefore, we can split this leaf using the platform feature and obtain the decision node shown in figure 9.16.

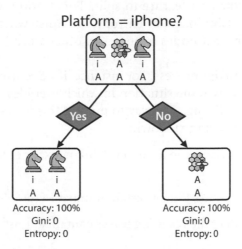

Figure 9.16 We can split the right leaf of the tree in figure 9.15 using platform and obtain two pure datasets. Each one of them has an accuracy of 100% and a Gini index and entropy of 0.

After this split, we are done, because we can't improve our splits any further. Thus, we obtain the tree in figure 9.17.

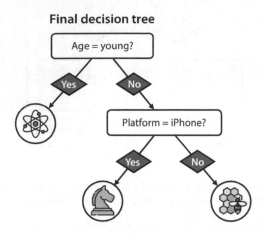

Final decision tree

Figure 9.17   The resulting decision tree has two nodes and three leaves. This tree predicts every point in the original dataset correctly.

This is the end of our process, and we have built a decision tree that classifies our entire dataset. We almost have all the pseudocode for the algorithm, except for some final details which we see in the next section.

Last step: When to stop building the tree and other hyperparameters

In the previous section, we built a decision tree by recursively splitting our dataset. Each split was performed by picking the best feature to split. This feature was found using any of the following metrics: accuracy, Gini index, or entropy. We finish when the portion of the dataset corresponding to each of the leaf nodes is pure—in other words, when all the samples on it have the same label.

Many problems can arise in this process. For instance, if we continue splitting our data for too long, we may end up with an extreme situation in which every leaf contains very few samples, which can lead to serious overfitting. The way to prevent this is to introduce a stopping condition. This condition can be any of the following:

1. Don't split a node if the change in accuracy, Gini index, or entropy is below some threshold.

2. Don't split a node if it has less than a certain number of samples.

3. Split a node only if both of the resulting leaves contain at least a certain number of samples.

4. Stop building the tree after you reach a certain depth.

All of these stopping conditions require a hyperparameter. More specifically, these are the hyperparameters corresponding to the previous four conditions:

1. The minimum amount of change in accuracy (or Gini index, or entropy)

2. The minimum number of samples that a node must have to split it

3. The minimum number of samples allowed in a leaf node

4. The maximum depth of the tree

The way we pick these hyperparameters is either by experience or by running an exhaustive search where we look for different combinations of hyperparameters and choose the one that performs best in our validation set. This process is called *grid search*, and we'll study it in more detail in the section "Tuning the hyperparameters to find the best model: Grid search" in chapter 13.

The decision tree algorithm: How to build a decision tree and make predictions with it

Now we are finally ready to state the pseudocode for the decision tree algorithm, which allows us to train a decision tree to fit a dataset.

Pseudocode for the decision tree algorithm

Inputs:

- A training dataset of samples with their associated labels

- A metric to split the data (accuracy, Gini index, or entropy)

- One (or more) stopping condition

Output:

- A decision tree that fits the dataset

Procedure:

- Add a root node, and associate it with the entire dataset. This node has level 0. Call it a leaf node.

- Repeat until the stopping conditions are met at every leaf node:

  - Pick one of the leaf nodes at the highest level.

  - Go through all the features, and select the one that splits the samples corresponding to that node in an optimal way, according to the selected metric. Associate that feature to the node.

  - This feature splits the dataset into two branches. Create two new leaf nodes, one for each branch, and associate the corresponding samples to each of the nodes.

- If the stopping conditions allow a split, turn the node into a decision node, and add two new leaf nodes underneath it. If the level of the node is i, the two new leaf nodes are at level $i + 1$.

- If the stopping conditions don't allow a split, the node becomes a leaf node. To this leaf node, associate the most common label among its samples. That label is the prediction at the leaf.

Return:

- The decision tree obtained.

To make predictions using this tree, we simply traverse down it, using the following rules:

- Traverse the tree downward. At every node, continue in the direction that is indicated by the feature.

- When arriving at a leaf, the prediction is the label associated with the leaf (the most common among the samples associated with that leaf in the training process).

This is how we make predictions using the app-recommendation decision tree we built previously. When a new user comes, we check their age and their platform, and take the following actions:

- If the user is young, then we recommend them Atom Count.

- If the user is an adult, then we check their platform.

    - If the platform is Android, then we recommend Beehive Count.

    - If the platform is iPhone, then we recommend Check Mate Mate.

aside   The literature contains terms like *Gini gain* and *information gain* when training decision trees. The Gini gain is the difference between the weighted Gini impurity index of the leaves and the Gini impurity index (entropy) of the decision node we are splitting. In a similar way, the information gain is the difference between the weighted entropy of the leaves and the entropy of the root. The more common way to train decision trees is by maximizing the Gini gain or the information gain. However, in this chapter, we train decision trees by, instead, minimizing the weighted Gini index or the weighted entropy. The training process is exactly the same, because the Gini impurity index (entropy) of the decision node is constant throughout the process of splitting that particular decision node.

Beyond questions like yes/no

In the section "The solution: Building an app-recommendation system," we learned how to build a decision tree for a very specific case in which every feature was categorical and binary (meaning that it has only two classes, such as the platform of the user). However, almost the same algorithm works to build a decision tree with categorical features with more classes (such as dog/cat/bird) and even with numerical features (such as age or average income). The main step to modify is the step in which we split the dataset, and in this section, we show you how.

Splitting the data using non-binary categorical features, such as dog/cat/bird

Recall that when we want to split a dataset based on a binary feature, we simply ask one yes-or-no question of the form, "Is the feature X?" For example, when the feature is the platform, a question to ask is "Is the user an iPhone user?" If we have a feature with more than two classes, we just ask several questions. For example, if the input is an animal that could be a dog, a cat, or a bird, then we ask the following questions:

- Is the animal a dog?

- Is the animal a cat?

- Is the animal a bird?

No matter how many classes a feature has, we can split it into several binary questions (figure 9.18).

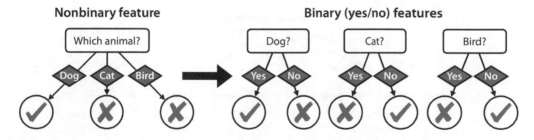

Figure 9.18 When we have a nonbinary feature, for example, one with three or more possible categories, we instead turn it into several binary (yes-or-no) features, one for each category. For example, if the feature is a dog, the answers to the three questions "Is it a dog?," "Is it a cat?," and "Is it a bird?" are "yes," "no," and "no."

Each of the questions splits the data in a different way. To figure out which of the three questions gives us the best split, we use the same methods as in the section "First step to build the model": accuracy, Gini index, or entropy. This process of turning a nonbinary categorical feature into several binary features is called *one-hot encoding*. In the section "Turning categorical data into numerical data" in chapter 13, we see it used in a real dataset.

Splitting the data using continuous features, such as age

Recall that before we simplified our dataset, the "age" feature contained numbers. Let's get back to our original table and build a decision tree there (table 9.3).

Table 9.3 Our original app recommendation dataset with the platform and (numerical) age of the users. This is the same as table 9.1.

Platform	Age	App
iPhone	15	Atom Count
iPhone	25	Check Mate Mate
Android	32	Beehive Finder
iPhone	35	Check Mate Mate
Android	12	Atom Count
Android	14	Atom Count

The idea is to turn the Age column into several questions of the form, "Is the user younger than X?" or "Is the user older than X?" It seems like we have infinitely many questions to ask, because there are infinitely many numbers, but notice that many of these questions split the data in the same way. For example, asking, "Is the user younger than 20?" and "Is the user younger than 21," gives us the same split. In fact, only seven splits are possible, as illustrated in figure 9.19.

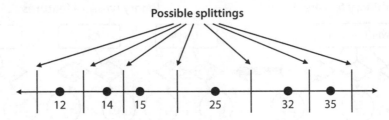

Figure 9.19 A graphic of the seven possible ways to split the users by age. Note that it doesn't matter where we put the cutoffs, as long as they lie between consecutive ages (except for the first and last cutoff).

As a convention, we'll pick the midpoints between consecutive ages to be the age for splitting. For the endpoints, we can pick any random value that is out of the interval. Thus, we have seven possible questions that split the data into two sets, as shown in table 9.4. In this table, we have also calculated the accuracy, the Gini impurity index, and the entropy of each of the splits.

Notice that the fourth question ("Is the user younger than 20?") gives the highest accuracy, the lowest weighted Gini index, and the lowest weighted entropy and, therefore, is the best split that can be made using the "age" feature.

Table 9.4 The seven possible questions we can pick, each with the corresponding splitting. In the first set, we put the users who are younger than the cutoff, and in the second set, those who are older than the cutoff.

Question	First set (yes)	Second set (no)	Labels	Weighted accuracy	Weighted Gini impurity index	Weighted entropy
Is the user younger than 7?	empty	12, 14, 15, 25, 32, 35	{}, {A,A,A,C,B,C}	3/6	0.611	1.459
Is the user younger than 13?	12	14, 15, 25, 32, 35	{A}, {A,A,C,B,C}	3/6	0.533	1.268
Is the user younger than 14.5?	12, 14	15, 25, 32, 35	{A,A} {A,C,B,C}	4/6	0.417	1.0
Is the user younger than 20?	**12, 14, 15**	**25, 32, 35**	**{A,A,A}, {C,B,C}**	**5/6**	**0.222**	**0.459**
Is the user younger than 28.5?	12, 14, 15, 25	32, 35	{A,A,A,C}, {B,C}	4/6	0.416	0.874
Is the user younger than 33.5?	12, 14, 15, 25, 32	35	{A,A,A,C,B}, {C}	4/6	0.467	1.145
Is the user younger than 100?	12, 14, 15, 25, 32, 35	empty	{A,A,A,C,B,C}, {}	3/6	0.611	1/459

Carry out the calculations in the table, and verify that you get the same answers. The entire calculation of these Gini indices is in the following notebook: https://github.com/luisguiserrano/manning/blob/master/Chapter_9_Decision_Trees/Gini_entropy_calculations.ipynb.

For clarity, let's carry out the calculations of accuracy, weighted Gini impurity index, and weighted entropy for the third question. Notice that this question splits the data into the following two sets:

- **Set 1** (younger than 14.5)
  - Ages: 12, 14
  - Labels: {A, A}

- **Set 2** (14.5 and older):
  - Ages: 15, 25, 32, 25
  - Labels: {A, C, B, C}

Accuracy calculation

The most common label in set 1 is "A" and in set 2 is "C," so these are the predictions we'll make for each of the corresponding leaves. In set 1, every element is predicted correctly, and in set 2, only two elements are predicted correctly. Therefore, this decision stump is correct in four out of the six data points, for an accuracy of 4/6 = 0.667.

For the next two calculations, notice the following:

- Set 1 is pure (all its labels are the same), so its Gini impurity index and entropy are both 0.

- In set 2, the proportions of elements with labels "A," "B," and "C" are $\frac{1}{4}$, $\frac{1}{4}$, and $\frac{2}{4} = \frac{1}{2}$, respectively.

Weighted Gini impurity index calculation

The Gini impurity index of the set {A, A} is 0.

The Gini impurity index of the set {A, C, B, C} is $1 - \left(\frac{1}{4}\right)^2 - \left(\frac{1}{4}\right)^2 - \left(\frac{1}{2}\right)^2 = 0.625$.

The weighted average of the two Gini impurity indices is $\frac{2}{6} \cdot 0 + \frac{4}{6} \cdot 0.625 = 0.417$.

Accuracy calculation

The entropy of the set {A, A} is 0.

The entropy of the set {A, C, B, C} is $-\frac{1}{4}\log_2\left(\frac{1}{4}\right) - \frac{1}{4}\log_2\left(\frac{1}{4}\right) - \frac{1}{2}\log_2\left(\frac{1}{2}\right) = 1.5$.

The weighted average of the two entropies is $\frac{2}{6} \cdot 0 + \frac{4}{6} \cdot 1.5 = 1.0$.

A numerical feature becomes a series of yes-or-no questions, which can be measured and compared with the other yes-or-no questions coming from other features, to pick the best one for that decision node.

> **aside** This app-recommendation model is very small, so we could do it all by hand. However, to see it in code, please check this notebook: https://github.com/luisguiserrano/manning/blob/master/Chapter_9_Decision_Trees/App_recommendations.ipynb. The notebook uses the Scikit-Learn package, which we introduce in more detail in the section "Using Scikit-Learn to build a decision tree."

The graphical boundary of decision trees

In this section, I show you two things: how to build a decision tree geometrically (in two dimensions) and how to code a decision tree in the popular machine learning package Scikit-Learn.

Recall that in classification models, such as the perceptron (chapter 5) or the logistic classifier (chapter 6), we plotted the boundary of the model that separated the points with labels 0 and 1, and it turned out to be a straight line. The boundary of a decision tree is also nice, and when the data is two-dimensional, it is formed by a combination of vertical and horizontal lines. In this section, we illustrate this with an example. Consider the dataset in figure 9.20, where the points with label 1 are triangles, and the points with label 0 are squares. The horizontal and vertical axes are called x_0 and x_1, respectively.

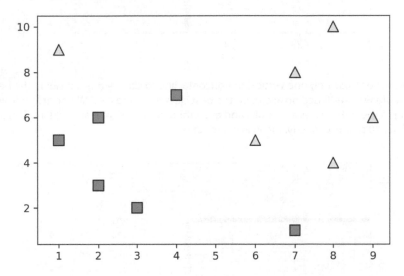

Figure 9.20 A dataset with two features (x_0 and x_1) and two labels (triangle and square) in which we will train a decision tree

If you had to split this dataset using only one horizontal or vertical line, what line would you pick? There could be different lines, according to the criteria you would use to measure the effectiveness of a solution. Let's go ahead and select a vertical line at $x_0 = 5$. This leaves mostly triangles to the right of it and mostly squares to the left of it, with the exception of two misclassified points, one square and one triangle (figure 9.21). Try checking all the other possible vertical and horizontal lines, compare them using your favorite metric (accuracy, Gini index, and entropy), and verify that this is the line that best divides the points.

Now let's look at each half separately. This time, it's easy to see that two horizontal lines at $x_1 = 8$ and $x_1 = 2.5$ will do the job on the left and the right side, respectively. These lines completely divide the dataset into squares and triangles. Figure 9.22 illustrates the result.

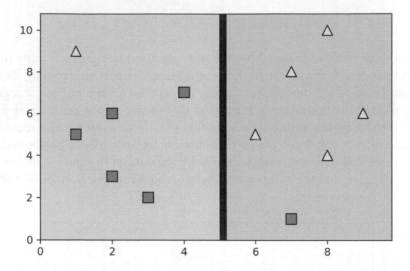

Figure 9.21   If we have to use only one vertical or horizontal line to classify this dataset in the best possible way, which one would we use? Based on accuracy, the best classifier is the vertical line at $x_0 = 5$, where we classify everything to the right of it as a triangle, and everything to the left of it as a square. This simple classifier classifies 8 out of the 10 points correctly, for an accuracy of 0.8.

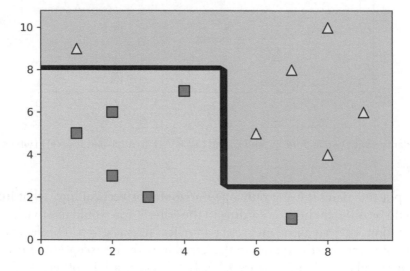

Figure 9.22   The classifier in figure 9.21 leaves us with two datasets, one at each side of the vertical line. If we had to classify each one of them, again using one vertical or horizontal line, which one would we choose? The best choices are horizontal lines at $x_1 = 8$ and $x_1 = 2.5$, as the figure shows.

What we did here was build a decision tree. At every stage, we picked from each of the two features (x_0 and x_1) and selected the threshold that best splits our data. In fact, in the next subsection, we use Scikit-Learn to build the same decision tree on this dataset.

Using Scikit-Learn to build a decision tree

In this section, we learn how to use a popular machine learning package called Scikit-Learn (abbreviated sklearn) to build a decision tree. The code for this section follows:

- **Notebook:** Graphical_example.ipynb
  - https://github.com/luisguiserrano/manning/blob/master/Chapter_9_Decision_Trees/Graphical_example.ipynb

We begin by loading the dataset as a Pandas DataFrame called `dataset` (introduced in chapter 8), with the following lines of code:

```
import pandas as pd
dataset = pd.DataFrame({
    'x_0':[7,3,2,1,2,4,1,8,6,7,8,9],
    'x_1':[1,2,3,5,6,7,9,10,5,8,4,6],
    'y': [0,0,0,0,0,0,1,1,1,1,1,1]})
```

Now we separate the features from the labels as shown here:

```
features = dataset[['x_0', 'x_1']]
labels = dataset['y']
```

To build the decision tree, we create a `DecisionTreeClassifier` object and use the `fit` function, as follows:

```
decision_tree = DecisionTreeClassifier()
decision_tree.fit(features, labels)
```

We obtained the plot of the tree, shown in figure 9.23, using the `display_tree` function in the utils.py file.

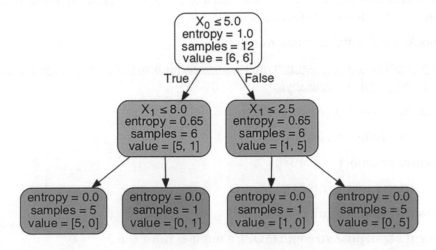

Figure 9.23 The resulting decision tree of depth 2 that corresponds to the boundary in figure 9.22. It has three nodes and four leaves.

Notice that the tree in figure 9.23 corresponds precisely to the boundary in figure 9.22. The root node corresponds to the first vertical line at $x_0 = 5$, with the points at each side of the line corresponding to the two branches. The two horizontal lines at $x_1 = 8.0$ and $x_1 = 2.5$ on the left and right halves of the plot correspond to the two branches. Furthermore, at each node we have the following information:

- **Gini:** the Gini impurity index of the labels at that node

- **Samples:** the number of data points (samples) corresponding to that node

- **Value:** the number of data points of each of the two labels at that node

As you can see, this tree has been trained using the Gini index, which is the default in Scikit-Learn. To train it using entropy, we can specify it when building the `DecisionTree` object, as follows:

```
decision_tree = DecisionTreeClassifier(criterion='entropy')
```

We can specify more hyperparameters when training the tree, which we see in the next section with a much bigger example.

Real-life application: Modeling student admissions with Scikit-Learn

In this section, we use decision trees to build a model that predicts admission to graduate schools. The dataset can be found in Kaggle (see appendix C for the link). As in the section "The graphical boundary of decision trees," we'll use Scikit-Learn to train the decision tree and Pandas to handle the dataset. The code for this section follows:

- **Notebook:** University_admissions.ipynb

    - https://github.com/luisguiserrano/manning/blob/master/Chapter_9_Decision_Trees/University_Admissions.ipynb

- **Dataset:** Admission_Predict.csv

The dataset has the following features:

- **GRE score:** a number out of 340

- **TOEFL score:** a number out of 120

- **University rating:** a number from 1 to 5

- **Statement of purpose strength (SOP):** a number from 1 to 5

- **Undergraduate grade point average (CGPA):** a number from 1 to 10

- **Letter of recommendation strength (LOR):** a number from 1 to 5
- **Research experience:** Boolean variable (0 or 1)

The labels on the dataset are the chance of admission, which is a number between 0 and 1. To have binary labels, we'll consider every student with a chance of 0.75 or higher as "admitted," and any other student as "not admitted."

The code for loading the dataset into a Pandas DataFrame and performing this preprocessing step is shown next:

```
import pandas as pd
data = pd.read_csv('Admission_Predict.csv', index_col=0)
data['Admitted'] = data['Chance of Admit'] >= 0.75
data = data.drop(['Chance of Admit'], axis=1)
```

The first few rows of the resulting dataset are shown in table 9.5.

Table 9.5 A dataset with 400 students and their scores in standardized tests, grades, university ratings, letters of recommendations, statements of purpose, and information about their chances of being admitted to graduate school

GRE score	TOEFL score	University rating	SOP	LOR	CGPA	Research	Admitted
337	118	4	4.5	4.5	9.65	1	True
324	107	4	4.0	4.5	8.87	1	True
316	104	3	3.0	3.5	8.00	1	False
322	110	3	3.5	2.5	8.67	1	True
314	103	2	2.0	3.0	8.21	0	False

As we saw in the section "The graphical boundary of decision trees," Scikit-Learn requires that we enter the features and the labels separately. We'll build a Pandas DataFrame called `features` containing all the columns except the Admitted column, and a Pandas Series called `labels` containing only the Admitted column. The code follows:

```
features = data.drop(['Admitted'], axis=1)
labels = data['Admitted']
```

Now we create a `DecisionTreeClassifier` object (which we call `dt`) and use the `fit` method. We'll train it using the Gini index, as shown next, so there is no need to specify the `criterion` hyperparameter, but go ahead and train it with entropy and compare the results with those that we get here:

```
from sklearn.tree import DecisionTreeClassifier
dt = DecisionTreeClassifier()
dt.fit(features, labels)
```

To make predictions, we can use the `predict` function. For example, here is how we make predictions for the first five students:

```
dt.predict(features[0:5])
Output: array([ True,  True, False,  True, False])
```

However, the decision tree we just trained massively overfits. One way to see this is by using the `score` function and realizing that it scores 100% in the training set. In this chapter, we won't test the model, but will try building a testing set and verifying that this model overfits. Another way to see the overfitting is to plot the tree and notice that its depth is 10 (see the notebook). In the next section, we learn about some hyperparameters that help us prevent overfitting.

Setting hyperparameters in Scikit-Learn

To prevent overfitting, we can use some of the hyperparameters that we learned in the section "Last step: When to stop building the tree and other hyperparameters," such as the following:

- `max_depth`: the maximum allowed depth.

- `max_features`: the maximum number of features considered at each split (useful for when there are too many features, and the training process takes too long).

- `min_impurity_decrease`: the decrease in impurity must be higher than this threshold to split a node.

- `min_impurity_split`: when the impurity at a node is lower than this threshold, the node becomes a leaf.

- `min_samples_leaf`: the minimum number of samples required for a leaf node. If a split leaves a leaf with less than this number of samples, the split is not performed.

- `min_samples_split`: the minimum number of samples required to split a node.

Play around with these parameters to find a good model. We'll use the following:

- `max_depth = 3`

- `min_samples_leaf = 10`

- `min_samples_split = 10`

```
dt_smaller = DecisionTreeClassifier(max_depth=3,
    min_samples_leaf=10, min_samples_split=10)
dt_smaller.fit(features, labels)
```

The resulting tree is illustrated in figure 9.24. Note that in this tree, all the edges to the right correspond to "False" and to the left to "True."

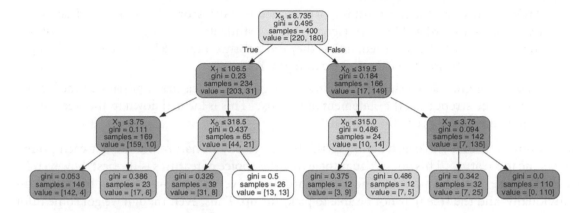

Figure 9.24   A decision tree of depth 3 trained in the student admissions dataset

The prediction given at each of the leaves is the label corresponding to the majority of the nodes in that leaf. In the notebook, each node has a color assigned to it, ranging from orange to blue. The orange nodes are those with more points with label 0, and the blue nodes are those with label 1. Notice that the white leaf, in which there are the same number of points with labels 0 and 1. For this leaf, any prediction has the same performance. In this case, Scikit-Learn defaults to the first class in the list, which in this case is false.

To make a prediction, we use the `predict` function. For example, let's predict the admission for a student with the following numbers:

- GRE score: 320
- TOEFL score: 110
- University rating: 3
- SOP: 4.0
- LOR: 3.5
- CGPA: 8.9
- Research: 0 (no research)

```
dt_smaller.predict([[320, 110, 3, 4.0, 3.5, 8.9, 0]])
Output: array([ True])
```

The tree predicts that the student will be admitted.

From this tree, we can infer the following things about our dataset:

- The most important feature is the sixth column (X_5), corresponding to the CGPA, or the grades. The cutoff grade is 8.735 out of 10. In fact, most of the predictions to the right of the root node are "admit" and to the left are "not admit," which implies that CGPA is a very strong feature.

- After this feature, the two most important ones are GRE score (X_0) and TOEFL score (X_1), both standardized tests. In fact, among the students who got good grades, most of them are likely to be admitted, unless they did poorly on the GRE, as accounted for by the sixth leaf from the left in the tree in figure 9.24.

- Aside from grades and standardized tests, the only other feature appearing in the tree is SOP, or the strength of the statement of purpose. This is located down in the tree, and it didn't change the predictions much.

Recall, however, that the construction of the tree is greedy in nature, namely, at each point it selects the top feature. This doesn't guarantee that the choice of features is the best, however. For example, there could be a combination of features that is very strong, yet none of them is strong individually, and the tree may not be able to pick this up. Thus, even though we got some information about the dataset, we should not yet throw away the features that are not present in the tree. A good feature selection algorithm, such as L1 regularization, would come in handy when selecting features in this dataset.

Decision trees for regression

In most of this chapter, we've used decision trees for classification, but as was mentioned earlier, decision trees are good regression models as well. In this section, we see how to build a decision tree regression model. The code for this section follows:

- **Notebook:** Regression_decision_tree.ipynb
  - https://github.com/luisguiserrano/manning/blob/master/Chapter_9_Decision_Trees/Regression_decision_tree.ipynb

Consider the following problem: we have an app, and we want to predict the level of engagement of the users in terms of how many days per week they used it. The only feature we have is the user's age. The dataset is shown in table 9.6, and its plot is in figure 9.25.

Table 9.6   A small dataset with eight users, their age, and their engagement with our app. The engagement is measured in the number of days when they opened the app in one week.

Age	Engagement
10	7
20	5
30	7
40	1
50	2
60	1
70	5
80	4

From this dataset, it seems that we have three clusters of users. The young users (ages 10, 20, 30) use the app a lot, the middle-aged users (ages 40, 50, 60) don't use it very much, and the older users (ages 70, 80) use it sometimes. Thus, a prediction like this one would make sense:

- If the user is 34 years old or younger, the engagement is 6 days per week.
- If the user is between 35 and 64, the engagement is 1 day per week.
- If the user is 65 or older, the engagement is 3.5 days per week.

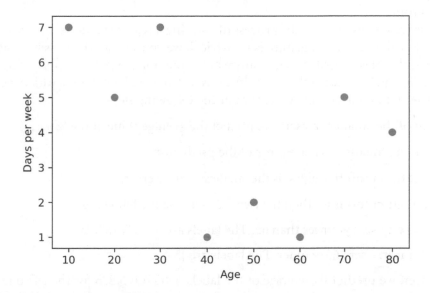

Figure 9.25 The plot of the dataset in table 9.6, where the horizontal axis corresponds to the age of the user and the vertical axis to the number of days per week that they engaged with the app

The predictions of a regression decision tree look similar to this, because the decision tree splits our users into groups and predicts a fixed value for each of the groups. The way to split the users is by using the features, exactly like we did for classification problems.

Lucky for us, the algorithm used for training a regression decision tree is very similar to the one we used for training a classification decision tree. The only difference is that for classification trees, we used accuracy, Gini index, or entropy, and for regression trees, we use the mean square error (MSE). The mean square error may sound familiar—we used it to train linear regression models in the section "How do we measure our results? The error function" in chapter 3.

Before we get into the algorithm, let's think about it conceptually. Imagine that you have to fit a line as close as possible to the dataset in figure 9.25. But there is a catch—the line must be horizontal. Where should we fit this horizontal line? It makes sense to fit it in the "middle" of the dataset—in other words, at a height equal to the average of the labels, which is 4. That is a very simple classification model, which assigns to every point the same prediction of 4.

Now, let's go a bit further. If we had to use two horizontal segments, how should we fit them as close as possible to the data? We might have several guesses, with one being to put a high bar for the points to the left of 35 and a low bar to the right of 35. That represents a decision stump that asks the question, "Are you younger than 35?" and assigns predictions based on how the user answered that question.

What if we could split each of these two horizontal segments into two more—where should we locate them? We can continue following this process until we have broken down the users into several groups in which their labels are very similar. We then predict the average label for all the users in that group.

The process we just followed is the process of training a regression decision tree. Now let's get more formal. Recall that when a feature is numerical, we consider all the possible ways to split it. Thus, the possible ways to split the age feature are using, for example, the following cutoffs: 15, 25, 35, 45, 55, 65, and 75. Each of these cutoffs gives us two smaller datasets, which we call the left dataset and the right dataset. Now we carry out the following steps:

1. For each of the smaller datasets, we predict the average value of the labels.

2. We calculate the mean square error of the prediction.

3. We select the cutoff that gives us the smallest square error.

For example, if our cutoff is 65, then the two datasets are the following:

- **Left dataset:** users younger than 65. The labels are {7, 5, 7, 1, 2, 1}.

- **Right dataset:** users 65 or older. The labels are {5,4}.

For each dataset, we predict the average of the labels, which is 3.833 for the left one and 4.5 for the right one. Thus, the prediction for the first six users is 3.833, and for the last two is 4.5. Now, we calculate the MSE as follows:

$$MSE = \frac{1}{8}[(7 - 3.833)^2 + (5 - 3.833)^2 + (7 - 3.833)^2 + (1 - 3.833)^2 + (2 - 3.833)^2$$

$$+ (1 - 3.833)^2 + (5 - 4.5)^2 + (4 - 4.5)^2]$$

$$= 5.167$$

In table 9.7, we can see the values obtained for each of the possible cutoffs. The full calculations are at the end of the notebook for this section.

Table 9.7 The nine possible ways to split the dataset by age using a cutoff. Each cutoff splits the dataset into two smaller datasets, and for each of these two, the prediction is given by the average of the labels. The mean square error (MSE) is calculated as the average of the squares of the differences between the labels and the prediction. Notice that the splitting with the smallest MSE is obtained with a cutoff of 35. This gives us the root node in our decision tree.

Cutoff	Labels left set	Labels right set	Prediction left set	Prediction right set	MSE
0	{}	{7,5,7,1,2,1,5,4}	None	4.0	5.25
15	{7}	{5,7,1,2,1,5,4}	7.0	3.571	3.964
25	{7,5}	{7,1,2,1,5,4}	6.0	3.333	3.917
35	**{7,5,7}**	**{1,2,1,5,4}**	**6.333**	**2.6**	**1.983**
45	{7,5,7,1}	{2,1,5,4}	5.0	3.0	4.25
55	{7,5,7,1,2}	{1,5,4}	4.4	3.333	4.983
65	{7,5,7,1,2,1}	{5,4}	3.833	4.5	5.167
75	{7,5,7,1,2,1,5}	{4}	4.0	4.0	5.25
100	{7,5,7,1,2,1,5,4}	{}	4.0	none	5.25

The best cutoff is at 35 years old, because it gave us the prediction with the least mean square error. Thus, we've built the first decision node in our regression decision tree. The next steps are to continue splitting the left and right datasets recursively in the same fashion. Instead of doing it by hand, we'll use Scikit-Learn as before.

First, we define our features and labels. We can use arrays for this, as shown next:

```
features = [[10],[20],[30],[40],[50],[60],[70],[80]]
labels = [7,5,7,1,2,1,5,4]
```

Now, we build a regression decision tree of maximum depth 2 using the `DecisionTreeRegressor` object as follows:

```
from sklearn.tree import DecisionTreeRegressor
dt_regressor = DecisionTreeRegressor(max_depth=2)
dt_regressor.fit(features, labels)
```

The resulting decision tree is shown in figure 9.26. The first cutoff is at 35, as we had already figured out. The next two cutoffs are at 15 and 65. At the right of figure 9.26, we can also see the predictions for each of these four resulting subsets of the data.

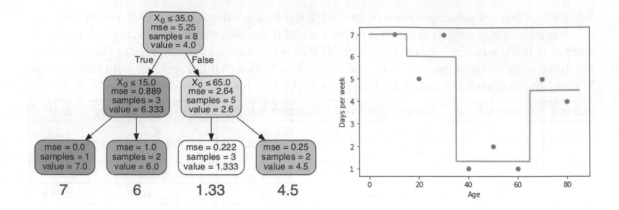

Figure 9.26   Left: The resulting decision tree obtained in Scikit-Learn. This tree has three decision nodes and four leaves. Right: The plot of the predictions made by this decision tree. Note that the cutoffs are at ages 35, 15, and 65, corresponding to the decision nodes in the tree. The predictions are 7, 6, 1.33, and 4.5, corresponding to the leaves in the tree.

Applications

Decision trees have many useful applications in real life. One special feature of decision trees is that, aside from predicting, they give us a lot of information about our data, because they organize it in a hierarchical structure. Many times, this information is of as much or even more value as the capacity of making predictions. In this section, we see some examples of decision trees used in real life in the following fields:

- Health care
- Recommendation systems

Decision trees are widely used in health care

Decision trees are widely used in medicine, not only to make predictions but also to identify features that are determinant in the prediction. You can imagine that in medicine, a black box saying "the patient is sick" or "the patient is healthy" is not good enough. However, a decision tree comes with a great deal of information about why the prediction was made. The patient could be sick based on their symptoms, family medical history, habits, or many other factors.

Decision trees are useful in recommendation systems

In recommendation systems, decision trees are also useful. One of the most famous recommendation systems problems, the Netflix prize, was won with the help of decision trees. In 2006, Netflix held a competition that involved building the best possible recommendation system to predict user ratings of their movies. In 2009, they awarded $1,000,000 USD to the winner, who improved the Netflix algorithm by over 10%. The way they did this was using gradient-boosted decision trees to combine more than 500 different models. Other recommendation engines use decision trees to study the engagement of their users and figure out the demographic features to best determine engagement.

In chapter 12, we will learn more about gradient-boosted decision trees and random forests. For now, the best way to imagine them is as a collection of many decision trees working together to make the best predictions.

Summary

- Decision trees are important machine learning models, used for classification and regression.

- The way decision trees work is by asking binary questions about our data and making a prediction based on the answers to those questions.

- The algorithm for building decision trees for classification consists of finding the feature in our data that best determines the label and iterating over this step.

- We have several ways to tell if a feature determines the label best. The three that we learned in this chapter are accuracy, Gini impurity index, and entropy.

- The Gini impurity index measures the purity of a set. In that way, a set in which every element has the same label has a Gini impurity index of 0. A set in which every element has a different label has a Gini impurity label close to 1.

- Entropy is another measure for the purity of a set. A set in which every element has the same label has an entropy of 0. A set in which half of the elements have one label and the other half has another label has an entropy of 1. When building a decision tree, the difference in entropy before and after a split is called information gain.

- The algorithm for building a decision tree for regression is similar to the one used for classification. The only difference is that we use the mean square error to select the best feature to split the data.

- In two dimensions, regression tree plots look like the union of several horizontal lines, where each horizontal line is the prediction for the elements in a particular leaf.

- Applications of decision trees range very widely, from recommendation algorithms to applications in medicine and biology.

Exercises

Exercise 9.1

In the following spam-detection decision tree model, determine whether an email from your mom with the subject line, "Please go to the store, there's a sale," will be classified as spam.

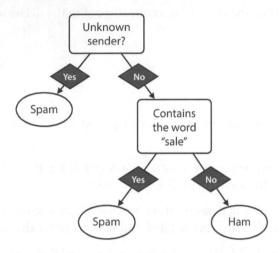

Exercise 9.2

Our goal is to build a decision tree model to determine whether credit card transactions are fraudulent. We use the dataset of credit card transactions below, with the following features:

- **Value:** value of the transaction.

- **Approved vendor:** the credit card company has a list of approved vendors. This variable indicates whether the vendor is in this list.

	Value	Approved vendor	Fraudulent
Transaction 1	$100	Not approved	Yes
Transaction 2	$100	Approved	No
Transaction 3	$10,000	Approved	No
Transaction 4	$10,000	Not approved	Yes
Transaction 5	$5,000	Approved	Yes
Transaction 6	$100	Approved	No

Build the first node of the decision tree with the following specifications:

a. Using the Gini impurity index

b. Using entropy

Exercise 9.3

A dataset of patients who have tested positive or negative for COVID-19 follows. Their symptoms are cough (C), fever (F), difficulty breathing (B), and tiredness (T).

	Cough (C)	Fever (F)	Difficulty breathing (B)	Tiredness (T)	Diagnosis
Patient 1		X	X	X	Sick
Patient 2	X	X		X	Sick
Patient 3	X		X	X	Sick
Patient 4	X	X	X		Sick
Patient 5	X			X	Healthy
Patient 6		X	X		Healthy
Patient 7		X			Healthy
Patient 8				X	Healthy

Using accuracy, build a decision tree of height 1 (a decision stump) that classifies this data. What is the accuracy of this classifier on the dataset?

Combining building blocks to gain more power: Neural networks | 10

In this chapter

- what is a neural network
- the architecture of a neural network: nodes, layers, depth, and activation functions
- training neural networks using backpropagation
- potential problems in training neural networks, such as the vanishing gradient problem and overfitting
- techniques to improve neural network training, such as regularization and dropout
- using Keras to train neural networks for sentiment analysis and image classification
- using neural networks as regression models

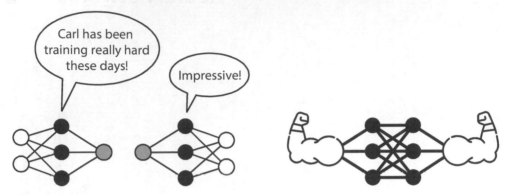

In this chapter, we learn *neural networks*, also called *multilayer perceptrons*. Neural networks are one of the most popular (if not the most popular) machine learning models out there. They are so useful that the field has its own name: *deep learning*. Deep learning has numerous applications in the most cutting-edge areas of machine learning, including image recognition, natural language processing, medicine, and self-driving cars. Neural networks are meant to, in a broad sense of the word, mimic how the human brain operates. They can be very complex, as figure 10.1 shows.

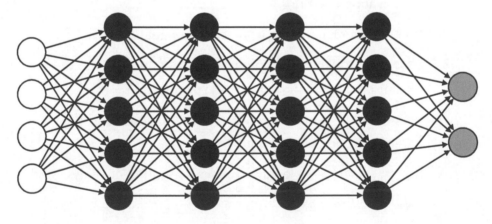

Figure 10.1   A neural network. It may look complicated, but in the next few pages, we will demystify this image.

The neural network in figure 10.1 may look scary with lots of nodes, edges, and so on. However, we can understand neural networks in much simpler ways. One way to see them is as a collection of perceptrons (which we learned in chapters 5 and 6). I like to see neural networks as compositions of linear classifiers that give rise to nonlinear classifiers. In low dimensions, the linear classifiers would look like lines or planes, and the nonlinear classifiers would look like complicated curves or surfaces. In this chapter, we discuss the intuition behind neural networks and the details about how they work, and we also code neural networks and use them for several applications such as image recognition.

Neural networks are useful for classification and regression. In this chapter, we focus mostly on classification neural networks, but we also learn the small changes needed to make them work for regression. First, a bit of terminology. Recall that in chapter 5, we learned the perceptron, and in chapter 6, we learned the logistic classifier. We also learned that they are called the discrete and continuous perceptrons. To refresh your memory, the output of the discrete perceptron is either 0 or 1, and the output of a continuous perceptron is any number in the interval (0,1). To calculate this output, the discrete perceptron uses the step function (the section "The step function and activation functions" in chapter 5), and the continuous perceptron uses the sigmoid function (the section "A probability approach to classification: The sigmoid function" in chapter 6). In this chapter, we refer to both classifiers as perceptrons, and when needed, we specify whether we are talking about a discrete or a continuous perceptron.

The code for this chapter is available in this GitHub repository: https://github.com/luisguiserrano/manning/tree/master/Chapter_10_Neural_Networks.

Neural networks with an example: A more complicated alien planet

In this section, we learn what a neural network is using a familiar sentiment analysis example from chapters 5 and 6. The scenario is the following: we find ourselves on a distant planet populated by aliens. They seem to speak a language formed by two words, *aack* and *beep*, and we want to build a machine learning model that helps us determine whether an alien is happy or sad based on the words they say. This is called sentiment analysis, because we need to build a model to analyze the sentiment of the aliens. We record some aliens talking and manage to identify by other means whether they are happy or sad, and we come up with the dataset shown in in table 10.1.

Table 10.1   Our dataset, in which each row represents an alien. The first column represents the sentence they uttered. The second and third columns represent the number of appearances of each of the words in the sentence. The fourth column represents the alien's mood.

Sentence	Aack	Beep	Mood
"Aack"	1	0	Sad
"Aack aack"	2	0	Sad
"Beep"	0	1	Sad
"Beep beep"	0	2	Sad
"Aack beep"	1	1	Happy
"Aack aack beep"	2	1	Happy
"Beep aack beep"	1	2	Happy
"Beep aack beep aack"	2	2	Happy

This looks like a nice enough dataset, and we should be able to fit a classifier to this data. Let's plot it first, as shown in figure 10.2.

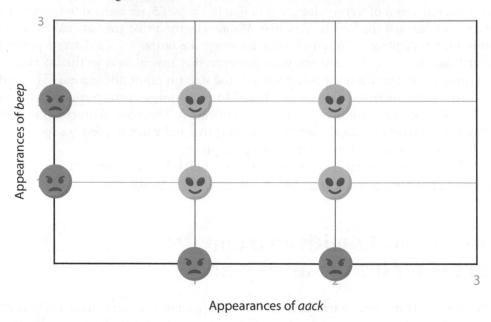

Figure 10.2   The plot of the dataset in table 10.1. The horizontal axis corresponds to the number of appearances of the word *aack*, and the vertical axis to the number of appearances of the word *beep*. The happy faces correspond to the happy aliens, and the sad faces to the sad aliens.

From figure 10.2, it looks like we won't be able to fit a linear classifier to this data. In other words, drawing a line that splits the happy and the sad faces apart would be impossible. What can we do? We've learned other classifiers that can do the job, such as the naive Bayes classifier (chapter 8) or decision trees (chapter 9). But in this chapter, we stick with perceptrons. If our goal is to separate the points in figure 10.2, and one line won't do it, what then is better than one line? What about the following:

1. Two lines

2. A curve

These are examples of neural networks. Let's begin by seeing why the first one, a classifier using two lines, is a neural network.

Solution: If one line is not enough, use two lines to classify your dataset

In this section, we explore a classifier that uses two lines to split the dataset. We have many ways to draw two lines to split this dataset, and one of these ways is illustrated in figure 10.3. Let's call them line 1 and line 2.

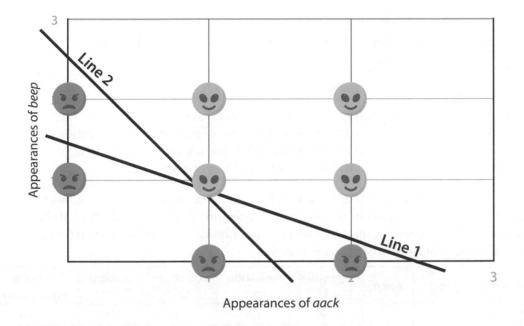

Figure 10.3 The happy and the sad points in our dataset cannot be divided by one line. However, drawing two lines separates them well—the points above both lines can be classified as happy, and the remaining points as sad. Combining linear classifiers this way is the basis for neural networks.

We can define our classifier as follows:

Sentiment analysis classifier

A sentence is classified as happy if its corresponding point is above the two lines shown in figure 10.3. If it is below at least one of the lines, it is classified as sad.

Now, let's throw in some math. Can we think of two equations for these lines? Many equations would work, but let's use the following two (where x_a is the number of times the word *aack* appears in the sentence, and x_b is the number of times *beep* appears).

- **Line 1:** $6x_a + 10x_b - 15 = 0$
- **Line 2:** $10x_a + 6x_b - 15 = 0$

aside: How did WE find these equations?   Notice that line 1 passes through the points $(0, 1.5)$ and $(2.5, 0)$. Therefore, the slope, defined as the change in the horizontal axis divided by the change in the vertical axis, is precisely $\dfrac{-1.5}{2.5} = -\dfrac{3}{5}$. The y-intercept—namely, the height at which the line crosses the vertical axis—is 1.5. Therefore, the equation of this line is $x_b = -\dfrac{3}{5} x_a + 1.5$. By manipulating this equation, we get $6x_a + 10x_b - 15 = 0$. We can take a similar approach to find the equation for line 2.

Therefore, our classifier becomes the following:

Sentiment analysis classifier

A sentence is classified as happy if both of the following two inequalities hold:

- **Inequality 1:** $6x_a + 10x_b - 15 \geq 0$

- **Inequality 2:** $10x_a + 6x_b - 15 \geq 0$

If at least one of them fails, then the sentence is classified as sad.

As a consistency check, table 10.2 contains the values of each of the two equations. At the right of each equation, we check whether the equation's value is larger than or equal to 0. The right-most column checks whether both values are larger than or equal to 0.

Table 10.2   The same dataset as in table 10.1, but with some new columns. The fourth and the sixth columns correspond to our two lines. The fifth and seventh column check if the equation of each of the lines at each of the data points gives a non-negative value. The last column checks if the two values obtained are both non-negative.

Sentence	Aack	Beep	Equation 1	Equation 1 ≥ 0?	Equation 2	Equation 2 ≥ 0?	Both equations ≥ 0
"Aack"	1	0	−9	No	−5	No	No
"Aack aack"	2	0	−3	No	5	Yes	No
"Beep"	0	1	−5	No	−9	No	No
"Beep beep"	0	2	5	Yes	3	No	No
"Aack beep"	1	1	1	Yes	1	Yes	Yes
"Aack aack beep"	1	2	11	Yes	7	Yes	Yes
"Beep aack beep"	2	1	7	Yes	11	Yes	Yes
"Beep aack beep aack"	2	2	17	Yes	17	Yes	Yes

Note that the right-most column in table 10.2 (yes/no) coincides with the right-most column in table 10.1 (happy/sad). This means the classifier managed to classify all the data correctly.

Why two lines? Is happiness not linear?

In chapters 5 and 6, we managed to infer things about the language based on the equations of the classifiers. For example, if the weight of the word *aack* was positive, we concluded that it was likely a happy word. What about now? Could we infer anything about the language in this classifier that contains two equations?

The way we could think of two equations is that maybe on the alien planet, happiness is not a simple linear thing but is instead based on two things. In real life, happiness can be based on many things: it can be based on having a fulfilling career combined with a happy family life and food on the table. It could be based on having coffee and a doughnut. In this case, let's say that the two aspects of happiness are career and family. For an alien to be happy, it needs to have *both*.

It turns out that in this case, both career happiness and family happiness are simple linear classifiers, and each is described by one of the two lines. Let's say that line 1 corresponds to career happiness and line 2 to family happiness. Thus, we can think of alien happiness as the diagram in figure 10.4. In this diagram, career happiness and family happiness are joined by an AND operator, which checks whether both are true. If they are, then the alien is happy. If any of them fails, the alien is unhappy.

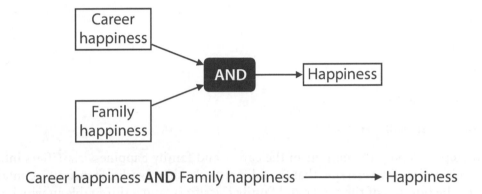

Figure 10.4   The happiness classifier is formed by the career happiness classifier, the family happiness classifier, and an AND operator. If both the career and family happiness classifiers output a Yes, then so does the happiness classifier. If any of them outputs a No, then the happiness classifier also outputs a No.

The family and career happiness classifiers are both perceptrons, because they are given by the equation of a line. Can we turn this AND operator into another perceptron? The answer is yes, and we'll see how in the next subsection.

Figure 10.4 is starting to look like a neural network. Just a few more steps and a little bit more math, and we'll get to something looking much more like figure 10.1 at the beginning of the chapter.

Combining the outputs of perceptrons into another perceptron

Figure 10.4 hints at a combination of perceptrons, in which we plug in the outputs of two perceptrons as inputs into a third perceptron. This is how neural networks are built, and in this section, we see the math behind it.

In the section "The step function and activation functions" in chapter 5, we defined the step function, which returns 0 if the input is negative and 1 if the input is positive or zero. Notice that because we are using the step function, these are discrete perceptrons. Using this function, we can define the family and career happiness classifiers as follows:

Career happiness classifier
Weights:

- *Aack*: 6

- *Beep*: 10

Bias: −15

Score of a sentence: $6x_a + 10x_b - 15$

Prediction: $F = step(6x_a + 10x_b - 15)$

Family happiness classifier

Weights:

- *Aack*: 10

- *Beep*: 6

Bias: −15

Score of a sentence: $10x_a + 6x_b - 15$

Prediction: $C = step(10x_a + 6x_b - 15)$

The next step is to plug the outputs of the career and family happiness classifiers into a new happiness classifier. Try verifying that the following classifier works. Figure 10.5 contains two tables with the outputs of the career and family classifiers, and a third table in which the first two columns are the outputs of the career and family classifier, and the last column is the output of the happiness classifier. Each of the tables in figure 10.5 corresponds to a perceptron.

Career classifier

x_a	x_b	$6x_a + 10x_b - 15$	$C = step(6x_a + 10x_b - 15)$
1	0	−9	0
2	0	−3	0
0	1	−5	0
0	2	5	1
1	1	1	1
1	2	11	1
2	1	7	1
2	2	17	1

Family classifier

x_a	x_b	$10x_a + 6x_b - 15$	$F = step(10x_a + 6x_b - 15)$
1	0	−5	0
2	0	5	1
0	1	−9	0
0	2	3	0
1	1	1	1
1	2	7	1
2	1	11	1
2	2	17	1

Happiness classifier

C	F	$1 \cdot C + 1 \cdot F - 1.5$	$\hat{y} = step(C + F - 1.5)$
0	0	−1.5	0
0	1	−0.5	0
0	0	−1.5	0
1	0	−0.5	0
1	1	0.5	1
1	1	0.5	1
1	1	0.5	1
1	1	0.5	1

Figure 10.5 Three perceptron classifiers, one for career happiness, one for family happiness, and one for happiness, which combines the two previous ones. The outputs of the career and family perceptrons are inputs into the happiness perceptron.

Happiness classifier

Weights:

- Career: 1
- Family: 1

Bias: –1.5

Score of a sentence: $1 \cdot C + 1 \cdot F - 1.5$

Prediction: $\hat{y} = step(1 \cdot C + 1 \cdot F - 1.5)$

This combination of classifiers is a neural network. Next, we see how to make this look like the image in figure 10.1.

A graphical representation of perceptrons

In this section, I show you how to represent perceptrons graphically, which gives rise to the graphical representation of neural networks. We call them neural networks because their basic unit, the perceptron, vaguely resembles a neuron.

A neuron comprises three main parts: the soma, the dendrites, and the axon. In broad terms, the neuron receives signals coming from other neurons through the dendrites, processes them in the soma, and sends a signal through the axon to be received by other neurons. Compare this to a perceptron, which receives numbers as inputs, applies a mathematical operation to them (normally consisting of a sum composed with an activation function), and outputs a new number. This process is illustrated in figure 10.6.

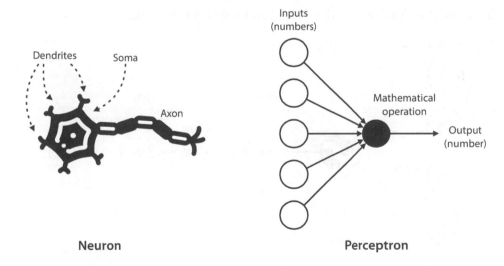

Figure 10.6   A perceptron is loosely based on a neuron. Left: A neuron with its main components: the dendrites, the soma, and the axon. Signals come in through the dendrites, get processed in the soma, and get sent to other neurons through the axon. Right: A perceptron. The nodes in the left correspond to numerical inputs, the node in the middle performs a mathematical operation and outputs a number.

More formally, recall the definition of a perceptron from chapters 5 and 6, in which we had the following entities:

- **Inputs:** $x_1, x_2, \ldots, x_n$
- **Weights:** $w_1, w_2, \ldots, w_n$
- **Bias:** b
- **An activation function:** Either the step function (for discrete perceptrons) or the sigmoid function (for continuous perceptrons). (Later in this chapter we learn other new activation functions.)
- **A prediction:** Defined by the formula $\hat{y} = f(w_1 x_1 + w_2 x_2 + \cdots + w_n x_n + b)$, where f is the corresponding activation function

The way these are located in the diagram is illustrated in figure 10.7. On the left, we have the input nodes, and on the right, we have the output node. The input variables go on the input nodes. The final input node doesn't contain a variable, but it contains a value of 1. The weights are located on the edges connecting the input nodes with the output node. The weight corresponding to the final input node is the bias. The mathematical operations for calculating the prediction happen inside the output node, and this node outputs the prediction.

For example, the perceptron defined by the equation $\hat{y} = \sigma(3x_1 - 2x_2 + 4x_3 + 2)$ is illustrated in figure 10.7. Notice that in this perceptron, the following steps are performed:

- The inputs are multiplied with their corresponding weights and added to obtain $3x_1 - 2x_2 + 4x_3$.
- The bias is added to the previous equation, to obtain $3x_1 - 2x_2 + 4x_3 + 2$.
- The sigmoid activation function is applied to obtain the output $\hat{y} = \sigma(3x_1 - 2x_2 + 4x_3 + 2)$.

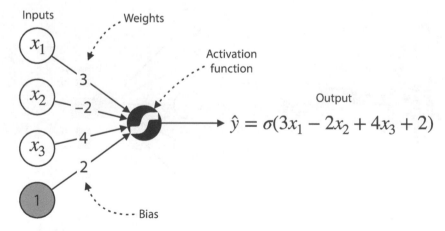

Figure 10.7   A visual representation of a perceptron. The inputs (features and bias) appear as nodes on the left, and the weights and bias are on the edges connecting the input nodes to the main node in the middle. The node in the middle takes the linear combination of the weights and the inputs, adds the bias, and applies the activation function, which in this case is the sigmoid function. The output is the prediction given by the formula $\hat{y} = \sigma(3x_1 - 2x_2 + 4x_3 + 2)$.

For example, if the input to this perceptron is the point $(x_1, x_2, x_3) = (1, 3, 1)$, then the output is $\sigma(3 \cdot 1 - 2 \cdot 3 + 4 \cdot 1 + 2) = \sigma(3) = 0.953$.

If this perceptron was defined using the step function instead of the sigmoid function, the output would be $step(3 \cdot 1 - 2 \cdot 3 + 4 \cdot 1 + 2) = step(3) = 1$.

This graphical representation makes perceptrons easy to concatenate, as we see in the next section.

A graphical representation of neural networks

As we saw in the previous section, a neural network is a concatenation of perceptrons. This structure is meant to loosely emulate the human brain, in which the output of several neurons becomes the input to another neuron. In the same way, in a neural network, the output of several perceptrons becomes the input of another perceptron, as illustrated in figure 10.8.

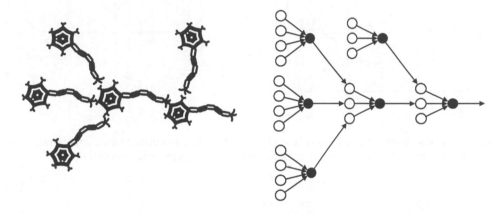

Figure 10.8   Neural networks are meant to (loosely) emulate the structure of the brain. Left: The neurons are connected inside the brain in a way that the output of a neuron becomes the input to another neuron. Right: The perceptrons are connected in a way that the output of a perceptron becomes the input to another perceptron.

The neural network we built in the previous section, in which we concatenate the career perceptron and the family perceptron with the happiness perceptron, is illustrated in figure 10.9.

Notice that in the diagram in figure 10.9, the inputs to the career and family perceptrons are repeated. A cleaner way to write this, in which these inputs don't get repeated, is illustrated in figure 10.10.

Notice that these three perceptrons use the step function. We did this only for educational purposes, because in real life, neural networks never use the step function as an activation function, because it makes it impossible for us to use gradient descent (more on this in the section "Training neural networks"). The sigmoid function, however, is widely used in neural networks, and in the section "Different activation functions," we learn some other useful activation functions used in practice.

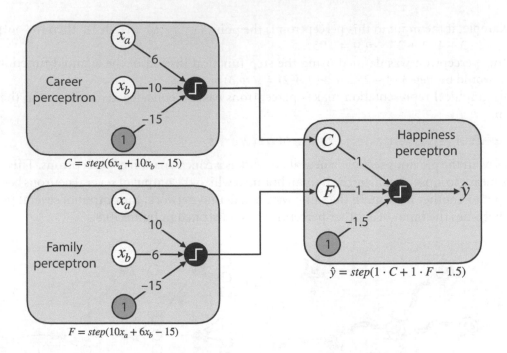

Figure 10.9 When we connect the outputs of the career and family perceptrons into the happiness perceptron, we get a neural network. This neural network uses the step function as an activation function.

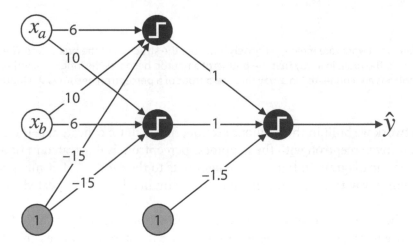

Figure 10.10 A cleaned-up version of the diagram in figure 10.9. In this diagram, the features x_a and x_b, and the bias are not repeated. Instead, each of them connects to both of the nodes at the right, nicely combining the three perceptrons into the same diagram.

The boundary of a neural network

In chapters 5 and 6, we studied the boundaries of perceptrons, which are given by lines. In this section, we see what the boundaries of neural networks look like.

Recall from chapters 5 and 6 that both the discrete perceptron and the continuous perceptron (logistic classifier) have a linear boundary given by the linear equation defining them. The discrete perceptron assigns predictions of 0 and 1 to the points according to what side of the line they are. The continuous perceptron assigns a prediction between 0 and 1 to every point in the plane. The points over the line get a prediction of 0.5, the points on one side of the line get predictions higher than 0.5, and the points on the other side get predictions lower than 0.5. Figure 10.11 illustrates the discrete and continuous perceptrons corresponding to the equation $10x_a + 6x_b - 15 = 0$.

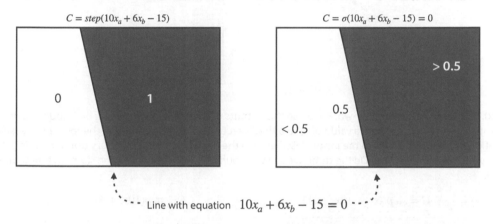

Figure 10.11 The boundary of a perceptron is a line. Left: For a discrete perceptron, the points on one side of the line are given a prediction of 0, and the points on the other side a prediction of 1. Right: For a continuous perceptron, the points are all given a prediction in the interval (0,1). In this example, the points at the very left get predictions close to 0, those at the very right get predictions close to 1, and those over the line get predictions of 0.5.

We can also visualize the output of a neural network in a similar way. Recall that the output of the neural network with the step activation function is the following:

- If $6x_a + 10x_b - 15 \geq 0$ and $10x_a + 6x_b - 15 \geq 0$, then the output is 1.
- Otherwise, the output is 0.

This boundary is illustrated in the left side of figure 10.12 using two lines. Notice that it's expressed as a combination of the boundaries of the two input perceptrons and the bias node. The boundary obtained with the step activation function is made by broken lines, whereas the one obtained with the sigmoid activation function is a curve.

To study these boundaries more carefully, check the following notebook: https://github.com/luisguiserrano/manning/blob/master/Chapter_10_Neural_Networks/Plotting_Boundaries.ipynb. In this notebook, the boundaries of the two lines and the two neural networks are plotted with the step and sigmoid activation functions, as illustrated in figure 10.13.

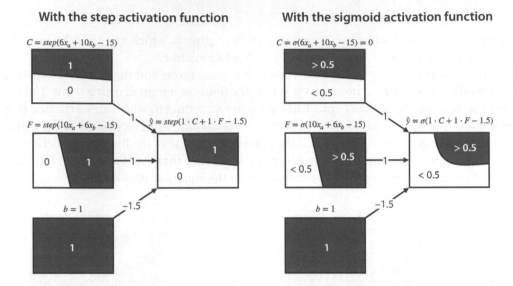

Figure 10.12   To build a neural network, we use the outputs of two perceptrons and a bias node (represented by a classifier that always outputs a value of 1) to a third perceptron. The boundary of the resulting classifier is a combination of the boundaries of the input classifiers. On the left, we see the boundary obtained using the step function, which is a broken line. On the right, we see the boundary obtained using the sigmoid function, which is a curve.

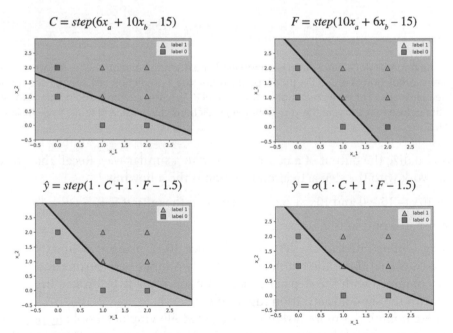

Figure 10.13   The plots of the boundaries of the classifiers. Top: The two linear classifiers, the career (left) and family (right) classifiers. Bottom: The two neural networks, using the step function (left) and the sigmoid function (right).

Note that the neural network with the sigmoid activation function actually doesn't fit the entire dataset well, because it misclassifies the point (1,1), as shown in the bottom right of figure 10.13. Try changing the weights in a way that it fits this point well. (See exercise 10.3 at the end of the chapter.)

The general architecture of a fully connected neural network

In the previous sections, we saw an example of a small neural network, but in real life, neural networks are much larger. The nodes are arranged in layers, as illustrated in figure 10.14. The first layer is the input layer, the final layer is the output layer, and all the layers in between are called the hidden layers. The arrangement of nodes and layers is called the *architecture* of the neural network. The number of layers (excluding the input layer) is called the *depth* of the neural network. The neural network in figure 10.14 has a depth of 3, and the following architecture:

- An input layer of size 4

- A hidden layer of size 5

- A hidden layer of size 3

- An output layer of size 1

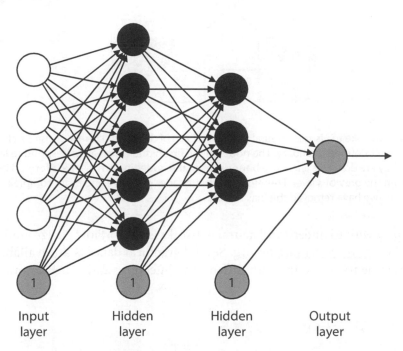

Figure 10.14   The general architecture of a neural network. The nodes are divided into layers, where the leftmost layer is the input layer, the rightmost layer is the output layer, and all the layers in between are hidden layers. All the nodes in a layer are connected to all the (non-bias) nodes in the next layer.

Neural networks are often drawn without the bias nodes, but it is assumed they are part of the architecture. However, we don't count bias nodes in the architecture. In other words, the size of a layer is the number of non-bias nodes in that layer.

Notice that in the neural network in figure 10.14, every node in a layer is connected to every (non-bias) node in the next layer. Furthermore, no connections happen between nonconsecutive layers. This architecture is called *fully connected*. For some applications, we use different architectures where not all the connections are there, or where some nodes are connected between nonconsecutive layers—see the section "Other architectures for more complex dialects" to read about some of them. However, in this chapter, all the neural networks we build are fully connected.

Picture the boundary of a neural network like the one shown in figure 10.15. In this diagram, you can see the classifier corresponding to each node. Notice that the first hidden layer is formed by linear classifiers, and the classifiers in each successive layer are slightly more complex than those in the previous ones.

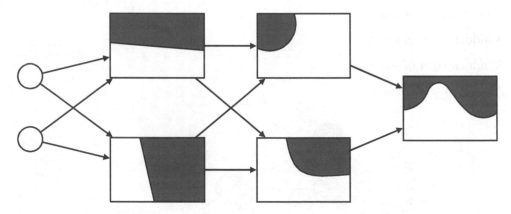

Figure 10.15 The way I like to visualize neural networks. Each of the nodes corresponds to a classifier, and this classifier has a well-defined boundary. The nodes in the first hidden layer all correspond to linear classifiers (perceptrons), so they are drawn as lines. The boundaries of the nodes in each layer are formed by combining the boundaries from the previous layer. Therefore, the boundaries get more and more complex in each hidden layer. In this diagram, we have removed the bias nodes.

A great tool to play with to understand neural networks is TensorFlow Playground, which can be found at https://playground.tensorflow.org. Several graphical datasets are available there, and it is possible to train neural networks with different architectures and hyperparameters.

Training neural networks

In this chapter, we've seen how neural networks look in general and that they're not as mysterious as they sound. How do we train one of these monsters? In theory, the process is not complicated, although it can be computationally expensive. We have several tricks and heuristics we can use to speed it up. In this section, we learn this training process. Training a neural network is not that different from training other models, such as the perceptron or the logistic classifier. We begin by initializing all the weights and biases at random. Next, we define an error function to measure the performance of the neural network. Finally, we repeatedly use the error function to tune in the weights and biases of the model to reduce the error function.

Error function: A way to measure how the neural network is performing

In this section, we learn about the error function used to train neural networks. Luckily, we've seen this function before—the log-loss function from the section "Logistic classifiers" in chapter 6. Recall that the formula for the log loss is

$$log\ loss = -y\ ln(\hat{y}) - (1 - y)\ ln(1 - \hat{y}),$$

where y is the label and $\hat{y}$ the prediction.

As a refresher, a good reason for using log loss for classification problems is that it returns a small value when the prediction and the label are close and a large value when they are far.

Backpropagation: The key step in training the neural network

In this section, we learn the most important step in the process of training a neural network. Recall that in chapters 3, 5, and 6 (linear regression, perceptron algorithm, and logistic regression), we used gradient descent to train our models. This is also the case for neural networks. The training algorithm is called the *backpropagation algorithm*, and its pseudocode follows:

Pseudocode for the backpropagation algorithm

- Initialize the neural network with random weights and biases.

- Repeat many times:

  - Calculate the loss function and its gradient (namely, the derivatives with respect to each one of the weights and biases).

  - Take a small step in the direction opposite to the gradient to decrease the loss function by a small amount.

- The weights you obtain correspond to a neural network that (likely) fits the data well.

The loss function of a neural network is complicated, because it involves the logarithm of the prediction, and the prediction itself is a complicated function. Furthermore, we need to calculate the derivative with respect to many variables, corresponding to each of the weights and biases of the neural network. In appendix B, "Using gradient descent to train neural networks," we go over the mathematical details of the backpropagation algorithm for a neural network with one hidden layer or arbitrary size. See some recommended resources in appendix C to go deep into the math of backpropagation for deeper neural networks. In practice, great packages, such as Keras, TensorFlow, and PyTorch, have implemented this algorithm with great speed and performance.

Recall that when we learned linear regression models (chapter 3), discrete perceptrons (chapter 5), and continuous perceptrons (chapter 6), the process always had a step where we moved a line in the way we needed to model our data well. This type of geometry is harder to visualize for neural networks, because it happens in much higher dimensions. However, we can still form a mental picture of backpropagation, and for this, we need to focus on only one of the nodes of the neural network and one data point. Imagine a classifier like the one on the right in figure 10.16. This classifier is obtained from the three classifiers on the left (the bottom one corresponds to the bias, which we represent by a classifier that always returns a prediction of 1). The resulting classifier misclassifies the point, as is shown. From the three input classifiers, the first one classifies the point well, but the other two don't. Thus, the backpropagation step will increase the weight on the edge corresponding to the top classifier and decrease those corresponding to the two classifiers at the bottom. This ensures the resulting classifier will look more like the top one, and thus, its classification for the point will improve.

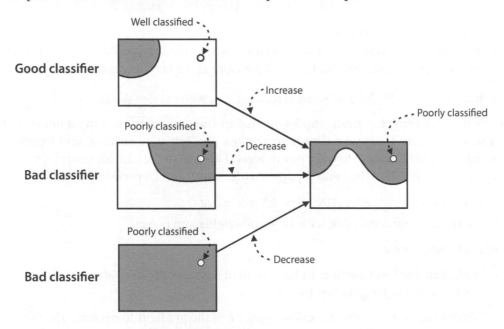

Figure 10.16   A mental picture of backpropagation. At each step of the training process, the weights of the edges are updated. If a classifier is good, its weight gets increased by a small amount, and if it is bad, its weight gets decreased.

Potential problems: From overfitting to vanishing gradients

In practice, neural networks work very well. But, due to their complexity, many problems arise with their training. Luckily, we can have a solution for the most pressing ones. One problem that neural networks have is overfitting—really big architectures can potentially memorize our data without generalizing it well. In the next section, we see some techniques to reduce overfitting when training neural networks.

Another serious problem that neural networks can have is vanishing gradients. Notice that the sigmoid function is very flat on the ends, which signifies that the derivatives (tangents to the curve) are too flat (see figure 10.17). This means their slopes are very close to zero.

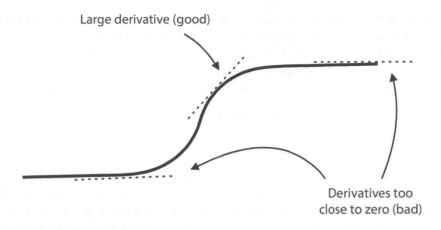

Large derivative (good)

Derivatives too
close to zero (bad)

Figure 10.17 The sigmoid function is flat at the ends, which means that for large positive and negative values, its derivative is very small, hampering the training.

During the backpropagation process, we compose many of these sigmoid functions (which means we plug in the output of a sigmoid function as the input to another sigmoid function repeatedly). As expected, this composition results in derivatives that are very close to zero, which means the steps taken during backpropagation are tiny. If this is the case, it may take us a very long time to get to a good classifier, which is a problem.

We have several solutions to the vanishing gradient problem, and so far one of the most effective ones is to change the activation function. In the section "Different activation functions," we learn some new activation functions to help us deal with the vanishing gradient problem.

Techniques for training neural networks: Regularization and dropout

As mentioned in the previous section, neural networks are prone to overfitting. In this section, we discuss some techniques to decrease the amount of overfitting during the training of neural networks.

How do we pick the correct architecture? This is a difficult question, with no concrete answer. The rule of thumb is to err on the side of picking a larger architecture than we may need and then apply techniques to reduce the amount of overfitting that your network may have. In some way it is like picking a pair of pants, where the only choices you have are too small or too big. If we pick pants that are too small, there is not much we can do. On the other hand, if we pick pants that are too big, we can wear a belt to make them fit better. It's not ideal, but it's all we have for now. Picking the correct architecture based on the dataset is a complicated problem, and a lot of research is currently being done in this direction. To learn more about this, check out the resources in appendix C.

Regularization: A way to reduce overfitting by punishing higher weights

As we learned in chapter 4, we can use L1 and L2 regularization to decrease overfitting in regression and classification models, and neural networks are no exception. The way one applies regularization in neural networks is the same as one would apply it in linear regression—by adding a regularization term to the error function. If we are doing L1 regularization, the regularization term is equal to the regularization parameter (λ) times the sum of the absolute values of all the weights of our model (not including the biases). If we are doing L2 regularization, then we take the sum of squares instead of absolute values. As an example, the L2 regularization error of the neural network in the example in the section "Neural networks with an example" is

$$log\ loss + \lambda \cdot (6^2 + 10^2 + 10^2 + 6^2 + 1^2 + 1^2) = log\ loss + 274\lambda.$$

Dropout: Making sure a few strong nodes are not dominating the training

Dropout is an interesting technique used to reduce overfitting in neural networks, and to understand it, let's consider the following analogy: imagine that we are right-handed, and we like to go to the gym. After some time, we start noticing that our right bicep is growing a lot, but our left one is not. We then start paying more attention to our training and realize that because we are right-handed, we tend to always pick up the weights with the right arm, and we're not allowing the left arm to do much exercise. We decide that enough is enough, so we take a drastic measure. Some days we decide to tie our right hand to our back and force ourselves to do the entire routine without using the right arm. After this, we start seeing that the left arm starts to grow, as desired. Now, to get both arms to work, we do the following: every day before heading to the gym, we flip two coins, one for each arm. If the left coin falls on heads, we tie the left arm to our back, and if the right arm falls on heads, we tie the right arm to our back. Some days we'll work with both arms, some days with only one, and some days with none (those are leg days, perhaps). The randomness of the coins will make sure that, on average, we are working both arms almost equally.

Dropout uses this logic, except instead of arms, we are training the weights in the neural network. When a neural network has too many nodes, some of the nodes pick up patterns in the data that are useful for making good predictions, whereas other nodes pick up patterns that are noisy or irrelevant. The dropout process removes some of the nodes randomly at every epoch and performs one gradient descent step on the remaining ones. By dropping some of the nodes at each epoch, it is likely that sometimes we may drop the ones that have picked up the useful patterns, thus forcing the other nodes to pick up the slack.

To be more specific, the dropout process attaches a small probability p to each of the neurons. In each epoch of the training process, each neuron is removed with probability p, and the neural network is trained only with the remaining ones. Dropout is used only on the hidden layers, not on the input or output layers. The dropout process is illustrated in figure 10.18, where some neurons are removed in each of four epochs of training.

Dropout has had great success in the practice, and I encourage you to use it every time you train a neural network. The packages that we use for training neural networks make it easy to use, as we'll see later in this chapter.

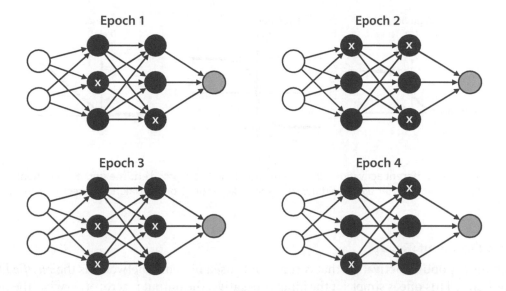

Figure 10.18 The dropout process. At different epochs, we pick random nodes to remove from the training to give all the nodes an opportunity to update their weights and not have a few single nodes dominating the training.

Different activation functions: Hyperbolic tangent (tanh) and the rectified linear unit (ReLU)

As we saw in the section "Potential problems," the sigmoid function is a bit too flat, which causes problems with vanishing gradients. A solution to this problem is to use different activation functions. In this section, we cover two different activation functions that are crucial to improve our training process: the hyperbolic tangent (tanh) and the rectified linear unit (ReLU)

Hyperbolic tangent (tanh)

The *hyperbolic tangent* function tends to work better than the sigmoid function in practice, due to its shape, and is given by the following formula:

$$\tanh(x) = \frac{e^x - e^{-x}}{e^x + e^{-x}}$$

Tanh is a bit less flat than sigmoid, but it still has a similar shape, as is shown in figure 10.19. It provides an improvement over sigmoid, but it still suffers from the vanishing gradient problem.

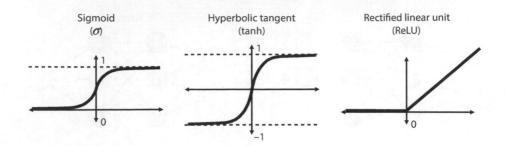

Figure 10.19   Three different activation functions used in neural networks. Left: The sigmoid function, represented by the Greek letter *sigma*. Middle: The hyperbolic tangent, or tanh. Right: The rectified linear unit, or ReLU.

Rectified linear unit (ReLU)

A much more popular activation that is commonly used in neural networks is the *rectified linear unit*, or ReLU. This one is simple: if the input is negative, the output is zero; otherwise, the output is equal to the input. In other words, it leaves nonnegative numbers alone and turns all the negative numbers into zero. For $x \geq 0$, $ReLU(x) = x$, and for $x < 0$, $ReLU(x) = 0$. ReLU is a good solution to the vanishing gradient problem, because its derivative is 1 when the input is positive, and thus, it is widely used in large neural networks.

The great thing about these activation functions is that we can combine different ones in the same neural network. In one of the most common architectures, every node uses the ReLU activation function except for the last one, which uses the sigmoid. The reason for this sigmoid at the end is that if our problem is a classification problem, the output of the neural network must be between 0 and 1.

Neural networks with more than one output: The softmax function

So far, the neural networks we've worked with have had only one output. However, it is not hard to build a neural network that produces several outputs using the softmax function that we learned in the section "Classifying into multiple classes: The softmax function" in chapter 6. The softmax function is a multivariate extension of the sigmoid, and we can use it to turn scores into probabilities.

The best way to illustrate the softmax function is with an example. Imagine that we have a neural network whose job is to determine whether an image contains an aardvark, a bird, a cat, or a dog. In the final layer, we have four nodes, one corresponding to each animal. Instead of applying the sigmoid function to the scores coming from the previous layer, we apply the softmax function to all of them. For example, if the scores are 0, 3, 1, and 1, softmax returns the following:

- Probability(aardvark) $= \dfrac{e^0}{e^0 + e^3 + e^1 + e^1} = 0.0377$

- Probability(bird) $= \dfrac{e^3}{e^0 + e^3 + e^1 + e^1} = 0.7573$

- Probability(cat) = $\dfrac{e^1}{e^0 + e^3 + e^1 + e^1} = 0.1025$

- Probability(dog) = $\dfrac{e^1}{e^0 + e^3 + e^1 + e^1} = 0.1025$

These results indicate that the neural network strongly believes that the image corresponds to a bird.

Hyperparameters

Like most machine learning algorithms, neural networks use many hyperparameters that we can fine-tune to get them to work better. These hyperparameters determine how we do our training, namely, how long we want the process to go, at what speed, and how we choose to enter our data into the model. Some of the most important hyperparameters in neural networks follow:

- **Learning rate η:** the size of the step that we use during our training

- **Number of epochs:** the number of steps we use for our training

- **Batch vs. mini-batch vs. stochastic gradient descent:** how many points at a time enter the training process—namely, do we enter the points one by one, in batches, or all at the same time?

- **Architecture:**
  - The number of layers in the neural network
  - The number of nodes per layer
  - The activation functions used in each node

- **Regularization parameters:**
  - L1 or L2 regularization
  - The regularization term λ

- **Dropout probability p**

We tune these hyperparameters in the same way we tune them for other algorithms, using methods such as grid search. In chapter 13, we elaborate on these methods more with a real-life example.

Coding neural networks in Keras

Now that we learned the theory behind neural networks, it's time to put them in practice! Many great packages have been written for neural networks, such as Keras, TensorFlow, and PyTorch. These three are powerful, and in this chapter, we'll use Keras due to its simplicity. We'll build two neural networks for two different datasets. The first dataset contains points with two features and labels of 0 and 1. The dataset is two-dimensional, so we'll be able to look at the nonlinear boundary created by the model. The second dataset is a common dataset used in image recognition called the MNIST (Modified National Institute of Standards and Technology) dataset. The MNIST dataset contains handwritten digits that we can classify using a neural network.

A graphical example in two dimensions

In this section, we'll train a neural network in Keras on the dataset shown in figure 10.20. The dataset contains two labels, 0 and 1. The points with label 0 are drawn as squares, and those with label 1 are drawn as triangles. Notice that the points with label 1 are located mostly at the center, whereas the points with label 0 are located on the sides. For this type of dataset, we need a classifier with a nonlinear boundary, which makes it a good example for a neural network. The code for this section follows:

- **Notebook:** Graphical_example.ipynb
  - https://github.com/luisguiserrano/manning/blob/master/Chapter_10_Neural_Networks/Graphical_example.ipynb

- **Dataset:** one_circle.csv

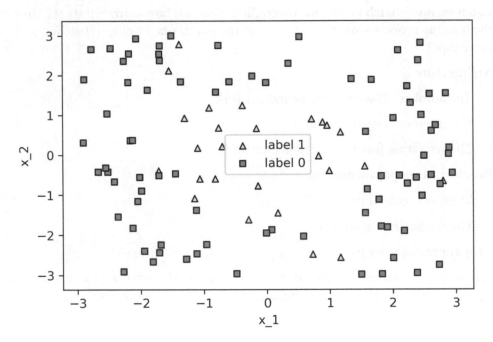

Figure 10.20 Neural networks are great for nonlinearly separable sets. To test this, we'll train a neural network on this circular dataset.

Before we train the model, let's look at some random rows in our data. The input will be called x, with features x_1 and x_2, and the output will be called y. Table 10.3 has some sample data points. The dataset has 110 rows.

Table 10.3   The dataset with 110 rows, two features, and labels of 0 and 1

x_1	x_2	y
−0.759416	2.753240	0
−1.885278	1.629527	0
...	...	...
0.729767	−2.479655	1
−1.715920	−0.393404	1

Before we build and train the neural networks, we must do some data preprocessing.

Categorizing our data: Turning nonbinary features into binary ones

In this dataset, the output is a number between 0 and 1, but it represents two classes. In Keras, it is recommended to categorize this type of output. This simply means that points with label 0 will now have a label [1,0], and points with label 1 will now have a label [0,1]. We do this using the `to_categorical` function as follows:

```
from tensorflow.keras.utils import to_categorical
categorized_y = np.array(to_categorical(y, 2))
```

The new labels are called `categorized_y`.

The architecture of the neural network

In this section, we build the architecture of the neural network for this dataset. Deciding which architecture to use is not an exact science, but it is normally recommended to go a little bigger rather than a little smaller. For this dataset, we'll use the following architecture with two hidden layers (figure 10.21):

- Input layer
  - Size: 2
- First hidden layer
  - Size:128
  - Activation function: ReLU
- Second hidden layer
  - Size: 64
  - Activation function: ReLU
- Output layer
  - Size: 2
  - Activation function: softmax

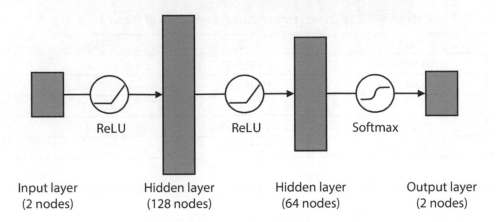

Figure 10.21   The architecture that we will use to classify our dataset. It contains two hidden layers: one of 128 and one of 64 nodes. The activation function between them is a ReLU, and the final activation function is a softmax.

Furthermore, we'll add dropout layers between our hidden layers with a dropout probability of 0.2, to prevent overfitting.

Building the model in Keras

Building the neural network takes only a few lines of code in Keras. First we import the necessary packages and functions as follows:

```
from tensorflow.keras.models import Sequential
from tensorflow.keras.layers import Dense, Dropout, Activation
```

Now, on to define the model with the architecture that we have defined in the previous subsection. First, we define the model with the following line:

```
model = Sequential()
model.add(Dense(128, activation='relu', input_shape=(2,)))
model.add(Dropout(.2))
model.add(Dense(64, activation='relu'))
model.add(Dropout(.2))
model.add(Dense(2, activation='softmax'))
```

Defines the model

Adds the first hidden layer with a ReLU activation function

Adds a dropout with a probability of 0.2

Adds the second hidden layer with a ReLU activation function

Adds the output layer with a softmax activation function

Once the model is defined, we can compile it, as shown here:

```
model.compile(loss = 'categorical_crossentropy', optimizer='adam',
    metrics=['accuracy'])
```

The parameters in the `compile` function follow:

- `loss = 'categorical_crossentropy'`: this is the loss function, which we have defined as the log loss. Because our labels have more than one column, we need to use the multivariate version for the log loss function, called *categorical cross-entropy*.

- `optimizer = 'adam'`: packages like Keras have many built-in tricks that help us train a model in an optimal way. It's always a good idea to add an optimizer to our training. Some of the best ones are Adam, SGD, RMSProp, and AdaGrad. Try this same training with other optimizers, and see how they do.

- `metrics = ['accuracy']`: As the training goes, we get reports on how the model is doing at each epoch. This flag allows us to define what metrics we want to see during the training, and for this example, we've picked the accuracy.

When we run the code, we get a summary of the architecture and number of parameters, as follows:

```
Model: "sequential"

_____
Layer (type)                 Output Shape              Param #
=================================================================
dense (Dense)                (None, 128)               384
_____
dropout (Dropout)            (None, 128)               0
_____
dense_1 (Dense)              (None, 64)                8256
_____
dropout_1 (Dropout)          (None, 64)                0
_____
dense_2 (Dense)              (None, 2)                 130
=================================================================
Total params: 8,770
Trainable params: 8,770
Non-trainable params: 0
_____
```

Each row in the previous output is a layer (dropout layers are treated as separate layers for description purposes). The columns correspond to the type of the layer, the shape (number of nodes), and the number of parameters, which is precisely the number of weights plus the number of biases. This model has a total of 8,770 trainable parameters.

Training the model

For training, one simple line of code suffices, shown next:

```
model.fit(x, categorized_y, epochs=100, batch_size=10)
```

Let's examine each of the inputs to this fit function.

- `x` and `categorized_y`: the features and labels, respectively.

- `epochs`: the number of times we run backpropagation on our whole dataset. Here we do it 100 times.

- `batch_size`: the length of the batches that we use to train our model. Here we are introducing our data to the model in batches of 10. For a small dataset like this one, we don't need to input it in batches, but in this example, we are doing it for exposure.

As the model trains, it outputs some information at each epoch, namely, the loss (error function) and the accuracy. For contrast, notice next how the first epoch has a high loss and a low accuracy, whereas the last epoch has much better results in both metrics:

```
Epoch 1/100
11/11 [==============================] - 0s 2ms/step - loss: 0.5473 -
     accuracy: 0.7182
...
Epoch 100/100
11/11 [==============================] - 0s 2ms/step - loss: 0.2110 -
     accuracy: 0.9000
```

The final accuracy of the model on the training is 0.9. This is good, although remember that accuracy must be calculated in the testing set instead. I won't do it here, but try splitting the dataset into a training and a testing set and retraining this neural network to see what testing accuracy you obtain. Figure 10.22 shows the plot of the boundary of the neural network.

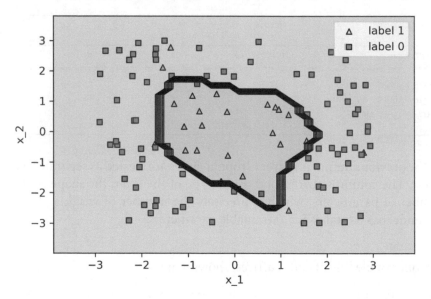

Figure 10.22 The boundary of the neural network classifier we trained. Notice that it correctly classifies most of the points, with a few exceptions.

Note that the model managed to classify the data pretty well, encircling the triangles and leaving the squares outside. It made some mistakes, due to noisy data, but this is OK. The rigged boundary hints to small levels of overfitting, but in general it seems like a good model.

Training a neural network for image recognition

In this section, we learn how to train a neural network for image recognition. The dataset we use is MNIST, a popular dataset for image recognition, which contains 70,000 handwritten digits from 0 to 9. The label of each image is the corresponding digit. Each grayscale image comes as a 28-by-28 matrix of numbers between 0 and 255, where 0 represents white, 255 represents black, and any number in between represents a shade of gray. The code for this section follows:

- **Notebook:** Image_recognition.ipynb

  - https://github.com/luisguiserrano/manning/blob/master/Chapter_10_Neural_Networks/Image_recognition.ipynb

- **Dataset:** MNIST (comes preloaded with Keras)

Loading the data

This dataset comes preloaded in Keras, so it is easy to load it into NumPy arrays. In fact, it has already been separated into training and testing sets of sizes 60,000 and 10,000, respectively. The following lines of code will load them into NumPy arrays:

```
from tensorflow import keras
(x_train, y_train), (x_test, y_test) = keras.datasets.mnist.load_data()
```

In figure 10.23, you can see the first five images in the dataset with their labels.

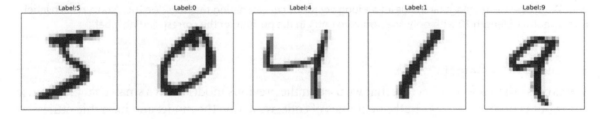

Figure 10.23 Some examples of handwritten digits in MNIST with their labels

Preprocessing the data

Neural networks receive vectors as input instead of matrices, so we must turn each 28-by-28 image into a long vector of length $28^2 = 784$. We can use the reshape function for this, as shown next:

```
x_train_reshaped = x_train.reshape(-1, 28*28)
x_test_reshaped = x_test.reshape(-1, 28*28)
```

As with the previous example, we must also categorize the labels. Because the label is a number between 0 and 9, we must turn that into a vector of length 10, in which the entry corresponding to the label is a 1 and the rest are 0. We can do this with the following lines of code:

```
y_train_cat = to_categorical(y_train, 10)
y_test_cat = to_categorical(y_test, 10)
```

This process is illustrated in figure 10.24.

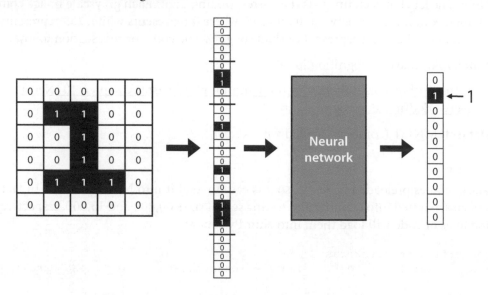

Figure 10.24   Before training the neural network, we preprocess the images and the labels in the following way. We shape the rectangular image into a long vector by concatenating the rows. We then convert each label into a vector of length 10 with only one non-zero entry in the position of the corresponding label.

Building and training the model

We can use the same architecture that we used in the previous model, with a small change, because the input is now of size 784. In the next lines of code, we define the model and its architecture:

```
model = Sequential()
model.add(Dense(128, activation='relu', input_shape=(28*28,)))
model.add(Dropout(.2))
model.add(Dense(64, activation='relu'))
model.add(Dropout(.2))
model.add(Dense(10, activation='softmax'))
```

Now we compile and train the model for 10 epochs with a batch size of 10, as shown here. This model has 109,386 trainable parameters, so training for 10 epochs may take a few minutes on your computer.

```
model.compile(loss = 'categorical_crossentropy', optimizer='adam',
    metrics=['accuracy'])
model.fit(x_train_reshaped, y_train_cat, epochs=10, batch_size=10)
```

Looking at the output, we can see that the model has a training accuracy of 0.9164, which is good, but let's evaluate the testing accuracy to make sure the model is not overfitting.

Evaluating the model

We can evaluate the accuracy in the testing set by making predictions in the testing dataset and comparing them with the labels. The neural network outputs vectors of length 10 with the probabilities it assigns to each of the labels, so we can obtain the predictions by looking at the entry of maximum value in this vector, as follows:

```
predictions_vector = model.predict(x_test_reshaped)
predictions = [np.argmax(pred) for pred in predictions_vector]
```

When we compare these to the labels, we get a testing accuracy of 0.942, which is quite good. We can do better than this with more complicated architectures, such as convolutional neural networks (see more of this in the next section), but it's good to know that with a small, fully connected neural network, we can do quite well in an image recognition problem.

Let's now look at some predictions. In figure 10.25, we can see a correct one (left) and an incorrect one (right). Notice that the incorrect one is a poorly written image of a number 3, which also looks a bit like an 8.

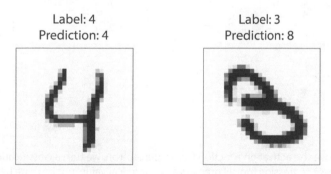

Figure 10.25 Left: An image of a 4 that has been correctly classified by the neural network. Right: An image of a 3 that has been incorrectly classified as an 8.

With this exercise, we can see that the process of training such a large neural network is simple with a few lines of code in Keras! Of course, there is much more one can do here. Play with the notebook, add more layers to the neural network, change the hyperparameters, and see how high you can improve the testing accuracy for this model!

Neural networks for regression

Throughout this chapter, we've seen how to use neural networks as a classification model, but neural networks are just as useful as regression models. Luckily, we have only two small tweaks to apply to a classification neural network to obtain a regression neural network. The first tweak is to remove the final sigmoid function from the neural network. The role of this function is to turn the input into a number between 0 and 1, so if we remove it, the neural network will be able to return any number. The second tweak is to change the error function to the absolute error or the mean square error, because these are the error functions associated with regression. Everything else will remain the same, including the training process.

As an example, let's look at the perceptron in figure 10.7 in the section "A graphical representation of perceptrons." This perceptron makes the prediction $\hat{y} = \sigma(3x_1 - 2x_2 + 4x_3 + 2)$. If we remove the sigmoid activation function, the new perceptron makes the prediction $\hat{y} = 3x_1 - 2x_2 + 4x_3 + 2$. This perceptron is illustrated in figure 10.26. Notice that this perceptron represents a linear regression model.

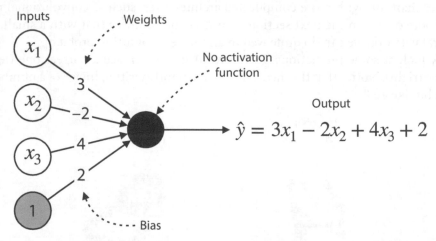

Figure 10.26   If we remove the activation function from a perceptron, we turn a classification model into a linear regression model. The linear regression model predicts any numerical value, not just one between 0 and 1.

To illustrate this process, we train a neural network in Keras on a familiar dataset: the dataset of housing prices in Hyderabad. Recall that in the section "Real-life application: Using Turi Create to predict housing prices in India," in chapter 3, we trained a linear regression model to fit this dataset. The code for this section follows:

- **Notebook:** House_price_predictions_neural_network.ipynb
  - https://github.com/luisguiserrano/manning/blob/master/Chapter_10_Neural_Networks/House_price_predictions_neural_network.ipynb
- **Dataset:** Hyderabad.csv

The details for loading the dataset and splitting the dataset into features and labels can be found in the notebook. The architecture of the neural network that we'll use follows:

- An input layer of size 38 (the number of columns in the dataset)

- A hidden layer of size 128 with a ReLU activation function and a dropout parameter of 0.2

- A hidden layer of size 64 with a ReLU activation function and a dropout parameter of 0.2

- An output layer of size 1 with no activation function

```
model = Sequential()
model.add(Dense(38, activation='relu', input_shape=(38,)))
model.add(Dropout(.2))
model.add(Dense(128, activation='relu'))
model.add(Dropout(.2))
model.add(Dense(64, activation='relu'))
model.add(Dropout(.2))
model.add(Dense(1))
```

To train the neural network, we use the mean square error function and the Adam optimizer. We'll train for 10 epochs using a batch size of 10, as shown here:

```
model.compile(loss = 'mean_squared_error', optimizer='adam')
model.fit(features, labels, epochs=10, batch_size=10)
```

This neural network reports a root mean square error of 5,535,425 in the training dataset. Study this model further by adding a testing set, and play with the architecture, and see how much you can improve it!

Other architectures for more complex datasets

Neural networks are useful in many applications, perhaps more so than any other machine learning algorithm currently. One of the most important qualities of neural networks is their versatility. We can modify the architectures in very interesting ways to better fit our data and solve our problem. To find out more about these architectures, check out *Grokking Deep Learning* by Andrew Trask (Manning, 2019) and a set of videos available in appendix C or at https:// serrano.academy/neural-networks/.

How neural networks see: Convolutional neural networks (CNN)

As we learned in this chapter, neural networks are great with images, and we can use them in many applications, such as the following:

- **Image recognition:** the input is an image, and the output is the label on the image. Some famous datasets used for image recognition follow:

  - MNIST: handwritten digits in 28-by-28 gray scale images

  - CIFAR-10: color images, with 10 labels such as airplane, automobile, and so on, in 32-by-32 images

- CIFAR-100: similar to CIFAR-10, but with 100 labels such as aquatic mammals, flowers, and so on

- **Semantic segmentation:** the input is an image, and the output is not only the labels of the things found in the image but also their location inside the image. Normally, the neural network outputs this location as a bounded rectangle in the image.

In the section "Training a neural network for image recognition," we built a small, fully connected neural network that classified the MNIST dataset quite well. However, for more complicated images, such as pictures and faces, a neural network like this one won't do well because turning the image into a long vector loses a lot of information. For these complicated images, we need different architectures, and this is where convolutional neural networks come to help us.

For the details on neural networks, review the resources in appendix C, but here is a rough outline of how they work. Imagine that we have a large image that we want to process. We take a smaller window, say 5-by-5, or 7-by-7 pixels, and swipe it through the large image. Every time we pass it through, we apply a formula called a *convolution*. Thus, we end with a slightly smaller filtered image, which in some way summarizes the previous one—a convolutional layer. A convolutional neural network consists of several of these convolutional layers, followed by some fully connected layers.

When it comes to complicated images, we normally wouldn't go about training a neural network from scratch. A useful technique called *transfer learning* consists of starting with a pretrained network and using our data to tweak some of its parameters (usually the last layer). This technique tends to work well and at a low computational cost. Networks such as InceptionV3, ImageNet, ResNet, and VGG have been trained by companies and research groups with large computational power, so it's highly recommended for us to use them.

How neural networks talk: Recurrent neural networks (RNN), gated recurrent units (GRU), and long short-term memory networks (LSTM)

One of the most fascinating applications of neural networks is when we can get them to talk to us or understand what we say. This involves listening to what we say or reading what we write, analyzing it, and being able to respond or act. The ability for computers to understand and process language is called *natural language processing*. Neural networks have had a lot of success in natural language processing. The sentiment analysis example at the beginning of this chapter is part of natural language processing, because it entails understanding sentences and determining whether they have positive or negative sentiment. As you can imagine, many more cutting-edge applications exist, such as the following:

- **Machine translation:** translating sentences from various languages into others.

- **Speech recognition:** decoding human voice and turning it into text.

- **Text summarization:** summarizing large texts into a few paragraphs.

- **Chatbots:** a system that can talk to humans and answer questions. These are not yet perfected, but useful chatbots operate in specific topics, such as customer support.

The most useful architectures that work well for processing texts are *recurrent neural networks*, and some more advanced versions of them called *long short-term memory networks* (LSTM) and *gated recurrent units* (GRU). To get an idea of what they are, imagine a neural network where the output is plugged back into the network as part of the inputs. In this way, neural networks have a memory, and when trained properly, this memory can help them make sense of the topic in the text.

How neural networks paint paintings: Generative adversarial networks (GAN)

One of the most fascinating applications of neural networks is generation. So far, neural networks (and most other ML models in this book) have worked well in predictive machine learning, namely, being able to answer questions such as "How much is that?" or "Is this a cat or a dog?" However, in recent years, many advances have occurred in a fascinating area called *generative machine learning*. Generative machine learning is the area of machine learning that teaches the computer how to create things, rather than simply answer questions. Actions such as painting a painting, composing a song, or writing a story represent a much higher level of understanding of the world.

Without a doubt, one of the most important advances in the last few years has been the development of *generative adversarial networks*, or GANs. Generative adversarial networks have shown fascinating results when it comes to image generation. GANs consist of two competing networks, the generator and the discriminator. The generator attempts to generate real-looking images, whereas the discriminator tries to tell the real images and the fake images apart. During the training process, we feed real images to the discriminator, as well as fake images generated by the generator. When applied to a dataset of human faces, this process results in a generator that can generate some very real-looking faces. In fact, they look so real that humans often have a hard time telling them apart. Test yourself against a GAN—www.whichfaceisreal.com.

Summary

- Neural networks are a powerful model used for classification and regression. A neural network consists of a set of perceptrons organized in layers, where the output of one layer serves as input to the next layer. Their complexity allows them to achieve great success in applications that are difficult for other machine learning models.

- Neural networks have cutting-edge applications in many areas, including image recognition and text processing.

- The basic building block of a neural network is the perceptron. A perceptron receives several values as inputs, and outputs one value by multiplying the inputs by weights, adding a bias, and applying an activation function.

- Popular activation functions include sigmoid, hyperbolic tangent, softmax, and the rectified linear unit (ReLU). They are used between layers in a neural network to break linearity and help us build more complex boundaries.

- The sigmoid function is a simple function that sends any real number to the interval between 0 and 1. The hyperbolic tangent is similar, except the output is the interval between –1 and 1. Their goal is to squish our input into a small interval so that our answers can be interpreted as a category. They are mostly used for the final (output) layer in a neural network. Due to the flatness of their derivatives, they may cause problems with vanishing gradients.

- The ReLU function is a function that sends negative numbers to 0, and non-negative numbers to themselves. It showed great success in reducing the vanishing gradient problem, and thus it is used more in training neural networks than the sigmoid function or the hyperbolic tangent function.

- Neural networks have a very complex structure, which makes them hard to train. The process we use to train them, called backpropagation, has shown great success. Backpropagation consists of taking the derivative of the loss function and finding all the partial derivatives with respect to all the weights of the model. We then use these derivatives to update the weights of the model iteratively to improve its performance.

- Neural networks are prone to overfitting and other problems such as vanishing gradients, but we can use techniques such as regularization and dropout to help reduce these problems.

- We have some useful packages to train neural networks, such as Keras, TensorFlow, and PyTorch. These packages make it very easy for us to train neural networks, because we have to define only the architecture of the model and the error functions, and they take care of the training. Furthermore, they have many built-in cutting-edge optimizers that we can take advantage of.

Exercises

Exercise 10.1

The following image shows a neural network in which all the activations are sigmoid functions.

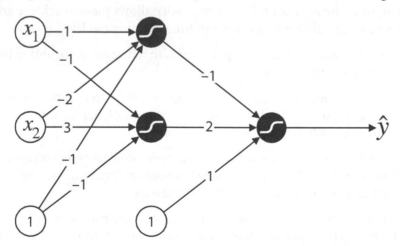

What would this neural network predict for the input (1,1)?

Exercise 10.2

As we learned in exercise 5.3, it is impossible to build a perceptron that mimics the XOR gate. In other words, it is impossible to fit the following dataset with a perceptron and obtain 100% accuracy:

x_1	x_2	y
0	0	0
0	1	1
1	0	1
1	1	0

This is because the dataset is not linearly separable. Using a neural network of depth 2, build a perceptron that mimics the XOR gate shown previously. As the activation functions, use the step function instead of the sigmoid function to get discrete outputs.

  hint This will be hard to do using a training method; instead, try eyeballing the weights. Try (or search online how) to build an XOR gate using AND, OR, and NOT gates, and use the results of exercise 5.3 to help you.

Exercise 10.3

At the end of the section "A graphical representation of neural networks," we saw that the neural network in figure 10.13 with the activation function doesn't fit the dataset in table 10.1 because the point (1,1) is misclassified.

  a. Verify that this is the case.

  b. Change the weights so that the neural network classifies every point correctly.

In this chapter

- what a support vector machine is

- which of the linear classifiers for a dataset has the best boundary

- using the kernel method to build nonlinear classifiers

- coding support vector machines and the kernel method in
  Scikit-Learn

Experts recommend the kernel method when attempting to separate chicken datasets.

In this chapter, we discuss a powerful classification model called the *support vector machine* (SVM for short). An SVM is similar to a perceptron, in that it separates a dataset with two classes using a linear boundary. However, the SVM aims to find the linear boundary that is located as far as possible from the points in the dataset. We also cover the kernel method, which is useful when used in conjunction with an SVM, and it can help classify datasets using highly nonlinear boundaries.

In chapter 5, we learned about linear classifiers, or perceptrons. With two-dimensional data, these are defined by a line that separates a dataset consisting of points with two labels. However, we may have noticed that many different lines can separate a dataset, and this raises the following question: how do we know which is the best line? In figure 11.1, we can see three different linear classifiers that separate this dataset. Which one do you prefer, classifier 1, 2, or 3?

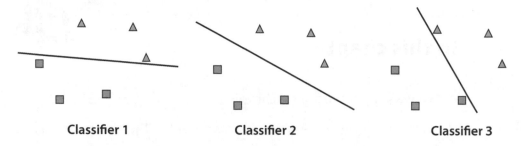

Figure 11.1   Three classifiers that classify our data set correctly. Which should we prefer, classifier 1, 2, or 3?

If you said classifier 2, we agree. All three lines separate the dataset well, but the second line is better placed. The first and third lines are very close to some of the points, whereas the second line is far from all the points. If we were to wiggle the three lines around a little bit, the first and the third may go over some of the points, misclassifying some of them in the process, whereas the second one will still classify them all correctly. Thus, classifier 2 is more robust than classifiers 1 and 3.

This is where support vector machines come into play. An SVM classifier uses two parallel lines instead of one line. The goal of the SVM is twofold; it tries to classify the data correctly and also tries to space the lines as much as possible. In figure 11.2, we can see the two parallel lines for the three classifiers, together with their middle line for reference. The two external (dotted) lines in classifier 2 are the farthest from each other, which makes this classifier the best one.

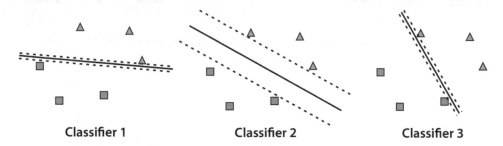

Figure 11.2   We draw our classifier as two parallel lines, as far apart from each other as possible. We can see that classifier 2 is the one where the parallel lines are the farthest away from each other. This means that the middle line in classifier 2 is the one best located between the points.

We may want to visualize an SVM as the line in the middle that tries to stay as far as possible from the points. We can also imagine it as the two external parallel lines trying to stay as far away from each other as possible. In this chapter, we'll use both visualizations at different times, because each of them is useful in certain situations.

How do we build such a classifier? We can do this in a similar way as before, with a slightly different error function and a slightly different iterative step.

note In this chapter, all the classifiers are discrete, namely, their output is 0 or 1. Sometimes they are described by their prediction $\hat{y} = step(f(x))$, and other times by their boundary equation $f(x) = 0$, namely, the graph of the function that attempts to separate our data points into two classes. For example, the perceptron that makes the prediction $\hat{y} = step(3x_1 + 4x_2 - 1)$ sometimes is described only by the linear equation $3x_1 + 4x_2 - 1 = 0$. For some classifiers in this chapter, especially those in the section "Training SVMs with nonlinear boundaries: The kernel method," the boundary equation will not necessarily be a linear function.

In this chapter, we see this theory mostly on datasets of one and two dimensions (points on a line or on the plane). However, support vector machines work equally well in datasets of higher dimensions. The linear boundaries in one dimension are points and in two dimensions are lines. Likewise, the linear boundaries in three dimensions are planes, and in higher dimensions, they are hyperplanes of one dimension less than the space in which the points live. In each of these cases, we try to find the boundary that is the farthest from the points. In figure 11.3, you can see examples of boundaries for one, two, and three dimensions.

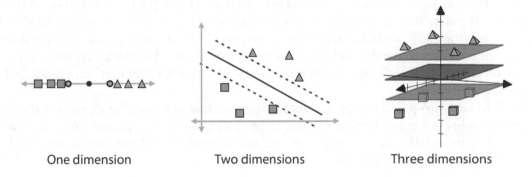

One dimension   Two dimensions   Three dimensions

Figure 11.3 Linear boundaries for datasets in one, two, and three dimensions. In one dimension, the boundary is formed by two points, in two dimensions by two lines, and in three dimensions by two planes. In each of the cases, we try to separate these two as much as possible. The middle boundary (point, line, or plane) is illustrated for clarity.

All the code for this chapter is in this GitHub repository: https://github.com/luisguiserrano/manning/tree/master/Chapter_11_Support_Vector_Machines.

Using a new error function to build better classifiers

As is common in machine learning models, SVMs are defined using an error function. In this section, we see the error function of SVMs, which is very special, because it tries to maximize two things at the same time: the classification of the points and the distance between the lines.

To train an SVM, we need to build an error function for a classifier consisting of two lines, spaced as far apart as possible. When we think of building an error function, we should always ask ourselves: "What do we want the model to achieve?" The following are the two things we want to achieve:

- Each of the two lines should classify the points as best as possible.

- The two lines should be as far away from each other as possible.

The error function should penalize any model that doesn't achieve these things. Because we want two things, our SVM error function should be the sum of two error functions: the first one penalizes points that are misclassified, and the second one penalizes lines that are too close to each other. Therefore, our error function can look like this:

$$\text{Error} = \text{Classification Error} + \text{Distance Error}$$

In the next two sections, we develop each one of these two terms separately.

Classification error function: Trying to classify the points correctly

In this section, we learn the classification error function. This is the part of the error function that pushes the classifier to correctly classify the points. In short, this error is calculated as follows. Because the classifier is formed by two lines, we think of them as two separate discrete perceptrons (chapter 5). We then calculate the total error of this classifier as the sum of the two perceptron errors (section "How to compare classifiers? The error function" in chapter 5). Let's take a look at an example.

The SVM uses two parallel lines, and luckily, parallel lines have similar equations; they have the same weights but a different bias. Thus, in our SVM, we use the central line as a frame of reference L with equation $w_1x_1 + w_2x_2 + b = 0$, and construct two lines, one above it and one below it, with the respective equations:

- L+: $w_1x_1 + w_2x_2 + b = 1$, and

- L−: $w_1x_1 + w_2x_2 + b = -1$

As an example, figure 11.4 shows the three parallel lines, L, L+, and L−, with the following equations:

- L: $2x_1 + 3x_2 - 6 = 0$

- L+: $2x_1 + 3x_2 - 6 = 1$

- L−: $2x_1 + 3x_2 - 6 = -1$

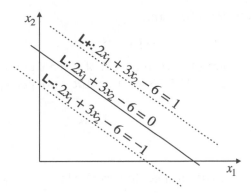

Figure 11.4 Our main line L is the one in the middle. We build the two parallel equidistant lines L+ and L– by slightly changing the equation of L.

Our classifier now consists of the lines L+ and L–. We can think of L+ and L– as two independent perceptron classifiers, and each of them has the same goal of classifying the points correctly. Each classifier comes with its own perceptron error function, so the classification function is defined as the sum of these two error functions, as illustrated in figure 11.5.

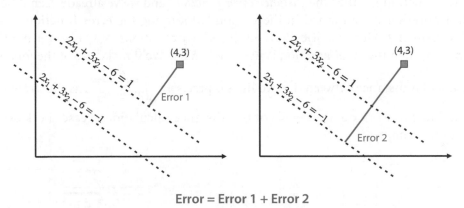

Error = Error 1 + Error 2

Figure 11.5 Now that our classifier consists of two lines, the error of a misclassified point is measured with respect to both lines. We then add the two errors to obtain the classification error. Note that the error is not the length of the perpendicular segment to the boundary, as illustrated, but it is proportional to it.

Notice that in an SVM, *both* lines have to classify the points well. Therefore, a point that is between the two lines is always misclassified by one of the lines, so it does not count as a correctly classified point by the SVM.

Recall from the section "How to compare classifiers? The error function" in chapter 5 that the error function for the discrete perceptron with prediction $\hat{y} = step(w_1 x_1 + w_2 x_2 + b)$ at the point (p, q) is given by the following:

- 0 if the point is correctly classified, and

- $|w_1x_1 + w_2x_2 + b|$ if the point is incorrectly classified

As an example, consider the point (4,3) with a label of 0. This point is incorrectly classified by both of the perceptrons in figure 11.5. Note that the two perceptrons give the following predictions:

- L+: $\hat{y} = step(2x_1 + 3x_2 - 7)$

- L−: $\hat{y} = step(2x_1 + 3x_2 - 5)$

Therefore, its classification error with respect to this SVM is

$$|2 \cdot 4 + 3 \cdot 3 - 7| + |2 \cdot 4 + 3 \cdot 3 - 5| = 10 + 12 = 22.$$

Distance error function: Trying to separate our two lines as far apart as possible

Now that we have created an error function that measures classification errors, we need to build one that looks at the distance between the two lines and raises an alarm if this distance is small. In this section, we discuss a surprisingly simple error function that is large when the two lines are close and small when they are far.

   This error function is called the *distance error function*, and we've already seen it before; it is the regularization term we learned in the section "Modifying the error function to solve our problem" in chapter 4. More specifically, if our lines have equations $w_1x_1 + w_2x_2 + b = 1$ and $w_1x_1 + w_2x_2 + b = -1$, then the error function is $w_1^2 + w_2^2$. Why? We'll make use of the following fact: the perpendicular distance between the two lines is precisely $\frac{2}{\sqrt{w_1^2 + w_2^2}}$, as illustrated in figure

11.6. If you'd like to work out the details of this distance calculation, please check exercise 11.1 at the end of this chapter.

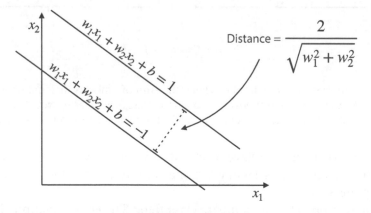

Figure 11.6   The distance between the two parallel lines can be calculated based on the equations of the lines.

Knowing this, notice the following:

- When $w_1^2 + w_2^2$ is large, $\dfrac{2}{\sqrt{w_1^2 + w_2^2}}$ is small.

- When $w_1^2 + w_2^2$ is small, $\dfrac{2}{\sqrt{w_1^2 + w_2^2}}$ is large.

Because we want the lines to be as far apart as possible, this term $w_1^2 + w_2^2$ is a good error function, as it gives us large values for the bad classifiers (those where the lines are close) and small values for the good classifiers (those where the lines are far).

In figure 11.7, we can see two examples of SVM classifiers. Their equations follow:

- SVM 1:
  - L+: $3x_1 + 4x_2 + 5 = 1$
  - L–: $3x_1 + 4x_2 + 5 = -1$
- SVM 2:
  - L+: $30x_1 + 40x_2 + 50 = 1$
  - L–: $30x_1 + 40x_2 + 50 = 1$

Their distance error functions are shown next:

- SVM 1:
  - Distance error function = $3^2 + 4^2 = 25$
- SVM 2:
  - Distance error function = $30^2 + 40^2 = 2500$

Notice also from figure 11.7 that the lines are much closer in SVM 2 than in SVM 1, which makes SVM 1 a much better classifier (from the distance perspective). The distance between the lines in SVM 1 is $\dfrac{2}{\sqrt{3^2 + 4^2}} = 0.4$, whereas in SVM 2 it is $\dfrac{2}{\sqrt{30^2 + 40^2}} = 0.04$.

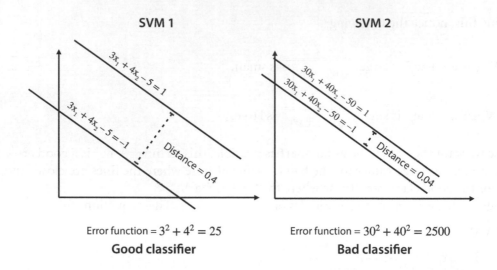

Figure 11.7   Left: An SVM where the lines are at distance 0.4 apart, with an error of 25. Right: An SVM where the lines are at distance 0.04 apart, with an error of 2500. Notice that in this comparison, the classifier on the left is much better than the one on the right, because the lines are farther apart from each other. This results in a smaller distance error.

Adding the two error functions to obtain the error function

Now that we've built a classification error function and a distance error function, let's see how to combine them to build an error function that helps us make sure that we have achieved both goals: classify our points well and with two lines that are far apart from each other.

To obtain this error function, we add the classification error function and the distance error function and get the following formula:

$$\text{Error} = \text{Classification Error} + \text{Distance Error}$$

A good SVM that minimizes this error function must then try to make as few classification errors as possible, while simultaneously trying to keep the lines as far apart as possible.

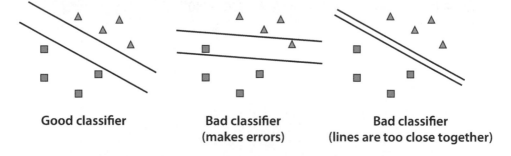

Figure 11.8   Left: A good SVM consisting of two well-spaced lines that classifies all the points correctly. Middle: A bad SVM that misclassifies two points. Right: A bad SVM that consists of two lines that are too close together.

In figure 11.8, we can see three SVM classifiers for the same dataset. The one on the left is a good classifier, because it classifies the data well and the lines are far apart, reducing the likelihood of errors. The one in the middle makes some errors (because there is a triangle underneath the top line and a square over the bottom line), so it is not a good classifier. The one on the right classifies the points correctly, but the lines are too close together, so it is also not a good classifier.

Do we want our SVM to focus more on classification or distance? The C parameter can help us

In this section, we learn a useful technique to tune and improve our model, which involves introducing the C parameter. The *C parameter* is used in cases where we want to train an SVM that pays more attention to classification than to distance (or the other way around).

So far it seems that all we have to do to build a good SVM classifier is to keep track of two things. We want to make sure the classifier makes as few errors as possible, while keeping the lines as far apart as possible. But what if we have to sacrifice one for the benefit of the other? In figure 11.9, we have two classifiers for the same dataset. The one on the left makes some errors, but the lines are far apart. The one on the right makes no errors, but the lines are too close together. Which one should we prefer?

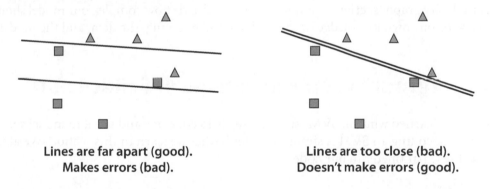

Lines are far apart (good).
Makes errors (bad).

Lines are too close (bad).
Doesn't make errors (good).

Figure 11.9 Both of these classifiers have one pro and one con. The one on the left consists of well-spaced lines (pro), but it misclassifies some points (con). The one on the right consists of lines that are too close together (con), but it classifies all the points correctly (pro).

It turns out that the answer for this depends on the problem we are solving. Sometimes we want a classifier that makes as few errors as possible, even if the lines are too close, and sometimes we want a classifier that keeps the lines apart, even if it makes a few errors. How do we control this? We use a parameter which we call the C parameter. We slightly modify the error formula by multiplying the classification error by C, to get the following formula:

$$\text{Error formula} = C \cdot (\text{Classification Error}) + (\text{Distance Error})$$

If C is large, then the error formula is dominated by the classification error, so our classifier focuses more on classifying the points correctly. If C is small, then the formula is dominated by the distance error, so our classifier focuses more on keeping the lines far apart.

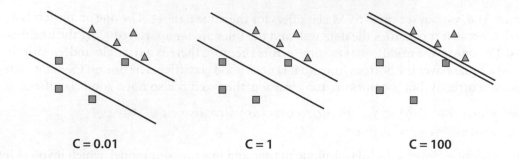

Figure 11.10   Different values of C toggle between a classifier with well-spaced lines and one that classifies points correctly. The classifier on the left has a small value of C (0.01), and the lines are well spaced, but it makes mistakes. The classifier on the right has a large value of C (100), and it classifies points correctly, but the lines are too close together. The classifier in the middle makes one mistake but finds two lines that are well spaced apart.

In figure 11.10, we can see three classifiers: one with a large value of C that classifies all points correctly, one with a small value of C that keeps the lines far apart, and one with C = 1, which tries to do both. In real life, C is a hyperparameter that we can tune using methods such as the model complexity graph (section "A numerical way to decide how complex our model should be" in chapter 4) or our own knowledge of the problem we're solving, the data, and the model.

Coding support vector machines in Scikit-Learn

Now that we've learned what an SVM is, we are ready to code one and use it to model some data. In Scikit-Learn, coding an SVM is simple and that's what we learn in this section. We also learn how to use the C parameter in our code.

Coding a simple SVM

We start by coding a simple SVM in a sample dataset and then we'll add more parameters. The dataset is called linear.csv, and its plot is shown in figure 11.11. The code for this section follows:

- **Notebook:** SVM_graphical_example.ipynb
  - https://github.com/luisguiserrano/manning/blob/master/Chapter_11_Support_Vector_Machines/SVM_graphical_example.ipynb
- **Dataset:** linear.csv

We first import from the svm package in Scikit-Learn and load our data as follows:

```
from sklearn.svm import SVC
```

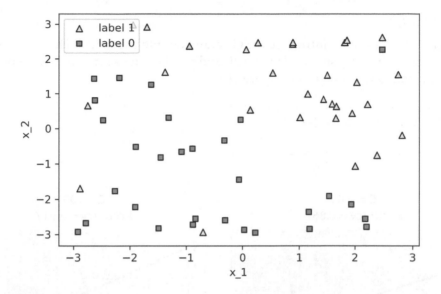

Figure 11.11 An almost linearly separable dataset, with some outliers

Then, as shown in the next code snippet, we load our data into two Pandas DataFrames called `features` and `labels`, and then we define our model called `svm_linear` and train it. The accuracy we obtain is 0.933, and the plot is shown in figure 11.12.

```
svm_linear = SVC(kernel='linear')
svm_linear.fit(features, labels)
```

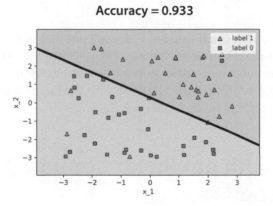

Figure 11.12 The plot of the SVM classifier we've built in Scikit-Learn consists of a line. The accuracy of this model is 0.933.

The C parameter

In Scikit-Learn, we can easily introduce the C parameter into the model. Here we train and plot two models, one with a very small value of 0.01, and another one with a large value of 100, which is shown in the following code and in figure 11.13:

```
svm_c_001 = SVC(kernel='linear', C=0.01)
svm_c_001.fit(features, labels)

svm_c_100 = SVC(kernel='linear', C=100)
svm_c_100.fit(features, labels)
```

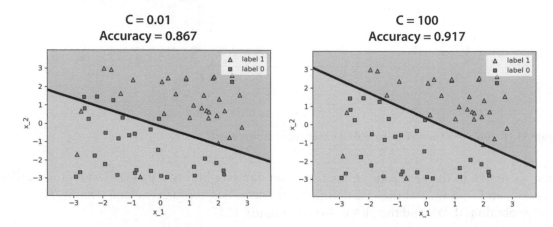

Figure 11.13   The classifier on the left has a small value of C, and it spaced the line well between the points, but it makes some mistakes. The classifier on the right has a large value of C, and it makes no mistakes, although the line passes too close to some of the points.

We can see that the model with a small value of C doesn't put that much emphasis on classifying the points correctly, and it makes some mistakes, as is evident in its low accuracy (0.867). It is hard to tell in this example, but this classifier puts a lot of emphasis on the line being as far away from the points as possible. In contrast, the classifier with the large value of C tries to classify all the points correctly, which reflects on its higher accuracy.

Training SVMs with nonlinear boundaries: The kernel method

As we've seen in other chapters of this book, not every dataset is linearly separable, and many times we need to build nonlinear classifiers to capture the complexity of the data. In this section, we study a powerful method associated with SVMs called the *kernel method*, which helps us build highly nonlinear classifiers.

If we have a dataset and find that we can't separate it with a linear classifier, what can we do? One idea is to add more columns to this dataset and hope that the richer dataset is linearly separable. The kernel method consists of adding more columns in a clever way, building a linear classifier on this new dataset and later removing the columns we added while keeping track of the (now nonlinear) classifier.

That was quite a mouthful, but we have a nice geometric way to see this method. Imagine that the dataset is in two dimensions, which means that the input has two columns. If we add a third column, the dataset is now three-dimensional, like if the points on your paper all of a sudden start flying into space at different heights. Maybe if we raise the points at different heights in a clever way, we can separate them with a plane. This is the kernel method, and it is illustrated in figure 11.14.

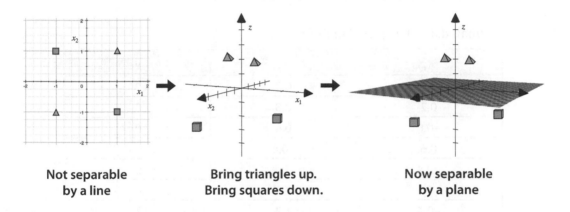

**Not separable
by a line**

**Bring triangles up.
Bring squares down.**

**Now separable
by a plane**

Figure 11.14 Left: The set is not separable by a line. Middle: We look at it in three dimensions, and proceed to raise the two triangles and lower the two squares. Right: Our new dataset is now separable by a plane. (Source: Image created with the assistance of Grapher™ from Golden Software, LLC; https://www.goldensoftware.com/products/grapher.)

Kernels, feature maps, and operator theory

The theory behind the kernel method comes from a field in mathematics called *operator theory*. A kernel is a similarity function, which, in short, is a function that tells us if two points are similar or different (e.g., close or far). A kernel can give rise to a *feature map*, which is a map between the space where our dataset lives and a (usually) higher-dimensional space.

The full theory of kernels and feature maps is not needed to understand the classifiers. If you'd like to delve into these more, see the resources in appendix C. For the purpose of this chapter, we look at the kernel method as a way of adding columns to our dataset to make the points separable. For example, the dataset in figure 11.14 has two columns, x_1 and x_2, and we have added the third column with the value $x_1 x_2$. Equivalently, it can also be seen as the function that sends the point (x_1, x_2) in the plane to the point $(x_1, x_2, x_1 x_2)$ in space. Once the points belong in 3-D space, we can separate them using the plane seen on the right of figure 11.14. To study this example more in detail, see exercise 11.2 at the end of the chapter.

The two kernels and their corresponding features maps we see in this chapter are the *polynomial kernel* and the *radial basis function* (RBF) *kernel*. Both of them consist of adding columns to our dataset in different, yet very effective, ways.

Using polynomial equations to our benefit: The polynomial kernel

In this section, we discuss the polynomial kernel, a useful kernel that will help us model nonlinear datasets. More specifically, the kernel method helps us model data using polynomial equations such as circles, parabolas, and hyperbolas. We'll illustrate the polynomial kernel with two examples.

Example 1: A circular dataset

For our first example, let's try to classify the dataset in table 11.1.

Table 11.1   A small dataset, depicted in figure 11.15

x_1	x_2	y
0.3	0.3	0
0.2	0.8	0
−0.6	0.4	0
0.6	−0.4	0
−0.4	−0.3	0
0	−0.8	0
−0.4	1.2	1
0.9	−0.7	1
−1.1	−0.8	1
0.7	0.9	1
−0.9	0.8	1
0.6	−1	1

The plot is shown in figure 11.15, where the points with label 0 are drawn as squares and those with label 1 are drawn as triangles.

When we look at the plot in figure 11.15, it is clear that a line won't be able to separate the squares from the triangles. However, a circle would (seen in figure 11.16). Now the question is, if a support vector machine can draw only linear boundaries, how can we draw this circle?

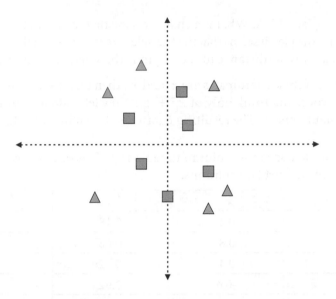

Figure 11.15 Plot of the dataset in table 11.1. Note that it is not separable by a line. Therefore, this dataset is a good candidate for the kernel method.

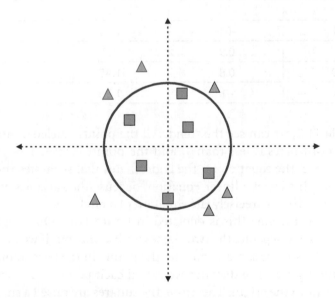

Figure 11.16 The kernel method gives us a classifier with a circular boundary, which separates these points well.

To draw this boundary, let's think. What is a characteristic that separates the squares from the triangles? From observing the plot, it seems that the triangles are farther from the origin than the circles. The formula that measures the distance to the origin is the square root of the sum of the squares of the two coordinates. If these coordinates are x_1 and x_2, then this distance is $\sqrt{x_1^2 + x_2^2}$. Let's forget about the square root, and think only of $x_1^2 + x_2^2$. Now let's add a column to table 11.1 with this value and see what happens. The resulting dataset is shown in table 11.2.

Table 11.2   We have added one more column to table 11.1. This one consists of the sum of the squares of the values of the first two columns.

x_1	x_2	$x_1^2 + x_2^2$	y
0.3	0.3	0.18	0
0.2	0.8	0.68	0
−0.6	0.4	0.52	0
0.6	−0.4	0.52	0
−0.4	−0.3	0.25	0
0	−0.8	0.64	0
−0.4	1.2	1.6	1
0.9	−0.7	1.3	1
−1.1	−0.8	1.85	1
0.7	0.9	1.3	1
−0.9	0.8	1.45	1
0.6	−1	1.36	1

After looking at table 11.2, we can see the trend. All the points labeled 0 satisfy that the sum of the squares of the coordinates is less than 1, and the points labeled 1 satisfy that this sum is greater than 1. Therefore, the equation on the coordinates that separates the points is precisely $x_1^2 + x_2^2 = 1$. Note that this is not a linear equation, because the variables are raised to a power greater than one. In fact, this is precisely the equation of a circle.

The geometric way to imagine this is depicted in figure 11.17. Our original set lives in the plane, and it is impossible to separate the two classes with a line. But if we raise each point (x_1, x_2) to the height $x_1^2 + x_2^2$, this is the same as putting the points in the paraboloid with equation $z = x_1^2 + x_2^2$ (drawn in the figure). The distance we raised each point is precisely the square of the distance from that point to the origin. Therefore, the squares are raised a small amount, because they are close to the origin, and the triangles are raised a large amount, because they are far away from the origin. Now the squares and triangles are far away from each other, and therefore, we can separate them with the horizontal plane at height 1—in other words, the plane with equation $z = 1$. As a final step, we project everything down to the plane. The intersection between the paraboloid and the plane becomes the circle of equation $x_1^2 + x_2^2 = 1$. Notice that this equation is not linear, because it has quadratic terms. Finally, the prediction this classifier makes is given by $\hat{y} = step(x_1^2 + x_2^2 - 1)$.

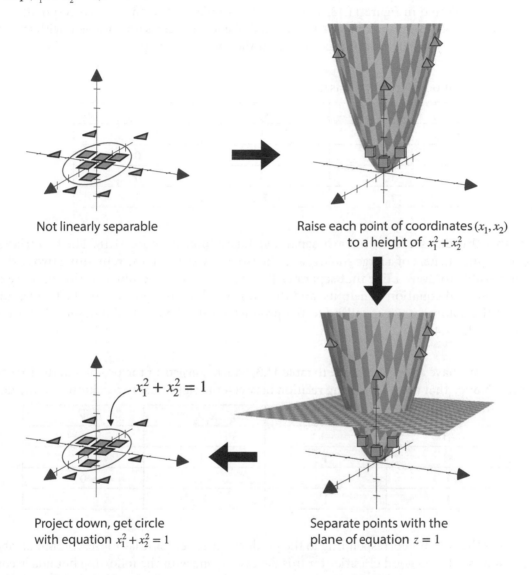

Not linearly separable

Raise each point of coordinates (x_1, x_2) to a height of $x_1^2 + x_2^2$

$x_1^2 + x_2^2 = 1$

Project down, get circle with equation $x_1^2 + x_2^2 = 1$

Separate points with the plane of equation $z = 1$

Figure 11.17 The kernel method. Step 1: We start with a dataset that is not linearly separable. Step 2: Then we raise each point by a distance that is the square of its distance to the origin. This creates a paraboloid. Step 3: Now the triangles are high, whereas the squares are low. We proceed to separate them with a plane at height 1. Step 4. We project everything down. The intersection between the paraboloid and the plane creates a circle. The projection of this circle gives us the circular boundary of our classifier. (Source: Image created with the assistance of Grapher™ from Golden Software, LLC; https://www.goldensoftware.com/products/grapher.)

Example 2: The modified XOR dataset

Circles are not the only figure we can draw. Let's consider a very simple dataset, illustrated in table 11.3 and plotted in figure 11.18. This dataset is similar to the one that corresponds to the XOR operator from exercises 5.3 and 10.2. If you'd like to solve the same problem with the original XOR dataset, you can do it in exercise 11.2 at the end of the chapter.

Table 11.3   The modified XOR dataset

x_1	x_2	y
−1	−1	1
−1	1	0
1	−1	0
1	1	1

To see that this dataset is not linearly separable, take a look at figure 11.18. The two triangles lie on opposite corners of a large square, and the two squares lie on the remaining two corners. It is impossible to draw a line that separates the triangles from the squares. However, we can use a polynomial equation to help us, and this time we'll use the product of the two features. Let's add the column corresponding to the product x_1x_2 to the original dataset. The result is shown in table 11.4.

Table 11.4   We have added a column to table 11.3, which consists of the product of the first two columns. Notice that there is a strong relation between the rightmost two columns on the table.

x_1	x_2	x_1x_2	y
−1	−1	1	1
−1	1	−1	0
1	−1	−1	0
1	1	1	1

Notice that the column corresponding to the product x_1x_2 is very similar to the column of labels. We can now see that a good classifier for this data is the one with the following boundary equation: $x_1x_2 = 1$. The plot of this equation is the union of the horizontal and vertical axes, and the reason for this is that for the product x_1x_2 to be 0, we need that $x_1 = 0$ or $x_2 = 0$. The prediction this classifier makes is given by $\hat{y} = step(x_1x_2)$, and it is 1 for points in the northeast and southwest quadrants of the plane, and 0 elsewhere.

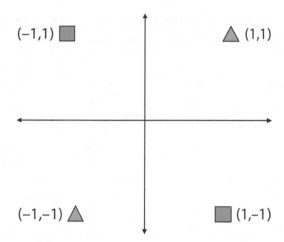

Figure 11.18 The plot of the dataset in table 11.3. The classifier that separates the squares from the triangles has boundary equation $x_1x_2 = 0$, which corresponds to the union of the horizontal and vertical axes.

Going beyond quadratic equations: The polynomial kernel

In both of the previous examples, we used a polynomial expression to help us classify a dataset that was not linearly separable. In the first example, this expression was $x_1^2 + x_2^2$, because that value is small for points near the origin and large for points far from the origin. In the second example, the expression was x_1x_2, which helped us separate points in different quadrants of the plane.

How did we find these expressions? In a more complicated dataset, we may not have the luxury to look at a plot and eyeball an expression that will help us out. We need a method or, in other words, an algorithm. What we'll do is consider all the possible monomials of degree 2 (quadratic), containing x_1 and x_2. These are the following three monomials: x_1^2, x_1x_2, and x_2^2. We call these new variables x_3, x_4, and x_5, and we treat them as if they had no relation with x_1 and x_2 whatsoever. Let's apply this to the first example (the circle). The dataset in table 11.1 with these new columns added is shown in table 11.5.

We can now build an SVM that classifies this enhanced dataset. The way to train an SVM is using the methods learned in the last section. I encourage you to build such a classifier using Scikit-Learn, Turi Create, or the package of your choice. By inspection, here is one equation of a classifier that works:

$$0x_1 + 0x_2 + 1x_3 + 0x_4 + 1x_5 - 1 = 0$$

Table 11.5   We have added three more columns to table 11.1, one corresponding to each of the monomials of degree 2 on the two variables x_1 and x_2. These monomials are x_1^2, $x_1 x_2$, and x_2^2.

x_1	x_2	$x_3 = x_1^2$	$x_4 = x_1 x_2$	$x_5 = x_2^2$	y
0.3	0.3	0.09	0.09	0.09	0
0.2	0.8	0.04	0.16	0.64	0
−0.6	0.4	0.36	−0.24	0.16	0
0.6	−0.4	0.36	−0.24	0.16	0
−0.4	−0.3	0.16	0.12	0.09	0
0	−0.8	0	0	0.64	0
−0.4	1.2	0.16	−0.48	1.44	1
0.9	−0.7	0.81	−0.63	0.49	1
−1.1	−0.8	1.21	0.88	0.64	1
0.7	0.9	0.49	0.63	0.81	1
−0.9	0.8	0.81	−0.72	0.64	1
0.6	−1	0.36	−0.6	1	1

Remembering that $x_3 = x_1^2$ and $x_5 = x_2^2$, we get the desired equation of the circle, as shown next:

$$x_1^2 + x_2^2 = 1$$

If we want to visualize this process geometrically, like we've done with the previous ones, it gets a little more complicated. Our nice two-dimensional dataset became a five-dimensional dataset. In this one, the points labelled 0 and 1 are now far away, and can be separated with a four-dimensional hyperplane. When we project this down to two dimensions, we get the desired circle.

The polynomial kernel gives rise to the map that sends the 2-D plane to the 5-D space. The map is the one that sends the point (x_1, x_2) to the point $(x_1, x_2, x_1^2, x_1 x_2, x_2^2)$. Because the maximum degree of each monomial is 2, we say that this is the polynomial kernel of degree 2. For the polynomial kernel, we always have to specify the degree.

What columns do we add to the dataset if we are using a polynomial kernel of higher degree, say, k? We add one column for each monomial in the given set of variables, of degree less than or equal to k. For example, if we are using the degree 3 polynomial kernel on the variables x_1 and x_2, we are adding columns corresponding to the monomials $\{x_1, x_2, x_1^2, x_1 x_2, x_2^2, x_1^3, x_1^2 x_2, x_1 x_2^2, x_2^3\}$. We can also do this for more variables in the same way. For example, if we use the degree 2 polynomial kernel on the variables x_1, x_2, and x_3, we are adding columns with the following monomials: $\{x_1, x_2, x_3, x_1^2, x_1 x_2, x_1 x_3, x_2^2, x_2 x_3, x_3^2\}$.

Using bumps in higher dimensions to our benefit: The radial basis function (RBF) kernel

The next kernel that we'll see is the radial basis function kernel. This kernel is tremendously useful in practice, because it can help us build nonlinear boundaries using certain special functions centered at each of the data points. To introduce the RBF kernel, let's first look at the one-dimensional example shown in figure 11.19. This dataset is not linearly separable—the square lies exactly between the two triangles.

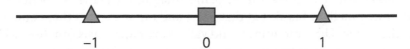

Figure 11.19   A dataset in one dimension that can't be classified by a linear classifier. Notice that a linear classifier is a point that divides the line into two parts, and there is no point that we can locate on the line that leaves all the triangles on one side and the square on the other side.

The way we will build a classifier for this dataset is to imagine building a mountain or a valley on each of the points. For the points labeled 1 (the triangles), we'll put a mountain, and for those labeled 0 (the square), we'll put a valley. These mountains and valleys are called *radial basis functions*. The resulting figure is shown at the top of figure 11.20. Now, we draw a mountain range such that at every point, the height is the sum of all the heights of the mountains and valleys at that point. We can see the resulting mountain range at the bottom of figure 11.20. Finally, the boundary of our classifier corresponds to the points at which this mountain range is at height zero, namely, the two highlighted points in the bottom. This classifier classifies anything in the interval between those two points as a square and everything outside of the interval as a triangle.

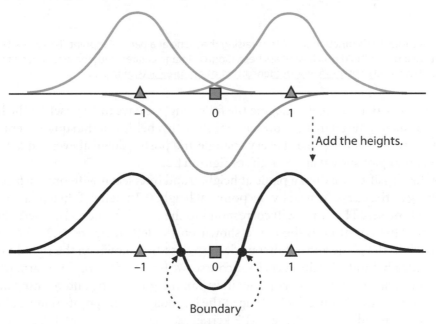

Figure 11.20   Using an SVM with the RBF kernel to separate a nonlinear dataset in one dimension. Top: We draw a mountain (radial basis function) at each point with label 1 and a valley at each point of label 0. Bottom: We add the radial basis functions from the top figure. The resulting function intersects the axis twice. The two points of intersection are the boundary of our SVM classifier. We classify each point between them as a square (label 0) and every point outside as a triangle (label 1).

This (plus some math around it which comes in the next section) is the essence of the RBF kernel. Now let's use it to build a similar classifier in a two-dimensional dataset.

To build the mountains and valleys on the plane, imagine the plane as a blanket (as illustrated in figure 11.21). If we pinch the blanket at that point and raise it, we get the mountain. If we push it down, we get the valley. These mountains and valleys are radial basis functions. They are called radial basis functions because the value of the function at a point is dependent only on the distance between the point and the center. We can raise the blanket at any point we like, and that gives us one different radial basis function for each point. The *radial basis function kernel* (also called RBF kernel) gives rise to a map that uses these radial functions to add several columns to our dataset in a way that will help us separate it.

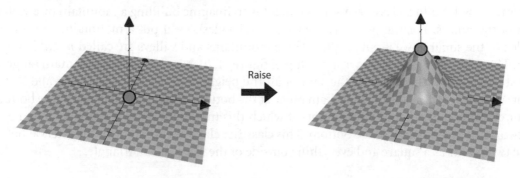

Figure 11.21   A radial basis function consists of raising the plane at a particular point. This is the family of functions that we'll use to build nonlinear classifiers. (Source: Image created with the assistance of Grapher™ from Golden Software, LLC; https://www.goldensoftware.com/products/grapher.)

How do we use this as a classifier? Imagine the following: we have the dataset on the left of figure 11.22, where, as usual, the triangles represent points with label 1, and the squares represent points with label 0. Now, we lift the plane at every triangle and push it down at every square. We get the three-dimensional plot shown on the right of figure 11.22.

To create the classifier, we draw a plane at height 0 and intersect it with our surface. This is the same as looking at the curve formed by the points at height 0. Imagine if there is a landscape with mountains and the sea. The curve will correspond to the coastline, namely, where the water and the land meet. This coastline is the curve shown on the left in figure 11.23. We then project everything back to the plane and obtain our desired classifier, shown on the right in figure 11.23.

That is the idea behind the RBF kernel. Of course, we have to develop the math, which we will do in the next few sections. But in principle, if we can imagine lifting and pushing down a blanket, and then building a classifier by looking at the boundary of the points that lie at a particular height, then we can understand what an RBF kernel is.

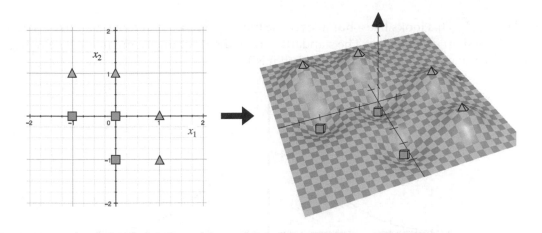

Figure 11.22 Left: A dataset in the plane that is not linearly separable. Right: We have used the radial basis functions to raise each of the triangles and lower each of the squares. Notice that now we can separate the dataset by a plane, which means our modified dataset is linearly separable. (Source: Image created with the assistance of Grapher™ from Golden Software, LLC; https://www.goldensoftware.com/products/grapher.)

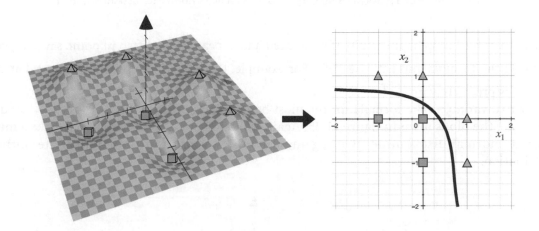

Figure 11.23 Left: If we look at the points at height 0, they form a curve. If we think of the high points as land and the low points as the sea, this curve is the coastline. Right: When we project (flatten) the points back to the plane, the coastline is now our classifier that separates the triangles from the squares. (Source: Image created with the assistance of Grapher™ from Golden Software, LLC; https://www.goldensoftware.com/products/grapher.)

A more in-depth look at radial basis functions

Radial basis functions can exist in any number of variables. At the beginning of this section, we saw them in one and two variables. For one variable, the simplest radial basis function has the formula $y = e^{-x^2}$. This looks like a bump over the line (figure 11.24). It looks a lot like a standard normal (Gaussian) distribution. The standard normal distribution is similar, but it has a slightly different formula, so that the area underneath it is 1.

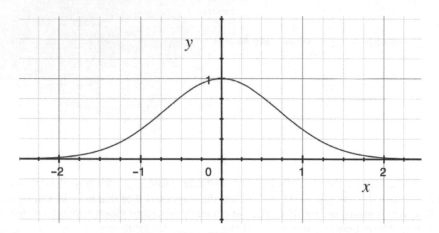

Figure 11.24   An example of a radial basis function. It looks a lot like a normal (Gaussian) distribution.

Notice that this bump happens at 0. If we wanted it to appear at any different point, say p, we can translate the formula and get $y = e^{-(x-p)^2}$. For example, the radial basis function centered at the point 5 is precisely $y = e^{-(x-5)^2}$.

For two variables, the formula for the most basic radial basis function is $z = e^{-(x^2+y^2)}$, and it looks like the plot shown in figure 11.25. Again, you may notice that it looks a lot like a multivariate normal distribution. It is, again, a modified version of the multivariate normal distribution.

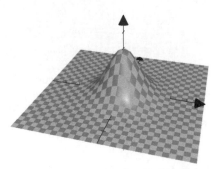

Figure 11.25   A radial basis function on two variables. It again looks a lot like a normal distribution. (Source: Image created with the assistance of Grapher™ from Golden Software, LLC; https://www.goldensoftware.com/products/grapher.)

This bump happens exactly at the point (0,0). If we wanted it to appear at any different point, say (p, q), we can translate the formula, and get $y = e^{-\left[(x-p)^2 + (y-q)^2\right]}$. For example, the radial basis function centered at the point (2, –3) is precisely $y = e^{-\left[(x-2)^2 + (y+3)^2\right]}$.

For n variables, the formula for the basic radial basis function is $y = e^{-\left(x_1^2 + \cdots + x_n^2\right)}$. We can't draw a plot in $n + 1$ dimensions, but if we imagine pinching an n-dimensional blanket and lifting it up with our fingers, that's how it looks. However, because the algorithm that we use is purely mathematical, the computer has no trouble running it in as many variables as we want. As usual, this n-dimensional bump is centered at 0, but if we wanted it centered at the point $(p_1, \ldots, p_n)$, the formula is $y = e^{-\left[(x_1 - p_1)^2 + \cdots + (x_n - p_n)^2\right]}$.

A measure of how close points are: Similarity

To build an SVM using the RBF kernel, we need one notion: the notion of *similarity*. We say that two points are similar if they are close to each other, and not similar if they are far away (figure 11.26). In other words, the similarity between two points is high if they are close to each other and low if they are far away from each other. If the pair of points are the same point, then the similarity is 1. In theory, the similarity between two points that are an infinite distance apart is 0.

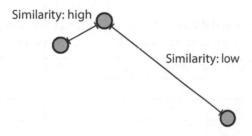

Figure 11.26   Two points that are close to each other are defined to have high similarity. Two points that are far away are defined to have low similarity.

Now we need to find a formula for similarity. As we can see, the similarity between two points decreases as the distance between them increases. Thus, many formulas for similarity would work, as long as they satisfy that condition. Because we are using exponential functions in this section, let's define it as follows. For points p and q, the similarity between p and q is as follows:

$$similarity(p,q) = e^{-distance(p,q)^2}$$

That looks like a complicated formula for similarity, but there is a very nice way to look at it. If we want to find the similarity between two points, say p and q, this similarity is precisely the height of the radial basis function centered at p and applied at the point q. This is, if we pinch the blanket at point p and lift it, then the height of the blanket at point q is high if the q is close to p and low if q is far from p. In figure 11.27, we can see this for one variable, but imagine it in any number of variables by using the blanket analogy.

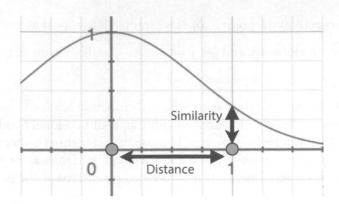

Figure 11.27 The similarity is defined as the height of a point in the radial basis function, where the input is the distance. Note that the higher the distance, the lower the similarity, and vice versa.

Training an SVM with the RBF kernel

Now that we have all the tools to train an SVM using the RBF kernel, let's see how to put it all together. Let's first look at the simple dataset displayed in figure 11.19. The dataset itself appears in table 11.6.

Table 11.6 The one-dimensional dataset shown in figure 11.19. Note that it isn't linearly separable, because the point with label 0 is right between the two points with label 1.

Point	x	y (label)
1	−1	1
2	0	0
3	1	1

As we saw, this dataset is not linearly separable. To make it linearly separable, we'll add a few columns. The three columns we are adding are the similarity columns, and they record the similarity between the points. The similarity between two points with x-coordinates x_1 and x_2 is measured as $e^{(x_1-x_2)^2}$, as indicated in the section "Using bumps in higher dimensions to our benefit." For example, the similarity between points 1 and 2 is $e^{(-1-0)^2}$ =0.368. In the Sim1 column, we'll record the similarity between point 1 and the other three points, and so on. The extended dataset is shown in table 11.7.

Table 11.7 We extend the dataset in table 11.6 by adding three new columns. Each column corresponds to the similarity of all points with respect to each point. This extended dataset lives in a four-dimensional space, and it is linearly separable.

Point	x	Sim1	Sim2	Sim3	y
1	−1	1	0.368	0.018	1
2	0	0.368	1	0.368	0
3	1	0.018	0.368	1	1

This extended dataset is now linearly separable! Many classifiers will separate this set, but in particular, the one with the following boundary equation will:

$$\hat{y} = step(Sim1 - Sim2 + Sim3)$$

Let's verify this by predicting the label at every point as shown next:

- **Point 1:** $\hat{y} = step(1 - 0.368 + 0.018) = step(0.65) = 1$
- **Point 2:** $\hat{y} = step(0.368 - 1 + 0.368) = step(-0.264) = 0$
- **Point 3:** $\hat{y} = step(0.018 - 0.368 + 1) = step(0.65) = 1$

Furthermore, because $Sim1 = e^{(x+1)^2}$, $Sim2 = e^{(x-0)^2}$, and $Sim3 = e^{(x-1)^2}$ then our final classifier makes the following predictions:

$$\hat{y} = step\left(e^{(x+1)^2} - e^{x^2} + e^{(x-1)^2}\right)$$

Now, let's do this same procedure but in two dimensions. This section does not require code, but the calculations are large, so if you'd like to take a look at them, they are in the following notebook: https://github.com/luisguiserrano/manning/blob/master/Chapter_11_Support_Vector_Machines/Calculating_similarities.ipynb.

Table 11.8 A simple dataset in two dimensions, plotted in figure 11.28. We'll use an SVM with an RBF kernel to classify this dataset.

Point	x_1	x_2	y
1	0	0	0
2	−1	0	0
3	0	−1	0
4	0	1	1
5	1	0	1
6	−1	1	1
7	1	−1	1

Consider the dataset in table 11.8, which we already classified graphically (figures 11.22 and 11.23). For convenience, it is plotted again in figure 11.28. In this plot, the points with label 0 appear as squares and those with label 1 as triangles.

Notice that in the first column of table 11.8 and in figure 11.28, we have numbered every point. This is not part of the data; we did it only for convenience. We will now add seven columns to this table. The columns are the similarities with respect to every point. For example, for point 1, we add a similarity column named Sim1. The entry for every point in this column is the amount of similarity between that point and point 1. Let's calculate one of them, for example, the similarity with point 6. The distance between point 1 and point 6, by the Pythagorean theorem follows:

$$distance(point\ 1, point\ 6) = \sqrt{(0+1)^2 + (0-1)^2} = \sqrt{2}$$

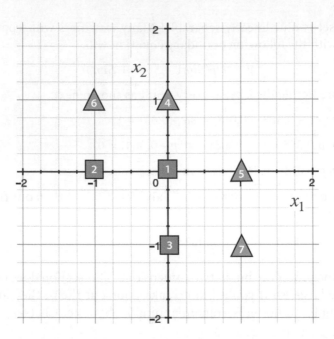

Figure 11.28 The plot of the dataset in table 11.8, where the points with label 0 are squares and those with label 1 are triangles. Notice that the squares and triangles cannot be separated with a line. We'll use an SVM with an RBF kernel to separate them with a curved boundary.

Therefore, the similarity is precisely

$$similarity(point\ 1,\ point\ 6) = e^{-distance(q,p)^2} = e^{-2} = 0.135.$$

This number goes in row 1 and column Sim6 (and by symmetry, also in row 6 and column Sim1). Fill in a few more values in this table to convince yourself that this is the case, or take a look at the notebook where the whole table is calculated. The result is shown in table 11.9.

Table 11.9 We have added seven similarity columns to the dataset in table 11.8. Each one records the similarities with all the other six points.

Point	x_1	x_2	Sim1	Sim2	Sim3	Sim4	Sim5	Sim6	Sim7	y
1	0	0	1	0.368	0.368	0.368	0.368	0.135	0.135	0
2	−1	0	0.368	1	0.135	0.135	0.018	0.368	0.007	0
3	0	−1	0.368	0.135	1	0.018	0.135	0.007	0.368	0
4	0	1	0.368	0.135	0.018	1	0.135	0.368	0.007	1
5	1	0	0.368	0.018	0.135	0.135	1	0.007	0.368	1
6	−1	1	0.135	0.368	0.007	0.367	0.007	1	0	1
7	1	−1	0.135	0.007	0.368	0.007	0.368	0	1	1

Notice the following things:

1. The similarity between each point and itself is always 1.

2. For each pair of points, the similarity is high when they are close in the plot and low when they are far.

3. The table consisting of the columns Sim1 to Sim7 is symmetric, because the similarity between p and q is the same as the similarity between q and p (as it depends only on the distance between p and q).

4. The similarity between points 6 and 7 appears as 0, but in reality, it is not. The distance between points 6 and 7 is $\sqrt{2^2 + 2^2} = \sqrt{8}$, so their similarity is $e^{-8} = 0.00033546262$, which rounds to zero because we are using three significant figures.

Now, on to building our classifier! Notice that for the data in the small table 11.8, no linear classifier works (because the points can't be split by a line), but on the much larger table 11.9, which has a lot more features (columns), we can fit such a classifier. We proceed to fit an SVM to this data. Many SVMs can classify this dataset correctly, and in the notebook, I've used Turi Create to build one. However, a simpler one works as well. This classifier has the following weights:

- The weights of x_1 and x_2 are 0.

- The weight of Sim p is 1, for $p = 1, 2$, and 3.

- The weight of Sim p is –1, for $p = 4, 5, 6$, and 7.

- The bias is $b = 0$.

We find the classifier was adding a label –1 to the columns corresponding to the points labeled 0, and a +1 to the columns corresponding to the points labeled 1. This is equivalent to the process of adding a mountain at any point of label 1 and a valley at every point of label 0, like in figure 11.29. To check mathematically that this works, take table 11.7, add the values of the columns Sim4, Sim5, Sim6, and Sim7, then subtract the values of the columns Sim1, Sim2 and Sim3. You'll notice that you get a negative number in the first three rows and a positive one in the last four rows. Therefore, we can use a threshold of 0, and we have a classifier that classifies this dataset correctly, because the points labeled 1 get a positive score, and the points labeled 0 get a negative score. Using a threshold of 0 is equivalent to using the coastline to separate the points in the plot in figure 11.29.

If we plug in the similarity function, the classifier we obtain is the following:

$$\hat{y} = step\left(-e^{x_1^2 + x_2^2} - e^{(x_1+1)^2 + x_2^2} - e^{x_1^2 + (x_2+1)^2} + e^{x_1^2 + (x_2-1)^2} + e^{(x_1-1)^2 + x_2^2} + e^{(x_1+1)^2 + (x_2-1)^2} + e^{(x_1-1)^2 + (x_2+1)^2}\right)$$

In summary, we found a dataset that was not linearly separable. We used radial basis functions and similarity between points to add several columns to the dataset. This helped us build a linear classifier (in a much higher-dimensional space). We then projected the higher-dimensional linear classifier into the plane to get the classifier we wanted. We can see the resulting curved classifier in figure 11.29.

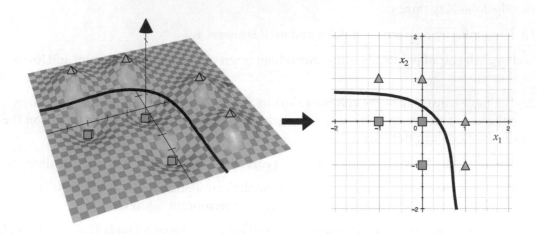

Figure 11.29   In this dataset, we raised each triangle and lowered each square. Then we drew a plane at height 0, which separates the squares and the triangles. The plane intersects the surface in a curved boundary. We then projected everything back down to two dimensions, and this curved boundary is the one that separates our triangles from our squares. The boundary is drawn at the right. (Source: Image created with the assistance of Grapher™ from Golden Software, LLC; https://www.goldensoftware.com/products/grapher.)

Overfitting and underfitting with the RBF kernel: The gamma parameter

At the beginning of this section, we mentioned that many different radial basis functions exist, namely one per point in the plane. There are actually many more. Some of them lift the plane at a point and form a narrow surface, and others form a wide surface. Some examples can be seen in figure 11.30. In practice, the wideness of our radial basis functions is something we want to tune. For this, we use a parameter called the *gamma parameter*. When gamma is small, the surface formed is very wide, and when it is large, the surface is very narrow.

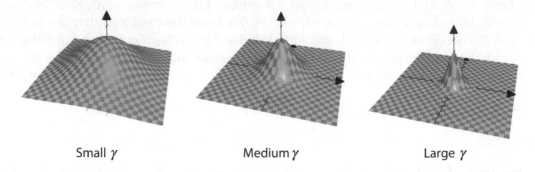

Small γ Medium γ Large γ

Figure 11.30   The gamma parameter determines how wide the surface is. Notice that for small values of gamma, the surface is very wide, and for large values of gamma, the surface is very narrow. (Source: Image created with the assistance of Grapher™ from Golden Software, LLC; https://www.goldensoftware.com/products/grapher.)

Gamma is a hyperparameter. Recall that hyperparameters are the specifications that we use to train our model. The way we tune this hyperparameter is using methods that we've seen before, such as the model complexity graph (the section "A numerical way to decide how complex our model should be" in chapter 4). Different values of gamma tend to overfit and underfit. Let's look back at the example at the beginning of this section, with three different values of gamma. The three models are plotted in figure 11.31.

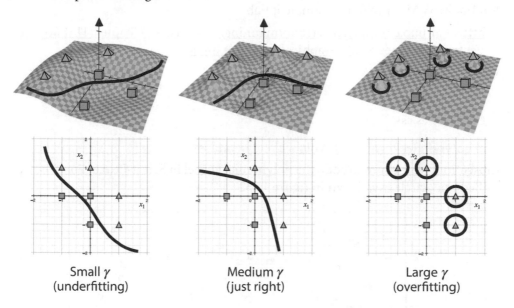

Small γ
(underfitting)

Medium γ
(just right)

Large γ
(overfitting)

Figure 11.31   Three SVM classifiers shown with an RBF kernel and different values of gamma. (Source: Image created with the assistance of Grapher™ from Golden Software, LLC; https://www.goldensoftware.com/products/grapher.)

Notice that for a very small value of gamma, the model overfits, because the curve is too simple, and it doesn't classify our data well. For a large value of gamma, the model vastly overfits, because it builds a tiny mountain for each triangle and a tiny valley for each square. This makes it classify almost everything as a square, except for the areas just around the triangles. A medium value of gamma seems to work well, because it builds a boundary that is simple enough, yet classifies the points correctly.

The equation for the radial basis function doesn't change much when we add the gamma parameter—all we have to do is multiply the exponent by gamma. In the general case, the equation of the radial basis function follows:

$$y = e^{-\gamma \left[(x_1 - p_1)^2 + \cdots + (x_n - p_n)^2 \right]}$$

Don't worry very much about learning this formula—just remember that even in higher dimensions, the bumps we make can be wide or narrow. As usual, there is a way to code this and make it work, which is what we do in the next section.

Coding the kernel method

Now that we've learned the kernel method for SVMs, we learn code them in Scikit-Learn and train a model in a more complex dataset using the polynomial and RBF kernels. To train an SVM in Scikit-Learn with a particular kernel, all we do is add the kernel as a parameter when we define the SVM. The code for this section follows:

- **Notebook:** SVM_graphical_example.ipynb
  - https://github.com/luisguiserrano/manning/blob/master/Chapter_11_Support_Vector_Machines/SVM_graphical_example.ipynb
- Datasets:
  - one_circle.csv
  - two_circles.csv

Coding the polynomial kernel to classify a circular dataset

In this subsection, we see how to code the polynomial kernel in Scikit-Learn. For this, we use the dataset called one_circle.csv, shown in figure 11.32.

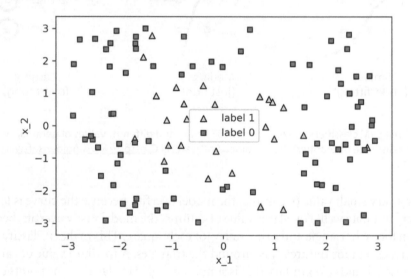

Figure 11.32   A circular dataset, with some noise. We will use an SVM with the polynomial kernel to classify this dataset.

Notice that aside from some outliers, this dataset is mostly circular. We train an SVM classifier where we specify the `kernel` parameter to be `poly`, and the `degree` parameter to be 2, as shown in the next code snippet. The reason we want the degree to be 2 is because the equation of a circle is a polynomial of degree 2. The result is shown in figure 11.33.

```
svm_degree_2 = SVC(kernel='poly', degree=2)
svm_degree_2.fit(features, labels)
```

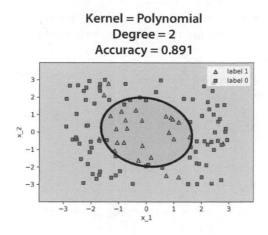

Figure 11.33 An SVM classifier with a polynomial kernel of degree 2

Notice that this SVM with a polynomial kernel of degree 2 manages to build a mostly circular region to bound the dataset, as desired.

Coding the RBF kernel to classify a dataset formed by two intersecting circles and playing with the gamma parameter

We've drawn a circle, but let's get more complicated. In this subsection, we learn how to code several SVMs with the RBF kernel to classify a dataset that has the shape of two intersecting circles. This dataset, called two_circles.csv, is illustrated in figure 11.34.

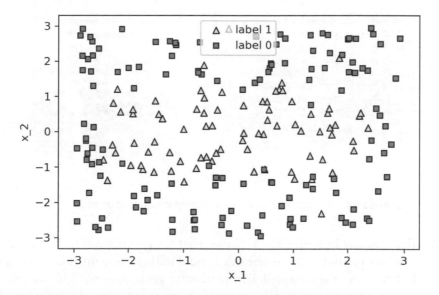

Figure 11.34 A dataset consisting of two intersecting circles, with some outliers. We will use an SVM with the RBF kernel to classify this dataset.

To use the RBF kernel, we specify `kernel = 'rbf'`. We can also specify a value for gamma. We'll train four different SVM classifiers, for the following values of gamma: 0.1, 1, 10, and 100, as shown next:

```
svm_gamma_01 = SVC(kernel='rbf', gamma=0.1)         ←——   Gamma = 0.1
svm_gamma_01.fit(features, labels)

svm_gamma_1 = SVC(kernel='rbf', gamma=1)            ←——   Gamma = 1
svm_gamma_1.fit(features, labels)

svm_gamma_10 = SVC(kernel='rbf', gamma=10)          ←——   Gamma = 10
svm_gamma_10.fit(features, labels)

svm_gamma_100 = SVC(kernel='rbf', gamma=100)        ←——   Gamma = 100
svm_gamma_100.fit(features, labels)
```

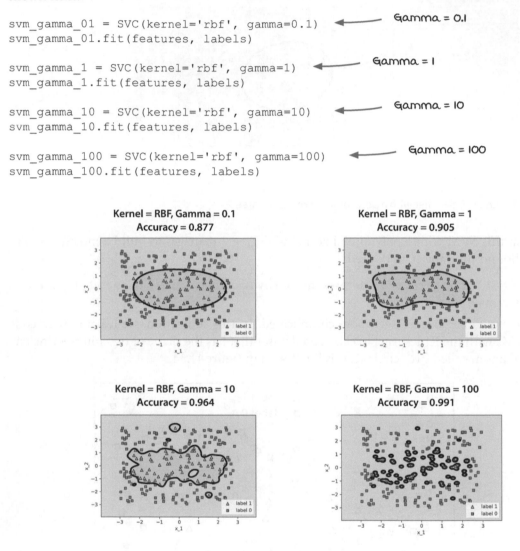

Figure 11.35   Four SVM classifiers with an RBF kernel and different values of gamma

The four classifiers appear in figure 11.35. Notice that for gamma = 0.1, the model underfits a little, because it thinks the boundary is one oval, and it makes some mistakes. Gamma = 1 gives a good model that captures the data well. By the time we get to gamma = 10, we can see that the model starts to overfit. Notice how it tries to classify every point correctly, including the outliers, which it encircles individually. By the time we get to gamma=100, we can see some serious overfitting. This classifier only surrounds each triangle with a small circular region and classifies everything else as a square. Thus, for this model, gamma = 1 seems to be the best value among the ones we tried.

Summary

- A support vector machine (SVM) is a classifier that consists of fitting two parallel lines (or hyperplanes), and trying to space them as far apart as possible, while still trying to classify the data correctly.

- The way to build support vector machines is with an error function that comprises two terms: the sum of two perceptron errors, one per parallel line, and the distance error, which is high when the two parallel lines are far apart and low when they are close together.

- We use the C parameter to regulate between trying to classify the points correctly and trying to space out the lines. This is useful while training because it gives us control over our preferences, namely, if we want to build a classifier that classifies the data very well, or a classifier with a well-spaced boundary.

- The kernel method is a useful and very powerful tool for building nonlinear classifiers.

- The kernel method consists of using functions to help us embed our dataset inside a higher-dimensional space, in which the points may be easier to classify with a linear classifier. This is equivalent to adding columns to our dataset in a clever way to make the enhanced dataset linearly separable.

- Several different kernels, such as the polynomial kernel and the RBF kernel, are available. The polynomial kernel allows us to build polynomial regions such as circles, parabolas, and hyperbolas. The RBF kernel allows us to build more complex curved regions.

Exercises

Exercise 11.1

(This exercise completes the calculation needed in the section "Distance error function.")

Show that the distance between the lines with equations $w_1 x_1 + w_2 x_1 + b = 1$ and $w_1 x_1 + w_2 x_1 + b = -1$ is precisely $\dfrac{2}{\sqrt{w_1^2 + w_2^2}}$.

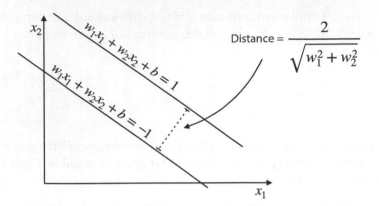

$$\text{Distance} = \frac{2}{\sqrt{w_1^2 + w_2^2}}$$

Exercise 11.2

As we learned in exercise 5.3, it is impossible to build a perceptron model that mimics the XOR gate. In other words, it is impossible to fit the following dataset (with 100% accuracy) with a perceptron model:

x_1	x_2	y
0	0	0
0	1	1
1	0	1
1	1	0

This is because the dataset is not linearly separable. An SVM has the same problem, because an SVM is also a linear model. However, we can use a kernel to help us out. What kernel should we use to turn this dataset into a linearly separable one? What would the resulting SVM look like?

hint   Look at example 2 in the section "Using polynomial equations to your benefit," which solves a very similar problem.

Combining models to maximize results: Ensemble learning | **12**

In this chapter

- what ensemble learning is, and how it is used to combine weak classifiers into a stronger one

- using bagging to combine classifiers in a random way

- using boosting to combine classifiers in a cleverer way

- some of the most popular ensemble methods: random forests, AdaBoost, gradient boosting, and XGBoost

Oh no, they've learned ensemble methods!!

After learning many interesting and useful machine learning models, it is natural to wonder if it is possible to combine these classifiers. Thankfully, we can, and in this chapter, we learn several ways to build stronger models by combining weaker ones. The two main methods we learn in this chapter are bagging and boosting. In a nutshell, bagging consists of constructing a few models in a random way and joining them together. Boosting, on the other hand, consists of building these models in a smarter way by picking each model strategically to focus on the previous models' mistakes. The results that these ensemble methods have shown in important machine learning problems has been tremendous. For example, the Netflix Prize, which was awarded to the best model that fits a large dataset of Netflix viewership data, was won by a group that used an ensemble of different models.

In this chapter, we learn some of the most powerful and popular bagging and boosting models, including random forests, AdaBoost, gradient boosting, and XGBoost. The majority of these are described for classification, and some are described for regression. However, most of the ensemble methods work in both cases.

A bit of terminology: throughout this book, we have referred to machine learning models as models, or sometimes regressors or classifiers, depending on their task. In this chapter, we introduce the term *learner*, which also refers to a machine learning model. In the literature, it is common to use the terms *weak learner* and *strong learner* when talking about ensemble methods. However, there is no difference between a machine learning model and a learner.

All the code for this chapter is available in this GitHub repository: https://github.com/luisguiserrano/manning/tree/master/Chapter_12_Ensemble_Methods.

With a little help from our friends

Let's visualize ensemble methods using the following analogy: Imagine that we have to take an exam that consists of 100 true/false questions on many different topics, including math, geography, science, history, and music. Luckily, we are allowed to call our five friends—Adriana, Bob, Carlos, Dana, and Emily—to help us. There is a small constraint, which is that all of them work full time, and they don't have time to answer all 100 questions, but they are more than happy to help us with a subset of them. What techniques can we use to get their help? Two possible techniques follow:

Technique 1: For each of the friends, pick several random questions, and ask them to answer them (make sure every question gets an answer from at least one of our friends). After we get the responses, answer the test by selecting the option that was most popular among those who answered that question. For example, if two of our friends answered "True" and one answered "False" on question 1, then we answer question 1 as "True" (if there are ties, we can pick one of the winning responses randomly).

Technique 2: We give the exam to Adriana and ask her to answer only the questions she is the surest about. We assume that those answers are good and remove them from the test. Now we give the remaining questions to Bob, with the same instructions. We continue in this fashion until we pass it to all the five friends.

Technique 1 resembles a bagging algorithm, and technique 2 resembles a boosting algorithm. To be more specific, bagging and boosting use a set of models called *weak learners* and combine them into a *strong learner* (as illustrated in figure 12.1).

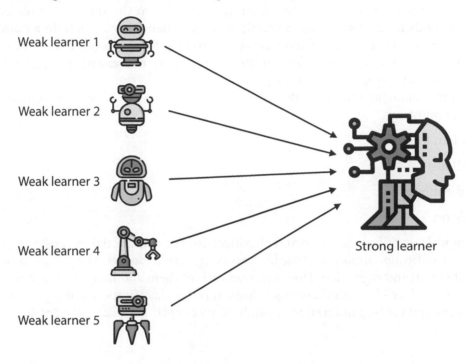

Figure 12.1   Ensemble methods consist of joining several weak learners to build a strong learner.

Bagging: Build random sets by drawing random points from the dataset (with replacement). Train a different model on each of the sets. These models are the weak learners. The strong learner is then formed as a combination of the weak models, and the prediction is done by voting (if it is a classification model) or averaging the predictions (if it is a regression model).

Boosting: Start by training a random model, which is the first weak learner. Evaluate it on the entire dataset. Shrink the points that have good predictions, and enlarge the points that have poor predictions. Train a second weak learner on this modified dataset. We continue in this fashion until we build several models. The way to combine them into a strong learner is the same way as with bagging, namely, by voting or by averaging the predictions of the weak learner. More specifically, if the learners are classifiers, the strong learner predicts the most common class predicted by the weak learners (thus the term *voting*), and if there are ties, by choosing randomly among them. If the learners are regressors, the strong learner predicts the average of the predictions given by the weak learners.

Most of the models in this chapter use decision trees (both for regression and classification) as the weak learners. We do this because decision trees lend themselves very well to this type of approach. However, as you read the chapter, I encourage you to think of how you would combine other types of models, such as perceptrons and SVMs.

We've spent an entire book building very good learners. Why do we want to combine several weak learners instead of simply building a strong learner from the start? One reason is that ensemble methods have been shown to overfit much less than other models. In a nutshell, it is easy for one model to overfit, but if you have several models for the same dataset, the combination of them overfits less. In a sense, it seems that if one learner makes a mistake, the others tend to correct it, and on average, they work better.

We learn the following models in this chapter. The first one is a bagging algorithm, and the last three are boosting:

- Random forests
- AdaBoost
- Gradient boosting
- XGBoost

All these models work for regression and classification. For educational purposes, we learn the first two as classification models and the last two as regression models. The process is similar for both classification and regression. However, read each of them and imagine how it would work in both cases. To learn how all these algorithms work for classification and regression, see the links to videos and reading material in appendix C that explain both cases in detail.

Bagging: Joining some weak learners randomly to build a strong learner

In this section we see one of the most well-known bagging models: a *random forest*. In a random forest, the weak learners are small decision trees trained on random subsets of the dataset. Random forests work well for classification and regression problems, and the process is similar. We will see random forests in a classification example. The code for this section follows:

- **Notebook:** Random_forests_and_AdaBoost.ipynb
    - https://github.com/luisguiserrano/manning/blob/master/Chapter_12_Ensemble_Methods/Random_forests_and_AdaBoost.ipynb

We use a small dataset of spam and ham emails, similar to the one we used in chapter 8 with the naive Bayes model. The dataset is shown in table 12.1 and plotted in figure 12.2. The features of the dataset are the number of times the words "lottery" and "sale" appear in the email, and the "yes/no" label indicates whether the email is spam (yes) or ham (no).

Table 12.1 Table of spam and ham emails, together with the number of appearances of the words "lottery" and "sale" on each email

Lottery	Sale	Spam
7	8	1
3	2	0
8	4	1
2	6	0
6	5	1
9	6	1
8	5	0
7	1	0
1	9	1
4	7	0
1	3	0
3	10	1
2	2	1
9	3	0
5	3	0
10	1	0
5	9	1
10	8	1

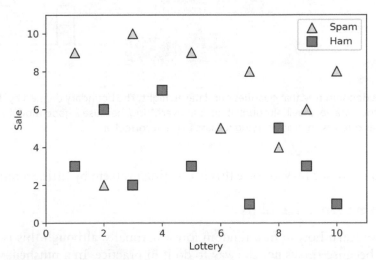

Figure 12.2 The plot of the dataset in table 12.1. Spam emails are represented by triangles and ham emails by squares. The horizontal and vertical axes represent the number of appearances of the words "lottery" and "sale," respectively.

First, (over)fitting a decision tree

Before we get into random forests, let's fit a decision tree classifier to this data and see how well it performs. Because we've learned this in chapter 9, figure 12.3 shows only the final result, but we can see the code in the notebook. On the left of figure 12.3, we can see the actual tree (quite deep!), and on the right, we can see the plot of the boundary. Notice that it fits the dataset very well, with a 100% training accuracy, although it clearly overfits. The overfitting can be noticed on the two outliers that the model tries to classify correctly, without noticing they are outliers.

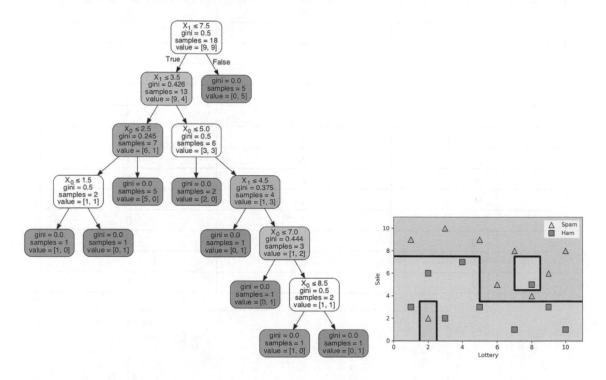

Figure 12.3   Left: A decision tree that classifies our dataset. Right: The boundary defined by this decision tree. Notice that it splits the data very well, although it hints at overfitting, because a good model would treat the two isolated points as outliers, instead of trying to classify them correctly.

In the next sections, we see how to solve this overfitting problem by fitting a random forest.

Fitting a random forest manually

In this section, we learn how to fit a random forest manually, although this is only for educational purposes, because this is not the way to do it in practice. In a nutshell, we pick random subsets from our dataset and train a weak learner (decision tree) on each one of them. Some data points may belong to several subsets, and others may belong to none. The combination of them is our strong learner. The way the strong learner makes predictions is by letting the weak learners vote. For this dataset, we use three weak learners. Because the dataset has 18 points, let's consider three subsets of 6 data points each, as shown in figure 12.4.

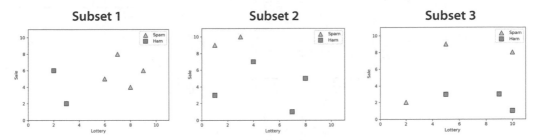

Figure 12.4   The first step to build a random forest is to split our data into three subsets. This is a splitting of the dataset shown in figure 12.2.

Next, we proceed to build our three weak learners. Fit a decision tree of depth 1 on each of these subsets. Recall from chapter 9 that a decision tree of depth 1 contains only one node and two leaves. Its boundary consists of a single horizontal or vertical line that splits the dataset as best as possible. The weak learners are illustrated in figure 12.5.

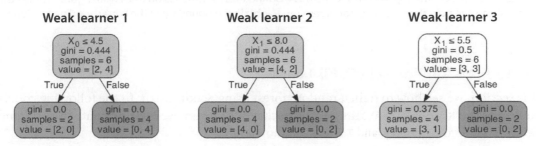

Figure 12.5   The three weak learners that form our random forest are decision trees of depth 1. Each decision tree fits one of the corresponding three subsets from figure 12.4.

We combine these into a strong learner by voting. In other words, for any input, each of the weak learners predicts a value of 0 or 1. The prediction the strong learner makes is the most common output of the three. This combination can be seen in figure 12.6, where the weak learners are on the top and the strong learner on the bottom.

Note that the random forest is a good classifier, because it classifies most of the points correctly, but it allows a few mistakes in order to not overfit the data. However, we don't need to train these random forests manually, because Scikit-Learn has functions for this, which we see in the next section.

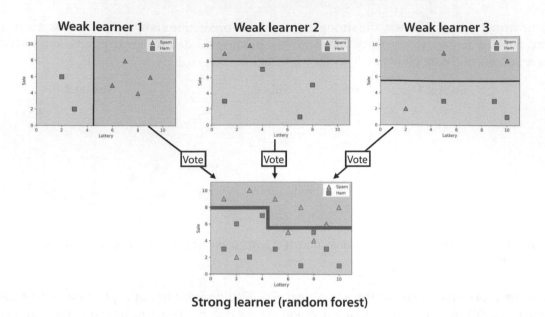

Figure 12.6   The way to obtain the predictions of the random forest is by combining the predictions of the three weak learners. On the top, we can see the three boundaries of the decision trees from figure 12.5. On the bottom, we can see how the three decision trees vote to obtain the boundary of the corresponding random forest.

Training a random forest in Scikit-Learn

In this section, we see how to train a random forest using Scikit-Learn. In the following code, we make use of the `RandomForestClassifier` package. To begin, we have our data in two Pandas DataFrames called `features` and `labels`, as shown next:

```
from sklearn.ensemble import RandomForestClassifier
random_forest_classifier = RandomForestClassifier(random_state=0,
    n_estimators=5, max_depth=1)
random_forest_classifier.fit(features, labels)
random_forest_classifier.score(features, labels)
```

In the previous code, we specified that we want five weak learners with the `n_estimators` hyperparameter. These weak learners are again decision trees, and we have specified that their depth is 1 with the `max_depth` hyperparameter. The plot of the model is shown in figure 12.7. Note how this model makes some mistakes but manages to find a good boundary, where the spam emails are those with a lot of appearances of the words "lottery" and "sale" (top right of the plot) and the ham emails are those with not many appearances of these words (bottom left of the figure).

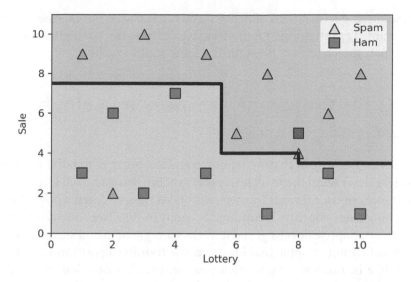

Figure 12.7 The boundary of the random forest obtained with Scikit-Learn. Notice that it classifies the dataset well, and it treats the two misclassified points as outliers, instead of trying to classify them correctly.

Scikit-Learn also allows us to visualize and plot the individual weak learners (see the notebook for the code). The weak learners are shown in figure 12.8. Notice that not all the weak learners are useful. For instance, the first one classifies every point as ham.

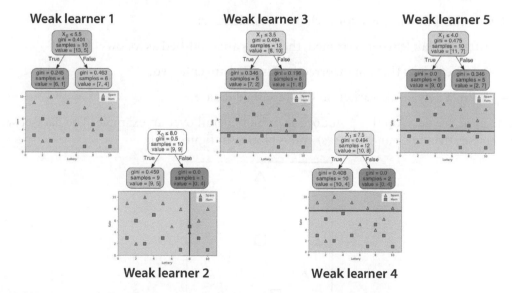

Figure 12.8 The random forest is formed by five weak learners obtained using Scikit-Learn. Each one is a decision tree of depth 1. They combine to form the strong learner shown in figure 12.7.

In this section, we used decision trees of depth 1 as weak learners, but in general, we can use trees of any depth we want. Try retraining this model using decision trees of higher depth by varying the `max_depth` hyperparameter, and see what the random forest looks like!

AdaBoost: Joining weak learners in a clever way to build a strong learner

Boosting is similar to bagging in that we join several weak learners to build a strong learner. The difference is that we don't select the weak learners at random. Instead, each learner is built by focusing on the weaknesses of the previous learners. In this section, we learn a powerful boosting technique called AdaBoost, developed by Freund and Schapire in 1997 (see appendix C for the reference). AdaBoost is short for adaptive boosting, and it works for regression and classification. However, we will use it in a classification example that illustrates the training algorithm very clearly.

In AdaBoost, like in random forests, each weak learner is a decision tree of depth 1. Unlike random forests, each weak learner is trained on the whole dataset, rather than on a portion of it. The only caveat is that after each weak learner is trained, we modify the dataset by enlarging the points that have been incorrectly classified, so that future weak learners pay more attention to these. In a nutshell, AdaBoost works as follows:

Pseudocode for training an AdaBoost model

- Train the first weak learner on the first dataset.

- Repeat the following step for each new weak learner:

  – After a weak learner is trained, the points are modified as follows:

    – The points that are incorrectly classified are enlarged.

  – Train a new weak learner on this modified dataset.

In this section, we develop this pseudocode in more detail over an example. The dataset we use has two classes (triangles and squares) and is plotted in figure 12.9.

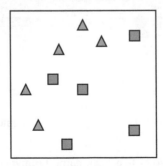

Figure 12.9   The dataset that we will classify using AdaBoost. It has two labels represented by a triangle and a square.

A big picture of AdaBoost: Building the weak learners

Over the next two subsections, we see how to build an AdaBoost model to fit the dataset shown in figure 12.9. First we build the weak learners that we'll then combine into one strong learner.

The first step is to assign to each of the points a weight of 1, as shown on the left of figure 12.10. Next, we build a weak learner on this dataset. Recall that the weak learners are decision trees of depth 1. A decision tree of depth 1 corresponds to the horizontal or vertical line that best splits the points. Several such trees do the job, but we'll pick one—the vertical line illustrated in the middle of figure 12.10—which correctly classifies the two triangles to its left and the five squares to its right, and incorrectly classifies the three triangles to its right. The next step is to enlarge the three incorrectly classified points to give them more importance under the eyes of future weak learners. To enlarge them, recall that each point initially has a weight of 1. We define the *rescaling factor* of this weak learner as the number of correctly classified points divided by the number of incorrectly classified points. In this case, the rescaling factor is $\frac{7}{3} = 2.33$. We proceed to rescale every misclassified point by this rescaling factor, as illustrated on the right of figure 12.10.

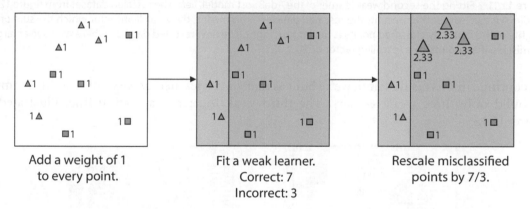

Add a weight of 1 to every point.

Fit a weak learner.
Correct: 7
Incorrect: 3

Rescale misclassified points by 7/3.

Figure 12.10   Fitting the first weak learner of the AdaBoost model. Left: The dataset, where each point gets assigned a weight of 1. Middle: A weak learner that best fits this dataset. Right: The rescaled dataset, where we have enlarged the misclassified points by a rescaling factor of 7/3.

Now that we've built the first weak learner, we build the next ones in the same manner. The second weak learner is illustrated in figure 12.11. On the left of the figure, we have the rescaled dataset. The second weak learner is one that fits this dataset best. What do we mean by that? Because points have different weights, we want the weak learner for which the sum of the weights of the correctly classified points is the highest. This weak learner is the horizontal line in the middle of figure 12.11. We now proceed to calculate the rescaling factor. We need to slightly modify its definition, because the points now have weights. The rescaling factor is the ratio between the sum of the weights of the correctly classified points and the sum of the weights of the incorrectly classified points. The first term is 2.33 + 2.33 + 2.33 + 1 + 1 + 1 + 1 = 11, and the second is 1 + 1 + 1 = 3. Thus, the rescaling factor is $\frac{11}{3} = 3.67$. We proceed to multiply the weights of the three misclassified points by this factor of 3.67, as illustrated on the right of figure 12.11.

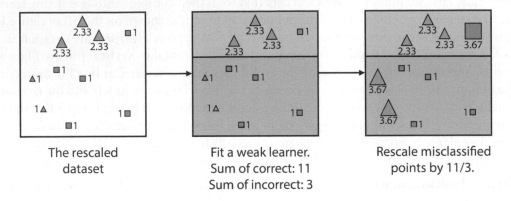

The rescaled dataset

Fit a weak learner.
Sum of correct: 11
Sum of incorrect: 3

Rescale misclassified points by 11/3.

Figure 12.11 Fitting the second weak learner of the AdaBoost model. Left: The rescaled dataset from figure 12.10. Middle: A weak learner that best fits the rescaled dataset—this means, the weak learner for which the sum of weights of the correctly classified points is the largest. Right: The new rescaled dataset, where we have enlarged the misclassified points by a rescaling factor of 11/3.

We continue in this fashion until we've built as many weak learners as we want. For this example, we build only three weak learners. The third weak learner is a vertical line, illustrated in figure 12.12.

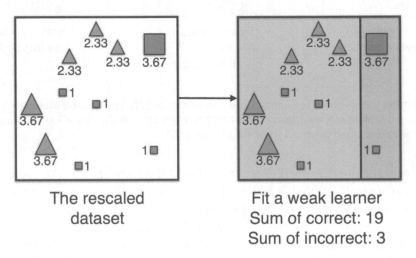

The rescaled dataset

Fit a weak learner
Sum of correct: 19
Sum of incorrect: 3

Figure 12.12 Fitting the third weak learner of the AdaBoost model. Left: The rescaled dataset from figure 12.11. Right: A weak learner that best fits this rescaled dataset.

This is how we build the weak learners. Now, we need to combine them into a strong learner. This is similar to what we did with random forests, but using a little more math, as shown in the next section.

Combining the weak learners into a strong learner

Now that we've built the weak learners, in this section, we learn an effective way to combine them into a strong learner. The idea is to get the classifiers to vote, just as they did in the random forest classifier, but this time, good learners get more of a say than poor learners. In the event that a classifier is *really* bad, then its vote will actually be negative.

To understand this, imagine we have three friends: Truthful Teresa, Unpredictable Umbert, and Lying Lenny. Truthful Teresa almost always tells the truth, Lying Lenny almost always lies, and Unpredictable Umbert says the truth roughly half of the time and lies the other half. Out of these three friends, which is the least useful one?

The way I see it, Truthful Teresa is very reliable, because she almost always tells the truth, so we can trust her. Among the other two, I prefer Lying Lenny. If he almost always lies when we ask him a yes-or-no question, we simply take as truth the opposite of what he tells us, and we'll be correct most of the time! On the other hand, Unpredictable Umbert serves us no purpose if we have no idea whether he's telling the truth or lying. In that case, if we were to assign a score to what each friend says, I'd give Truthful Teresa a high positive score, Lying Lenny a high negative score, and Unpredictable Umbert a score of zero.

Now imagine that our three friends are weak learners trained in a dataset with two classes. Truthful Teresa is a classifier with very high accuracy, Lying Lenny is one with very low accuracy, and Unpredictable Umbert is one with an accuracy close to 50%. We want to build a strong learner where the prediction is obtained by a weighted vote from the three weak learners. Thus, to each of the weak learners, we assign a score, and that is how much the vote of the learner will count in the final vote. Furthermore, we want to assign these scores in the following way:

- The Truthful Teresa classifier gets a high positive score.

- The Unpredictable Umbert classifier gets a score close to zero.

- The Lying Lenny classifier gets a high negative score.

In other words, the score of a weak learner is a number that has the following properties:

1. Is positive when the accuracy of the learner is greater than 0.5

2. Is 0 when the accuracy of the model is 0.5

3. Is negative when the accuracy of the learner is smaller than 0.5

4. Is a large positive number when the accuracy of the learner is close to 1

5. Is a large negative number when the accuracy of the learner is close to 0

To come up with a good score for a weak learner that satisfies properties 1–5 above, we use a popular concept in probability called the *logit*, or *log-odds*, which we discuss next.

Probability, odds, and log-odds

You may have seen in gambling that probabilities are never mentioned, but they always talk about *odds*. What are these odds? They are similar to probability in the following sense: if we run an experiment many times and record the number of times a particular outcome occurred, the probability of this outcome is the number of times it occurred divided by the total number of times we ran the experiment. The odds of this outcome are the number of times it occurred divided by the number of times it didn't occur.

For example, the probability of obtaining 1 when we roll a die is $\frac{1}{6}$, but the odds are $\frac{1}{5}$. If a particular horse wins 3 out of every 4 races, then the probability of that horse winning a race is $\frac{3}{4}$, and the odds are $\frac{3}{1} = 3$. The formula for odds is simple: if the probability of an event is x, then the odds are $\frac{x}{1-x}$. For instance, in the dice example, the probability is $\frac{1}{6}$ and the odds are

$$\frac{\frac{1}{6}}{1-\frac{1}{6}} = \frac{1}{5}.$$

Notice that because the probability is a number between 0 and 1, then the odds are a number between 0 and ∞.

Now let's get back to our original goal. We are looking for a function that satisfies properties 1–5 above. The odds function is close, but not quite there, because it outputs only positive values. The way to turn the odds into a function that satisfies properties 1–5 above is by taking the logarithm. Thus, we obtain the log-odds, also called the logit, defined as follows:

$$\text{log-odds}\,(x) = ln\,\frac{x}{1-x}$$

Figure 12.13 shows the graph of the log-odds function $y = ln\left(\frac{x}{1-x}\right)$. Notice that this function satisfies properties 1–5.

Therefore, all we need to do is use the log-odds function to calculate the score of each of the weak learners. We apply this log-odds function on the accuracy. Table 12.2 contains several values for the accuracy of a weak learner and the log-odds of this accuracy. Notice that, as desired, models with high accuracy have high positive scores, models with low accuracy have high negative scores, and models with accuracy close to 0.5 have scores close to 0.

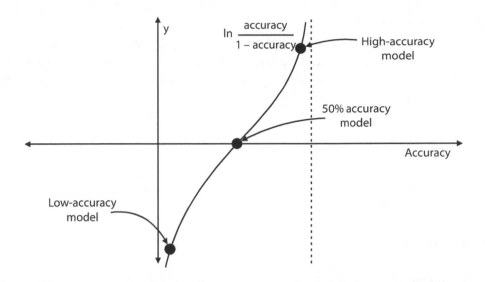

Figure 12.13 The curve shows the plot of the log-odds function with respect to the accuracy. Notice that for small values of the accuracy, the log-odds is a very large negative number, and for higher values of the accuracy, it is a very large positive number. When the accuracy is 50% (or 0.5), the log-odds is precisely zero.

Table 12.2 Several values for the accuracy of a weak classifier, with the corresponding score, calculated using the log-odds. Notice that the models with very low accuracy get large negative scores, the values with very high accuracy get large positive scores, and the values with accuracy close to 0.5 get scores close to 0.

Accuracy	Log-odds (score of the weak learner)
0.01	−4.595
0.1	−2.197
0.2	−1.386
0.5	0
0.8	1.386
0.9	2.197
0.99	4.595

Combining the classifiers

Now that we've settled on the log-odds as the way to define the scores for all the weak learners, we can proceed to join them to build the strong learner. Recall that the accuracy of a weak learner is the sum of the scores of the correctly classified points divided by the sum of the scores of all the points, as shown in figures 12.10–12.12.

- Weak learner 1:

    - Accuracy: $\dfrac{7}{10}$

    - Score: $ln\left(\dfrac{7}{3}\right) = 0.847$

- Weak learner 2:

    - Accuracy: $\dfrac{11}{14}$

    - Score: $ln\left(\dfrac{11}{3}\right) = 1.299$

- Weak learner 3:

    - Accuracy: $\dfrac{19}{22}$

    - Score: $ln\left(\dfrac{19}{3}\right) = 1.846$

The prediction that the strong learner makes is obtained by the weighted vote of the weak classifiers, where each classifier's vote is its score. A simple way to see this is to change the predictions of the weak learners from 0 and 1 to –1 and 1, multiplying each prediction by the score of the weak learner, and adding them. If the resulting prediction is greater than or equal to zero, then the strong learner predicts a 1, and if it is negative, then it predicts a 0. The voting process is illustrated in figure 12.14, and the predictions in figure 12.15. Notice also in figure 12.15 that the resulting classifier classified every point in the dataset correctly.

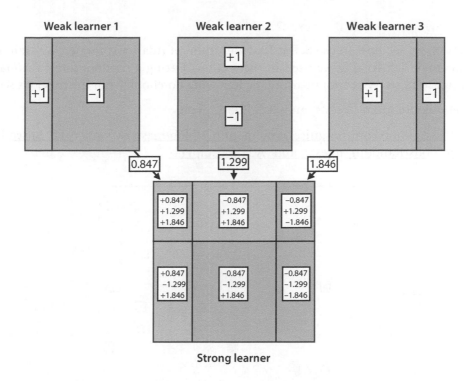

Figure 12.14 How to combine the weak learners into a strong learner in the AdaBoost model. We score each of the weak learners using the log-odds and make them vote based on their scores (the larger the score, the more voting power that particular learner has). Each of the regions in the bottom diagram has the sum of the scores of the weak learners. Note that to simplify our calculations, the predictions from the weak learners are +1 and −1, instead of 1 and 0.

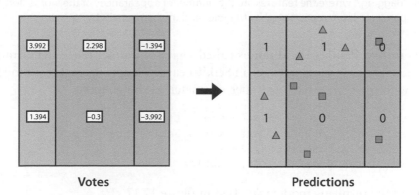

Figure 12.15 How to obtain the predictions for the AdaBoost model. Once we have added the scores coming from the weak learners (shown in figure 12.14), we assign a prediction of 1 if the sum of scores is greater than or equal to 0 and a prediction of 0 otherwise.

Coding AdaBoost in Scikit-Learn

In this section, we see how to use Scikit-Learn to train an AdaBoost model. We train it on the same spam email dataset that we used in the section "Fitting a random forest manually" and plotted in figure 12.16. We continue using the following notebook from the previous sections:

- **Notebook:** Random_forests_and_AdaBoost.ipynb

    - https://github.com/luisguiserrano/manning/blob/master/Chapter_12_Ensemble_Methods/Random_forests_and_AdaBoost.ipynb

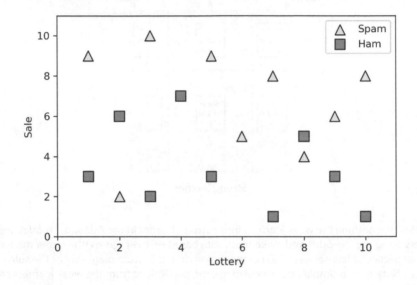

Figure 12.16   In this dataset, we train an AdaBoost classifier using Scikit-Learn. This is the same spam dataset from the section "Bagging," where the features are the number of appearances of the words "lottery" and "spam," and the spam emails are represented by triangles and the ham emails by squares.

The dataset is in two Pandas DataFrames called `features` and `labels`. The training is done using the `AdaBoostClassifier` package in Scikit-Learn. We specify that this model will use six weak learners with the `n_estimators` hyperparameter, as shown next:

```
from sklearn.ensemble import AdaBoostClassifier
adaboost_classifier = AdaBoostClassifier(n_estimators=6)
adaboost_classifier.fit(features, labels)
adaboost_classifier.score(features, labels)
```

The boundary of the resulting model is plotted in figure 12.17.

We can go a bit further and explore the six weak learners and their scores (see notebook for the code). Their boundaries are plotted in figure 12.18, and as is evident in the notebook, the scores of all the weak learners are 1.

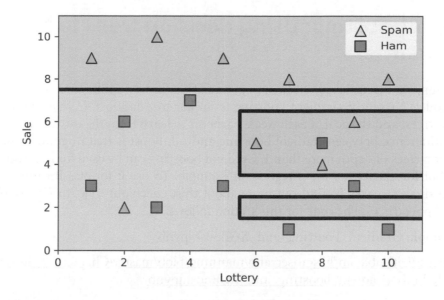

Figure 12.17 The result of the AdaBoost classifier on the spam dataset in figure 12.16. Notice that the classifier does a good job fitting the dataset and doesn't overfit much.

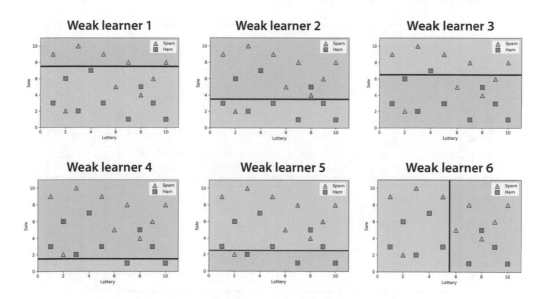

Figure 12.18 The six weak learners in our AdaBoost model. Each one of them is a decision tree of depth 1. They combine into the strong learner in figure 12.17.

Note that the strong learner in figure 12.17 is obtained by assigning a score of 1 to each of the weak learners in figure 12.18 and letting them vote.

Gradient boosting: Using decision trees to build strong learners

In this section, we discuss gradient boosting, one of the most popular and successful machine learning models currently. Gradient boosting is similar to AdaBoost, in that the weak learners are decision trees, and the goal of each weak learner is to learn from the mistakes of the previous ones. One difference between gradient boosting and AdaBoost is that in gradient boosting, we allow decision trees of depth more than 1. Gradient boosting can be used for regression and classification, but for clarity, we use a regression example. To use it for classification, we need to make some small tweaks. To find out more about this, check out links to videos and reading material in appendix C. The code for this section follows:

- **Notebook:** Gradient_boosting_and_XGBoost.ipynb
  - https://github.com/luisguiserrano/manning/blob/master/Chapter_12_Ensemble_Methods/Gradient_boosting_and_XGBoost.ipynb

The example we use is the same one as in the section "Decision trees for regression" in chapter 9, in which we studied the level of engagement of certain users with an app. The feature is the age of the user, and the label is the number of days that the user engages with the app (table 12.3). The plot of the dataset is shown in figure 12.19.

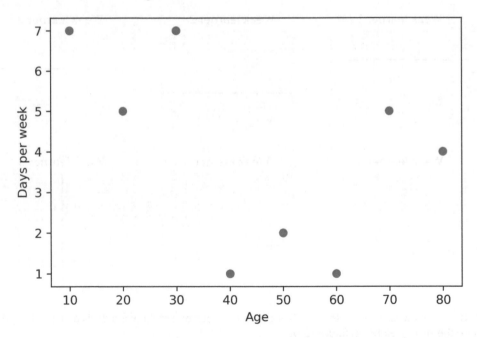

Figure 12.19   The plot of the user engagement dataset from table 12.3. The horizontal axis represents the age of the users, and the vertical axis represents the days per week that the user uses our app.

Table 12.3 A small dataset with eight users, their age, and their engagement with our app. The engagement is measured in the number of days when they opened the app in one week. We'll fit this dataset using gradient boosting.

Feature (age)	Label (engagement)
10	7
20	5
30	7
40	1
50	2
60	1
70	5
80	4

The idea of gradient boosting is that we'll create a sequence of trees that fit this dataset. The two hyperparameters that we'll use for now are the number of trees, which we set to five, and the learning rate, which we set to 0.8. The first weak learner is simple: it is the decision tree of depth 0 that best fits the dataset. A decision tree of depth 0 is simply a node that assigns the same label to each point in the dataset. Because the error function we are minimizing is the mean square error, then this optimal value for the prediction is the average value of the labels. The average value of the labels of this dataset is 4, so our first weak learner is a node that assigns a prediction of 4 to every point.

The next step is to calculate the residual, which is the difference between the label and the prediction made by this first weak learner, and fit a new decision tree to these residuals. As you can see, what this is doing is training a decision tree to fill in the gaps that the first tree has left. The labels, predictions, and residuals are shown in table 12.4.

The second weak learner is a tree that fits these residuals. The tree can be as deep as we'd like, but for this example, we'll make sure all the weak learners are of depth at most 2. This tree is shown in figure 12.20 (together with its boundary), and its predictions are in the rightmost column of table 12.4. This tree has been obtained using Scikit-Learn; see the notebook for the procedure.

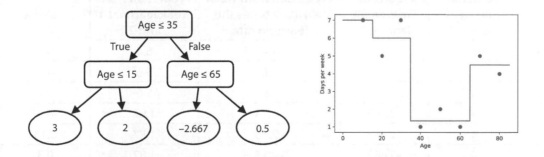

Figure 12.20 The second weak learner in the gradient boosting model. This learner is a decision tree of depth 2 pictured on the left. The predictions of this weak learner are shown on the plot on the right.

Table 12.4 The predictions from the first weak learner are the average of the labels. The second weak learner is trained to fit the residuals of the first weak learner.

Feature (age)	Label (engagement)	Prediction from weak learner 1	Residual	Prediction from weak learner 2
10	7	4	3	3
20	5	4	2	2
30	7	4	3	2
40	1	4	−3	−2.667
50	2	4	−2	−2.667
60	1	4	−3	−2.667
70	5	4	1	0.5
80	4	4	0	0.5

The idea is to continue in this fashion, calculating new residuals and training a new weak learner to fit these residuals. However, there's a small caveat—to calculate the prediction from the first two weak learners, we first multiply the prediction of the second weak learner by the learning rate. Recall that the learning rate we're using is 0.8. Thus, the combined prediction of the first two weak learners is the prediction of the first one (4) plus 0.8 times the prediction of the second one. We do this because we don't want to overfit by fitting our training data too well. Our goal is to mimic the gradient descent algorithm, by slowly walking closer and closer to the solution, and this is what we achieve by multiplying the prediction by the learning rate. The new residuals are the original labels minus the combined predictions of the first two weak learners. These are calculated in table 12.5.

Table 12.5 The labels, the predictions from the first two weak learners, and the residual. The prediction from the first weak learner is the average of the labels. The prediction from the second weak learner is shown in figure 12.20. The combined prediction is equal to the prediction of the first weak learner plus the learning rate (0.8) times the prediction of the second weak learner. The residual is the difference between the label and the combined prediction from the first two weak learners.

Label	Prediction from weak learner 1	Prediction from weak learner 2	Prediction from weak learner 2 times the learning rate	Prediction from weak learners 1 and 2	Residual
7	4	3	2.4	6.4	0.6
5	4	2	1.6	5.6	−0.6
7	4	2	1.6	5.6	1.4
1	4	−2.667	−2.13	1.87	−0.87
2	4	−2.667	−2.13	1.87	0.13
1	4	−2.667	−2.13	1.87	−0.87
5	4	0.5	0.4	4.4	0.6
4	4	0.5	0.4	4.4	−0.4

Now we can proceed to fit a new weak learner on the new residuals and calculate the combined prediction of the first two weak learners. We obtain this by adding the prediction for the first weak learner and 0.8 (the learning rate) times the sum of the predictions of the second and the third weak learner. We repeat this process for every weak learner we want to build. Instead of doing it by hand, we can use the `GradientBoostingRegressor` package in Scikit-Learn (the code is in the notebook). The next few lines of code show how to fit the model and make predictions. Note that we have set the depth of the trees to be at most 2, the number of trees to be five, and the learning rate to be 0.8. The hyperparameters used for this are `max_depth`, `n_estimators`, and `learning_rate`. Note, too, that if we want five trees, we must set the `n_estimators` hyperparameter to four, because the first tree isn't counted.

```
from sklearn.ensemble import GradientBoostingRegressor
gradient_boosting_regressor = GradientBoostingRegressor(max_depth=2,
    n_estimators=4, learning_rate=0.8)
gradient_boosting_regressor.fit(features, labels)
gradient_boosting_regressor.predict(features)
```

The plot for the resulting strong learner is shown in figure 12.21. Notice that it does a good job predicting the values.

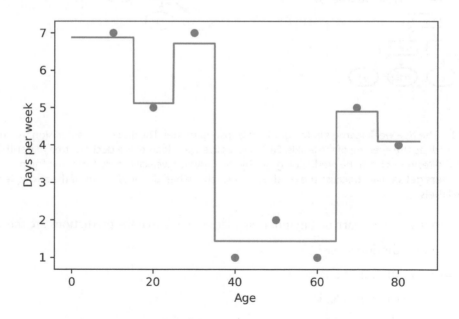

Figure 12.21 The plot of the predictions of the strong learner in our gradient boosting regressor. Note that the model fits the dataset quite well.

However, we can go a little further and actually plot the five weak learners we obtain. The details for this are in the notebook, and the five weak learners are shown in figure 12.22. Notice that the predictions of the last weak learners are much smaller than those of the first ones, because each weak learner is predicting the error of the previous ones, and these errors get smaller and smaller at each step.

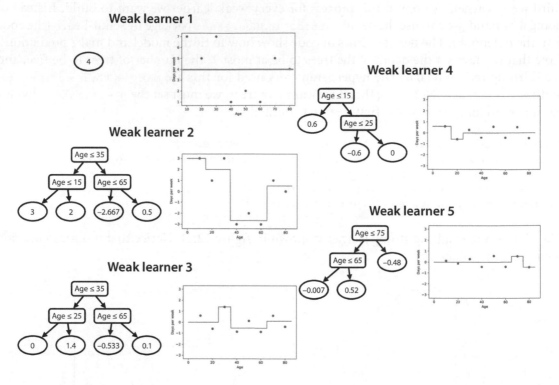

Figure 12.22   The five weak learners in the gradient boosting model. The first one is a decision tree of depth 0 that always predicts the average of the labels. Each successive weak learner is a decision tree of depth at most 2, which fits the residuals from the prediction given by the previous weak learners. Note that the predictions of the weak learners get smaller, because the residuals get smaller when the predictions of the strong learner get closer to the labels.

Finally, we can use Scikit-Learn or a manual calculation to see that the predictions are the following:

- Age = 10, prediction = 6.87
- Age = 20, prediction = 5.11
- Age = 30, prediction = 6.71
- Age = 40, prediction = 1.43
- Age = 50, prediction = 1.43
- Age = 60, prediction = 1.43
- Age = 70, prediction = 4.90
- Age = 80, prediction = 4.10

XGBoost: An extreme way to do gradient boosting

XGBoost, which stands for *extreme gradient boosting*, is one of the most popular, powerful, and effective gradient boosting implementations. Created by Tianqi Chen and Carlos Guestrin in 2016 (see appendix C for the reference), XGBoost models often outperform other classification and regression models. In this section, we discuss how XGBoost works, using the same regression example from the section "Gradient boosting: Using decision trees to build strong learners."

XGBoost uses decision trees as the weak learners, and just like in the previous boosting methods we learned, each weak learner is designed to focus on the weaknesses of the previous ones. More specifically, each tree is built to fit the residuals of the predictions of the previous trees. However, there are some small differences, such as the way we build the trees, which is using a metric called the *similarity score*. Furthermore, we add a pruning step to prevent overfitting, in which we remove the branches of the trees if they don't satisfy certain conditions. In this section, we cover this in more detail.

XGBoost similarity score: A new and effective way to measure similarity in a set

In this subsection, we see the main building block of XGBoost, which is a way to measure how similar the elements of a set are. This metric is aptly called the *similarity score*. Before we learn it, let's do a small exercise. Among the following three sets, which one has the most amount of similarity, and which one has the least?

- **Set 1:** {10, −10, 4}
- **Set 2:** {7, 7, 7}
- **Set 3:** {7}

If you said that set 2 has the most amount of similarity and set 1 has the least amount, your intuition is correct. In set 1, the elements are very different from each other, so this one has the least amount of similarity. Between sets 2 and 3, it's not so clear, because both sets have the same element, but a different number of times. However, set 2 has the number seven appearing three times, whereas set 3 has it appearing only once. Therefore, in set 2, the elements are more homogeneous, or more similar, than in set 3.

To quantify similarity, consider the following metric. Given a set $\{a_1, a_2, ..., a_n\}$, the similarity score is the square of the sum of the elements, divided by the number of elements, namely, $\frac{(a_1 + a_2 + \cdots + a_n)^2}{n}$. Let's calculate the similarity score for the three sets above, shown next:

- **Set 1:** $Similarity\ score = \frac{(10 - 10 + 4)^2}{3} = 5.33$
- **Set 2:** $Similarity\ score = \frac{(7 + 7 + 7)^2}{3} = 147$
- **Set 3:** $Similarity\ score = \frac{7^2}{1} = 49$

Note that as expected, the similarity score of set 2 is the highest, and that of set 1 is the lowest.

note   This similarity score is not perfect. One can argue that the set {1, 1, 1} is more similar than the set {7, 8, 9}, yet the similarity score of {1, 1, 1} is 3, and the similarity score of {7, 8, 9} is 192. However, for the purposes of our algorithm, this score still works. The main goal of the similarity score is to be able to separate the large and small values well, and this goal is met, as we'll see in the current example.

There is a hyperparameter λ associated with the similarity score, which helps prevent overfitting. When used, it is added to the denominator of the similarity score, which gives the formula $\dfrac{(a_1 + a_2 + \cdots + a_n)^2}{n + \lambda}$. Thus, for example, if $\lambda = 2$, the similarity score of set 1 is now $\dfrac{(10 - 10 + 4)^2}{3 + 2} = 3.2$. We won't use the λ hyperparameter in our example, but when we get to the code, we'll see how to set it to any value we want.

Building the weak learners

In this subsection, we see how to build each one of the weak learners. To illustrate this process, we use the same example from the section "Gradient boosting," shown in table 12.3. For convenience, the same dataset is shown in the two leftmost columns of table 12.6. This is a dataset of users of an app, in which the feature is the age of the users, and the label is the number of days per week in which they engage with the app. The plot of this dataset is shown in figure 12.19.

Table 12.6   The same dataset as in table 12.3, containing users, their age, and the number of days per week in which they engaged with our app. The third column contains the predictions from the first weak learner in our XGBoost model. These predictions are all 0.5 by default. The last column contains the residual, which is the difference between the label and the prediction.

Feature (age)	Label (engagement)	Prediction from the first weak learner	Residual
10	7	0.5	6.5
20	5	0.5	4.5
30	7	0.5	6.5
40	1	0.5	0.5
50	2	0.5	1.5
60	1	0.5	0.5
70	5	0.5	4.5
80	4	0.5	3.5

The process of training an XGBoost model is similar to that of training gradient boosting trees. The first weak learner is a tree that gives a prediction of 0.5 to each data point. After building this weak learner, we calculate the residuals, which are the differences between the label and the predicted label. These two quantities can be found in the two rightmost columns of table 12.6.

Before we start building the remaining trees, let's decide how deep we want them to be. To keep this example small, let's again use a maximum depth of 2. That means that when we get to depth 2, we stop building the weak learners. This is a hyperparameter, which we'll see in more detail in the section "Training an XGBoost model in Python."

To build the second weak learner, we need to fit a decision tree to the residuals. We do this using the similarity score. As usual, in the root node, we have the entire dataset. Thus, we begin by calculating the similarity score of the entire dataset as follows:

$$Similarity = \frac{(6.5+4.5+6.5+0.5+1.5+0.5+4.5+3.5)^2}{8} = 98$$

Now, we proceed to split the node using the age feature in all the possible ways, as we did with decision trees. For each split, we calculate the similarity score of the subsets corresponding to each of the leaves and add them. That is the combined similarity score corresponding to that split. The scores are the following:

Split for the root node, with dataset {6.5, 4.5, 6.5, 0.5, 1.5, 0.5, 4.5, 3.5}, and similarity score = 98:

- Split at 15:
  - Left node: {6.5}; similarity score: 42.25
  - Right node: {4.5, 6.5, 0.5, 1.5, 0.5, 4.5, 3.5}; similarity score: 66.04
  - Combined similarity score: 108.29
- Split at 25:
  - Left node: {6.5, 4.5}; similarity score: 60.5
  - Right node: {6.5, 0.5, 1.5, 0.5, 4.5, 3.5}; similarity score: 48.17
  - Combined similarity score: 108.67
- Split at 35:
  - Left node: {6.5, 4.5, 6.5}; similarity score: 102.08
  - Right node: {0.5, 1.5, 0.5, 4.5, 3.5}; similarity score: 22.05
  - **Combined similarity score: 124.13**
- Split at 45:
  - Left node: {6.5, 4.5, 6.5, 0.5}; similarity score: 81
  - Right node: {1.5, 0.5, 4.5, 3.5}; similarity score: 25
  - Combined similarity score: 106
- Split at 55:
  - Left node: {6.5, 4.5, 6.5, 0.5, 1.5}; similarity score: 76.05
  - Right node: {0.5, 4.5, 3.5}; similarity score: 24.08
  - Combined similarity score: 100.13

- Split at 65:
  - Left node: {6.5, 4.5, 6.5, 0.5, 1.5, 0.5}; similarity score: 66.67
  - Right node: {4.5, 3.5}; similarity score: 32
  - Combined similarity score: 98.67
- Split at 75:
  - Left node: {6.5, 4.5, 6.5, 0.5, 1.5, 0.5, 4.5}; similarity score: 85.75
  - Right node: {3.5}; similarity score: 12.25
  - Combined similarity score: 98

As shown in these calculations, the split with the best combined similarity score is at age = 35. This is going to be the split at the root node.

Next, we proceed to split the datasets at each of the nodes in the same way.

Split for the left node, with dataset {6.5, 4.5, 6.5} and similarity score 102.08:

- Split at 15:
  - Left node: {6.5}; similarity score: 42.25
  - Right node: {4.5, 6.5}; similarity score: 60.5
  - Similarity score: 102.75
- Split at 25:
  - Left node: {6.5, 4.5}; similarity score: 60.5
  - Right node: {6.5}; similarity score: 42.25
  - Similarity score: 102.75

Both splits give us the same combined similarity score, so we can use any of the two. Let's use the split at 15. Now, on to the right node.

Split for the right node, with dataset {0.5, 1.5, 0.5, 4.5, 3.5} and similarity score 22.05:

- Split at 45:
  - Left node: {0.5}; similarity score: 0.25
  - Right node: {1.5, 0.5, 4.5, 3.5}; similarity score: 25
  - Similarity score: 25.25
- Split at 55:
  - Left node: {0.5, 1.5}; similarity score: 2
  - Right node: {0.5, 4.5, 3.5}; similarity score: 24.08
  - Similarity score: 26.08

- Split at 65:
  - Left node: {0.5, 1.5, 0.5}; similarity score: 2.08
  - Right node: {4.5, 3.5}; similarity score: 32
  - **Similarity score: 34.08**
- Split at 75:
  - Left node: {0.5, 1.5, 0.5, 4.5}; similarity score: 12.25
  - Right node: {3.5}; similarity score: 12.25
  - Similarity score: 24.5

From here, we conclude that the best split is at age = 65. The tree now has depth 2, so we stop growing it, because this is what we decided at the beginning of the algorithm. The resulting tree, together with the similarity scores at the nodes, is shown in figure 12.23.

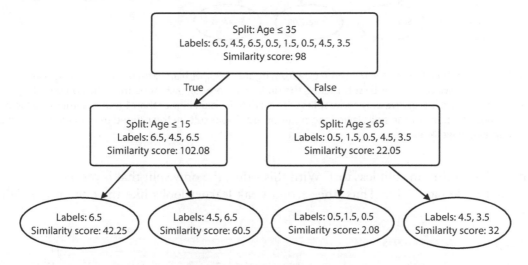

Figure 12.23 The second weak learner in our XGBoost classifier. For each of the nodes, we can see the split based on the age feature, the labels corresponding to that node, and the similarity score for each set of labels. The split chosen for each node is the one that maximizes the combined similarity score of the leaves. For each of the leaves, you can see the corresponding labels and their similarity score.

That's (almost) our second weak learner. Before we continue building more weak learners, we need to do one more step to help reduce overfitting.

Tree pruning: A way to reduce overfitting by simplifying the weak learners

A great feature of XGBoost is that it doesn't overfit much. For this, it uses several hyperparameters that are described in detail in the section "Training an XGBoost model in Python." One of them, the minimum split loss, prevents a split from happening if the combined similarity scores of the resulting nodes are not significantly larger than the similarity score of the original node. This difference is called the *similarity gain*. For example, in the root node of our tree, the similarity score is 98, and the combined similarity score of the nodes is 124.13. Thus, the similarity gain is 124.13 − 98 = 26.13. Similarly, the similarity gain of the left node is 0.67, and that of the right node is 12.03, as shown in figure 12.24.

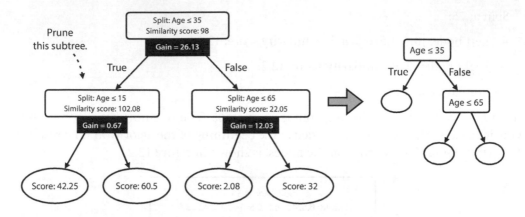

Figure 12.24   On the left, we have the same tree from figure 12.23, with an extra piece of information: the similarity gain. We obtain this by subtracting the similarity score for each node from the combined similarity score of the leaves. We only allow splits with a similarity gain higher than 1 (our minimum split loss hyperparameter), so one of the splits is no longer permitted. This results in the pruned tree on the right, which now becomes our weak learner.

We'll set the minimum split loss to 1. With this value, the only split that is prevented is the one on the left node (age ≤ 15). Thus, the second weak learner looks like the one on the right of figure 12.24.

Making the predictions

Now that we've built our second weak learner, it's time to use it to make predictions. We obtain predictions the same way we obtain them from any decision tree, namely, by averaging the labels in the corresponding leaf. The predictions for our second weak learner are seen in figure 12.25.

Now, on to calculate the combined prediction for the first two weak learners. To avoid overfitting, we use the same technique that we used in gradient boosting, which is multiplying the prediction of all the weak learners (except the first one) by the learning rate. This is meant to emulate the gradient descent method, in which we slowly converge to a good prediction after several iterations. We use a learning rate of 0.7. Thus, the combined prediction of the first two weak learners is equal to the prediction of the first weak learner plus the prediction of the second weak learner times 0.7. For example, for the first data point, this prediction is

$$0.5 + 5.83 \cdot 0.7 = 4.58.$$

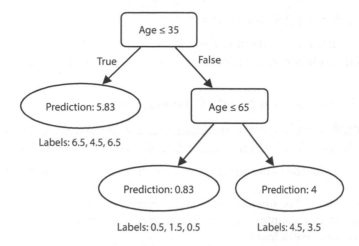

Figure 12.25   The second weak learner in our XGBoost model after being pruned. This is the same tree from figure 12.24, with its predictions. The prediction at each leaf is the average of the labels corresponding to that leaf.

The fifth column of table 12.7 contains the combined prediction of the first two weak learners.

Table 12.7   The labels, predictions from the first two weak learners, and the residual. The combined prediction is obtained by adding the prediction from the first weak learner (which is always 0.5) plus the learning rate (0.7) times the prediction from the second weak learner. The residual is again the difference between the label and the combined prediction.

Label (engagement)	Prediction from weak learner 1	Prediction from weak learner 2	Prediction from weak learner 2 times the learning rate	Combined prediction	Residual
7	0.5	5.83	4.08	4.58	2.42
5	0.5	5.83	4.08	4.58	0.42
7	0.5	5.83	4.08	4.58	2.42
1	0.5	0.83	0.58	1.08	−0.08
2	0.5	0.83	0.58	1.08	0.92
1	0.5	0.83	0.58	1.08	−0.08
5	0.5	4	2.8	3.3	1.7
4	0.5	4	2.8	3.3	0.7

Notice that the combined predictions are closer to the labels than the predictions of the first weak learner. The next step is to iterate. We calculate new residuals for all the data points, fit a tree to them, prune the tree, calculate the new combined predictions, and continue in this fashion. The number of trees we want is another hyperparameter that we can choose at the start. To continue building these trees, we resort to a useful Python package called `xgboost`.

Training an XGBoost model in Python

In this section, we learn how to train the model to fit the current dataset using the `xgboost` Python package. The code for this section is in the same notebook as the previous one, shown here:

- **Notebook:** Gradient_boosting_and_XGBoost.ipynb

    - https://github.com/luisguiserrano/manning/blob/master/Chapter_12_Ensemble_Methods/Gradient_boosting_and_XGBoost.ipynb

Before we start, let's revise the hyperparameters that we've defined for this model:

number of estimators   The number of weak learners. Note: in the `xgboost` package, the first weak learner is not counted among the estimators. For this example, we set it to 3, which will give us four weak learners.

maximum depth   The maximum depth allowed for each one of the decision trees (weak learners). We set it to 2.

lambda parameter   The number added to the denominator of the similarity score. We set it to 0.

minimum split loss   The minimum gain in similarity score to allow for a split to happen. We set it to 1.

learning rate   The predictions from the second to last weak learners are multiplied by the learning rate. We set it to 0.7.

With the following lines of code, we import the package, build a model called `XGBRegressor`, and fit it to our dataset:

```
import xgboost
from xgboost import XGBRegressor
xgboost_regressor = XGBRegressor(random_state=0,
                                 n_estimators=3,
                                 max_depth=2,
                                 reg_lambda=0,
                                 min_split_loss=1,
                                 learning_rate=0.7)
xgboost_regressor.fit(features, labels)
```

The plot of the model is shown in figure 12.26. Notice that it fits the dataset well.

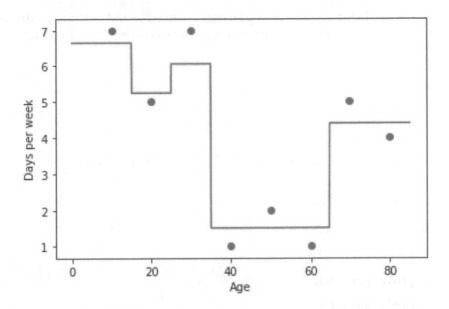

Figure 12.26 The plot of the predictions of our XGBoost model. Note that it fits the dataset well.

The `xgboost` package also allows us to look at the weak learners, and they appear in figure 12.24. The trees obtained in this fashion already have the labels multiplied by the learning rate of 0.7, which is clear when compared with the predictions of the tree obtained manually in figure 12.25 and the second tree from the left in figure 12.27.

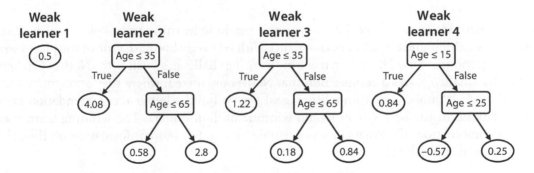

Figure 12.27 The four weak learners that form the strong learner in our XGBoost model. Note that the first one always predicts 0.5. The other three are quite similar in shape, which is a coincidence. However, notice that the predictions from each of the trees get smaller, because each time we are fitting smaller residuals. Furthermore, notice that the second weak learner is the same tree we obtained manually in figure 12.25, where the only difference is that in this tree, the predictions are already multiplied by the learning rate of 0.7.

Thus, to obtain the predictions of the strong learner, we need to add only the prediction of every tree. For example, for a user who is 20 years old, the predictions are the following:

- Weak learner 1: 0.5

- Weak learner 2: 4.08

- Weak learner 3: 1.22

- Weak learner 4: −0.57

Thus, the prediction is $0.5 + 5.83 + 1.22 − 0.57 = 5.23$. The predictions for the other points follow:

- Age = 10; prediction = 6.64

- Age = 20; prediction = 5.23

- Age = 30; prediction = 6.05

- Age = 40; prediction = 1.51

- Age = 50; prediction = 1.51

- Age = 60; prediction = 1.51

- Age = 70; prediction = 4.39

- Age = 80; prediction = 4.39

Applications of ensemble methods

Ensemble methods are some of the most useful machine learning techniques used nowadays because they exhibit great levels of performance with relatively low cost. One of the places where ensemble methods are used most is in machine learning challenges, such as the Netflix Challenge. The Netflix Challenge was a competition that Netflix organized, where they anonymized some data and made it public. The competitors' goal was to build a better recommendation system than Netflix itself; the best system would win one million dollars. The winning team used a powerful combination of learners in an ensemble to win. For more information on this, check the reference in appendix C.

Summary

- Ensemble methods consist of training several weak learners and combining them into a strong one. They are an effective way to build powerful models that have had great results with real datasets.

- Ensemble methods can be used for regression and for classification.

- There are two major types of ensemble methods: bagging and boosting.

- Bagging, or bootstrap aggregating, consists of building successive learners on random subsets of our data and combining them into a strong learner that makes predictions based on a majority vote.

- Boosting consists of building a sequence of learners, where each learner focuses on the weaknesses of the previous one, and combining them into a strong classifier that makes predictions based on a weighted vote of the learners.

- AdaBoost, gradient boosting, and XGBoost are three advanced boosting algorithms that produce great results with real datasets.

- Applications of ensemble methods range widely, from recommendation algorithms to applications in medicine and biology.

Exercises

Exercise 12.1

A boosted strong learner L is formed by three weak learners, L_1, L_2, and L_3. Their weights are 1, 0.4, and 1.2, respectively. For a particular point, L_1 and L_2 predict that its label is positive, and L_3 predicts that it's negative. What is the final prediction the learner L makes on this point?

Exercise 12.2

We are in the middle of training an AdaBoost model on a dataset of size 100. The current weak learner classifies 68 out of the 100 data points correctly. What is the weight that we'll assign to this learner in the final model?

In this chapter

- cleaning up and preprocessing data to make it readable by our model

- using Scikit-Learn to train and evaluate several models

- using grid search to select good hyperparameters for our model

- using k-fold cross-validation to be able to use our data for training and validation simultaneously

I'm not concerned. My model says I will survive!

Throughout this book, we've learned some of the most important algorithms in supervised learning, and we've had the chance to code them and use them to make predictions on several datasets. However, the process of training a model on real data requires several more steps, and this is what we discuss in this chapter.

One of the most fundamental jobs of a data scientist is cleaning and preprocessing the data. This is crucial because the computer can't fully do it. To clean data properly, it's necessary to have good knowledge of the data and of the problem being solved. In this chapter, we see some of the most important techniques for cleaning up and preprocessing data. Then we look more carefully into the features and apply some feature engineering that will get them ready for the model. As a next step, we split the model into training, validation, and testing sets, train several models on our dataset, and evaluate them. This way, we'll be able to pick the best-performing model for this dataset. Finally, we learn important methods such as grid search to find the best hyperparameters for our model.

We apply all these steps on a popular dataset for learning and practicing machine learning techniques: the Titanic dataset. We cover this dataset in depth in the following section. This chapter includes lots of coding. The two Python packages that we use are Pandas and Scikit-Learn, which we've used extensively throughout this book. The Pandas package is good for handling data, including opening files, loading data, and organizing it as tables, called DataFrames. The Scikit-Learn package is good for training and evaluating models, and it contains solid implementations of most of the algorithms we learn in this book.

The code and the dataset that we'll be working with throughout this whole chapter are the following:

- **Notebook:** End_to_end_example.ipynb

  - https://github.com/luisguiserrano/manning/blob/master/Chapter_13_End_to_end_example/End_to_end_example.ipynb

- **Dataset:** titanic.csv

The Titanic dataset

In this section, we load and study the dataset. Loading and handling data is a crucial skill for a data scientist, because the success of the model depends highly on how the data that feeds into it is preprocessed. We use the Pandas package to do this.

Throughout this chapter, we work with an example that is popular for learning machine learning: the Titanic dataset. At a high level, the dataset contains information about many of the passengers in the *Titanic*, including their name, age, marital status, port of embarkment, and class. Most importantly, it also contains information about the passenger's survival. This dataset can be found in Kaggle (www.kaggle.com), a popular online community with great datasets and contests, which I highly recommend you check out.

note The dataset we use is a historic dataset, which, as you may imagine, contains many societal biases from 1912. Historical datasets do not present the opportunity for revision or additional sampling to reflect current societal norms and understanding of the world. Some examples found here are the lack of inclusion of nonbinary genders, different treatment for passengers with respect to gender and social class, and many others. We'll evaluate this dataset as if it were a number table, because we believe that it is a very rich and commonly used dataset for building models and making predictions. However, as data scientists, it is our duty to always be mindful of biases in our data, such as those concerning race, gender identity, sexual orientation, social status, ability, nationality, beliefs, and many others, and to do everything in our power to ensure that the models we build will not perpetuate historical biases.

The features of our dataset

The Titanic dataset we are using contains the names and information of 891 passengers on the *Titanic*, including whether they survived. Here are the columns of the dataset:

- **PassengerID**: a number that identifies each passenger, from 1 to 891

- **Name:** the full name of the passenger

- **Sex:** the gender of the passenger (male or female)

- **Age:** the age of the passenger as an integer

- **Pclass:** the class in which the passenger was traveling: first, second, or third

- **SibSP:** the number of siblings and spouse of the passenger (0 if the passenger is traveling alone)

- **Parch:** the number of parents and children of the passenger (0 if the passenger is traveling alone)

- **Ticket:** the ticket number

- **Fare:** the fare the passenger paid in British pounds

- **Cabin:** the cabin in which the passenger was traveling

- **Embarked:** the port in which the passenger embarked: "C" for Cherbourg, "Q" for Queenstown, and "S" for Southampton

- **Survived:** information whether the passenger survived (1) or not (0)

Using Pandas to load the dataset

In this section, we learn how to open a dataset using Pandas and load it into a DataFrame, which is the object Pandas uses to store tables of data. I have downloaded the data from www.kaggle. com and stored it as a CSV (comma-separated values) file named titanic.csv. Before we do anything on Pandas, we must import Pandas with the following command:

```
import pandas
```

Now that we have loaded Pandas, we need to load the dataset. For storing datasets, Pandas uses two objects: the *DataFrame* and the *Series*. They are essentially the same thing, except that the Series is used for datasets of only one column, and the DataFrame is used for datasets of more than one column.

We can load the dataset as a DataFrame using the following command:

```
raw_data = pandas.read_csv('./titanic.csv', index_col="PassengerId")
```

This command stores the dataset into a Pandas DataFrame called `raw_data`. We call it raw data because our goal is to clean it and preprocess it later. Once we load it, we can see that the first rows look like table 13.1. In general, Pandas adds an extra column numbering all the elements in the dataset. Because the dataset already comes with this numbering, we can set this index to be that column by specifying `index_col="PassengerId"`. For this reason, we may see that in this dataset, the rows are indexed starting from 1 instead of starting from 0 as is more common in practice.

Table 13.1   The Titanic dataset contains information on the passengers on the Titanic, including whether they survived. Here we use Pandas to open the dataset and print out its rows and columns. Notice that it has 891 rows and 12 columns.

PassengerId	Survived	Pclass	Name	Sex	Age	SibSp	Parch	Ticket	Fare	Cabin	Embarked
1	0	3	Braund, Mr. Owen Harris	male	22.0	1	0	A/5 21171	7.2500	NaN	S
2	1	1	Cumings, Mrs. John Bradley (Florence Briggs Th...	female	38.0	1	0	PC 17599	71.2833	C85	C
3	1	3	Heikkinen, Miss Laina	female	26.0	0	0	STON/O2. 3101282	7.9250	NaN	S
...	...	...	...	...	...	...	...	...	...	...	...
890	1	1	Behr, Mr. Karl Howell	male	26.0	0	0	111369	30.0000	C148	C
891	0	3	Dooley, Mr. Patrick	male	32.0	0	0	370376	7.7500	NaN	Q

Saving and loading the dataset

Before we embark on studying our dataset, here's a small step that will help us. At the end of each section, we'll save the dataset in a CSV file, and we'll load it again at the beginning of the next section. This is so we can put down the book or quit the Jupyter Notebook and come back to work on it later at any checkpoint, without having to rerun all the commands from the beginning. With a small dataset like this one, it is not a big deal to rerun the commands, but imagine if we were processing large volumes of data. Serializing and saving data is important there, because it saves time and processing power.

Here are the names of the datasets saved at the end of each section:

- "The Titanic dataset": raw_data

- "Cleaning up our dataset": clean_data

- "Feature engineering": preprocessed_data

The commands for saving and loading follow:

```
tablename.to_csv('./filename.csv', index=None)
tablename = pandas.read_csv('./filename.csv')
```

When Pandas loads a dataset, it adds an index column that numbers each of the elements. We can ignore this column, but when we save the dataset, we must set the parameter `index=None` to avoid saving unnecessary index columns.

The dataset already has an index column called PassengerId. If we wanted to instead use this one as the default index column in Pandas, we could specify `index_col='PassengerId'` when we load the dataset (but we won't do this).

Using Pandas to study our dataset

In this section, I teach you some useful methods for studying our dataset. The first one is the length function, or `len`. This function returns the number of rows in the dataset as follows:

```
len(raw_data)
Output: 891
```

This means our dataset has 891 rows. To output the names of the columns, we use the `columns` property of a DataFrame, as follows:

```
raw_data.columns
Output: Index(['PassengerId', 'Survived', 'Pclass', 'Name', 'Sex', 'Age',
    'SibSp', 'Parch', 'Ticket', 'Fare', 'Cabin', 'Embarked'], dtype='object')
```

Now let's explore one of the columns. With the following command, we can explore the Survived column:

```
raw_data['Survived']
Output:
0, 1, 1, 1, 0, .., 0, 1, 0, 1, 0
Name: Survived, Length: 891, dtype: int64
```

The first column is the index of the passenger (1 to 891). The second one is a 0 if the passenger didn't survive, and a 1 if the passenger survived. However, if we wanted two columns—for example Name and Age—we can use the `next` command:

```
raw_data[['Name', 'Age']]
```

and this would return a DataFrame with only those two columns.

Now let's say we want to find out how many passengers survived. We can sum up the values in the Survived column using the `sum` function, as follows:

```
sum(raw_data['Survived'])
Output: 342
```

This indicates that out of the 891 passengers in our dataset, only 342 survived.

This is only the tip of the iceberg in terms of all the functionality that Pandas offers for handling datasets. Visit the documentation page at pandas.pydata.org to learn more about it.

Cleaning up our dataset: Missing values and how to deal with them

Now that we know how to handle DataFrames, we discuss some techniques to clean up our dataset. Why is this important? In real life, data can be messy, and feeding messy data into a model normally results in a bad model. It is important that before training models, the data scientist explores the dataset well and performs some cleanup to get the data ready for the models.

The first problem we encounter is datasets with missing values. Due to human or computer errors, or simply due to problems with data collection, datasets don't always come with all the values in them. Trying to fit a model to a dataset with missing values will probably result in an error. The Titanic dataset is not an exception when it comes to missing data. For example, let's look at the Cabin column of our dataset, shown here:

```
raw_data['Cabin']
Output:
0       NaN
1       C85
2       NaN
3       C123
4       NaN
       ...
886     NaN
887     B42
888     NaN
889     C148
890     NaN
Name: Cabin, Length: 891, dtype: object
```

Some cabin names are present, such as C123 or C148, but the majority of the values are NaN. NaN, or "not a number," means the entry is either missing, unreadable, or simply another type that can't be converted into a number. This could have happened because of clerical errors; one could imagine that the records of the *Titanic* are old and some information has been lost, or they simply didn't record the cabin number for every passenger to begin with. Either way, we don't want to have NaN values in our dataset. We are at a decision point: should we deal with these NaN values or remove the column completely? First let's check how many NaN values are in each column of our dataset. Our decision will depend on the answer to that question.

To find out how many values in each column are NaN, we use the `is_na` (or `is_null`) function. The `is_na` function returns a 1 if the entry is NaN, and a 0 otherwise. Therefore, if we sum over these values, we get the number of entries that are NaN in every column, as shown here:

```
raw_data.isna().sum()
```
Output:
```
PassengerId      0
Survived         0
Pclass           0
Name             0
Sex              0
Age            177
SibSp            0
Parch            0
Ticket           0
Fare             0
Cabin          687
Embarked         2
```

This tells us that the only columns with missing data are Age, which is missing 177 values; Cabin, which is missing 687 values; and Embarked, which is missing 2 values. We can deal with missing data using a few methods, and we'll apply different ones to different columns for this dataset.

Dropping columns with missing data

When a column is missing too many values, the corresponding feature may not be useful to our model. In this case, Cabin does not look like a good feature. Out of 891 rows, 687 don't have a value. This feature should be removed. We can do it with the `drop` function in Pandas as follows. We'll make a new DataFrame called `clean_data` to store the data we're about to clean up:

```
clean_data = raw_data.drop('Cabin', axis=1)
```

The arguments to the `drop` function follow:

- The name of the column we want to drop

- The `axis` parameter, which is 1 when we want to drop a column and 0 when we want to drop a row

We then assign the output of this function to the variable `clean_data`, indicating that we want to replace the old DataFrame called `data` by the new one with the deleted column.

How to not lose the entire column: Filling in missing data

We don't always want to delete columns with missing data, because we might lose important information. We can also fill in the data with values that would make sense. For example, let's take a look at the Age column, shown next:

```
clean_data['Age']
Output:
0       22.0
1       38.0
2       26.0
3       35.0
4       35.0
        ...
886     27.0
887     19.0
888     NaN
889     26.0
890     32.0
Name: Age, Length: 891, dtype: float64
```

As we calculated previously, the Age column is missing only 177 values out of 891, which is not that many. This column is useful, so let's not delete it. What can we do with these missing values, then? There are many things we can do, but the most common are filling them in with the average or the median of the other values. Let's do the latter. First, we calculate the median, using the median function, and we obtain 28. Next, we use the `fillna` function, which fills in the missing values with the value we give it, as shown in the next code snippet:

```
median_age = clean_data["Age"].median()
clean_data["Age"] = clean_data["Age"].fillna(median_age)
```

The third column that is missing values is Embarked, which is missing two values. What can we do here? There is no average we can use, because these are letters, not numbers. Luckily, only two rows are missing this number among 891 of them, so we are not losing too much information here. My suggestion is to lump all the passengers with no value in the Embarked column into the same class. We can call this class U, for "Unknown." The following line of code will do it:

```
clean_data["Embarked"] = clean_data["Embarked"].fillna('U')
```

Finally, we can save this DataFrame in a CSV file called clean_titanic_data to use in the next section:

```
clean_data.to_csv('./clean_titanic_data.csv', index=None)
```

Feature engineering: Transforming the features in our dataset before training the models

Now that we've cleaned our dataset, we are much closer to being able to train a model. However, we still need to do some important data manipulations, which we see in this section. The first is transforming the type of data from numerical to categorical, and vice versa. The second is feature selection, in which we manually decide which features to remove to improve the training of our model.

Recall from chapter 2 that there are two types of features, numerical and categorical. A numerical feature is one that is stored as numbers. In this dataset, features such as the age, fare, and class are numbers. A categorical feature is one that contains several categories, or classes. For example, the gender feature contains two classes: female and male. The embarked feature contains three classes, C for Cherbourg, Q for Queenstown, and S for Southampton.

As we have seen throughout this book, machine learning models take numbers as input. If that is the case, how do we input the word "female," or the letter "Q"? We need to have a way to turn categorical features into numerical features. Also, believe it or not, sometimes we may be interested in treating numerical features as categorical to aid us in our training, such as putting them in buckets, for example, age 1–10, 11–20, and so on. We cover this more in the section "Turning numerical data into categorical data."

Even more, when we think of a feature such as the passenger class (called Pclass), is this truly a numerical feature, or is it categorical? Should we think of class as a number between one and three, or as three classes: first, second, and third? We answer all those questions in this section.

In this section, we call the DataFrame `preprocessed_data`. The first few rows of this dataset are shown in table 13.2

Table 13.2 The first five rows of the cleaned-up dataset. We will proceed to preprocess this data for training.

PassengerId	Survived	Pclass	Name	Sex	Age	SibSp	Parch	Ticket	Fare	Embarked
1	0	3	Braund, Mr. Owen Harris	male	22.0	1	0	A/5 21171	7.2500	S
2	1	1	Cumings, Mrs. John Bradley (Florence Briggs Th...	female	38.0	1	0	PC 17599	71.2833	C
3	1	3	Heikkinen, Miss. Laina	female	26.0	0	0	STON/O2. 3101282	7.9250	S
4	1	1	Futrelle, Mrs. Jacques Heath (Lily May Peel)	female	35.0	1	0	113803	53.1000	S
5	0	3	Allen, Mr. William Henry	male	35.0	0	0	373450	8.0500	S

Turning categorical data into numerical data: One-hot encoding

As was mentioned previously, machine learning models perform a lot of mathematical operations, and to perform mathematical operations in our data, we must make sure all the data is numerical. If we have any columns with categorical data, we must turn them into numbers. In this section, we learn a way to do this effectively using a technique called *one-hot encoding*.

But before we delve into one-hot encoding, here's a question: why not simply attach a different number to each one of the classes? For example, if our feature has 10 classes, why not number them 0, 1, 2,..., 9? The reason is that this forces an order in the features that we may not want. For example, if the Embarked column has the three classes C, Q, and S, corresponding to Cherbourg, Queenstown, and Southampton, assigning the numbers 0, 1, and 2 to these would implicitly tell the model that the value of Queenstown is between the values of Cherbourg and Southampton, which is not necessarily true. A complex model may be able to deal with this implicit ordering, but simpler models (such as linear models, for example) will suffer. We'd like to make these values more independent of each other, and this is where one-hot encoding comes in.

One-hot encoding works in the following way: First, we look at how many classes the feature has and build as many new columns. For example, a column with two categories, female and male, would turn it into two columns, one for female and one for male. We can call these columns gender_male and gender_female for clarity. Then, we look at each passenger. If the passenger is female, then the gender_female column will have a 1, and the gender_male column will have a 0. If the passenger is male, then we do the opposite.

What if we have a column with more classes, such as the embarked column? Because that column has three classes (C for Cherbourg, Q for Queenstown, and S for Southampton), we simply make three columns called embarked_c, embarked_q, and embarked_s. In that way, if a passenger embarked in, say, Southampton, the third column will have a 1 and the other two a 0. This process is illustrated in figure 13.1.

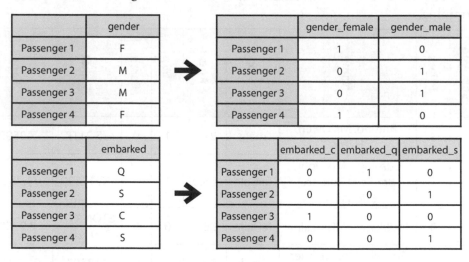

Figure 13.1 One-hot encoding our data to turn it all into numbers for the machine learning model to read. On the left, we have columns with categorical features such as gender or port of embarkment. On the right, we have turned these categorical features into numerical features.

The Pandas function `get_dummies` helps us with one-hot encoding. We use it to create some new columns, then we attach these columns to the dataset, and we must not forget to remove the original column, because that information is redundant. Next is the code to do one-hot encoding in the gender and the embarked columns:

Creates columns with the
one-hot encoded columns

Concatenates the
dataset with the
newly created
columns

```
gender_columns = pandas.get_dummies(data['Sex'], prefix='Sex')
embarked_columns = pandas.get_dummies(data["Pclass"], prefix="Pclass")

preprocessed_data = pandas.concat([preprocessed_data, gender_columns], axis=1)
preprocessed_data = pandas.concat([preprocessed_data, embarked_columns], axis=1)

preprocessed_data = preprocessed_data.drop(['Sex', 'Embarked'], axis=1)
```

Deletes the old columns
from the dataset

Sometimes this process can be expensive. Imagine having a column with 500 classes. That will add 500 new columns to our table! Not only that, but the rows will be very sparse, namely, they will contain mostly zeroes. Now imagine if we had many columns with hundreds of classes each—our table would become too big to handle. In this case, as a data scientist, use your criteria to make a decision. If there is enough computing power and storage space to handle thousands or perhaps millions of columns, then one-hot encoding is no problem. If these resources are limited, perhaps we can broaden our classes to produce fewer columns. For example, if we had a column with 100 animal types, we can lump them into six columns formed by mammals, birds, fish, amphibians, invertebrates, and reptiles.

Can we one-hot encode numerical features? If so, why would we want to?

Clearly, if a feature has categories such as male or female, our best strategy is to one-hot encode it. However, there are some numerical features for which we still may want to consider one-hot encoding. Let's look, for example, at the Pclass column. This column has the classes 0, 1, and 2, for first, second, and third class. Should we keep it as a numerical feature, or should we one-hot encode it as three features, Pclass1, Pclass2, and Pclass3? This is certainly debatable, and we can make good arguments on both sides. One may argue that we don't want to unnecessarily enlarge a dataset if it doesn't give the model a potential improvement in performance. There is a rule of thumb that we can use to decide whether to split a column into several columns. We can ask ourselves: is this feature directly correlated to the outcome? In other words, does increasing the value of the feature make it more likely (or less likely) for a passenger to survive? One would imagine that perhaps the higher the class, the more likely a passenger survived. Let's see if this is the case by doing some counting (see code in the notebook), shown next:

- In first class, 62.96% of the passengers survived.

- In second class, 47.28% of the passengers survived.

- In third class, 24.24% of the passengers survived.

Notice that the lowest possibility of survival is for the passengers in second class. Therefore, it is not true that increasing (or decreasing) the class automatically improves the chances of survival. For this reason, I suggest one-hot encoding this feature as follows:

```
categorized_pclass_columns = pd.get_dummies(preprocessed_data['Pclass'],
    prefix='Pclass')
preprocessed_data = pd.concat([preprocessed_data, categorized_pclass_columns],
    axis=1)
preprocessed_data = preprocessed_data.drop(['Pclass'], axis=1)
```

Turning numerical data into categorical data (and why would we want to do this?): Binning

In the previous section, we learned to turn categorical data into numerical data. In this section, we see how to go in the other direction. Why would we ever want this? Let's look at an example.

Let's look at the Age column. It's nice and numerical. A machine learning model answers the following question: "How much does age determine survival in the *Titanic*?" Imagine that we have a linear model for survival. Such a model would end up with one of the following two conclusions:

- The older the passenger is, the more likely they are to survive.

- The older the passenger is, the less likely they are to survive.

However, is this always the case? What if the relationship between age and survival is not as straightforward? What if the highest possibility of survival is when the passenger is between 20 and 30, and it's low for all other age groups. What if the lowest possibility of survival is between 20 and 30? We need to give the model all the freedom to determine which ages determine whether a passenger is more or less likely to survive. What can we do?

Many nonlinear models can deal with this, but we should still modify the Age column to something that gives the model more freedom to explore the data. A useful technique we can do is to bin the ages, namely, split them into several different buckets. For example, we can turn the age column into the following:

- From 0 to 10 years old

- From 11 to 20 years old

- From 21 to 30 years old

- From 31 to 40 years old

- From 41 to 50 years old

- From 51 to 60 years old

- From 61 to 70 years old

- From 71 to 80 years old

- 81 years old or older

This is similar to one-hot encoding, in the sense that it will turn the Age column into nine new columns. The code to do this follows:

```
bins = [0, 10, 20, 30, 40, 50, 60, 70, 80]
categorized_age = pandas.cut(preprocessed_data['Age'], bins)
preprocessed_data['Categorized_age'] = categorized_age
preprocessed_data = preprocessed_data.drop(["Age"], axis=1)
```

Feature selection: Getting rid of unnecessary features

In the subsection "Dropping columns with missing data," we dropped some columns in our table, because they had too many missing values. However, we should also drop some other columns, because they are not necessary for our model, or even worse, they may completely ruin our model! In this section, we discuss which features should be dropped. But before that, take a look at the features and think of which of them would be bad for our model. Here they are again:

- **PassengerID:** a unique number corresponding to every passenger
- **Name:** the full name of the passenger
- **Sex (two categories):** the gender of the passenger as male or female
- **Age (several categories):** the age of the passenger as an integer
- **Pclass (several categories):** the class in which the passenger was traveling: first, second, or third
- **SibSP:** the number of siblings and spouse of the passenger (0 if the passenger is traveling alone)
- **Parch:** the number of parents and children of the passenger (0 if the passenger is traveling alone)
- **Ticket:** the ticket number
- **Fare:** the fare the passenger paid in British pounds
- **Cabin:** the cabin in which the passenger was traveling
- **Embarked:** the port in which the passenger embarked: C for Cherbourg, Q for Queenstown, and S for Southampton
- **Survived:** information whether the passenger survived (1) or not (0)

First, let's look at the name feature. Should we consider it in our model? Absolutely not, and here is the reason: every passenger has a different name (perhaps with some very few exceptions, which are not significant). Therefore, the model would be trained to simply learn the names of the passengers who survived, and it wouldn't be able to tell us anything about new passengers whose names it hasn't seen. This model is memorizing the data—it is not learning anything meaningful about its features. This means it heavily overfits, and, therefore, we should completely get rid of the Name column.

The ticket and the PassengerID features have the same problem as the name feature, because there is a unique one for each passenger. We'll remove those two columns as well. The `drop` function will help us do this, as shown next:

```
preprocessed_data = preprocessed_data.drop(['Name', 'Ticket', 'PassengerId'],
    axis=1)
```

What about the Survived feature—shouldn't we get rid of that one, too? Definitely! Keeping the Survived column in our dataset while training will overfit, because the model will simply use this feature to determine whether the passenger survived. This is like cheating on a test by looking at the solution. We won't remove it yet from the dataset, because we will remove it when we split the dataset into features and labels later for training.

As usual, we can save this dataset in the csv file preprocessed_titanic_data.csv for use in the next section.

Training our models

Now that our data has been preprocessed, we can start training different models on the data. What models should we choose from the ones we've learned in this book: decision trees, support vector machines, logistic classifiers? The answer to this lies in evaluating our models. In this section, we see how to train several different models, evaluate them on a validation dataset, and pick the best model that fits our dataset.

As usual, we load our data from the file where we saved it in the previous section, as shown next. We'll call it `data`.

```
data = pandas.read_csv('preprocessed_titanic_data.csv')
```

Table 13.3 contains the first few rows of the preprocessed data. Notice that not all the columns are displayed because there are 27 of them.

Table 13.3   The first five rows of our preprocessed data, ready to be fed into the model. Note that it has 21 columns, many more than before. These extra columns were created when we one-hot encoded and binned several of the existing features.

Survived	SibSp	Parch	Fare	Sex_female	Sex_male	Pclass_C	Pclass_Q	Pclass_S	Pclass_U	...	Categorized_age_(10, 20]
0	1	0	7.25000	0	1	0	0	1	0	...	0
1	1	0	71.2833	1	0	1	0	0	0	...	0
1	0	0	7.9250	1	0	0	0	1	0	...	0
1	1	0	53.1000	1	0	0	0	1	0	...	0
0	0	0	8.0500	0	1	0	0	1	0	...	0

aside If you run the code from the notebook, you may get different numbers.

Splitting the data into features and labels, and training and validation

Our dataset is a table with the features and labels together. We need to perform two splits. First, we need to separate the features from the labels to feed this to the model. Next, we need to form a training and a testing set. This is what we cover in this subsection.

To split the dataset into two tables called `features` and `labels`, we use the `drop` function as follows:

```
features = data.drop(["Survived"], axis=1)
labels = data["Survived"]
```

Next, we split the data into training and validation sets. We'll use 60% of our data for training, 20% for validation, and 20% for testing. For splitting the data, we use the Scikit-Learn function `train_test_split`. In this function, we specify the percentage of data we want for validation with the `test_size` parameter. The output is the four tables called `features_train`, `features_test`, `labels_train`, `labels_test`.

If we wanted to split our data into 80% training and 20% testing, we would use the following code:

```
from sklearn.model_selection import train_test_split
features_train, features_test, labels_train, labels_test =
    train_test_split(features, labels, test_size=0.2)
```

However, because we want 60% training, 20% validation, and 20% testing, we need to use the `train_test_split` function twice: once for separating the training data, and once for splitting the validation and testing sets, as shown here:

```
features_train, features_validation_test, labels_train,
    labels_validation_test = train_test_split(features, labels,
    test_size=0.4)
features_validation, features_test, labels_validation,
    labels_test = train_test_split(features_validation_test,
    labels_validation_test, test_size=0.5)
```

aside You may see that in the notebook we have specified a fixed `random_state` in this function. The reason is that `train_test_split` shuffles the data when it splits it. We fix the random state to make sure we always get the same split.

We can check the lengths of these DataFrames, and notice that the length of the training set is 534, of the validation set is 178, and of the testing set is 179. Now, recall from chapter 4 that the Golden Rule is to never use our testing data for training or for making decisions on our models. Therefore, we'll save the test set for the very end, when we've decided what model to use. We'll use the training set for training the models and the validation set for taking any decisions on what model to choose.

Training several models on our dataset

We're finally getting to the fun part: training the models! In this section, we see how to train several different models in Scikit-Learn in just a few lines of code.

First, we start by training a logistic regression model. We can do this by creating an instance of `LogisticRegression` and using the `fit` method, as follows:

```
from sklearn.linear_model import LogisticRegression
lr_model = LogisticRegression()
lr_model.fit(features_train, labels_train)
```

Let's also train a decision tree, a naive Bayes model, a support vector machine, a random forest, a gradient boosted tree, and an AdaBoost model, as shown in the next code:

```
from sklearn.tree import DecisionTreeClassifier, GaussianNB, SVC,
    RandomForestClassifier, GradientBoostingClassifier, AdaBoostClassifier

dt_model = DecisionTreeClassifier()
dt_model.fit(features_train, labels_train)

nb_model = GaussianNB()
nb_model.fit(features_train, labels_train)

svm_model = SVC()
svm_model.fit(features_train, labels_train)

rf_model = RandomForestClassifier()
rf_model.fit(features_train, labels_train)

gb_model = GradientBoostingClassifier()
gb_model.fit(features_train, labels_train)

ab_model = AdaBoostClassifier()
ab_model.fit(features_train, labels_train)
```

Which model is better? Evaluating the models

Now that we've trained some models, we need to select the best one. In this section, we use different metrics to evaluate them using the validation sets. Recall that in chapter 7 we learned accuracy, recall, precision, and F_1-score. To refresh your memory, the definitions follow:

accuracy   The ratio between the number of correctly labeled points and the total number of points.

recall   Among the points with positive labels, the proportion of them that are correctly classified. In other words, Recall = TP / (TP + FN), where TP is the number of true positives and FN the number of false negatives.

precision   Among the points that have been classified as positive, the proportion of them that are correctly classified. In other words, Precision = TP / (TP + FP), where FP is the number of false positives.

F_1**-score**   The harmonic mean of precision and recall. This is a number between precision and recall, but it is closer to the smaller of the two.

Testing each model's accuracy

Let's start by evaluating the accuracy of these models. The `score` function in Scikit-Learn will do this, as shown next:

```
lr_model.score(features_validation, labels_validation)
Output:
0.7932960893854749
```

We calculate it for all the other models and get the following results, which I've rounded to two figures (see the notebook for the whole procedure):

Accuracy

- **Logistic regression:** 0.77
- **Decision tree:** 0.78
- **Naive Bayes:** 0.72
- **SVM:** 0.68
- **Random forest:** 0.7875
- **Gradient boosting:** 0.81
- **AdaBoost:** 0.76

This hints that the best model in this dataset is a gradient boosted tree, because it gives us the highest accuracy on the validation set (81%, which is good for the Titanic dataset). This is not surprising, because this algorithm normally performs very well.

You can follow a similar procedure to calculate the recall, precision, and F_1 score. I will let you do it for recall and precision, and we will do it together for F_1 score.

Testing each model's F_1-score

Here is how we check the F_1 score. First, we have to output the predictions of the model, using the `predict` function, and then we use the `f1_score` function, as follows:

Uses the model to make the predictions

```
lr_predicted_labels = lr_model.predict(features_validation)
f1_score(labels_validation, lr_predicted_labels)
Output:
0.6870229007633588
```

Calculates the F_1 score

As before, we can do this for all the models, and get the following:

F_1-**Score**

- **Logistic regression:** 0.69
- **Decision tree:** 0.71
- **Naive Bayes:** 0.63
- **Support vector machine:** 0.42
- **Random forest:** 0.68
- **Gradient boosting:** 0.74
- **AdaBoost:** 0.69

Again, the gradient boosted tree won with an F_1-score of 0.74. Given the fact that its numbers were much higher than the other models, we can safely conclude that among these eight models, gradient boosted trees is the best one. Notice that the tree-based models did well in general, which is not surprising, given the high nonlinearity of the dataset. It would be interesting to train a neural network and an XGBoost model on this dataset, too, and I encourage you to do so!

Testing the model

After comparing the models using the validation set, we have finally made up our minds, and we have chosen the gradient boosted tree as the best model for this dataset. Don't be surprised; gradient boosted trees (and their close cousin, XGBoost) win most competitions. But to see if we really did well or if we accidentally overfit, we need to give this model its final test: we need to test the model in the test set that we haven't touched yet.

First, let's evaluate the accuracy, as follows:

```
gb_model.score(features_test, labels_test)
Output:
0.8324022346368715
```

And now let's look at the F_1-score, shown next:

```
gb_predicted_test_labels = gb_model.predict(features_test)
f1_score(labels_test, gb_predicted_test_labels)
Output:
0.8026315789473685
```

These scores are quite good for the Titanic dataset. Thus, we can comfortably say that our model is good.

However, we trained these models without touching their hyperparameters, which means that Scikit-Learn picked some standard hyperparameters for them. Is there a way we can find the best hyperparameters for a model? In the next section, we learn that there is.

Tuning the hyperparameters to find the best model: Grid search

In the previous section, we trained several models and found that the gradient boosting tree performed best among them. However, we didn't explore many different combinations of hyperparameters, so we have room to improve in our training. In this section, we see a useful technique to search among many combinations of hyperparameters to find a good model for our data.

The performance of the gradient boosted tree was about as high as one can obtain for the Titanic dataset, so let's leave that one alone. The poor SVM, however, performed last, with an accuracy of 69% and an F_1-score of 0.42. We believe in SVMs, however, because they are a powerful machine learning model. Perhaps the bad performance of this SVM is due to the hyperparameters it is using. There may be a better combination of them that works.

> **aside**   Throughout this section, we make some choices of parameters. Some are based on experience, some on standard practices, and some are arbitrary. I encourage you to try following a similar procedure with any choices you decide to make and to try to beat the current scores of the models!

To improve the performance of our SVM, we use a method called *grid search*, which consists of training our model several times over different combinations of the hyperparameters and selecting the one that performs best on our validation set.

Let's begin by picking a kernel. In practice, I have found that the RBF (radial basis functions) kernel tends to perform well, so let's select that one. Recall from chapter 9 that the hyperparameter that goes with the RBF kernel is gamma, which is a real number. Let's try to train an SVM with two values for gamma, namely, 1 and 10. Why 1 and 10? Normally when we search for hyperparameters, we tend to do an exponential search, so we would try values such as 0.1, 1, 10, 100, 1000, and so on, as opposed to 1, 2, 3, 4, 5. This exponential search covers a larger space and gives us better chances of finding good hyperparameters, and doing this type of search is standard practice among data scientists.

Recall again from chapter 9 that another hyperparameter associated to SVMs is the C parameter. Let's also try to train models with C = 1 and C = 10. This gives us the following four possible models to train:

Model 1: kernel = RBF, gamma = 1, C = 1

Model 2: kernel = RBF, gamma = 1, C = 10

Model 3: kernel = RBF, gamma = 10, C = 1

Model 4: kernel = RBF, gamma = 10, C = 10

We can easily train all of those in our training set with the following eight lines of code:

```
svm_1_1 = SVC(kernel='rbf', C=1, gamma=1)
svm_1_1.fit(features_train, labels_train)
```

```
svm_1_10 = SVC(kernel='rbf', C=1, gamma=10)
svm_1_10.fit(features_train, labels_train)

svm_10_1 = SVC(kernel='rbf', C=10, gamma=1)
svm_10_1.fit(features_train, labels_train)

svm_10_10 = SVC(kernel='rbf', C=10, gamma=10)
svm_10_10.fit(features_train, labels_train)
```

Now we evaluate them, using accuracy (another arbitrary choice—we could also use F_1-score, precision, or recall). The scores are recorded in table 13.4.

Table 13.4   The grid search method is useful to search over many combinations of hyperparameters and pick the best model. Here we use a grid search to pick the best combination of parameters C and gamma in an SVM. We used accuracy to compare the models in the validation set. Notice that the best model among these is the one with gamma = 0.1 and C = 10, with an accuracy of 0.72.

	C = 1	**C = 10**
gamma = 0.1	0.69	**0.72**
gamma = 1	0.70	0.70
gamma = 10	0.67	0.65

Notice from table 13.4 that the best accuracy is 0.72, given by the model with gamma = 0.1 and C = 1. This is an improvement from the 0.68 we obtained previously when we didn't specify any hyperparameters.

If we had many more parameters, we simply make a grid with them and train all the possible models. Notice that as we explore more choices, the number of models rapidly increases. For example, if we wanted to explore five values for gamma and four values for C, we would have to train 20 models (five times four). We can also add more hyperparameters—for example, if there was a third hyperparameter that we wanted to try, and there were seven values for this one, we would have to train a total of 140 models (five times four times seven). As the number of models grows so quickly, it is important to pick the choices in such a way that it explores the hyperparameter space well, without training a huge number of models.

Scikit-Learn offers a simple way to do this: using the `GridSearchCV` object. First, we define the hyperparameters as a dictionary, where the key of the dictionary is the name of the parameter and the value corresponding to this key is the list of values we want to try for our hyperparameter. In this case, let's explore the following combinations of hyperparameters:

Kernel: RBF

C: 0.01, 0.1, 1, 10, 100

gamma: 0.01, 0.1, 1, 10, 100

The following code will do it:

```
svm_parameters = {'kernel': ['rbf'],
                  'C': [0.01, 0.1, 1 , 10, 100],
                  'gamma': [0.01, 0.1, 1, 10, 100]
                 }
svm = SVC()

svm_gs = GridSearchCV(estimator = svm,
                      param_grid = svm_parameters)

svm_gs.fit(features_train, labels_train)
```

A dictionary with the hyperparameters and the values we want to try

A regular SVM with no hyperparameters

A GridSearchCV object where we pass the SVM and the hyperparameter dictionary

We fit the GridSearchCV model in the same way that we fit a regular model in Scikit-Learn.

This trains 25 models with all the combinations of hyperparameters given in the hyperparameter dictionary. Now, we pick the best of these models and call it svm_winner. Let's calculate the accuracy of this model on the validation set as follows:

```
svm_winner = svm_gs.best_estimator_
svm_winner.score(features_validation, labels_validation)
Output:
0.7303370786516854
```

Our winning model achieved an accuracy of 0.73, which is better than the original 0.68. We could still improve this model by running a larger hyperparameter search, and I encourage you to try it yourself. For now, let's explore which hyperparameters were used by the last winning SVM model, as shown here:

```
svm_winner
Output:
SVC(C=10, break_ties=False, cache_size=200, class_weight=None, coef0=0.0,
    decision_function_shape='ovr', degree=3, gamma=0.01, kernel='rbf',
    max_iter=-1, probability=False, random_state=None, shrinking=True,
    tol=0.001, verbose=False)
```

The winning model used an RBF kernel with gamma = 0.01 and C = 10.

challenge   I encourage you to try using grid search on other models, and see how much you can improve the accuracy and F_1-score of the winning model! If you have a good score, run it on the Kaggle dataset and submit your predictions using this link: https://www.kaggle.com/c/titanic/submit.

One more thing: what is that *CV* at the end of GridSearchCV? It stands for *cross-validation*, which we learn in the next section.

Using *K*-fold cross-validation to reuse our data as training and validation

In this section, we learn an alternative to the traditional training-validation-testing method we've been using in this chapter. It is called *k-fold cross validation*, and it is useful in many situations, especially when our dataset is small.

Throughout this example, we used 60% of our data for training, 20% for validation, and a final 20% for testing. That works in practice, but it seems that we are losing some data, right? We end up training the model with only 60% of our data, which may hurt our model, especially when the dataset is small. *K*-fold cross-validation is a way to use all the data for training and testing, by recycling it several times. It works as follows:

1. Split the data into *k* equal (or almost equal) portions.

2. Train the model *k* times, using the union of *k* − 1 of the portions as the training set and the remaining one as a validation set.

3. The final score of that model is the average of the validation scores from the *k* steps.

Figure 13.2 shows a picture of fourfold cross-validation.

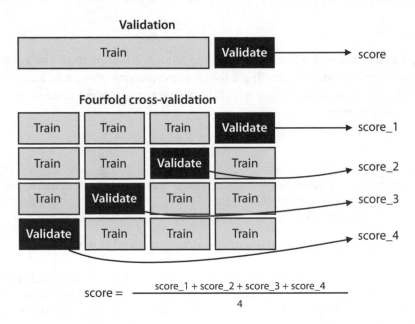

Figure 13.2 *K*-fold cross validation is a useful method that recycles our data to use it both as training and as validation. On the top, we see the classical training-validation split. On the bottom, we see an illustration of fourfold cross-validation in which we split the data into four equal (or almost equal) portions. We then train our model four times. Each time we pick three of the portions as the training set, and the remaining one as the validation set. The score of this model is the average of the four scores obtained on each of the validation sets.

This method is what is used in `GridSearchCV`, and the results of this process can be examined by typing `svm_gs.cv_results_`. We won't show the results here, because they are very long, but you can take a look at them in the notebook.

Summary

- Pandas is a useful Python package to open, manipulate, and save datasets.

- Cleaning up our data is necessary, because it may come with problems such as missing values.

- Features can be numerical or categorical. Numerical features are numbers, such as age. Categorical features are categories, or types, such as dog/cat/bird.

- Machine learning models take only numbers, so to feed categorical data to a machine learning model, we must turn it into numerical data. One way to do this is by one-hot encoding.

- In some situations, we may want to treat our numerical features as categorical features as well, which we can do by binning the data.

- It is important to use feature selection to remove unnecessary features in our data.

- Scikit-Learn is a useful package to train, test, and evaluate machine learning models.

- Before training the model, we must split the data into training, validation, and testing. We have Pandas functions for doing this.

- Grid search is a method used to find the best hyperparameters for a model. It consists of training several models over a (sometimes large) set of hyperparameters.

- *K*-fold cross-validation is a method used to recycle the data and use it as training and validation as well. It consists of training and testing several models on different portions of the data.

Exercises

Exercise 13.1

The repository contains a file called test.csv. This is a file with more passengers on the *Titanic*, except it doesn't have the Survived column.

1. Preprocess the data in this file as we did in this chapter.

2. Use any of the models to predict labels in this dataset. According to your model, how many passengers survived?

3. Comparing the performance of all the models in this chapter, how many passengers from the test set would you think actually survived?

Chapter 2: Types of machine learning

For the questions in this chapter, your answers don't need to match mine. If you have different ideas for models used in these applications, they might be great! I encourage you to look them up in the literature, and if they don't exist, try to implement them.

Exercise 2.1

For each of the following scenarios, state if it is an example of supervised or unsupervised learning. Explain your answers. In cases of ambiguity, pick one and explain why you picked it.

a. A recommendation system on a social network that recommends potential friends to a user

b. A system in a news site that divides the news into topics

c. The Google autocomplete feature for sentences

d. A recommendation system on an online retailer that recommends to users what to buy based on their past purchasing history

e. A system in a credit card company that captures fraudulent transactions

Solution

Depending on how you interpreted the problem and the dataset, each of these can be considered an example of supervised or unsupervised learning. It is completely OK (and encouraged!) to have different answers, as long as the reasoning behind them is correct.

a. This is an example of both supervised and unsupervised learning. Supervised learning: for a particular user, we can build a classification model where the label of every other user is positive if they are a potential friend and negative if they are not a potential friend. Unsupervised learning: we can cluster the users, where similar users share similar demographic or behavioral features. To a particular user, we can recommend other users in their cluster as potential friends.

b. This is also an example of both supervised and unsupervised learning. Supervised learning: a classification model where the label of each news article is the topic, for example, politics, sports, or science. Unsupervised learning: we can cluster the articles and then manually check if the topics in each cluster are similar. If this is the case, then we can manually label each cluster by the most common topic. There are some more advanced unsupervised learning techniques such as latent Dirichlet allocation, which you can learn in this video: https://www.youtube.com/watch?v=T05t-SqKArY.

c. This one is more of a supervised learning task. We can build a classification model in which the features are the last few words the user has typed, and the label is the next word they'll type. In that way, the prediction of the model is the word we'll suggest to the user.

d. This is similar to a), and it can be considered a supervised or an unsupervised learning problem. Supervised learning: for a particular user, we can build a classification model for all the products, where for each product, we predict whether the user will buy it. We can also build a regression model in which we predict how much money the user will spend on that particular product. Unsupervised learning: we can cluster the users. If a user has bought a product, we can recommend that same product to other users in the cluster. We can also cluster the products, and if a user has bought a product, we recommend products in the same cluster.

e. This one is more of a supervised learning task. We can build a classification model that predicts whether a certain transaction is fraudulent or not, based on the characteristics of that transaction. It can also be seen as an unsupervised learning task in which we cluster the transactions, and those left as outliers have a higher chance of being fraudulent.

Exercise 2.2

For each of the following applications of machine learning, would you use regression or classification to solve it? Explain your answers. In cases of ambiguity, pick one and explain why you picked it.

a. An online store predicting how much money a user will spend on their site

b. A voice assistant decoding voice and turning it into text

c. Selling or buying stock from a particular company

d. YouTube recommending a video to a user

Solution

a. Regression, because we are trying to predict the amount of money that the user spends, and this is a numerical feature.

b. Classification, because we are trying to predict whether the sentence the user has spoken is directed to Alexa, and this is a categorical feature.

c. This could be regression or classification. If we are trying to predict the expected gain or the expected risk to help us in our decision, it is regression. If we are trying to predict whether we should buy the stock, it is classification.

d. This can again be regression or classification. If we are trying to predict how much time the user will spend watching the video in order to recommend it, it is regression. If we are trying to predict whether the user will watch a video, it is classification.

Exercise 2.3

Your task is to build a self-driving car. Give at least three examples of machine learning problems that you would have to solve to build it. In each example, explain whether you are using supervised/unsupervised learning, and if supervised, whether you are using regression or classification. If you are using other types of machine learning, explain which ones and why.

Solution

- A classification model, which, based on the image, determines whether there are pedestrians, stop signs, lanes, other cars, and so on. This is a large area of machine learning called computer vision, which I highly encourage you to explore further!

- A similar classification model as the previous one, which determines what objects are around the car based on the signals from all the different sensors in the car (lidar, etc.)

- A machine learning model that finds the closest path to our desired destination. This is not precisely supervised or unsupervised learning. There are some more classical artificial intelligence algorithms such as A* (A-star) search that can be used here.

Chapter 3: Drawing a line close to our points: Linear regression

Exercise 3.1

A website has trained a linear regression model to predict the amount of minutes that a user will spend on the site. The formula they have obtained is

$$\hat{t} = 0.8d + 0.5m + 0.5y + 0.2a + 1.5$$

where $\hat{t}$ is the predicted time in minutes, and d, m, y, and a are indicator variables (namely, they take only the values 0 or 1) defined as follows:

- d is a variable that indicates if the user is on desktop.

- m is a variable that indicates if the user is on mobile device.

- y is a variable that indicates if the user is young (under 21 years old).

- a is a variable that indicates if the user is an adult (21 years old or older).

Example: If a user is 30 years old and on desktop, then $d = 1$, $m = 0$, $y = 0$, and $a = 1$.

If a 45-year-old user looks at the website from their phone, what is the expected time they will spend on the site?

Solution

In this case, the values of the variables are the following:

- $d = 0$ because the user is not on desktop.

- $m = 1$ because the user is on mobile.

- $y = 0$ because the user is not under 21.

- $a = 1$ because the user is over 21.

When we plug them into the formula, we get

$$\hat{t} = 0.8 \cdot 0 + 0.5 \cdot 1 + 0.5 \cdot 0 + 0.2 \cdot 1 + 1.5 = 2.2.$$

This means the model predicts that this user will spend 2.2 minutes on the website.

Exercise 3.2

Imagine that we trained a linear regression model in a medical dataset. The model predicts the expected lifetime of a patient. To each of the features in our dataset, the model would assign a weight.

a) For the following quantities, state if you believe the weight attached to this quantity is a positive number, a negative number, or zero. Note: if you believe that the weight is a very small number, whether positive or negative, you can say zero.

1. Number of hours of exercise the patient gets per week

2. Number of cigarettes the patient smokes per week

3. Number of family members with heart problems

4. Number of siblings of the patient

5. Whether or not the patient has been hospitalized

b) The model also has a bias. Do you think the bias is positive, negative, or zero?

Solution

a) We'll make some generalizations based on general medical knowledge. For a particular patient, the following are not necessarily true, but we'll make the assumption that they are true for the general population:

1. A patient who exercises a lot is expected to live longer than a similar patient who doesn't. Thus, this weight should be a positive number.

2. A patient who smokes many cigarettes a week is expected to live shorter than a similar patient who doesn't. Thus, this weight should be a negative number.

3. A patient who has many family members with heart problems has a higher likelihood of having heart problems, and thus they are expected to live shorter than a similar patient that doesn't have them. Thus, this weight should be a negative number.

4. The number of siblings tends to be independent of the expected lifetime, so we expect this weight to be a very small number, or zero.

5. A patient who has been hospitalized in the past is likely to have had previous health problems. Thus, their expected lifetime is shorter than a similar patient that hasn't been hospitalized before. Therefore, this weight should be a negative number. Of course, the hospitalization could be for a reason that doesn't affect expected lifetime (such as a broken leg), but on average, we can say that if a patient has been to the hospital in the past, they have a higher probability to have health problems.

b) The bias is the prediction for a patient for which every feature is zero (i.e., a patient who doesn't smoke, doesn't exercise, has zero family members with heart condition, zero siblings, and has never been hospitalized). Because this patient is expected to live a positive number of years, the bias of this model must be a positive number.

Exercise 3.3

The following is a dataset of houses with sizes (in square feet) and prices (in dollars).

	Size (s)	Prize (p)
House 1	100	200
House 2	200	475
House 3	200	400
House 4	250	520
House 5	325	735

Suppose we have trained the model where the prediction for the price of the house based on size is the following:

$$\hat{p} = 2s + 50$$

a. Calculate the predictions that this model makes on the dataset.

b. Calculate the mean absolute error of this model.

c. Calculate the root mean square error of this model.

Solution

a. The predicted prices based on the model follow:

    − House 1: $\hat{p} = 2 \cdot 100 + 50 = 250$

    − House 2: $\hat{p} = 2 \cdot 200 + 50 = 450$

    − House 3: $\hat{p} = 2 \cdot 200 + 50 = 450$

    − House 4: $\hat{p} = 2 \cdot 250 + 50 = 550$

    − House 5: $\hat{p} = 2 \cdot 325 + 50 = 700$

b. The mean absolute error is

$$\frac{1}{5}(|200 - 250| + |475 - 450| + |400 - 450| + |520 - 550| + |735 - 700|)$$

$$= \frac{1}{5}(50 + 25 + 50 + 30 + 35) = 38.$$

c. The mean square error is

$$\frac{1}{5}((200 - 250)^2 + (475 - 450)^2 + (400 - 450)^2 + (520 - 550)^2 + (735 - 700)^2)$$

$$= \frac{1}{5}(2500 + 625 + 2500 + 900 + 1225) = 1550.$$

Therefore, the root mean square error is $\sqrt{1550} = 39.37$.

Exercise 3.4

Our goal is to move the line with equation $\hat{y} = 2x + 3$ closer to the point $(x, y) = (5, 15)$ using the tricks we've learned in this chapter. For the following two problems, use the learning rate $\eta = 0.01$.

a. Apply the absolute trick to modify the line above to be closer to the point.

b. Apply the square trick to modify the line above to be closer to the point.

Solution

The prediction that this model makes at the point is $\hat{y} = 2 \cdot 5 + 3 = 13$.

a. Because the prediction is 13, which is smaller than the label 15, the point is underneath the line.

    In this model, the slope is $m = 2$ and the y-intercept is $b = 3$. The absolute trick involves adding $x\eta = 5 \cdot 0.01 = 0.05$ to the slope, and $\eta = 0.01$ to the y-intercept, thus obtaining the model with equation

$$\hat{y} = 2.05x + 3.01.$$

b. The square trick involves adding $(y - \hat{y})x\eta = (15 - 13) \cdot 5 \cdot 0.01 = 0.1$ to the slope, and $(y - \hat{y})\eta$ $= (15 - 13) \cdot 0.01 = 0.02$ to the y-intercept, thus obtaining the model with equation

$$\hat{y} = 2.1x + 3.02.$$

Chapter 4: Optimizing the training process: Underfitting, overfitting, testing, and regularization

Exercise 4.1

We have trained four models in the same dataset with different hyperparameters. In the following table we have recorded the training and testing errors for each of the models.

Model	Training error	Testing error
1	0.1	1.8
2	0.4	1.2
3	0.6	0.8
4	1.9	2.3

a. Which model would you select for this dataset?

b. Which model looks like it's underfitting the data?

c. Which model looks like it's overfitting the data?

Solution

a. The best model is the one with the smallest testing error, which is model 3.

b. Model 4 looks like it is underfitting because it has large training and testing errors.

c. Models 1 and 2 look like they are overfitting, because they have small training errors but large testing errors.

Exercise 4.2

We are given the following dataset:

x	y
1	2
2	2.5
3	6
4	14.5
5	34

We train the polynomial regression model that predicts the value of y as $\hat{y}$, where

$$\hat{y} = 2x^2 - 5x + 4.$$

If the regularization parameter is $\lambda = 0.1$ and the error function we've used to train this dataset is the mean absolute value (MAE), determine the following:

a. The lasso regression error of our model (using the L1-norm)

b. The ridge regression error of our model (using the L2-norm)

Solution

First we need to find the predictions to calculate the mean absolute error of the model. In the following table, we can find the prediction calculated by the formula $\hat{y} = 2x^2 - 5x + 4$, and the absolute value of the difference between the prediction and the label $|y - \hat{y}|$.

x	y	$\hat{y}$	$\|y - \hat{y}\|$
1	2	1	1
2	2.5	2	0.5
3	6	7	1
4	14.5	16	1.5
5	34	29	5

Thus, the mean absolute error is the average of the numbers in the fourth row, namely

$$\frac{1}{5}(1 + 0.5 + 1 + 1.5 + 5) = 1.8.$$

a. First we need to find the L1-norm of the polynomial. This is the sum of the absolute values of the nonconstant coefficients, namely, $|2| + |-5| = 7$. To find the L1-regularization cost of the model, we add the mean absolute error and the L1-norm times the regularization parameter, to obtain $1.8 + 0.1 \cdot 7 = 2.5$.

b. In a similar way, we find the L1-norm of the polynomial by adding the squares of nonconstant coefficients to get $2^2 + (-5)^2 = 29$. As before, the L2-regularization cost of the model is $1.8 + 0.1 \cdot 29 = 4.7$.

Chapter 5: Using lines to split our points: The perceptron algorithm

Exercise 5.1

The following is a dataset of patients who have tested positive or negative for COVID-19. Their symptoms are cough (C), fever (F), difficulty breathing (B), and tiredness (T).

	Cough (C)	Fever (F)	Difficulty breathing (B)	Tiredness (T)	Diagnosis (D)
Patient 1		X	X	X	Sick
Patient 2	X	X		X	Sick
Patient 3	X		X	X	Sick
Patient 4	X	X	X		Sick
Patient 5	X			X	Healthy
Patient 6		X	X		Healthy
Patient 7		X			Healthy
Patient 8				X	Healthy

Build a perceptron model that classifies this dataset.

> **hint** You can use the perceptron algorithm, but you may be able to eyeball a good perceptron model that works.

Solution

If we count how many symptoms each patient has, we notice that the sick patients show three or more symptoms, whereas the healthy patients show two or fewer symptoms. Thus, the following model works to predict the diagnosis D:

$$\hat{D} = step(C + F + B + T - 2.5)$$

Exercise 5.2

Consider the perceptron model that assigns to the point (x_1, x_2) the prediction $\hat{y} = step(2x_1 + 3x_2 - 4)$. This model has as a boundary line with equation $2x_1 + 3x_2 - 4 = 0$. We have the point $p = (1, 1)$ with label 0.

a. Verify that the point p is misclassified by the model.

b. Calculate the perceptron error that the model produces at the point p.

c. Use the perceptron trick to obtain a new model that still misclassifies p but that produces a smaller error. You can use $\eta = 0.01$ as the learning rate.

d. Find the prediction given by the new model at the point p, and verify that the perceptron error obtained is smaller than the original.

Solution

a. The prediction for the point p is

$$\hat{y} = step(2x_1 + 3x_2 - 4) = step(2 \cdot 1 + 3 \cdot 1 - 4) = step(1) = 1.$$

Because the label of the point is 0, the point is misclassified.

b. The perceptron error is the absolute value of the score. The score is $2x_1 + 3x_2 - 4 = 2 \cdot 1 + 3 \cdot 1 - 4 = 1$, so the perceptron error is 1.

c. The weights of the model are 2, 3, and −4, and the coordinates of the point are (1, 1). The perceptron trick does the following:

- Replaces 2 with $2 - 0.01 \cdot 1 = 1.99$

- Replaces 3 with $3 - 0.01 \cdot 1 = 2.99$

- Replaces −4 with $-1 - 0.01 \cdot 1 = -4.01$

Thus, the new model is the one that makes the prediction $\hat{y} = step(1.99x_1 + 2.99x_2 - 4.01)$.

d. Note that at our point, the new prediction is $\hat{y} = step(1.99x_1 + 2.99x_2 - 4.01) = step(0.97) = 0$, which means the model still misclassifies the point. However, the new perceptron error is $|1.99 \cdot 1 + 2.99 \cdot 1 - 4.01| = 0.97$, which is smaller than 1, the previous error.

Exercise 5.3

Perceptrons are particularly useful for building logical gates such as AND and OR.

a. Build a perceptron that models the AND gate. In other words, build a perceptron to fit the following dataset (where x_1, x_2 are the features and y is the label):

x_1	x_2	y
0	0	0
0	1	0
1	0	0
1	1	1

b. Similarly, build a perceptron that models the OR gate, given by the following dataset:

x_1	x_2	y
0	0	0
0	1	1
1	0	1
1	1	1

c. Show that there is no perceptron that models the XOR gate, given by the following dataset:

x_1	x_2	y
0	0	0
0	1	1
1	0	1
1	1	0

Solution

For simplicity, we plot the data points in the figure that follows.

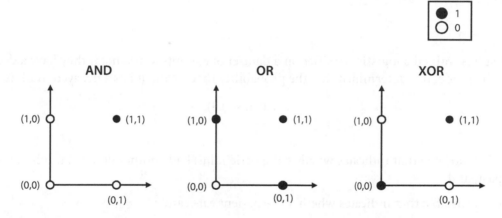

Note that a perceptron classifier is precisely a line that would split the black and white dots in the above plots.

For the AND and OR datasets, we can easily split the black and white points with a line, as seen next.

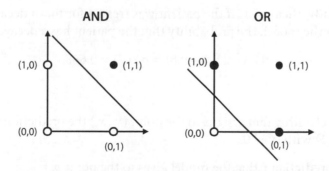

a. Many equations work for the line separating the AND dataset. We'll pick the line with equation $x_1 + x_2 - 1.5$. Thus, the perceptron that classifies this dataset makes the prediction $\hat{y} = step(x_1 + x_2 - 1.5)$.

b. Similarly, many equations work for the OR dataset, and we pick the line with equation $x_1 + x_2 - 0.5$. The equation for the prediction is $\hat{y} = step(x_1 + x_2 - 0.5)$.

c. Notice that the dataset for XOR is impossible to separate using a single line. Thus, there is no perceptron model that perfectly fits the XOR dataset. However, a combination of perceptrons can separate this dataset. These are also called multilayer perceptrons, or neural networks, and we'll see them in chapter 10. If you're curious, take a look at exercise 10.2.

Chapter 6: A continuous approach to splitting points: Logistic classifiers

Exercise 6.1

A dentist has trained a logistic classifier on a dataset of patients to predict if they have a decayed tooth. The model has determined that the probability that a patient has a decayed tooth is

$$\sigma(d + 0.5c - 0.8),$$

where

- d is a variable that indicates whether the patient has had another decayed tooth in the past, and

- c is a variable that indicates whether the patient eats candy.

For example, if a patient eats candy, then $c = 1$, and if they don't, then $c = 0$. What is the probability that a patient that eats candy and was treated for a decayed tooth last year has a decayed tooth today?

Solution

If the patient eats candy, then $c = 1$. If the patient was treated for tooth decay last year, then $d = 1$. Thus, according to the model, the probability that the patient has a decayed tooth is

$$\sigma(1 + 0.5 \cdot 1 - 0.8) = \sigma(0.7) = 0.668.$$

Exercise 6.2

Consider the logistic classifier that assigns to the point (x_1, x_2) the prediction $\hat{y} = \sigma(2x_1 + 3x_2 - 4)$, and the point $p = (1, 1)$ with label 0.

a. Calculate the prediction $\hat{y}$ that the model gives to the point p.

b. Calculate the log loss that the model produces at the point p.

c. Use the logistic trick to obtain a new model that produces a smaller log loss. You can use $\eta = 0.1$ as the learning rate.

d. Find the prediction given by the new model at the point p, and verify that the log loss obtained is smaller than the original.

Solution

a. The prediction is $\hat{y} = \sigma(2 \cdot 1 + 3 \cdot 1 - 4) = \sigma(1) = 0.731$

b. The log loss is

$$log\ loss = -y\ ln\ (\hat{y}) - (1 - y)\ ln\ (1 - \hat{y})$$

$$= -0\ ln\ (0.731) - (1 - 0)\ ln\ (1 - 0.731)$$

$$= 1.313.$$

c. Recall that the perceptron trick for the logistic regression model with prediction $\hat{y} = \sigma(w_1 x_1 + w_2 x_2 + b)$ gives us the following new weights:

- $w_i' = w_i + \eta(y - \hat{y})\ x_i$ for $i = 1,2$
- $b' = b + \eta(y - \hat{y})$ for $i = 1,2$

These are the values to plug into the previous formulas:

- $y = 0$
- $\hat{y} = 0.731$
- $w_1 = 2$
- $w_2 = 3$
- $b = -4$
- $\eta = 0.1$
- $x_1 = 1$
- $x_2 = 1$

We obtain the following new weights for our classifier:

- $w_1' = 2 + 0.1 \cdot (0 - 0.731) \cdot 1 = 1.9269$
- $w_2' = 3 + 0.1 \cdot (0 - 0.731) \cdot 1 = 2.9269$
- $b = -4 + 0.1 \cdot (0 - 0.731) = -4.0731$

Thus, our new classifier is the one that makes the prediction $\hat{y} = \sigma(1.9269x_1 + 2.9269x_2 - 4.0731)$.

The prediction at the point p is $\hat{y} = \sigma(1.9269 \cdot 1 + 2.9269 \cdot 1 - 4.0731) = 0.686$. Notice that because the label is 0, the prediction has improved from the original 0.731, to the actual 0.686.

d. The log loss for this prediction is $-y \ln(\hat{y}) - (1 - y) \ln(1 - \hat{y}) = -0 \ln(0.686) - (1 - 0)$ $\ln(1 - 0.686) = 1.158$. Note that this is smaller than the original log loss of 1.313.

Exercise 6.3

Using the first model in exercise 6.2, construct a point for which the prediction is 0.8.

> **hint**　First find the score that will give a prediction of 0.8, and recall that the prediction is $\hat{y} = \sigma(\text{score})$.

Solution

First, we need to find a score such that $\sigma(\text{score}) = 0.8$. This is equivalent to

$$\frac{e^{score}}{1 + e^{score}} = 0.8$$

$$e^{score} = 0.8(1 + e^{score})$$

$$e^{score} = 0.8 + 0.8 \cdot e^{score}$$

$$0.2e^{score} = 0.8$$

$$e^{score} = 4$$

$$score = \ln(4) = 1.386.$$

Recall that for the point (x_1, x_2), the score is $2x_1 + 3x_2 - 4$. Many points (x_1, x_2) satisfy that the score is 1.386, but in particular, let's pick one in which $x_2 = 0$ for convenience. We need to solve the equation $2x_1 + 3 \cdot 0 - 4 = 1.386$, which has as a solution, $x_1 = 2.693$. Thus, a point that gives a prediction of 0.8 is the point (2.693, 0).

Chapter 7: How do you measure classification models? Accuracy and its friends

Exercise 7.1

A video site has established that a particular user likes animal videos and absolutely nothing else. In the next figure, we can see the recommendations that this user got when logging in to the site.

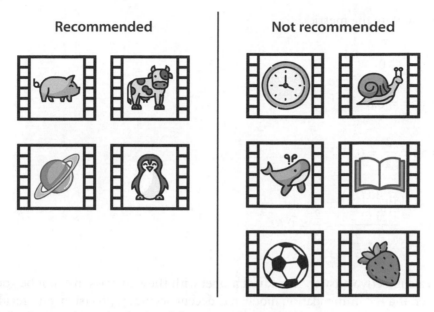

Recommended   Not recommended

If this is all the data we have on the model, answer the following questions:

a. What is the accuracy of the model?

b. What is the recall of the model?

c. What is the precision of the model?

d. What is the F_1-score of the model?

e. Would you say that this is a good recommendation model?

Solution

First, let's write the confusion matrix. In this case, we label the videos that are about animals as *positive*, and the videos that are recommended as *predicted positive*.

- There are four recommended videos. Out of them, three are about animals, which means they are good recommendations. The other one is not about animals, so it is a false positive.

- There are six videos that are not recommended. Out of them, two are about animals, which should have been recommended. Thus, they are false negatives. The other four are not about animals, so it was correct not to recommend them.

Thus, the confusion matrix is the following:

	Predicted positive (recommended)	Predicted negative (not recommended)
Positive (about animals)	3	2
Negative (not about animals)	1	4

Now we can calculate the metrics.

a. Accuracy $= \dfrac{7}{10} = 0.7$

b. Recall $= \dfrac{3}{5} = 0.6$

c. Precision $= \dfrac{3}{4} = 0.75$

d. F_1-score $= \dfrac{2\left(\dfrac{3}{4}\right)\left(\dfrac{3}{5}\right)}{\dfrac{3}{4} + \dfrac{3}{5}} = \dfrac{2}{3} = 0.67$

e. This is a subjective answer. A medical model with these metrics may not be good enough. However, if a recommendation model has decent accuracy, precision, and recall, it is considered a good model, because making a couple of mistakes in a recommendation model is not as crucial.

Exercise 7.2

Find the sensitivity and specificity of the medical model with the following confusion matrix:

	Predicted sick	**Predicted healthy**
Sick	120	22
Healthy	63	795

Solution

The sensitivity is the number of correctly predicted sick people divided by the total number of sick people. This is $\dfrac{120}{142} = 0.845$.

The specificity is the number of correctly predicted healthy people divided by the total number of healthy people. This is $\dfrac{795}{858} = 0.927$.

Exercise 7.3

For the following models, determine which error is worse, a false positive or a false negative. Based on that, determine which of the two metrics, precision or recall, we should emphasize when evaluating each of the models.

1. A movie recommendation system that predicts whether a user will watch a movie.

2. An image-detection model used in self-driving cars that detects whether an image contains a pedestrian.

3. A voice assistant at home that predicts whether the user gave it an order.

Solution

note   In all of the following models, a false negative and a false positive are bad, and we want to avoid both of them. However, we show an argument for which one of the two is worse. These are all conceptual questions, so if you have a different idea, as long as you can argue it well, it is valid! These are the kind of discussions that arise in a team of data scientists, and it is important to have healthy opinions and arguments supporting each point of view.

1. In this model, we label the movies that the user wants to watch as positives. A false positive occurs any time we recommend a movie that the user doesn't want to watch. A false negative occurs any time there is a movie that the user wants to watch, but we don't recommend it. Which is worse, a false negative or a false positive? Because the homepage shows many recommendations and the user ignores most of them, this model has many false negatives that don't affect the user experience much. However, if there is a great movie that the user would like to watch, it is crucial to recommend it to them. Therefore, in this model, a false negative is worse than a false positive, so we should evaluate this model using **recall**.

2. In this model, we label the existence of a pedestrian as a positive. A false positive occurs when there is no pedestrian, but the car thinks there is a pedestrian. A false negative occurs when the car doesn't detect a pedestrian that is in front of the car. In the case of a false negative, the car may hit a pedestrian. In the case of a false positive, the car may brake unnecessarily, which may or may not lead to an accident. Although both are serious, it is much worse to hit a pedestrian. Therefore, in this model, a false negative is worse than a false positive, so we should evaluate this model using **recall**.

3. In this model, we label a voice command as a positive. A false positive occurs when the user is not talking to the voice assistant, but the voice assistant responds. A false negative occurs when the user is talking to the voice assistant, but the voice assistant doesn't respond. As a personal choice, I prefer to have to repeat to my voice assistant than to have her speak to me out of the blue. Thus, in this model, a false positive is worse than a false negative, so we should evaluate this model using **precision**.

Exercise 7.4

We are given the following models:

1. A self-driving car model for detecting a pedestrian based on the image from the car's camera

2. A medical model for diagnosing a deadly illness based on the patient's symptoms

3. A recommendation system for movies based on the user's previous movies watched

4. A voice assistant that determines whether the user needs assistance given the voice command

5. A spam-detection model that determines whether an email is spam based on the words in the email

We are given the task of evaluating these models using F_β-scores. However, we haven't been given the values of β to use. What value of β would you use to evaluate each of the models?

Solution

Remember that for models in which precision is more important than recall, we use an F_β-score with a small value of β. In contrast, for models in which recall is more important than precision, we use an F_β-score with a large value of β.

> **note** If you have different scores than this solution, that is completely OK, as long as you have an argument for which is more important between precision and recall, and for the value of β that you choose.

- For the self-driving car and the medical models, recall is tremendously important because we want very few false negatives. Thus, I would use a large value of β, such as 4.

- For the spam-detection model, precision is important, because we want very few false positives. Thus, I would use a small value of β, such as 0.25.

- For the recommendation system, recall is more important (see exercise 7.3), although precision also matters. Thus, I would use a large value of β, such as 2.

- For the voice assistant, precision is more important, although recall also matters (see exercise 7.3). Thus, I would use a small value for β, such as 0.5.

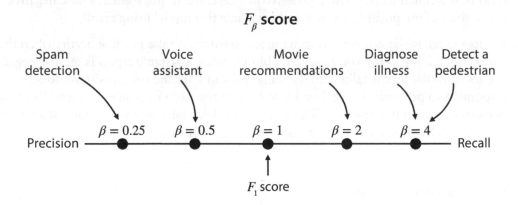

Chapter 8: Using probability to its maximum: The naive Bayes model

Exercise 8.1

For each pair of events A and B, determine whether they are independent or dependent. For (a) to (d), provide mathematical justification. For (e) and (f) provide verbal justification.

Throwing three fair coins:

    a. A: First one falls on heads. B: Third one falls on tails.

    b. A: First one falls on heads. B: There is an odd number of heads among the three throws.

Rolling two dice:

    c. A: First one shows a 1. B: Second one shows a 2.

    d. A: First one shows a 3. B: Second one shows a higher value than the first one.

For the following, provide a verbal justification. Assume that for this problem, we live in a place with seasons.

    e. A: It's raining outside. B: It's Monday.

    f. A: It's raining outside. B: It's June.

Solution

Some of the following can be deduced by intuition. However, sometimes intuition fails when determining whether two events are independent. For this reason, unless the events are obviously independent, we'll stick to checking whether two events A and B are independent if $P(A \cap B) = P(A)\,P(B)$.

    a. Because A and B correspond to tossing different coins, they are independent events.

    b. $P(A) = \dfrac{1}{2}$ because flipping a fair coin results in two equally likely scenarios. For the calculation of $P(B)$, we'll use "h" for heads and "t" for tails. This way, the event "hth" corresponds to the first and third coin toss landing on heads and the second one landing on tails. Thus, if we throw three coins, the eight equally likely possibilities are {hhh, hht, hth, htt, thh, tht, tth, ttt}. $P(B) = \dfrac{4}{8} = \dfrac{1}{2}$ because among the eight equally likely possibilities (hhh, hht, hth, htt, thh, tht, tth, ttt), only four of them have an odd number of heads, namely, {hhh, htt, tht, tth}. $P(A \cap B) = \dfrac{2}{4} = \dfrac{1}{2}$ because among the eight possibilities, only two satisfy that the first one falls on heads, and there are an odd number of heads, namely, {hhh, htt}. $P(A)\, P(B) = \dfrac{1}{4} = P(A \cap B)$, so the events A and B are independent.

c. Because A and B correspond to tossing different dice, they are independent events.

d. $P(A) = \dfrac{1}{6}$, because it corresponds to tossing a die and obtaining a particular value.

$P(B) = \dfrac{5}{12}$ for the following reason. Notice that the 36 equally likely possibilities for the scores of the two dice are {11, 12, 13, …, 56, 66}. In six of these, the two dice show the same value. The remaining 30 correspond to 15 in which the first value is higher, and 15 in which the second value is higher, by symmetry. Therefore, there are 15 scenarios in which the second die shows a higher value than the third one, so $P(B) = \dfrac{15}{36} = \dfrac{5}{12}$.

$P(A \cap B) = \dfrac{1}{2}$ for the following reason. If the first die falls on 3, we have a total of six equally likely scenarios, namely, {31, 32, 33, 34, 35, 36}. Out of these six, the second number is higher for three of them. Thus, $P(A \cap B) = \dfrac{3}{6} = \dfrac{1}{2}$. Because $P(A)\, P(B) \neq P(A \cap B)$, the events A and B are dependent.

e. For this problem, we'll make the assumption that A and B are independent, namely, that weather is not dependent on the day of the week. This is a fair assumption, given our knowledge of weather, but if we wanted to be surer, we could look at weather datasets and verify this by calculating the corresponding probabilities.

f. Because we've assumed that we live in a place with seasons, June is summer in the northern hemisphere and winter in the southern hemisphere. Depending on where we live, it may rain more in the winter or in the summer. Thus, we can assume that events A and B are dependent.

Exercise 8.2

There is an office where we have to go regularly for some paperwork. This office has two clerks, Aisha and Beto. We know that Aisha works there three days a week, and Beto works the other two However, the schedules change every week, so we never know which three days Aisha is there, and which two days Beto is there.

a. If we show up on a random day to the office, what is the probability that Aisha is the clerk?

We look from outside and notice that the clerk is wearing a red sweater, although we can't tell who the clerk is. We've been going to that office a lot, so we know that Beto tends to wear red more often than Aisha. In fact, Aisha wears red one day out of three (one-third of the time), and Beto wears red one day out of two (half of the time).

b. What is the probability that Aisha is the clerk, knowing that the clerk is wearing red today?

Solution

Let's use the following notation for events:

- A: the event that the clerk is Aisha

- B: The event that the clerk is Beto

- R: The event that the clerk is wearing red

a. Because Aisha works at the office three days and Beto works two days, the probability that Aisha is the clerk is $P(A) = \frac{3}{5}$, or 60%. In addition, the probability that Beto is the clerk is $P(B) = \frac{2}{5}$, or 40%.

b. Intuitively, because Beto wears red more often than Aisha, we imagine that the probability that the clerk is Aisha is lower than in part a). Let's check whether the math agrees with us. We know the clerk is wearing red, so we need to find the probability that the clerk is Aisha *knowing that* the clerk is wearing red. This is $P(A \mid R)$.

The probability that Aisha wears red is $\frac{1}{3}$, so $P(R \mid A) = \frac{1}{3}$. The probability that Beto wears red is $\frac{1}{2}$, so $P(R \mid B) = \frac{1}{2}$.

We can use Bayes theorem to obtain

$$P(A \mid R) = \frac{P(R \mid A)P(A)}{P(R \mid A)P(A) + P(R \mid B)P(B)} = \frac{\frac{1}{3} \cdot \frac{3}{5}}{\frac{1}{3} \cdot \frac{3}{5} + \frac{1}{2} \cdot \frac{2}{5}} = \frac{\frac{1}{5}}{\frac{1}{5} + \frac{1}{5}} = \frac{1}{2}, \text{ or } 50\%.$$

A similar calculation shows that the probability that Beto is the clerk is $P(B \mid R) = \frac{1}{2}$, or 50%.

In effect, the probability that Aisha is the clerk is smaller than the one obtained in part a), so our intuition was right.

Exercise 8.3

The following is a dataset of patients who have tested positive or negative for COVID-19. Their symptoms are cough (C), fever (F), difficulty breathing (B), and tiredness (T).

	Cough (C)	Fever (F)	Difficulty breathing (B)	Tiredness (T)	Diagnosis
Patient 1		X	X	X	Sick
Patient 2	X	X		X	Sick
Patient 3	X		X	X	Sick
Patient 4	X	X	X		Sick
Patient 5	X			X	Healthy
Patient 6		X	X		Healthy
Patient 7		X			Healthy
Patient 8				X	Healthy

The goal of this exercise is to build a naive Bayes model that predicts the diagnosis from the symptoms. Use the naive Bayes algorithm to find the following probabilities:

note   For the following questions, the symptoms that are not mentioned are completely unknown to us. For example, if we know that the patient has a cough, but nothing is said about their fever, it does not mean the patient doesn't have a fever.

a. The probability that a patient is sick given that the patient has a cough

b. The probability that a patient is sick given that the patient is not tired

c. The probability that a patient is sick given that the patient has a cough and a fever

d. The probability that a patient is sick given that the patient has a cough and a fever, but no difficulty breathing

Solution

For this problem, we have the following events:

*   C: the event that the patient has a cough

*   F: the event that the patient has a fever

*   B: the event that the patient has difficulty breathing

*   T: the event that the patient is tired

*   S: the event that the patient has been diagnosed as sick

*   H: the event that the patient has been diagnosed as healthy

Furthermore, A^c denotes the complement (opposite) of the event A. Thus, for example, T^c represents the event that the patient is not tired.

First, let's calculate $P(S)$ and $P(H)$. Note that because the dataset contains four healthy and four sick patients, both of these (prior) probabilities are $\frac{1}{2}$, or 50%.

a. Because four patients have a cough and three of them are sick, $P(S \mid C) = \frac{3}{4}$, or 75%.

Equivalently, we can use Bayes' theorem in the following way: first, we calculate $P(S \mid C) = \frac{3}{4}$ by noticing that there are four sick patients, and three of them have a cough.

We also notice that $P(C \mid H) = \frac{1}{4}$, because there are four healthy patients, and only one of them has a cough.

Now we can use the formula

$$P(S \mid C) = \frac{P(C \mid S)P(S)}{P(C \mid S)P(S) + P(C \mid H)P(H)} = \frac{\frac{3}{4} \cdot \frac{1}{2}}{\frac{3}{4} \cdot \frac{1}{2} + \frac{1}{4} \cdot \frac{1}{2}} = \frac{3}{4}.$$

b. Because three patients are not tired and only one of them is sick, $P(S \mid T^c) = \frac{1}{3}$, or 33.3%.

We can also use Bayes' theorem as before. Notice that $P(T^c \mid S) = \frac{1}{4}$ because only one out of the four sick patients is not tired. Also, $P(T^c \mid H) = \frac{2}{4}$, because two out of the four healthy patients are not tired.

By Bayes' theorem,

$$P(S \mid T^c) = \frac{P(T^c \mid S)P(S)}{P(T^c \mid S)P(S) + P(T^c \mid H)P(H)} = \frac{\frac{1}{4} \cdot \frac{1}{2}}{\frac{1}{4} \cdot \frac{1}{2} + \frac{2}{4} \cdot \frac{1}{2}} = \frac{\frac{1}{8}}{\frac{1}{8} + \frac{2}{8}} = \frac{1}{3}.$$

c. $C \cap F$ represents the event that the patient has a cough and a fever, so we need to calculate $P(S \mid C \cap F)$.

Recall from part a) that $P(S \mid C) = \frac{3}{4}$ and $P(C \mid H) = \frac{1}{4}$.

Now we need to calculate $P(F \mid S)$ and $P(F \mid H)$. Note that because there are four sick patients and three of them have a fever, $P(F \mid S) = \dfrac{3}{4}$. Similarly, two out of the four healthy patients have a fever, so $P(F \mid H) = \dfrac{2}{4} = \dfrac{1}{2}$.

We are ready to use the naive Bayes algorithm to estimate the probability that the patient is sick given that they have a cough and fever. Using the formula in the section "What about two words? The naive Bayes algorithm" in chapter 8, we get

$$P(S \mid C \cap F) = \frac{P(C \mid S)P(F \mid S)P(S)}{P(C \mid S)P(F \mid S)P(S) + P(C \mid H)P(F \mid H)P(H)}$$

$$= \frac{\dfrac{3}{4} \cdot \dfrac{3}{4} \cdot \dfrac{1}{2}}{\dfrac{3}{4} \cdot \dfrac{3}{4} \cdot \dfrac{1}{2} + \dfrac{1}{4} \cdot \dfrac{2}{4} \cdot \dfrac{1}{2}} = \frac{\dfrac{9}{32}}{\dfrac{9}{32} + \dfrac{2}{32}} = \frac{9}{11} \text{ or } 81.82\%.$$

d. For this exercise we need to find $P(S \mid C \cap F \cap B^c)$.

Note that because there are four sick patients and only one of them has no difficulty breathing, $P(B^c \mid S) = \dfrac{1}{4}$. Similarly, there are four healthy patients and three of them have no difficulty breathing, so $P(B^c \mid H) = \dfrac{3}{4}$.

As before, we can use the naive Bayes algorithm.

$$P(S \mid C \cap F \cap B^c) = \frac{P(C \mid S)P(F \mid S)P(B^c \mid S)P(S)}{P(C \mid S)P(F \mid S)P(B^c \mid S)P(S) + P(C \mid H)P(F \mid H)P(B^c \mid H)P(H)}$$

$$\frac{\dfrac{3}{4} \cdot \dfrac{3}{4} \cdot \dfrac{1}{4} \cdot \dfrac{1}{2}}{\dfrac{3}{4} \cdot \dfrac{3}{4} \cdot \dfrac{1}{4} \cdot \dfrac{1}{2} + \dfrac{1}{4} \cdot \dfrac{2}{4} \cdot \dfrac{3}{4} \cdot \dfrac{1}{2}} = \frac{\dfrac{9}{32}}{\dfrac{9}{32} + \dfrac{6}{32}} = \frac{9}{15} \text{, or } 60\%.$$

Chapter 9: Splitting data by asking questions: Decision trees

Exercise 9.1

In the following spam-detection decision tree model, determine whether an email from your mom with the subject line "Please go to the store, there's a sale," will be classified as spam.

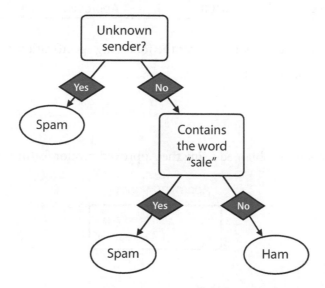

Solution

First we check whether the sender is unknown. Because the sender is our mom, the sender is not unknown. Thus, we take the branch on the right. We must check whether the email contains the word "sale." The email contains the word "sale," so the classifier (incorrectly) classifies it as spam.

Exercise 9.2

Our goal is to build a decision tree model to determine whether credit card transactions are fraudulent. We use the dataset of credit card transactions below, with the following features:

- **Value:** value of the transaction.

- **Approved vendor:** the credit card company has a list of approved vendors. This variable indicates whether the vendor is in this list.

	Value	Approved vendor	Fraudulent
Transaction 1	$100	Not approved	Yes
Transaction 2	$100	Approved	No
Transaction 3	$10,000	Approved	No
Transaction 4	$10,000	Not approved	Yes
Transaction 5	$5,000	Approved	Yes
Transaction 6	$100	Approved	No

Build the first node of the decision tree under the following specifications:

a. Using the Gini impurity index

b. Using entropy

Solution

In both cases, the best split is obtained using the Approved vendor feature, as in the next image.

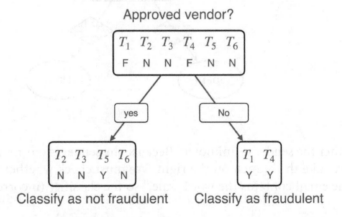

Let's call the transactions T_1, T_2, T_3, T_4, T_5, and T_6.

First, let's look at all the following splits we can make. The split using Approved vendor is easy, because this is a categorical variable with two categories. The Value column is more complicated—we can use it to split the data in two possible ways. One is when the cutoff is some value between $100 and $5,000, and the other one when it is some value between $5,000 and $10,000. To summarize, these are all the possible splits:

- **Value 1:** where the cutoff value is between $100 and $5,000. The two classes here are $\{T_1, T_2, T_6\}$ and $\{T_3, T_4, T_5\}$.

- **Value 2:** where the cutoff value is some value between $5,000 and $10,000. The two classes here are $\{T_1, T_2, T_5, T_6\}$ and $\{T_3, T_4\}$.

- **Approved vendor:** the two classes are "approved" and "not approved," or equivalently, $\{T_2, T_3, T_5, T_6\}$ and $\{T_1, T_4\}$.

a. Let's calculate the Gini impurity index for each one of the following four splits:

Value 1: cutoff value between \$100 and \$5,000

Note that for the first class $\{T_1, T_2, T_6\}$, the labels in the Fraudulent column are {"yes", "no", "no"}. The Gini impurity index of this split is $1-\left(\dfrac{1}{3}\right)^2-\left(\dfrac{2}{3}\right)^2=\dfrac{4}{9}$.

Note that for the second class $\{T_3, T_4, T_5\}$, the labels in the Fraudulent column are {"no", "yes", "yes"}. The Gini impurity index of this split is $1-\left(\dfrac{2}{3}\right)^2-\left(\dfrac{1}{3}\right)^2=\dfrac{4}{9}$.

Thus, the weighted Gini impurity index for this split is $\dfrac{3}{6}\cdot\dfrac{4}{9}+\dfrac{3}{6}\cdot\dfrac{4}{9}=\dfrac{4}{9}=0.444$.

Value 2: cutoff value between \$5,000 and \$10,000

For the first class $\{T_1, T_2, T_5, T_6\}$, the labels in the Fraudulent column are {"yes", "no", "yes", "no"}. The Gini impurity index of this split is $1-\left(\dfrac{2}{4}\right)^2-\left(\dfrac{2}{4}\right)^2=\dfrac{1}{2}$.

Note that for the second class $\{T_3, T_4\}$, the labels in the Fraudulent column are {"no", "yes"}. The Gini impurity index of this split is $1-\left(\dfrac{1}{2}\right)^2-\left(\dfrac{1}{2}\right)^2=\dfrac{1}{2}$.

Thus, the weighted Gini impurity index for this split is $\dfrac{4}{6}\cdot\dfrac{1}{2}+\dfrac{2}{6}\cdot\dfrac{1}{2}=\dfrac{1}{2}=0.5$.

Approved vendor:

For the first class $\{T_2, T_3, T_5, T_6\}$, the labels in the Fraudulent column are {"no", "no", "yes," "no"}. The Gini impurity index of this split is $1-\left(\dfrac{3}{4}\right)^2-\left(\dfrac{1}{4}\right)^2=\dfrac{6}{16}$.

For the second class $\{T_1, T_4\}$, the labels in the Fraudulent column are {"yes", "yes"}. The Gini impurity index of this split is $1 - 1^2 = 0$.

Thus, the weighted Gini impurity index for this split is $\dfrac{4}{6}\cdot\dfrac{6}{16}+\dfrac{2}{6}\cdot 0=\dfrac{1}{4}=0.25$.

Notice that out of these three values, the lowest is 0.25, corresponding to the Approved vendor column. This implies that the best way to split this data is using the Approved vendor feature.

b. For this part, we've done most of the heavy lifting already. We'll follow the same procedure as in part a), except calculating the entropy at each stage instead of the Gini impurity index.

Value 1: cutoff value between $100 and $5,000

The entropy of the set {"yes", "no", "no"} is $-\frac{1}{3}log_2\left(\frac{1}{3}\right)-\frac{2}{3}log_2\left(\frac{2}{3}\right)=0.918$.

The entropy of the set {"no", "yes", "yes"} is also $-\frac{2}{3}log_2\left(\frac{2}{3}\right)-\frac{1}{3}log_2\left(\frac{1}{3}\right)=0.918$.

Thus, the weighted entropy for this split is $\frac{3}{6}\cdot0.918+\frac{3}{6}\cdot0.918=0.918$.

Value 2: cutoff value between $5,000 and $10,000

The entropy of the set {"yes", "no", "yes", "no"} is $-\frac{2}{4}log_2\left(\frac{2}{4}\right)-\frac{2}{4}log_2\left(\frac{2}{4}\right)=1$.

The entropy of the set {"no", "yes"} is $-\frac{1}{2}log_2\left(\frac{1}{2}\right)-\frac{1}{2}log_2\left(\frac{1}{2}\right)=1$.

Thus, the weighted entropy for this split is $\frac{4}{6}\cdot1+\frac{2}{6}\cdot1=1$.

Approved vendor:

The entropy of the set {"no", "no", "yes", "no"} is $-\frac{1}{4}log_2\left(\frac{1}{4}\right)-\frac{3}{4}log_2\left(\frac{3}{4}\right)=0.811$.

The entropy of the set {"yes", "yes"} is $-\frac{2}{2}log_2\left(\frac{2}{2}\right)=0$.

Thus, the weighted entropy for this split is $\frac{4}{6}\cdot0.811+\frac{2}{6}\cdot0=0.541$.

Notice that among these three, the smallest entropy is 0.541, corresponding to the Approved vendor column. Thus, the best way to split this data is, again, using the Approved vendor feature.

Exercise 9.3

A dataset of patients who have tested positive or negative for COVID-19 follows. Their symptoms are cough (C), fever (F), difficulty breathing (B), and tiredness (T).

	Cough (C)	Fever (F)	Difficulty breathing (B)	Tiredness (T)	Diagnosis
Patient 1		X	X	X	Sick
Patient 2	X	X		X	Sick
Patient 3	X		X	X	Sick
Patient 4	X	X	X		Sick
Patient 5	X			X	Healthy
Patient 6		X	X		Healthy
Patient 7		X			Healthy
Patient 8				X	Healthy

Using accuracy, build a decision tree of height 1 (a decision stump) that classifies this data. What is the accuracy of this classifier on the dataset?

Solution

Let's call the patients P_1 up to P_8. The sick patients will be denoted by "s," and the healthy ones by "h."

First notice that the first split can be any of the four features C, F, B, and T. Let's first calculate the accuracy of the classifier obtained by splitting the data on feature C, namely, the classifier we build based on the question, "Does the patient have a cough?"

Splitting based on the C feature:

- Patients with a cough: $\{P_2, P_3, P_4, P_5\}$. Their labels are $\{s, s, s, h\}$.
- Patients without a cough: $\{P_1, P_6, P_7, P_8\}$. Their labels are $\{s, h, h, h\}$.

Looking at this, we can see that the most accurate classifier (only based on the C feature) is the one that classifies every person with a cough as sick and every person without a cough as healthy. This classifier correctly classifies six out of the eight patients (three sick and three healthy), so its accuracy is 6/8, or 75%.

Now, let's follow the same procedure with the other three features.

Splitting based on the F feature:

- Patients with a fever: $\{P_1, P_2, P_4, P_6, P_7\}$. Their labels are $\{s, s, s, h, h\}$.
- Patients without a fever: $\{P_3, P_5, P_8\}$. Their labels are $\{s, h, h\}$.

Looking at this, we can see that the most accurate classifier (only based on the F feature) is the one that classifies every patient with a fever as sick and every patient without a fever as healthy. This classifier correctly classifies five out of the eight patients (three sick and two healthy), so its accuracy is 5/8, or 62.5%.

Splitting based on the B feature:

- Patients showing difficulty breathing: $\{P_1, P_3, P_4, P_5\}$. Their labels are $\{s, s, s, h\}$.

- Patients not showing difficulty breathing: $\{P_2, P_6, P_7, P_8\}$. Their labels are $\{s, h, h, h\}$.

Looking at this, we can see that the most accurate classifier (based only on the T feature) is the one that classifies every patient showing difficulty breathing as sick and every patient not showing difficulty breathing as healthy. This classifier correctly classifies six out of the eight patients (three sick and three healthy), so its accuracy is 6/8, or 75%.

Splitting based on the T feature:

- Patients that are tired: $\{P_1, P_2, P_3, P_5, P_8\}$. Their labels are $\{s, s, s, h, h\}$.

- Patients that are not tired: $\{P_4, P_5, P_7\}$. Their labels are $\{s, h, h\}$.

Looking at this, we can see that the most accurate classifier (based only on the F feature) is the one that classifies every tired patient as sick and every patient that is not tired as healthy. This classifier correctly classifies five out of the eight patients (three sick and two healthy), so its accuracy is 5/8, or 62.5%.

Note that the two features that give us the best accuracy are C (cough) and B (difficulty breathing). The decision tree will pick one of these at random. Let's pick the first one, C. After we split the data using the C feature, we obtain the following two datasets:

- Patients with a cough: $\{P_2, P_3, P_4, P_5\}$. Their labels are $\{s, s, s, h\}$.

- Patients without a cough: $\{P_1, P_6, P_7, P_8\}$. Their labels are $\{s, h, h, h\}$.

This gives us our tree of depth 1 that classifies the data with a 75% accuracy. The tree is depicted in the next figure.

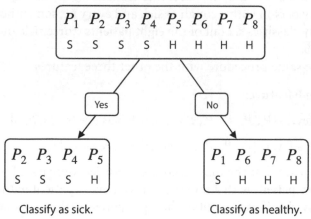

$$\text{Accuracy} = \frac{6}{8} = 75\%$$

Chapter 10: Combining building blocks to gain more power: Neural networks

Exercise 10.1

The following image shows a neural network in which all the activations are sigmoid functions.

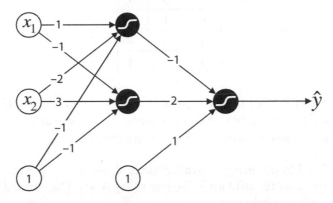

What would this neural network predict for the input (1,1)?

Solution

Let's call the outputs of the middle nodes h_1 and h_2. These are calculated as follows:

$$h_1 = \sigma(1 \cdot x_1 - 2 \cdot x_2 - 1)$$

$$h_2 = \sigma(-1 \cdot x_1 + 3 \cdot x_2 - 1)$$

Plugging in $x_1 = 1$ and $x_2 = 1$, we get the following:

$$h_1 = \sigma(-2) = 0.119$$

$$h_2 = \sigma(1) = 0.731$$

The final layer is

$$\hat{y} = \sigma(-1 \cdot h_1 + 2 \cdot h_2 + 1).$$

Replacing the values previously obtained for h_1 and h_2, we get

$$\hat{y} = \sigma(-0.119 + 2 \cdot 0.731 + 1) = \sigma(2.343) = 0.912.$$

Thus, the output of the neural network is 0.912.

Exercise 10.2

As we learned in exercise 5.3, it is impossible to build a perceptron that mimics the XOR gate. In other words, it is impossible to fit the following dataset with a perceptron and obtain 100% accuracy:

x_1	x_2	y
0	0	0
0	1	1
1	0	1
1	1	0

This is because the dataset is not linearly separable. Using a neural network of depth 2, build a perceptron that mimics the XOR gate shown previously. As the activation functions, use the step function instead of the sigmoid function to get discrete outputs.

> **hint**   This will be hard to do using a training method; instead, try eyeballing the weights. Try (or search online how) to build an XOR gate using AND, OR, and NOT gates, and use the results of exercise 5.3 to help you.

Solution

Note that the following combination of AND, OR, and NOT gates forms an XOR gate (where the NAND gate is the combination of an AND gate and a NOT gate).

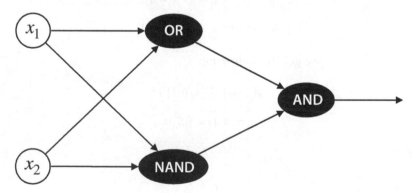

The following truth table illustrates it.

x_1	x_2	$h_1 = x_1$ OR x_2	$h_2 = x_1$ NAND x_2	h_1 AND h_2	x_1 XOR x_2
0	0	0	1	0	0
0	1	1	1	1	1
1	0	1	1	1	1
1	1	1	0	0	0

As we did in exercise 5.3, here are perceptrons that mimic the OR, NAND, and AND gates. The NAND gate is obtained by negating all the weights in the AND gate.

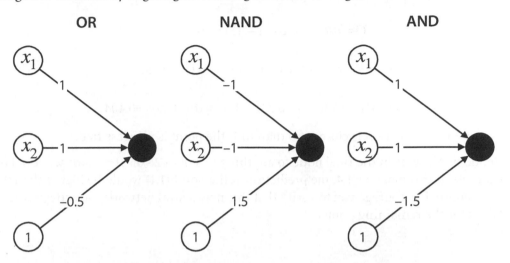

Joining these together, we get the neural network shown in the next figure.

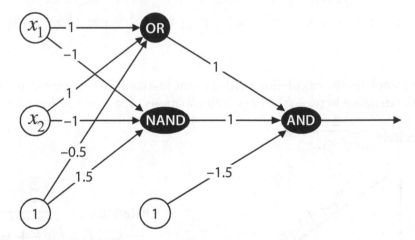

I encourage you to verify that this network does indeed mimic the XOR logic gate. This is done by inputting the four vectors (0,0), (0,1), (1,0), (1,1) through the network and verifying that the outputs are 0, 1, 1, 0.

Exercise 10.3

At the end of the section "A graphical representation of neural networks," we saw that the neural network in figure 10.13 with the activation function doesn't fit the dataset in table 10.1, because the point (1,1) is misclassified.

a. Verify that this is the case.

b. Change the weights so that the neural network classifies every point correctly.

Solution

a. For the point $(x_a, x_b) = (1, 1)$, the predictions are the following:

$$C = \sigma(6 \cdot 1 + 10 \cdot 1 - 15) = \sigma(1) = 0.731$$

$$F = \sigma(10 \cdot 1 + 6 \cdot 1 - 15) = \sigma(1) = 0.731$$

$$\hat{y} = \sigma(1 \cdot 0.731 + 1 \cdot 0.731 - 1.5) = \sigma(-0.39) = 0.404$$

Because the prediction is closer to 0 than to 1, the point is misclassified.

b. Reducing the bias in the final node to anything less than $2 \cdot 0.731 = 1.461$ will do. For example, if this bias was 1.4, the prediction at the point (1,1) would be higher than 0.5. As an exercise, I encourage you to verify that this new neural network correctly predicts the labels for the remaining points.

Chapter 11: Finding boundaries with style: Support vector machines and the kernel method

Exercise 11.1

(This exercise completes the calculation needed in the section "Distance error function.")

Show that the distance between the lines with equations $w_1 x_1 + w_2 x_2 + b = 1$ and $w_1 x_1 + w_2 x_2 + b = -1$ is precisely $\dfrac{2}{\sqrt{w_1^2 + w_2^2}}$.

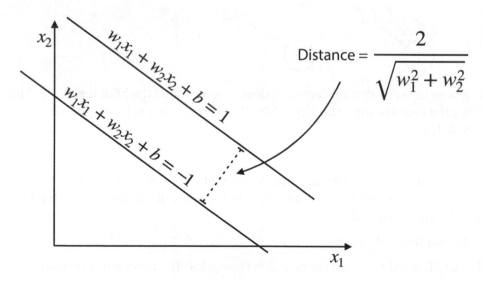

Solution

First, let us call the lines as follows:

- L_1 is the line with equation $w_1x_1 + w_2x_2 + b = 1$.
- L_2 is the line with equation $w_1x_1 + w_2x_2 + b = -1$.

Note that we can rewrite the equation $w_1x_1 + w_2x_2 + b = 0$ as $x_2 = -\dfrac{w_1x_1}{w_2} - \dfrac{b}{w_2}$, with slope $-\dfrac{w_1}{w_2}$.

Any perpendicular to this line has slope $\dfrac{w_2}{w_1}$. In particular, the line with equation $x_2 = \dfrac{w_2}{w_1} x_1$ is per
pendicular to both L_1 and L_2. We'll call this line L_3.

Next, we solve for the points of intersection of L_3 with each of the lines L_1 and L_2. The point of intersection of L_1 and L_3 is the solution to the following equations:

- $w_1x_1 + w_2x_2 + b = 1$

- $x_2 = \dfrac{w_2}{w_1} x_1$

We can plug the second equation into the first one, to obtain

$$w_1x_1 + w_2 \cdot \frac{w_2}{w_1} x_1 + b = 1,$$

and subsequently solve for x_1 to obtain

$$x_1 = \frac{1-b}{2w_1}.$$

Therefore, because every point in L_2 has the form $(x, \dfrac{w_1}{w_2} x)$, the point of intersection of L_1 and L_3

is the point with coordinates $\left(\dfrac{1-b}{w_1}, \dfrac{1-b}{w_2} \right)$.

A similar calculation will show that the point of intersection of L_2 and L_3 is the point with coordinates $\left(\dfrac{1-b}{w_1}, \dfrac{1-b}{w_2} \right)$.

To find the distance between these two points, we can use the Pythagorean theorem. This distance is

$$\sqrt{\left(\frac{1-b}{w_1} - \frac{-1-b}{w_1} \right)^2 + \left(\frac{1-b}{w_2} - \frac{-1-b}{w_2} \right)^2} = \sqrt{\left(\frac{2}{w_1} \right)^2 + \left(\frac{2}{w_2} \right)^2} = \frac{2}{\sqrt{w_1^2 + w_2^2}},$$

as desired.

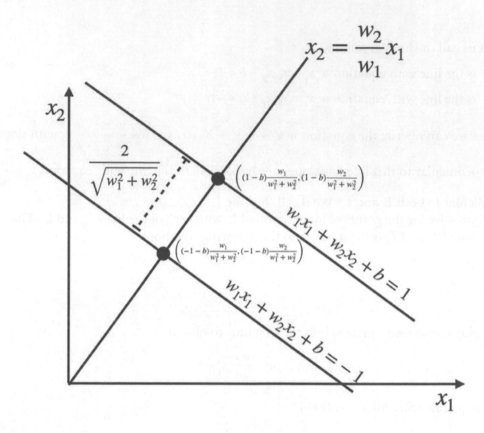

Exercise 11.2

As we learned in exercise 5.3, it is impossible to build a perceptron model that mimics the XOR gate. In other words, it is impossible to fit the following dataset (with 100% accuracy) with a perceptron model:

x_1	x_2	y
0	0	0
0	1	1
1	0	1
1	1	0

This is because the dataset is not linearly separable. An SVM has the same problem, because an SVM is also a linear model. However, we can use a kernel to help us out. What kernel should we use to turn this dataset into a linearly separable one? What would the resulting SVM look like?

hint   Look at example 2 in the section "Using polynomial equations to your benefit," which solves a very similar problem.

Solution

Considering the polynomial kernel of degree two, we get the following dataset:

x_1	x_2	x_1^2	$x_1 x_2$	x_2^2	y
0	0	0	0	0	0
0	1	0	0	1	1
1	1	1	0	0	1
1	1	1	1	1	0

Several classifiers work on this modified dataset. For example, the one with equation $\hat{y} = step(x_1 + x_2 - 2x_1x_2 - 0.5)$ classifies the data correctly.

Chapter 12: Combining models to maximize results: Ensemble learning

Exercise 12.1

A boosted strong learner L is formed by three weak learners, L_1, L_2, and L_3. Their weights are 1, 0.4, and 1.2, respectively. For a particular point, L_1 and L_2 predict that its label is positive, and L_3 predicts that it's negative. What is the final prediction the learner L makes on this point?

Solution

Because L_1 and L_2 predicted that the label is positive and L_3 predicted that it is negative, the sum of votes is

$$1 + 0.4 - 1.2 = 0.2.$$

This result is positive, which means that the strong learner predicts that the label of this point is positive.

Exercise 12.2

We are in the middle of training an AdaBoost model on a dataset of size 100. The current weak learner classifies 68 out of the 100 data points correctly. What is the weight that we'll assign to this learner in the final model?

Solution

This weight is the log odds, or the natural logarithm of the odds. The odds are 68/32, because the classifier classifies 68 points correctly and misclassifies the remaining 32. Therefore, the weight assigned to this weak learner is

$$weight = ln\left(\frac{68}{32}\right) = 0.754.$$

Chapter 13: Putting it all in practice: A real-life example of data engineering and machine learning

Exercise 13.1

The repository contains a file called test.csv. This is a file with more passengers on the *Titanic*, except it doesn't have the Survived column.

1. Preprocess the data in this file as we did in this chapter.

2. Use any of the models to predict labels in this dataset. According to your model, how many passengers survived?

3. Comparing the performance of all the models in this chapter, how many passengers from the test set would you think actually survived?

Solution

The solution is at the end of the following notebook: https://github.com/luisguiserrano/manning/tree/master/Chapter_13_End_to_end_example.

The math behind gradient descent:
Coming down a mountain
using derivatives and slopes

In this appendix, we'll go over the mathematical details of gradient descent. This appendix is fairly technical, and understanding it is not required to follow the rest of the book. However, it is here to provide a sense of completeness for the readers who wish to understand the inner workings of some of the core machine learning algorithms. The mathematics knowledge required for this appendix is higher than for the rest of the book. More specifically, knowledge of vectors, derivatives, and the chain rule is required.

In chapters 3, 5, 6, 10, and 11, we used gradient descent to minimize the error functions in our models. More specifically, we used gradient descent to minimize the following error functions:

- Chapter 3: the absolute and square error functions in a linear regression model

- Chapter 5: the perceptron error function in a perceptron model

- Chapter 6: the log loss in a logistic classifier

- Chapter 10: the log loss in a neural network

- Chapter 11: the classification (perceptron) error and the distance (regularization) error in an SVM

As we learned in chapters 3, 5, 6, 10, and 11, the error function measures how poorly the model is doing. Thus, finding the minimum value for this error function—or at least a really small value, even if it's not the minimum—will be instrumental in finding a good model.

The analogy we used was that of descending a mountain—Mount Errorest, shown in figure B.1. The scenario is the following: You are somewhere on top of a mountain, and you'd like to get to the bottom of this mountain. It is very cloudy, so you can't see far around you. The best bet you can have is to descend from the mountain one step at a time. You ask yourself, "If I were to take only one step, in which direction should I take it to descend the most?" You find that direction and take that step. Then you ask the same question again, and take another step, and you repeat the process many times. It is imaginable that if you always take the one step that helps you descend the most, that you must get to a low place. You may need a bit of luck to actually get to the bottom of the mountain, as opposed to getting stuck in a valley, but we'll deal with this later in the section "Getting stuck on local minima."

Figure B.1   In the gradient descent step, we want to descend from a mountain called Mount Errorest.

Throughout the following sections we'll describe the mathematics behind gradient descent and use it to help us train several machine learning algorithms by decreasing their error functions.

Using gradient descent to decrease functions

The mathematical formalism of gradient descent follows: say you want to minimize the function $f(x_1, x_2, ..., x_n)$ on the n variables $x_1, x_2, ..., x_n$. We assume the function is continuous and differentiable over each of the n variables.

We are currently standing at the point p with coordinates $(p_1, p_2, ..., p_n)$, and we wish to find the direction in which the function decreases the most, in order to take that step. This is illustrated in figure B.2. To find the direction in which the function decreases the most, we use the *gradient* of the function. The gradient is the n-dimensional vector formed by the partial derivatives of f with respect to each of the variables $x_1, x_2, ..., x_n$. This gradient is denoted as ∇f, as follows:

$$\nabla f = \left(\frac{\partial f}{\partial x_1}, \frac{\partial f}{\partial x_2}, ..., \frac{\partial f}{\partial x_n} \right)$$

The gradient is a vector that points in the direction of greatest growth, namely, the direction in which the function *increases* the most. Thus, the negative of the gradient is the direction in which the function *decreases* the most. This is the step we want to take. We determine the size of the step using the *learning rate* we learned in chapter 3 and which we denote with η. The gradient descent step consists of taking a step of length $\eta|\nabla f|$ in the direction of the negative of the gradient ∇f. Thus, if our original point was p, after applying the gradient descent step, we obtain the point $p - \eta \nabla f$. Figure B.2 illustrates the step that we've taken to decrease the function f.

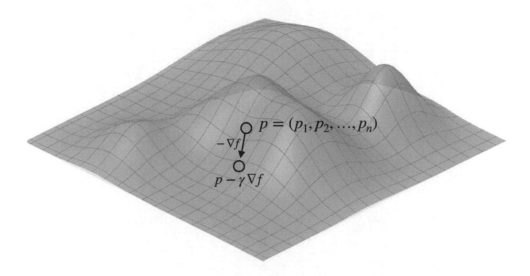

Figure B.2 We were originally at the point *p*. We take a step in the direction of the negative of the gradient and end up at a new point. This is the direction in which the function decreases the most. (Source: Image created with the assistance of Grapher™ from Golden Software, LLC; https://www.goldensoftware.com/products/grapher.)

Now that we know how to take one step to slightly decrease the function, we can simply repeat this process many times to minimize our function. Thus, the pseudocode of the gradient descent algorithm is the following:

Pseudocode for the gradient descent algorithm

Goal: To minimize the function *f*.

Hyperparameters:

- Number of epochs (repetitions) N
- Learning rate η

Process:

- Pick a random point p_0.
- For $i = 0, \ldots, N-1$:
  - Calculate the gradient $\nabla f(p_i)$.
  - Pick the point $p_{i+1} = p_i - \eta \nabla f(p_i)$.
- End with the point p_n.

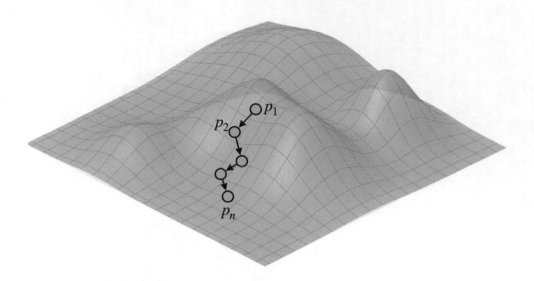

Figure B.3   If we repeat the gradient descent step many times, we have a high chance of finding the minimum value of the function. In this figure, p_1 represents the starting point and p_n the point we have obtained using gradient descent. (Source: Image created with the assistance of Grapher™ from Golden Software, LLC; <u>https://www.goldensoftware.com/products/grapher</u>.)

Does this process *always* find the minimum of the function? Unfortunately, no. Several problems may occur when trying to minimize a function using gradient descent, such as getting stuck at a local minimum (a valley). We'll learn a very useful technique to deal with this problem in the section "Getting stuck on local minima."

Using gradient descent to train models

Now that we know how gradient descent helps us minimize (or at least, find small values for) a function, in this section we see how to use it to train some machine learning models. The models we'll train follow:

- Linear regression (from chapter 3).
- Perceptron (from chapter 5).
- Logistic classifier (from chapter 6).
- Neural network (from chapter 10).
- Regularization (from chapters 4 and 11). This one is not a model, but we can still see the effects that a gradient descent step has on a model that uses regularization.

The way we use gradient descent to train a model is by letting f be the corresponding error function of the model and using gradient descent to minimize f. The value of the error function is calculated over the dataset. However, as we saw in the sections "Do we train using one point at a time or many" in chapter 3, "Stochastic, mini-batch, and batch gradient descent" in chapter 6, and "Hyperparameters" in chapter 10, if the dataset is too large, we can speed up training by splitting the dataset into mini-batches of (roughly) the same size and, at each step, picking a different mini-batch on which to calculate the error function.

Here is some notation we'll use in this appendix. Most of the terms have been introduced in chapters 1 and 2:

- The **size** of the dataset, or the number of rows, is m.

- The **dimension** of the dataset, or number of columns, is n.

- The dataset is formed by **features** and **labels**.

- The **features** are the m vectors $x_i = (x_1^{(i)}, x_2^{(i)}, ..., x_n^{(i)})$ for $i = 1, 2, ..., m$.

- The **labels** y_i, for $i = 1, 2, ..., m$.

- The **model** is given by the vector of n weights $w = (w_1, w_2, ..., w_n)$ and the bias b (a scalar) (except when the model is a neural network, which will have more weights and biases).

- The **predictions** $\hat{y}_i$, for $i = 1, 2, ..., m$.

- The **learning rate** of the model is η.

- The **mini-batches** of data are $B_1, B_2, ..., B_l$, for some number l. Each mini-batch has length q. The points in one mini-batch (for notational convenience) are denoted $x^{(1)}, ..., x^{(q)}$, and the labels are $y_1, ..., y_q$.

The gradient descent algorithm that we'll use for training models follows:

Gradient descent algorithm for training machine learning models

Hyperparameters:

- Number of epochs (repetitions) N

- Learning rate η

Process:

- Pick random weights $w_1, w_2, ..., w_n$ and a random bias b.

- For $i = 0, ..., N - 1$:

  - For each of the mini-batches $B_1, B_2, ..., B_l$:

    - Calculate the error function $f(w, b)$ on that particular mini-batch.

    - Calculate the gradient $\nabla f(w_1, ..., w_n, b) = \left(\dfrac{\partial f}{\partial w_1}, ..., \dfrac{\partial f}{\partial w_n}, \dfrac{\partial f}{\partial b} \right)$.

– Replace the weights and bias as follows:

– w_i gets replaced by $w_i' = w_i - \eta \dfrac{\partial f}{\partial w_i}$.

– b gets replaced by $b' = b - \eta \dfrac{\partial f}{\partial b}$.

Throughout the following subsections, we will perform this process in detail for each of the following models and error functions:

- Linear regression model with the mean absolute error function (the following section)

- Linear regression model with the mean square error function (the following section)

- Perceptron model with the perceptron error function (the section "Using gradient descent to train classification models")

- Logistic regression model with the log loss function (the section "Using gradient descent to train classification models")

- Neural network with the log loss function (the section "Using gradient descent to train neural networks")

- Models with regularization (the section "Using gradient descent for regularization")

Using gradient descent to train linear regression models

In this section, we use gradient descent to train a linear regression model, using both of the error functions we've learned previously: the mean absolute error and the mean square error. Recall from chapter 3 that in linear regression, the predictions $\hat{y}_1, \hat{y}_2, \ldots, \hat{y}_q$ are given by the following formula:

$$\hat{y}_i = \sum_{j=1}^{n} w_j x_j^{(i)} + b$$

The goal of our regression model is to find the weights $w_1, \ldots, w_n$, which produce predictions that are really close to the labels. Thus, the error function helps by measuring how far $\hat{y}$ is from y for a particular set of weights. As we've seen in sections "The absolute error" and "The square error" in chapter 3, we have two different ways to calculate this distance. The first is the absolute value $|\hat{y} - y|$, and the second one is the square of the difference $(\hat{y} - y)^2$. The first one gives rise to the mean absolute error, and the second one to the mean square error. Let's study them separately.

Training a linear regression model using gradient descent to reduce the mean absolute error

In this subsection, we'll calculate the gradient of the mean absolute error function and use it to apply gradient descent and train a linear regression model. The mean absolute error is a way to tell how far apart $\hat{y}$ and y are. It was first defined in the section "The absolute error" in chapter 3, and its formula follows:

$$MAE(w,b,x,y) = \frac{1}{q}\sum_{i=1}^{q} |\hat{y}_l - y_i|$$

For convenience, we'll abbreviate $MAE(w, b, x, y)$ as MAE. To use gradient descent to reduce MAE, we need to calculate the gradient ∇MAE, which is the vector containing the n + 1 partial derivatives of MAE with respect to $w_1, \ldots, w_n, b$,

$$\nabla MAE = \left(\frac{\partial MAE}{\partial w_1}, \ldots, \frac{\partial MAE}{\partial w_n}, \frac{\partial MAE}{\partial b} \right).$$

We'll calculate these partial derivatives using the chain rule. First, notice that

$$\frac{\partial MAE}{\partial w_j} = \frac{1}{q}\sum_{i=1}^{q} \frac{\partial |\hat{y}_i - y_i|}{\partial w_j}.$$

The derivative of $f(x) = |x|$ is the sign function $sgn(x) = \frac{|x|}{x}$, which is +1 when x is positive and −1 when x is negative (it is undefined at 0, but for convenience we can define it to be 0). Thus, we can rewrite the previous equation as

$$\frac{\partial MAE}{\partial w_j} = \frac{1}{q}\sum_{i=1}^{q} sgn(\hat{y}_i - y_i)\frac{\partial \hat{y}_i}{\partial w_j}.$$

To calculate this value, let's focus on the final part of the equation, namely, the $\frac{\partial \hat{y}_i}{\partial w_j}$. Since $\hat{y}_i = \sum_{j=1}^{n} w_j x_j^{(i)}$, then

$$\frac{\partial \hat{y}_i}{\partial w_j} = \sum_{j=1}^{n} \frac{\partial \left(w_j x_j^{(i)}\right)}{\partial w_j} = x_j^{(i)}.$$

This is because the derivative of w_j with respect to w_i, is 1 if $j = i$ and 0 otherwise. Thus, replacing on the derivative, we get the following:

$$\frac{\partial MAE}{\partial w_i} = \frac{1}{q}\sum_{i=1}^{q} sgn\left(\hat{y}_i - y_i\right)x_j^{(i)}$$

Using a similar analysis, we can calculate the derivative of $MAE(w, b)$ with respect to b to be

$$\frac{\partial MAE}{\partial b} = \frac{1}{q}\sum_{i=1}^{q} sgn\left(\hat{y}_i - y_i\right).$$

The gradient descent step is the following:

Gradient descent step:

Replace (w, b) by (w', b'), where

- $w_j' = w_j + \dfrac{1}{q}\sum_{i=1}^{q} \eta sgn(y_i - \hat{y}_i)x_j^{(i)}$ for $i = 1, 2, \ldots, n$

- $b' = b + \eta\sum_{i=1}^{q} sgn(y_i - \hat{y}_i)$

Notice something interesting: if the mini-batch has size $q = 1$ and consists only of the point $x = (x_1, x_2, \ldots, x_n)$ with label y and prediction $\hat{y}$, then the step is defined as follows:

Replace (w, b) by (w', b'), where

- $w_j' = w_j + \eta\, sgn(y - \hat{y})x_j$
- $b' = b + \eta\, sgn(y - \hat{y})$

This is precisely the simple trick we used in the section "The simple trick" in chapter 3 to train our linear regression algorithm.

Training a linear regression model using gradient descent to reduce the mean square error

In this subsection, we'll calculate the gradient of the mean square error function and use it to apply gradient descent and train a linear regression model. The mean square error is another way to tell how far apart $\hat{y}$ and y are. It was first defined in the section "The square error" in chapter 3 and its formula is

$$MSE(w,b,x,y) = \frac{1}{2m}\sum_{i=1}^{q}(\hat{y}_i - y_i)^2.$$

For convenience, we'll abbreviate $MSE(w, b, x, y)$ as MSE. To calculate the gradient ∇MSE, we can follow the same procedure as we did for the mean absolute error described earlier, with the exception that the derivative of $f(x) = x^2$ is $2x$. Therefore, the derivative of MSE with respect to w_j is

$$\frac{\partial MSE}{\partial w_j} = \frac{1}{2q}\sum_{i=1}^{q}\frac{\partial(\hat{y}_i - y_i)^2}{\partial w_j} = \frac{1}{2q}\sum_{i=1}^{q}2(\hat{y}_i - y_i)\frac{\partial \hat{y}_i}{\partial w_j} = \frac{1}{q}\sum_{i=1}^{q}(\hat{y}_i - y_i)\frac{\partial \hat{y}_i}{\partial w_j}.$$

Similarly, the derivative of $MSE(w, b)$ with respect to b is

$$\frac{\partial MSE}{\partial b} = \frac{1}{2q}\sum_{i=1}^{q}\frac{\partial(\hat{y}_i - y_i)^2}{\partial b} = \frac{1}{2q}\sum_{i=1}^{q}2(\hat{y}_i - y_i)\frac{\partial \hat{y}_i}{\partial b} = \frac{1}{q}\sum_{i=1}^{q}(\hat{y}_i - y_i)\frac{\partial \hat{y}_i}{\partial b}.$$

Gradient descent step:

Replace (w, b) by (w', b'), where

- $w_j' = w_j + \eta \dfrac{1}{q} \sum_{i=1}^{q} (y_i - \hat{y}_i) x_j^{(i)}$ for $i = 1, 2, \ldots, n$

- $b' = b + \eta \dfrac{1}{q} \sum_{i=1}^{q} (y_i - \hat{y}_i)$

Notice again that if the mini-batch has size $q = 1$ and consists only of the point $x = (x_1, x_2, \ldots, x_n)$ with label y and prediction $\hat{y}$, then the step is defined as follows:

Replace (w, b) by (w', b'), where

- $w_j' = w_j + \eta(y - \hat{y}) x_j$
- $b' = b + \eta(y - \hat{y})$

This is precisely the square trick we used in the section "The square trick" in chapter 3 to train our linear regression algorithm.

Using gradient descent to train classification models

In this section we learn how to use gradient descent to train classification models. The two models that we'll train are the perceptron model (chapter 5) and the logistic regression model (chapter 6). Each one of them has its own error function, so we will develop them separately.

Training a perceptron model using gradient descent to reduce the perceptron error

In this subsection, we'll calculate the gradient of the perceptron error function and use it to apply gradient descent and train a perceptron model. In the perceptron model, the predictions are $\hat{y}_1$, $\hat{y}_2, \ldots, \hat{y}_q$ where each $\hat{y}_i$ is 0 or 1. To calculate the predictions, we first need to remember the step function $step(x)$, introduced in chapter 5. This function takes as an input any real number x and outputs 0 if $x < 0$ and 1 if $x \geq 0$. Its graph is shown in figure B.4.

$$step(x) = \begin{cases} 0 \text{ if } x < 0 \\ 1 \text{ if } x \geq 0 \end{cases}$$

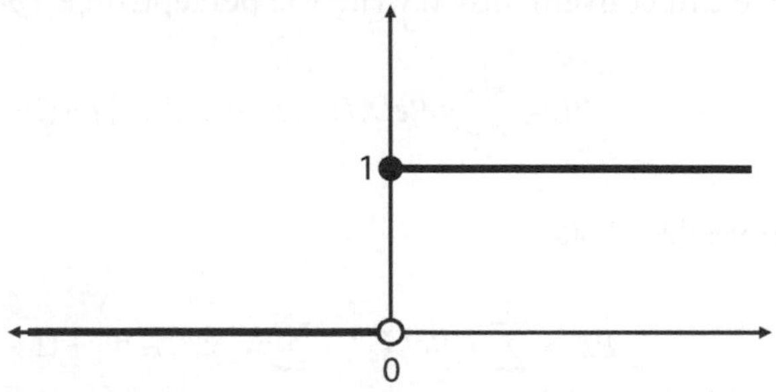

Figure B.4 The step function. For negative numbers it outputs 0, and for non-negative numbers it outputs 1.

The model gives each point a *score*. The score that the model with weights $(w_1, w_2, \ldots, w_n)$ and bias b gives to the point $x^{(i)} = (x_1^{(i)}, x_n^{(i)}, \ldots, x_n^{(i)})$ is $score(w,b,x^{(i)}) = \sum_{j=1}^{n} w_j x_j^{(i)} + b$. The predictions $\hat{y}_i$ are given by the following formula:

$$\hat{y}_i = step(score(w,b,x^{(i)})) = step\left(\sum_{j=1}^{n} w_j x_j^{(i)} + b \right)$$

In other words, the prediction is 1 if the score is positive, and 0 otherwise.

The perceptron error function is called $PE(w, b, x, y)$, which we'll abbreviate as PE. It was first defined in the section "How to compare classifiers? The error function" in chapter 5. By construction, it is a large number if the model made a bad prediction, and a small number (in this case, actually 0) if the model made a good prediction. The error function is defined as follows.

- $PE(w, b, x, y) = 0$ if $\hat{y} = y$

- $PE(w, b, x, y) = |score(w, b, x)|$ if $\hat{y} \neq y$

In other words, if the point is correctly classified, the error is zero. If the point is incorrectly classified, the error is the absolute value of the score. Thus, misclassified points with scores of low absolute value produce a low error, and misclassified points with scores of high absolute value produce a high error. This is because the absolute value of the score of a point is proportional to the distance between that point and the boundary. Thus, the points with low error are points that are close to the boundary, whereas points with high error are far from the boundary.

To calculate the gradient ∇PE, we can use the same rule as before. One thing we should notice is that the derivative of the absolute value function $|x|$ is 1 when $x \geq 0$ and 0 when $x < 0$. This derivative is undefined at 0, which is a problem with our calculations, but in practice, we can arbitrarily define it as 1 without any problems.

In chapter 10, we introduced the $ReLU(x)$ (rectified linear unit) function, which is 0 when $x < 0$ and x when $x \geq 0$. Notice that there are two ways in which a point can be misclassified:

- If $y = 0$ and $\hat{y} = 1$. This means $score(w, b, x) \geq 0$.

- If $y = 1$ and $\hat{y} = 0$. This means $score(w, b, x) < 0$.

Thus, we can conveniently rewrite the perceptron error as

$$PE = \sum_{i=1}^{q} y_i ReLU(-score(w,b,x)) + (1-y_i)ReLU(score(w,b,x)),$$

or in more detail, as

$$PE = \sum_{i=1}^{q} y_i ReLU\left(-\sum_{j=1}^{n} w_j x_j^{(i)} - b \right) + (1-y_i)ReLU\left(\sum_{j=1}^{n} w_j x_j^{(i)} + b \right).$$

Now we can proceed to calculate the gradient ∇PE using the chain rule. An important observation that we'll use and that the reader can verify is that the derivative of $ReLU(x)$ is the step function $step(x)$. This gradient is

$$\frac{\partial PE}{\partial w_j} = \sum_{i=1}^{q} y_i step\left(-\sum_{j=1}^{n} w_j x_j^{(i)} - b \right)(-x_j^{(i)}) + (1-y_i)step\left(\sum_{j=1}^{n} w_j x_j^{(i)} + b \right)x_j^{(i)},$$

which we can rewrite as

$$\frac{\partial PE}{\partial w_j} = \sum_{i=1}^{q} -y_i x_j^{(i)} step(-score(w,b,x)) + (1-y_i)x_j^{(i)} step(score(w,b,x)).$$

This looks complicated, but it's actually not that hard. Let's analyze each summand from the right-hand side of the previous expression. Notice that $step(score(w, b, x))$ is 1 if and only if $score(w, b, x) > 0$, and otherwise, it is 0. This is precisely when $\hat{y} = 1$. Similarly, $step(-score(w, b, x))$ is 1 if and only if $score(w, b, x) < 0$, and otherwise, it is 0. This is precisely when $\hat{y} = 0$. Therefore

- If $\hat{y}_i = 0$ and $y_i = 0$:

$$-y_i x_j^{(i)} step(-score(w,b,x)) + (1-y_i)x_j^{(i)} step(score(w,b,x)) = 0$$

- If $\hat{y}_i = 1$ and $y_i = 1$:

$$-y_i x_j^{(i)} step(-score(w,b,x)) + (1-y_i)x_j^{(i)} step(score(w,b,x)) = 0$$

- If $\hat{y}_i = 0$ and $y_i = 1$:

$$-y_i x_j^{(i)} step(-score(w,b,x)) + (1-y_i)x_j^{(i)} step(score(w,b,x)) = -x_j^{(i)}$$

- If $\hat{y}_i = 1$ and $y_i = 0$:

$$-y_i x_j^{(i)} step(-score(w,b,x)) + (1-y_i)x_j^{(i)} step(score(w,b,x)) = x_j^{(i)}$$

This means that when calculating $\frac{\partial PE}{\partial w_j}$, only the summands coming from misclassified points will add value.

In a similar manner,

$$\frac{\partial PE}{\partial b} = \sum_{i=1}^{q} -y_i step(-score(w,b,x)) + (1-y_i)step(score(w,b,x)).$$

Thus, the gradient descent step is defined as follows:

Gradient descent step:

Replace (w, b) by (w', b'), where

- $w_j' = w_j + \eta \sum\limits_{i=1}^{q} -y_i x_j^{(i)} step(-score(w,b,x)) + (1-y_i)x_j^{(i)} step(score(w,b,x))$, and

- $b' = b + \eta \sum\limits_{i=1}^{q} -y_i step(-score(w,b,x)) + (1-y_i)step(score(w,b,x))$.

And again, looking at the right-hand side of the previous expression

- If $\hat{y}_i = 0$ and $y_i = 0$:

$$-y_i step\left(-score\left(w,b,x\right)\right) + \left(1-y_i\right)step\left(score\left(w,b,x\right)\right) = 0$$

- If $\hat{y}_i = 1$ and $y_i = 1$:

$$-y_i step\left(-score\left(w,b,x\right)\right) + \left(1-y_i\right)step\left(score\left(w,b,x\right)\right) = 0$$

- If $\hat{y}_i = 0$ and $y_i = 1$:

$$-y_i step\left(-score\left(w,b,x\right)\right) + \left(1-y_i\right)step\left(score\left(w,b,x\right)\right) = -1$$

- If $\hat{y}_i = 1$ and $y_i = 0$:

$$-y_i step\left(-score\left(w,b,x\right)\right) + \left(1-y_i\right)step\left(score\left(w,b,x\right)\right) = 1$$

This all may not mean very much, but one can code this to calculate all the entries of the gradient. Notice again that if the mini-batch has size $q = 1$ and consists only of the point $x = (x_1, x_2, ..., x_n)$ with label y and prediction $\hat{y}$, then the step is defined as follows:

Gradient descent step:

- If the point is correctly classified, don't change w and b.

- If the point has label $y = 0$ and is classified as $\hat{y} = 1$:

  - Replace w by $w' = w - \eta x$.

  - Replace b by $b' = w - \eta$.

- If the point has label $y = 1$ and is classified as $\hat{y} = 0$:

  - Replace w by $w' = w + \eta x$.

  - Replace b by $b' = w + \eta$.

Note that this is precisely the perceptron trick described in the section "The perceptron trick" in chapter 5.

Training a logistic regression model using gradient descent to reduce the log loss

In this subsection, we'll calculate the gradient of the log loss function and use it to apply gradient descent and train a logistic regression model. In the logistic regression model, the predictions are $\hat{y}_1, \hat{y}_2, \ldots, \hat{y}_q$ where each $\hat{y}_i$ is some real number in between 0 and 1. To calculate the predictions, we first need to remember the sigmoid function $\sigma(x)$, introduced in chapter 6. This function takes as an input any real number x and outputs some number between 0 and 1. If x is a large positive number, then $\sigma(x)$ is close to 1. If x is a large negative number, then $\sigma(x)$ is close to 0. The formula for the sigmoid function is

$$\sigma(x) = \frac{1}{1+e^{-x}}.$$

The graph of $\sigma(x)$ is illustrated in figure B.5.

The predictions of the logistic regression model are precisely the output of the sigmoid function, namely, for $i = 1, 2, \ldots, q$ they are defined as follows:

$$\hat{y}_i = \sigma(score(w,b,x^{(i)})) = \sigma\left(\sum_{j=1}^{n} w_j x_j^{(i)} + b\right)$$

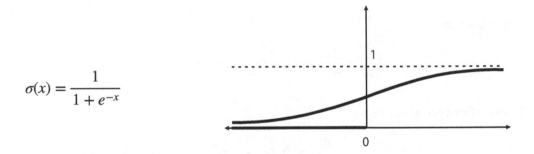

$$\sigma(x) = \frac{1}{1+e^{-x}}$$

Figure B.5 The sigmoid function always outputs a number between 0 and 1. The output for negative numbers is close to 0, and the output for positive numbers is close to 1.

The log loss is denoted as $LL(w, b, x, y)$, which we'll abbreviate as LL. This error function was first defined in the section "The dataset and the predictions" in chapter 6. It is similar to the perceptron error function because by construction, it is a large number if the model made a bad prediction and a small number if the model made a good prediction. The log loss function is defined as

$$LL = -\sum_{i=1}^{q} y_i log(\hat{y}_i) + (1-y_i)log(1-\hat{y}_i).$$

We can proceed to calculate the gradient ∇LL using the chain rule. Before this, let's note that the derivative of the sigmoid function can be written as $\sigma'(x) = \sigma(x)|1 - \sigma(x)|$. The details on the last calculation can be worked out using the quotient rule for differentiation, and they are left to the reader. Using this, we can calculate the derivative of $\hat{y}_i$ with respect to w_j. Because $\hat{y}_i = \sigma\left(\sum_{j=1}^{n}(w_j x_j^{(i)} + b)\right)$, then by the chain rule,

$$\frac{\partial \hat{y}_i}{\partial w_j} = \sigma\left(\sum_{j=1}^{n}(w_j x_j^{(i)} + b)\right)\left[1 - \sigma\left(\sum_{j=1}^{n}(w_j x_j^{(i)} + b)\right)\right] x j^i = y_i(1 - y_i)x j^i.$$

Now, on to develop the log loss. Using the chain rule again, we get

$$\frac{\partial LL}{\partial w_j} = -\sum_{i=1}^{q} y_i \frac{1}{\hat{y}_i}\frac{\partial \hat{y}_i}{\partial w_j} - (1 - y_i)\frac{-1}{1 - \hat{y}_i}\frac{\partial \hat{y}_i}{\partial w_j}.$$

And by the previous calculation for $\dfrac{\partial \hat{y}_i}{\partial w_j}$,

$$\frac{\partial LL}{\partial w_j} = \sum_{i=1}^{q} -y_i \frac{1}{\hat{y}_i}\hat{y}_i(1 + \hat{y}_i)x_j^{(i)} + (1 - y_i)\frac{-1}{1 - \hat{y}_i}\hat{y}_i(1 - \hat{y}_i)x_j^{(i)}.$$

Simplifying, we get

$$\frac{\partial LL}{\partial w_j} = \sum_{i=1}^{q} -y_i(1 - \hat{y}_i)x_j^{(i)} + (1 - y_i)\hat{y}_i x_j^{(i)},$$

which simplifies even more as

$$\frac{\partial LL}{\partial w_j} = \sum_{i=1}^{q}(\hat{y}_i - y_i)x_j^{(i)}.$$

Similarly, taking the derivative with respect to b, we get

$$\frac{\partial LL}{\partial b} = \sum_{i=1}^{q}(\hat{y}_i - y_i).$$

Therefore, the gradient descent step becomes the following:

Gradient descent step:

Replace (w, b) by (w', b'), where

- $w' = w + \eta \sum_{i=1}^{q} (y_i - \hat{y}_i) x^{(i)}$, and

- $b' = b + \eta \sum_{i=1}^{q} (y_i - \hat{y}_i)$.

Notice that when the mini-batches are of size 1, the gradient descent step becomes the following:

Replace (w, b) by (w', b'), where

- $w' = w + \eta (y - \hat{y}) x^{(i)}$, and

- $b' = b + \eta (y - \hat{y})$.

This is precisely the logistic regression trick we learned in the section "How to find a good logistic classifier?" in chapter 6.

Using gradient descent to train neural networks

In the section "Backpropagation" in chapter 10, we went over backpropagation—the process of training a neural network. This process consists of repeating a gradient descent step to minimize the log loss. In this subsection, we see how to actually calculate the derivatives to perform this gradient descent step. We'll perform this process in a neural network of depth 2 (one input layer, one hidden layer, and one output layer), but the example is big enough to show how these derivatives are calculated in general. Furthermore, we'll apply gradient descent on the error for only one point (in other words, we'll do stochastic gradient descent). However, I encourage you to work out the derivatives for a neural network of more layers, and using mini-batches of points (mini-batch gradient descent).

In our neural network, the input layer consists of m input nodes, the hidden layer consists of n hidden nodes, and the output layer consists of one output node. The notation in this subsection is different than in the other ones, for the sake of simplicity, as follows (and illustrated in figure B.6):

- The input is the point with coordinates $x_1, x_2, \ldots, x_m$.

- The first hidden layer has weights V_{ij} and biases b_j, for $i = 1, 2, \ldots, m$ and $j = 1, 2, \ldots, n$.

- The second hidden layer has weights W_j for $j = 1, 2, \ldots, n$, and bias c.

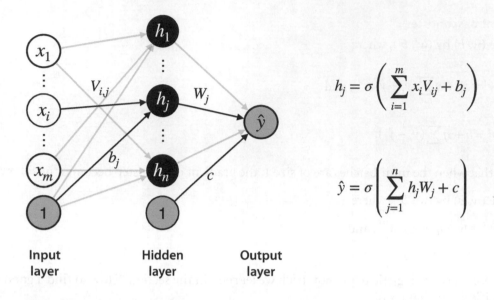

$$h_j = \sigma\left(\sum_{i=1}^{m} x_i V_{ij} + b_j\right)$$

$$\hat{y} = \sigma\left(\sum_{j=1}^{n} h_j W_j + c\right)$$

Figure B.6 The process of calculating a prediction using a neural network with one hidden layer and sigmoid activation functions

The way the output is calculated is via the following two equations:

- $h_j = \sigma\left(\sum_{i=1}^{m} x_i V_{ij} + b_j\right)$

- $\hat{y} = \sigma\left(\sum_{j=1}^{n} h_j W_j + c\right)$

To ease the calculation of the derivatives, we use the following helper variables r_j and s:

- $r_j = \sum_{i=1}^{m} x_i V_{ij} + b_j$
- $h_j = \sigma(r_j)$
- $s = \sum_{j=1}^{n} h_j W_j + c$
- $\hat{y} = \sigma(s)$

In that way, we can calculate the following partial derivatives (recalling that the derivative of the sigmoid function is $\sigma'(x) = \sigma'(x)[1 - \sigma(x)]$ and that the log loss is $L(y, \hat{y}) = -y\,ln(\hat{y}) - (1-y)\,ln(1-\hat{y})$—we'll call it L for convenience):

1. $\dfrac{\partial L}{\partial \hat{y}} = -y\dfrac{1}{\hat{y}} - (1-y)\dfrac{-1}{1-\hat{y}} = \dfrac{-(y-\hat{y})}{\hat{y}(1-\hat{y})}$

2. $\dfrac{\partial \hat{y}}{\partial s} = \sigma(s)[1 - \sigma(s)] = y(1-y)$

3. $\dfrac{\partial s}{\partial W_j} = h_j$, and $\dfrac{\partial s}{\partial b_j} = 1$

4. $\dfrac{\partial s}{\partial h_j} = W_j$

5. $\dfrac{\partial h_j}{\partial r_j} = \sigma(r_j)[1 - \sigma(r_j)] = hj(1 - hj)$

6. $\dfrac{\partial r_j}{\partial V_{ij}} = x_i$ and $\dfrac{\partial r_j}{\partial b_j} = 1$

To simplify our calculations, notice that if we multiply equations 1 and 2 and use the chain rule, we get

7. $\dfrac{\partial L}{\partial s} = \dfrac{\partial L}{\partial \hat{y}} \dfrac{\partial \hat{y}}{\partial s} = \dfrac{-(y - \hat{y})}{\hat{y}(1 - \hat{y})} \hat{y}(1 - \hat{y}) = -(y - \hat{y}).$

Now, we can use the chain rule and equations 3–7 to calculate the derivatives of the log loss with respect to the weights and biases as follows:

8. $\dfrac{\partial L}{\partial W_j} = \dfrac{\partial L}{\partial s} \dfrac{\partial s}{\partial W_j} = -(y - \hat{y})h_j$

9. $\dfrac{\partial L}{\partial c} = \dfrac{\partial L}{\partial s} \dfrac{\partial s}{\partial c} = -(y - \hat{y})$

10. $\dfrac{\partial L}{\partial V_{ij}} = \dfrac{\partial L}{\partial s} \dfrac{\partial s}{\partial h_j} \dfrac{\partial h_j}{\partial r_j} \dfrac{\partial r_j}{\partial V_{ij}} = -(y - \hat{y})W_j h_j (1 - h_j)x_i$

11. $\dfrac{\partial L}{\partial b_j} = \dfrac{\partial L}{\partial s} \dfrac{\partial s}{\partial h_j} \dfrac{\partial h_j}{\partial r_j} \dfrac{\partial r_j}{\partial b_j} = -(y - \hat{y})W_j h_j (1 - h_j)$

Using the previous equations, the gradient descent step is the following:

Gradient descent step for neural networks:

- Replace V_{ij} by $V_{ij} - \eta \dfrac{\partial L}{\partial V_{ij}} = V_{ij} + \eta(y - \hat{y})W_j h_j (1 - h_j)x_i$.

- Replace b_j by $b_j - \eta \dfrac{\partial L}{\partial b_j} = b_j + \eta(y - \hat{y})W_j h_j (1 - h_j)$.

- Replace W_j by $W_j + \eta \dfrac{\partial L}{\partial W_j} = W_j + \eta(y - \hat{y})h_j$.

- Replace c by $c + \eta \dfrac{\partial L}{\partial c} = c + \eta(y - \hat{y})$.

The previous equations are quite complicated, and so are the equations of backpropagation for neural networks of even more layers. Thankfully, we can use PyTorch, TensorFlow, and Keras to train neural networks without having to calculate all the derivatives.

Using gradient descent for regularization

In the section "Modifying the error function to solve our problem" in chapter 4, we learned regularization as a way to decrease overfitting in machine learning models. Regularization consists of adding a regularization term to the error function, which helps reduce overfitting. This term could be the L1 or the L2 norm of the polynomial used in the model. In the section "Techniques for training neural networks" in chapter 10, we learned how to apply regularization to train neural networks by adding a similar regularization term. Later, in the section "Distance error function" in chapter 11, we learned the distance error function for SVMs, which ensured that the two lines in the classifier stayed close to each other. The distance error function had the same form of the L2 regularization term.

However, in the section "An intuitive way to see regularization" in chapter 4, we learned a more intuitive way to see regularization. In short, every gradient descent step that uses regularization is decreasing the values of the coefficients of the model by a slight amount. Let's look at the math behind this phenomenon.

For a model with weights w_1, w_2, ..., w_n, the regularization terms were the following:

- L1 regularization: $W_1 = |w_1| + |w_2| + \cdots + |w_n|$
- L2 regularization: $W_2 = w_1^2 + w_2^2 + \cdots + w_n^2$

Recall that in order to not alter the coefficients too drastically, the regularization term is multiplied by a regularization parameter λ. Thus, when we apply gradient descent, the coefficients are modified as follows:

- L1 regularization: w_i is replaced by $w_i - \nabla W_1$
- L2 regularization: w_i is replaced by $w_i - \nabla W_2$

Where ∇ denotes the gradient of the regularization term. In other words, $\nabla(b_1,\ldots,b_n) = \left(\dfrac{\partial b_1}{\partial a_1},\ldots,\dfrac{\partial b_n}{\partial a_n} \right)$. Since $\dfrac{\partial |w_i|}{\partial w_i} = sgn(w_i)$, and $\dfrac{\partial w_i^2}{\partial w_i} = 2w_i$, then the gradient descent step is the following:

Gradient descent step for regularization:

- L1 regularization: Replace a_i by $a_i - \lambda \dfrac{\partial a_i}{\partial a_i} = a_i - \lambda \cdot sgn(a_i)$.

- L2 regularization: Replace a_i by $a_i - \lambda \dfrac{\partial a_i}{\partial a_i} = a_i - 2\lambda a_i = (1 - 2\lambda)a_i$.

Notice that this gradient descent step always reduces the absolute value of the coefficient a_i. In L1 regularization, we are subtracting a small value from a_i if it is a_i positive and adding a small value if it is negative. In L2 regularization, we are multiplying a_i by a number that is slightly smaller than 1.

Getting stuck on local minima: How it happens, and how we solve it

As was mentioned at the beginning of this appendix, the gradient descent algorithm doesn't necessarily find the minimum value of the function. As an example, look at figure B.7. Let's say that we want to find the minimum of the function in this figure using gradient descent. Because the first step in gradient descent is to start on a random point, we'll start at the point labeled "Starting point."

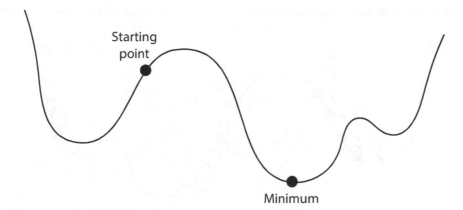

Figure B.7 We're standing at the point labeled "Starting point." The minimum value of the function is the point labeled "Minimum." Will we be able to reach this minimum using gradient descent?

Figure B.8 shows the path that the gradient descent algorithm will take to find the minimum. Note that it succeeds in finding the closest local minimum to that point, but it completely misses the global minimum on the right.

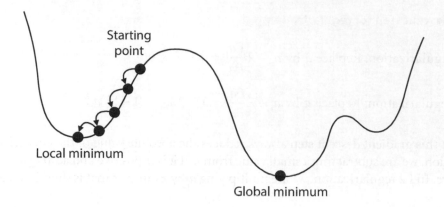

Figure B.8   Unfortunately, gradient descent didn't help us find the minimum value of this function. We did manage to go down, but we got stuck at a local minimum (valley). How can we solve this problem?

How do we solve this problem? We can use many techniques to fix this, and in this section, we learn a common one called *random restart*. The solution is to simply run the algorithm several times, always starting at a different random point, and picking the minimum value that was found overall. In figure B.9, we use random restart to find the global minimum on a function (note that this function is defined only on the interval pictured, and thus, the lowest value in the interval is indeed the global minimum). We have chosen three random starting points, one illustrated by a circle, one by a square, and one by a triangle. Notice that if we use gradient descent on each of these three points, the square manages to find the global minimum of the function.

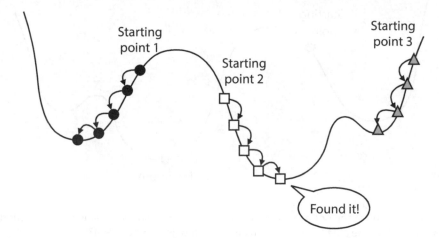

Figure B.9   The random restart technique illustrated. The function is defined only on this interval, with three valleys, and the global minimum located in the second valley. Here we run the gradient descent algorithm with three different starting points: the circle, the square, and the triangle. Notice that the square managed to find the global minimum of the function.

This method is still not guaranteed to find the global minimum, because we may be unlucky and pick only points that get stuck in valleys. However, with enough random starting points, we have a much higher chance of finding the global minimum. And even if we can't find the global minimum, we may still be able to find a good enough local minimum that will help us train a good model.

These references can also be found in https://serrano.academy/grokking-machine-learning/.

General references

- GitHub repository: www.github.com/luisguiserrano/manning
- YouTube videos: www.youtube.com/c/LuisSerrano
- General information: https://serrano.academy
- Book information: https://serrano.academy/grokking-machine-learning

Courses

- Udacity machine learning nanodegree: http://mng.bz/4KE5
- Coursera machine learning course: https://www.coursera.org/learn/machine-learning
- Coursera machine learning specialization (University of Washington): http://mng.bz/Xryl
- End-to-end machine learning: https://end-to-end-machine-learning.teachable.com/courses

Blogs and YouTube channels

- Machine learning videos by Brandon Rohrer: https://www.youtube.com/user/BrandonRohrer
- StatQuest with Josh Starmer: https://www.youtube.com/user/joshstarmer
- Chris Olah blog: https://colah.github.io/
- Jay Alammar blog: https://jalammar.github.io/
- Alexis Cook blog: https://alexisbcook.github.io/
- Dhruv Parthasarathy blog: https://medium.com/@dhruvp
- 3Blue1Brown: http://youtube.com/c/3blue1brown
- Machine Learning Mastery: https://machinelearningmastery.com
- Andrej Karpathy blog: http://karpathy.github.io/

Books

- *Pattern Recognition and Machine Learning,* by Christopher Bishop: http://mng.bz/g1DZ

Chapter 1

Videos

- General machine learning videos: https://serrano.academy/general-machine-learning/
- A friendly introduction to machine learning video: www.youtube.com/watch?v=IpGxLWOIZy4
- Monty Python spam sketch: www.youtube.com/watch?v=zLih-WQwBSc

Chapter 2

Videos

- Supervised machine learning videos: https://serrano.academy/linear-models/
- Unsupervised machine learning videos: https://serrano.academy/unsupervised-learning/
- Generative machine learning videos: https://serrano.academy/generative-models

- Reinforcement learning videos: https://serrano.academy/reinforcement-learning
- Deep learning videos: https://serrano.academy/neural-networks

Books

- *Grokking Deep Reinforcement Learning,* by Miguel Morales: http://mng.bz/5Zy4

Courses

- UCL course on reinforcement learning, by David Silver: https://www.davidsilver.uk/teaching/
- Udacity Deep Reinforcement Learning Nanodegree Program: http://mng.bz/6mMG

Chapter 3

Code

- GitHub repository: http://mng.bz/o8lN

Datasets

- Hyderabad housing dataset:
  - Creator: Ruchi Bhatia
  - Date: 2020/08/27
  - Version: 4
  - Retrieved from http://mng.bz/nrdv
  - License: CC0: Public Domain

Videos

- Linear regression video: http://mng.bz/v4Rx
- Polynomial regression video: https://www.youtube.com/watch?v=HmmkA-EFaW0

Chapter 4

Code

- GitHub repository: http://mng.bz/4KXB

Videos

- Machine learning: Testing and error metrics: https://www.youtube.com/watch?v=aDW44NPhNw0

- Lasso (L1) regression (StatQuest): https://www.youtube.com/watch?v=NGf0voTMlcs

- Ridge (L2) regression (StatQuest): https://www.youtube.com/watch?v=Q81RR3yKn30

Chapter 5

Code

- GitHub repository: http://mng.bz/Qqpm

Videos

- Logistic regression and the perceptron algorithm video: https://www.youtube.com/watch?v=jbluHIgBmBo

- Hidden Markov models video: https://www.youtube.com/watch?v=kqSzLo9fenk

Chapter 6

Code

- GitHub repository: http://mng.bz/Xr9Y

Datasets

- IMDB movie extensive reviews dataset

  - Creator: Stefano Leone

  - Date: 2019/11/24

  - Version: 2

  - Retrieved from https://www.kaggle.com/stefanoleone992/imdb-extensive-dataset

  - License: CC0: Public Domain

Videos

- Logistic regression and the perceptron algorithm video: https://www.youtube.com/watch?v=jbluHIgBmBo
- Cross entropy (StatQuest): https://www.youtube.com/watch?v=6ArSys5qHAU
- Cross entropy (Aurélien Géron): https://www.youtube.com/watch?v=ErfnhcEV1O8

Chapter 7

Videos

- Machine learning: Testing and error metrics: https://www.youtube.com/watch?v=aDW44NPhNw0

Chapter 8

Code

- GitHub repository: http://mng.bz/yJRJ

Datasets

- Spam filter dataset
  - Creator: Karthik Veerakumar
  - Date: 2017/07/14
  - Version: 1
  - Retrieved from https://www.kaggle.com/karthickveerakumar/spam-filter
  - Visibility: Public

Videos

- Naive Bayes: https://www.youtube.com/watch?v=Q8l0Vip5YUw

Chapter 9

Code

- GitHub repository: http://mng.bz/MvM2

Datasets

- Admissions dataset
    - Creator: Mohan S. Acharya
    - Date: 2018/03/03
    - Version: 2
    - Retrieved from http://mng.bz/aZlJ
    - Article: Mohan S. Acharya, Asfia Armaan, and Aneeta S Antony, "A Comparison of Regression Models for Prediction of Graduate Admissions," IEEE International Conference on Computational Intelligence in Data Science (2019).
    - License: CC0: Public Domain

Videos

- Decision trees (StatQuest): https://www.youtube.com/watch?v=7VeUPuFGJHk
- Regression decision trees (StatQuest): https://www.youtube.com/watch?v=g9c66TUylZ4
- Decision trees (Brandon Rohrer): https://www.youtube.com/watch?v=9w16p4QmkAI
- Gini impurity index: https://www.youtube.com/watch?v=u4IxOk2ijSs
- Shannon entropy and information gain: https://www.youtube.com/watch?v=9r7FIXEAGvs

Blog posts

- Shannon entropy, information gain, and picking balls from buckets: http://mng.bz/g1lR

Chapter 10

Code

- GitHub repository: http://mng.bz/ePAJ

Datasets

- MNIST dataset. Deng, L. "The MNIST Database of Handwritten Digit images for Machine Learning Research." *IEEE Signal Processing Magazine* 29, no. 6 (2012): 141–42. http://yann.lecun.com/exdb/mnist/

- Hyderabad housing dataset (see references for chapter 3)

Videos

- Deep learning and neural networks: https://www.youtube.com/watch?v=BR9h47Jtqyw

- Convolutional neural networks: https://www.youtube.com/watch?v=2-Ol7ZB0MmU

- Recurrent neural networks: https://www.youtube.com/watch?v=UNmqTiOnRfg

- How neural networks work (Brandon Rohrer): https://www.youtube.com/watch?v=ILsA4nyG7I0

- Recurrent neural networks (RNN) and long short-term memory (LSTM) (Brandon Rohrer): https://www.youtube.com/watch?v=WCUNPb-5EYI

Books

- *Grokking Deep Learning*, by Andrew Trask: https://www.manning.com/books/grokking-deep-learning

- *Deep Learning*, by Ian Goodfellow, Yoshua Bengio, and Aaron Courville: https://www.deeplearningbook.org/

Courses

- Udacity deep learning course: http://mng.bz/p9lP

Blog posts

- "Using Transfer Learning to Classify Images with Keras," by Alexis Cook: http://mng.bz/OQgP

- "Global Average Pooling Layers for Object Localization," by Alexis Cook: http://mng.bz/Ywj7

- "A Brief History of CNNs in Image Segmentation: From R-CNN to Mask R-CNN," by Dhruv Parthasarathy: http://mng.bz/GOnN

- "Neural networks, Manifolds, and Topology," by Chris Olah: http://mng.bz/zERZ

- "Understanding LSTM Networks," by Chris Olah: http://mng.bz/01nz

- "How GPT3 Works: Visualizations and Animations," by Jay Alammar: http://mng.bz/KoXn

- "How to Configure the Learning Rate When Training Deep Learning Neural Networks," by Jason Brownlee: http://mng.bz/9ae8

- "Setting the Learning Rate of Your Neural Network," by Jeremy Jordan: http://mng.bz/WBKX

- "Selecting the Best Architecture for Artificial Neural Networks," by Ahmed Gad: http://mng.bz/WBKX

- "A Recipe for Training Neural Networks," by Andrej Karpathy: http://mng.bz/80gg

Tools

- TensorFlow playground: https://playground.tensorflow.org/

Chapter 11

Code

- GitHub repository: http://mng.bz/ED6r

Videos

- Support vector machines: https://www.youtube.com/watch?v=Lpr__X8zuE8

- The polynomial kernel (StatQuest): https://www.youtube.com/watch?v=Toet3EiSFcM

- The radial (RBF) kernel (StatQuest): https://www.youtube.com/watch?v=Qc5IyLW_hns

Blog posts

- "Kernels and Feature Maps: Theory and Intuition," by Xavier Bourret Sicotte: http://mng.bz/N4aX

Chapter 12

Code

- GitHub repository: http://mng.bz/DK50

Videos

- Random forests (StatQuest): https://www.youtube.com/watch?v=J4Wdy0Wc_xQ

- AdaBoost (StatQuest): https://www.youtube.com/watch?v=LsK-xG1cLYA

- Gradient boosting (StatQuest): https://www.youtube.com/watch?v=3CC4N4z3GJc

- XGBoost (StatQuest): https://www.youtube.com/watch?v=OtD8wVaFm6E

Articles and blog posts

- "A Decision-Theoretic Generalization of Online Learning and an Application to Boosting," by Yoav Freund and Robert Shapire, *Journal of Computer and System Sciences*, 55, 119–139. http://mng.bz/l9Bz

- "Explaining AdaBoost," by Robert Schapire: http://rob.schapire.net/papers/explaining -adaboost.pdf

- "XGBoost: A Scalable Tree Boosting System," by Tiani Chen and Carlos Guestrin. KDD '16: Proceedings of the 22nd ACM SIGKDD International Conference on Knowledge Discovery and Data Mining, August 2016, 785–794. https://doi.org/10.1145/ 2939672.2939785

- "Winning the Netflix Prize: A Summary," by Edwin Chen: http://mng.bz/B1jq

Chapter 13

Code

- GitHub repository: http://mng.bz/drlz

Datasets

- Titanic dataset:

  - Retrieved from https://www.kaggle.com/c/titanic/data

Graphics and image icons

Graphics and image icons were provided by the following creators from flaticon.com:

- IFC—hiker, mountain range: Freepik; flag: Good Ware

- Preface—musician: photo3idea_studio; mathematician: Freepik

- Figure 1.2—person: Eucalyp; computer: Freepik

- Figure 1.4—person: ultimatearm

- Figures 1.5, 1.6, 1.7, 1.8, 1.9—person on computer: Freepik

- Figures 2.1, 2.2, 2.3, 2.4—dog: Freepik; cat: Smashicons

- Figures 2.2, 2.3, 2.4—factory: DinosoftLabs

- Figures 2.5, 2.6—envelope: Freepik

- Figure 2.7—house: Vectors Market

- Figure 2.8—map point: Freepik

- Figures 2.11, 2.12—robot, mountain: Freepik; dragon: Eucalyp; Treasure: Smashicons

- Figures 3.3, 3.4, 3.5—house: Vectors Market

- Figures 3.20, 3.21, 3.22—hiker, mountain range: Freepik; flag, bulb: Good Ware

- Figure 4.1—Godzilla: Freepik; swatter: Smashicons; fly: Eucalyp; bazooka: photo3idea_studio

- Figure 4.6—house: Vectors Market; bandage, shingles: Freepik; titanium rod: Vitaly Gorbachev

- Figures 5.1, 5.2, 5.3, 5.4, 5.5, 5.6, 5.10, 5.11, 5.12, 5.13, 5.16, 5.17, 5.18, 5.19, 5.20, 5.21, 5.22, 5.23, 5.24, 6.1, 6.4, 6.5, 6.6, 10.2, 10.3—happy face, sad face, neutral face: Vectors Market

- Figures 5.15, 5.16—hiker: Freepik; bulb: Good Ware

- Figure 7.11 (in the exercises)—various animals: surang; book: Good Ware; clock, strawberry, planet, soccer ball: Freepik; video: monkik

- Figure 8.4—chef hat: Vitaly Gorbachev; wheat, bread: Freepik

- Figures 8.5, 8.6, 8.7, 8.8, 8.9, 8.10, 8.11, 8.12, 8.13—envelope: Smashicons

- Figures 9.6, 9.7, 9.8, 9.9, 9.12, 9.13, 9.15, 9.16, 9.17—atom: mavadee; beehive: Smashicons; chess knight: Freepik

- Figures 9.13, 9.17—handbag: Gregor Cresnar

- Joke in chapter 10—arms with muscle: Freepik

- Joke in chapter 11—corn, chicken: Freepik; chicken: monkik

- Joke in chapter 12—shark, fish: Freepik

- Figure 12.1—big robot: photo3idea_studio; small robots: Freepik

- Joke in chapter 13—ship: Freepik

index

Hands-on projects for learning your way

liveProjects are an exciting way to develop your skills that's just like learning on-the-job.

In a Manning liveProject you tackle a real-world IT challenge and work out your own solutions. To make sure you succeed, you'll get 90 days full and unlimited access to a hand-picked list of Manning book and video resources.

Here's how liveProject works:

- **Achievable milestones.** Each project is broken down into steps and sections so you can keep track of your progress.

- **Collaboration and advice.** Work with other liveProject participants through chat, working groups, and peer project reviews.

- **Compare your results.** See how your work shapes up against an expert implementation by the liveProject's creator.

- **Everything you need to succeed.** Datasets and carefully selected learning resources come bundled with every liveProject.

- **Build your portfolio.** All liveProjects teach skills that are in-demand from industry. When you're finished, you'll have the satisfaction that comes with success and a real project to add to your portfolio.

Explore dozens of data, development, and cloud engineering liveProjects at www.manning.com!